SHADOW OF LIBERATION

SHADOW OF LIBERATION

Contestation and Compromise in the
Economic and Social Policy of the African
National Congress, 1943–1996

Vishnu Padayachee and Robert van Niekerk

WITS UNIVERSITY PRESS

Published in South Africa by:
Wits University Press
1 Jan Smuts Avenue
Johannesburg 2001

www.witspress.co.za

First published 2019

http://dx.doi.org.10.18772/12019103955

978-1-77614-395-5 (Paperback)
978-1-77614-396-2 (Web PDF)
978-1-77614-397-9 (EPUB)
978-1-77614-398-6 (Mobi)

Project manager: Alison Paulin
Copyeditor: Sally Hines
Proofreader: Alison Paulin
Indexer: Margaret Ramsay
Cover design: Hybrid Creative
Typesetter: Newgen
Typeset in 10 point MinionPro-Regular

CONTENTS

ACRONYMS AND ABBREVIATIONS   vii
PREFACE   ix
ACKNOWLEDGEMENTS   xvii

CHAPTER 1: The Context of Economic and Social Policy-Making in the ANC   1

CHAPTER 2: African Claims, the Freedom Charter and Social Democracy, 1943–1960   9

CHAPTER 3: Incarceration, Exile and Homecoming, c.1960–c.1991   27

CHAPTER 4: Economic Policy Debates during a Decade of Liberation, 1985–1993   73

CHAPTER 5: On the Way to GEAR, 1994–1996   109

CHAPTER 6: Making Sense of the Economic Policy Debates   143

CHAPTER 7: South African Reserve Bank Independence   179

CHAPTER 8: The Politics of Health Policy-Making in the Transition Era, 1990–1996 199

CHAPTER 9: Interpretation and Conclusion   227

NOTES   235
BIBLIOGRAPHY   241
INDEX   263

ACRONYMS AND ABBREVIATIONS

ANC	African National Congress
BEE	black economic empowerment
CCFF	Compensatory and Contingency Financing Facility
CEAS	Central Economic Advisory Services
CIA	Central Intelligence Agency
Codesa	Convention for a Democratic South Africa
Codesria	Council for the Development of Social Science Research in Africa
Cosatu	Congress of South African Trade Unions
CPGB	Communist Party of Great Britain
CPSA	Communist Party of South Africa
CPSU	Communist Party of the Soviet Union
CREFSA	Centre for Research into Economics and Finance in Southern Africa
CSS	Central Statistical Service
DBSA	Development Bank of Southern Africa
DEP	Department of Economic Planning
ECA	Economic Commission for Africa
EDP	Economic Development Plan
EROSA	Economic Research on South Africa
ET	Economic Trends Research Group
FFC	Financial and Fiscal Commission
GDP	gross domestic product
GEAR	Growth, Employment and Redistribution
GNP	gross national product
GNU	Government of National Unity
HBU	historically black university
IDRC	International Development Research Centre
IFP	Inkatha Freedom Party
IMF	International Monetary Fund
LAPC	Land and Agricultural Policy Centre

LSE	London School of Economics
MDM	mass democratic movement
MEC	Mineral Energy Complex
MERG	Macroeconomic Research Group
MK	uMkhonto we Sizwe
Nafcoc	National African Federated Chamber of Commerce and Industry
NAMDA	National Medical and Dental Association
NEC	National Executive Committee
Nedlac	National Economic Development and Labour Council
NEM	Normative Economic Model
NGO	non-governmental organisation
NHS	national health service
NIEP	National Institute for Economic Policy
NOFP	net open forward position
NP	National Party
Numsa	National Union of Metalworkers of South Africa
NWC	National Working Committee
PAC	Pan Africanist Congress
PHC	Primary Health Care
RDP	Reconstruction and Development Programme
RTG	Ready to Govern
SACP	South African Communist Party
Sanco	South African National Civic Organisation
SARB	South African Reserve Bank
SDR	Special Drawing Rights
SOAS	School of Oriental and African Studies
TEC	Transitional Executive Council
UCT	University of Cape Town
UDF	United Democratic Front
UK	United Kingdom
UN	United Nations
Unisa	University of South Africa
US	United States
UWC	University of the Western Cape
Wits	University of the Witwatersrand

PREFACE

In the pall of a destructive preceding political era under Jacob Zuma, characterised by corruption of the body politic and the institutions of our democracy and by poor economic performance, the president of the African National Congress, Cyril Ramaphosa, has promised a 'new dawn' for South Africa. He advocates that '… we put behind us the era of diminishing trust in public institutions and weakened confidence in leaders. We should put all the negativity that has dogged our country behind us, because a new dawn, inspired by our collective memory of Nelson Mandela and the changes that are unfolding, is upon us' (*Vuk'unzenzele* 2018). We must ask what lessons have been learnt though from the political circumstances and policy choices made since democracy in 1994 in South Africa that require the arising of such a new dawn.

In contributing an answer, we feel an honest and forthright reflection is required of our recent economic and social policy-making history, in particular in the era of the democratic political transition between 1990 and 1996. Our book is therefore centred on the primary question that, given its historical state-led anti-inequality stance, how did the ANC in the 1990s come to do such a dramatic volte-face on economic and social policy and advocate for an essentially market-driven or neo-liberal approach. How did this U-turn happen? What were the forces that led the market-friendly charge? Indeed, as many have asked, did the ANC willingly go that way or was it pushed into such compromises?

We show here that the economic policy choices of the ANC leadership were based on a judgement that there was no alternative to the neo-liberalism that had dominated global policy debate since the early 1980s. Ironically, this approach, also referred to as the Washington Consensus, was slowly losing credibility following the publication of the Japanese-sponsored World Bank's *The East Asian Miracle* report (1993c). That report was highly critical of the core economic and social policy positions that emerged out of the Washington Consensus. This rethinking globally on failed macroeconomic policy in the early to mid-1990s was happening at precisely the time when the ANC was entering negotiations with the apartheid regime over a democratic constitution and the accompanying institutions of a post-apartheid state. The ANC, however, entered this global arena of fierce contestation over macroeconomic policy strategies and ideas unevenly schooled in economic policy debates and in economic theorising about their history.

In contrast to the ANC, the apartheid state was able to turn to its well-resourced economic institutions and supportive state agencies, such as the National Treasury, South African Reserve Bank, the Central Economic Advisory Services, the Development Bank, the Land Bank and other state institutions, to confound the ANC with powerful, albeit flawed, neo-liberal ideas and policy proposals, which they had begun earnestly to espouse and implement from the late 1970s. In that exercise of persuasion and power play, the apartheid state had the implicit backing of Western governments and global financial institutions, as well as that of a still powerful local capitalist class.

Apart from 'there was no alternative', at least two other arguments are raised in defence of the ANC leadership's neo-liberal choices. The first is that the state was in a fiscal crisis, so no alternative policy strategy could be entertained or financed based on a state-driven investment programme. The second was based on the view that implementing any state-led investment and redistributive social policy delivery programme would have relied on a largely untransformed apartheid state bureau-cracy and would have been undermined by that old guard.

Some have questioned the degree and depth of the fiscal crisis in historical and comparative context (see Michie and Padayachee 1997, 1998; Fine and Padayachee 2000). By examining alternative, yet fiscally responsible, policy frameworks, such as the ANC's own (later disowned) macroeconomic policy framework (MERG) and the Congress of South African Trade Unions (Cosatu) led Reconstruction and Development Programme (RDP), we show that the first view was fatally flawed. There were credible and imaginative policy alternatives, but they were not only eschewed, but imperiously discarded without deliberative debate within the ANC or its alliance partners. While we do not deal extensively with the second point referred to above, it is clear that this argument is something of a feeble cop-out. Surely, to be consistent with the culture of democratic accountability forged in the mass democratic movement, the right strategy was to agree, through demo-cratic debate, on an appropriate, progressive policy framework, and then consider the kind of state capability needed to give effect to it? The outcome by now, 25 years later, we maintain, would have resulted in far more genuinely emancipatory outcomes for the majority of our people. That approach is what the Afrikaner nationalists did in the lead-up to their own racist version of freedom in 1948 and thereafter (see, for example, Freund 2019). After 1959, Fidel Castro's Cuba did not throw up its arms in despair after inheriting Fulgencio Batista's bureaucracy, but set about radically and purposefully transforming the civil service to give effect to their revolutionary goals. The South West Africa People's Organisation was able to do this, too, in Namibia in anticipation of taking over government.

The example of Ethiopia's recent development experience may be useful in setting the MERG state-led investment programme in some comparative perspective. Ethiopia's impressive growth rates, which averaged 10 per cent per annum over the past decade after the global crisis of 2008, was driven by substantial public sector infrastructural investment. Ken Coutts and Christina Laskaridis (2019) show that contrary to the concern that high public sector investment would crowd out private sector investment, the latter kept pace with public investment, being lower than public investment (as a percentage of the GDP) in the first phase and appreciably higher in the second. The only concern raised by analysts was the risk of exposure to spiralling external debt, calling for careful management of the currency and reserves and policies aimed at increasing output and exports of both agriculture and industry (Coutts and Laskaridis 2019).

Over 30 years ago, the 'largely and dangerously'[1] ignored post-Keynesian scholar Hyman Minsky wrote: 'Economic issues must become a serious public matter and the subject of debate if new directions are to be undertaken. Meaningful reforms cannot be put over by an advisory and administrative elite that is itself the architect of the existing situation' (in Rapley 2017: 416).

This book eschews both singular and conspiratorial narratives about why certain economic and social policies were decided upon and adopted in this period. Instead, we favour an in-depth and 'no-holds-barred' account that contrasts and reflects on the ideologically varying vantage points of all the key protagonists in South Africa's transition to democracy until approximately 1996 with the introduction of the market-friendly Growth, Employment and Redistribution policy framework. Without sacrificing our own voice, we have tried to give voice deliberately and fairly to all sides involved in the debates. But to understand the 1990s shifts, we felt the need to take a longer, historically grounded approach.

The book, therefore, locates the period of ANC economic and social policy-making in the post-1990 era against a wider historically contextualised canvas of ANC policy-making since the 1940s – commencing with African Claims of 1943 through the Freedom Charter of 1955, the 1992 Ready to Govern policy document, the RDP Base Document and MERG's macroeconomic policy framework of the 1990s. This detailed contextual framework allows us to argue unequivocally that the historical policy orientation of ANC economic and social policy-making was firmly social democratic in character (even though, and with the possible exception of Albert Luthuli, not conceptualised in such specifically ideological terms).

Social democracy as applied here by us is located within a broad tradition of socialist thought characterised historically by the state-led universalised provision of public goods to all citizens and across social strata (such as a single state-run national health service provided free at the point of delivery), based on principles of social solidarity and inclusive social citizenship and with accompanying redistributive macroeconomic policies. In the indigenised social democratic policy strategy reflected in ANC policy thinking, historically the democratic state would play a critical and leading role in the reconstruction and development of South Africa.

It is instructive to acknowledge at this point that very shortly after its unbanning in 1990, the ANC was fully open to such bold, nuanced and imaginative social democratic thinking on policy alternatives, but that this impetus was rapidly eclipsed by an emerging residualist, market-friendly policy discourse that was eventually consolidated in the Growth, Employment and Re-distribution (GEAR) strategy of 1996. The openness to redistributive, social democratic policy thinking at this stage was represented by no less a commanding figure than Nelson Mandela in a seminal keynote address to the Consultative Business Movement on 23 May 1990 early after his release from incarceration (Mandela 1990). Here, in contrast to the tone and content of what was soon to follow from the ANC, is an open and flexible approach to economic policy options, albeit firmly anchored in the specificities of South Africa's own history and legacy. Apart from the focus on education, housing, skills and social policy interventions, Mandela's economic policy ideas as reflected in this 1990 speech are significant. He speaks of the need for a 'macroeconomic indicative national plan'; the recognition of gross inequalities arising out of imbalances in concentrations of corporate power and land distribution; a proposal for strengthening economic democracy through, for example, state representation on private boards; a focus on employment and centralised bargaining; the need for anti-trust legislation and a more progressive tax policy; the importance of successfully competing in global markets; the imperative to build a small and medium business sector; a focus on investment, industrial policy and a living wage; registering opposition to the late apartheid era government's policy of privatisation, and his concern about capital flight. He does not fail to recognise fiscal realities in his speech, though he clearly does not labour over or fetishise them at this stage. Most significantly, the ideas raised here by Mandela are all key elements of a redistributive, social democratic economic and social policy framework, closer, we argue, both to the original social democratic and emancipatory vision of the ANC as contained in its African Claims policy document of 1943 and the Freedom Charter of 1955, and to the vision articulated later in the Macroeconomic Research Group (MERG) and Reconstruction and Development Programme (RDP) in 1993.

Its historical alliance with the vocal and Marxist-Leninist-inspired South African Communist Party gave the appearance, however, that the ANC was ideologically more to the left of this position. The book describes how and why these social democratic policy alternatives were summarily abandoned through the new centralised and elitist leadership politics that gripped the ANC in the transition era, displacing the mass-based, democratic politics of accountability of the anti-apartheid era. Indeed, the consequences of this market-value-informed political elitism that took root in the mid-1990s was most eloquently expressed by iconic anti-apartheid liberation fighter and United Democratic Front (UDF) founder member, the late Johnny Issel:

> Our public appearances are carefully choreographed. These are the requirements of the market. It demands that we present ourselves as saleable commodities. As functionaries we are required to possess a certain measure of exchange value, like any other commodity for sale. Such are the dictates of the 'market'. And more better if it is 'packaged' in an Italian-designed suit and driven in a German-produced automobile. And if so, the exchange value increases and the market rewards a higher premium. But on the market not all goods up for sale are sought. Similarly, some of us discover that we are not appropriately packaged. And we begin to doubt our own worth, our own self-worth. Others seem to find somewhat more expedient ways, albeit criminal ways, to appropriate what the market has to offer (South African History Online 2011).

While the ANC clearly and correctly triumphed on the political front in securing a globally celebrated constitutional democracy, the egregious lack of attention to economic theory for most of its history, the lack of economic capacity within its ranks in contrast to the late apartheid state's capacity and skills, the almost criminal neglect of its mass democratic base, and the summary rejection of the recommendations of its own progressive think tanks, including MERG and the RDP Base Document, all combined to cripple the ANC's stance on economic and social policy from about mid-1993 and into the early democratic era.

We do not characterise these compromises by Nelson Mandela and the ANC leadership as some kind of 'betrayal' or 'selling out', as has become popular in some circles today. Yes, in our judgement there were many things the ANC could have done better, especially in respect of the way it cut itself off from its greatest strength, that is the mass democratic movement. But we accept that those comrades in leadership who took these policy decisions were genuinely convinced it offered the best hope for our people. In this respect, we cannot conclude on the basis of the evidence that there was a conscious and intentional 'sell-out' of the decades-long struggle to achieve an emancipated society in South Africa. Neither is there any conclusive evidence, apart from some speculation, of secret late night meetings involving the ANC, Western governments, the Bretton Woods institutions and local capital, which persuaded the ANC to adopt market-friendly economic and social policies. For us, the jury is still out on this point. The extensive available evidence we have reviewed could not substantiate such claims, yet we do not deny this possibility. Further research is needed before anyone can come to a definitive conclusion and it is our hope that our book will act as a spur to such research by interested scholars.

What is unassailable in our view, though, is that the values and principles of democratic debate, accountability and accompanying political selflessness, all key features of the progressive mass democratic movement in the struggle against apartheid, were near abandoned in the economic policy-making process of the transition era. This commitment, indeed insistence, on the need to deliberate and reach consensus on policy alternatives through our mass democratic political culture is reflected most tellingly in the views of Alec Erwin, then education officer of the National Union of Metalworkers of South Africa (Numsa), expressed at an Indaba with the ANC in Paris in 1989. Erwin said that 'central to our thinking is the development of a democratic political process that will entrench mass participation and involvement in the formulation and implementation of economic policy' (Erwin 1990: 206). We hold that there was a subsequent 'sell-out' of this commitment to a grassroots, mass democratic political culture informing the policy-making process. Apart from the impact on policy process and content itself, this shift has had devastating consequences for accountability, eroding the fabric of progressive South African political life and contributing substantively to the corrosion of the progressive body politic. The roots of this phenomenon, we argue, are to be found in the era of the political transition since 1990 and the early period of democracy following the 1994 elections, and then finally cohered and consolidated in the ruinous Zuma era.

In respect of economic and social policy and in the context of a 'negotiated revolution', the ANC was outgunned and outwitted by the far more powerful economic machinery of the late apartheid state and of local (white) capital. In our view, the role of the 'international economic community' in the form of the International

Monetary Fund and the World Bank in explaining the 'shift' has been exaggerated, as has been conclusively demonstrated in a recent paper by Padayachee and Fine (2018). An elitist team was assembled and entrusted by the ANC leadership with creating the policy and institutional foundations for realising the Freedom Charter, the ANC's long-term emancipatory vision for a South African good society. Through missteps and arrogance, that foundation could not be laid. We now live with the consequences.

Now, as we conclude our work in a post-Zuma South Africa, and with a new dawn based on a 'New Deal' being evoked by President Ramaphosa and his followers, there are worrying signs that none of the lessons of theory or history, or the lessons drawn from the vast post-2008 crisis literature, appear to have been learnt. It looks like 'business as usual' after the obscenely corrupt ten years of Zuma's administration brought post-apartheid South Africa virtually to its knees (Van Niekerk and Fine 2019).

We wish to conclude though, again, with the observation of Issel, who after forcefully rejecting all the trappings of political elitism in the ANC in the final years of his life, had these words to say in his poignant and final public speech: 'What spurred us on then – the need and urge for freedom – still burns within us and I think it will burn within us for a long time to come. And I want you to be strong comrades and don't be distracted by anything … Let us continue moving on and finally I believe we shall see what we had fought for' (YouTube 2011).

ACKNOWLEDGEMENTS

Many individuals and institutions contributed their time, energy and ideas towards the finalisation of this book. We thank especially the staff of the many archives we searched: particular thanks are owed to Vuyolwethu Feni-Fete, senior archivist at the National Heritage and Cultural Studies Centre at the University of Fort Hare (Alice); Gabriele Mohale, head archivist at the William Cullen Library at the University of the Witwatersrand (Johannesburg); and Huibre Lombard and her dedicated staff at the Archive of Contemporary History at the University of the Free State (Bloemfontein). Dr Abel Gwaindepi (Rhodes and Stellenbosch University) assisted with our archival work at the National Heritage Archives in Alice. Lee Smith and Robert Jacot-Guillarmod are acknowledged for their assistance in the editing of the volume.

Special thanks are due to those (all busy people) who allowed us to interview them. Their names and affiliations are recorded in the bibliography. This book would not have been possible without their contribution.

We also thank the following colleagues who provide us with leads and shared their ideas and reflections on the period of South Africa's transition and who supported us in many ways as we worked towards completion of the manuscript. They include, in no particular order, Ronnie Kasrils, Saleem Badat, Bradley Bordiss, Bill Freund, Jannie Rossouw, Jonathan Leape, Tulo Makwati, Imraan Valodia, Lumkile Mondi, Keith Breckenridge, Deenan Pillay, Anand Pillay, Patsy Pillay, Jonathan Klaaren, Yusuf Sayed, Ben Turok, Shepi Mati, Greg Ruiters, Verne Harris and Keith Hart. Ben Fine and John Sender gave hugely of their time and their powerful memories of key aspects of the economics of the transition, in which they were both deeply involved. Apart from being interviewed by us, they always responded timeously and enthusiastically to our email queries and questions.

We are immensely indebted to Karen Pampallis and Sally Hines for their thorough editing work and for turning our scrabbled thoughts into elegant text. We are also grateful to our project manager, Alison Paulin, for her painstaking and meticulous efforts in finalising the book with us, carried out with good humour, patience and wonderful consideration for what we were trying to achieve.

We thank our respective families in Durban and Makhanda (Grahamstown). Vishnu Padayachee thanks Nishi, Sonali, Dhirren and his mother for being supportive and for allowing him the dedicated space and time to work uninterruptedly at his study in Durban. Vishnu would also like to acknowledge with deep gratitude four generations of the Padayachee and Naidoo families, whose powerful contribution and selfless service to the educational, cultural and economic life of Umkomaas left an indelible mark on his world view and values.

Robert van Niekerk thanks Orla, Nia and Oisin for their patience and support while he completed this book over four years of research and writing. Robert would also like to thank his comrades and friends in the Lansdowne Youth Movement and the Cape Youth Congress where his political understanding of the African National Congress as an historical movement of emancipation was first shaped. In particular he remembers Robbie Waterwitch, a cherished friend, and Coline Williams, who both died very unexpectedly but bravely as young MK guerrilla fighters in 1989. Their sacrifice is not forgotten.

For a lifetime of dedication and sacrifice to the struggle for democracy in South Africa and for his courage, integrity and vision, we are honoured to dedicate this book to Tata Andrew Mlangeni.

COPYRIGHT ACKNOWLEDGEMENTS

Permission to publish extracts and information taken from the following journal articles is gratefully acknowledged:

Vishnu Padayachee & John Sender. 2018. Vella Pillay: Revolutionary Activism and Economic Policy Analysis. *Journal of Southern African Studies* 44(1): 149-165. DOI: 10.1080/03057070.2018.1405644. Reprinted by permission of the publisher, Taylor & Francis Ltd, http://www.tandfonline.com.

Vishnu Padayachee & Ben Fine. 2018. The role and influence of the IMF on economic policy in South Africa's transition to democracy: The 1993 Compensatory and Contingency Financing Facility revisited. *Review of African Political Economy* DOI: 10.1080/03056244.2018.1484352 Reprinted by permission of Informa UK Limited, trading as Taylor & Francis Group, www.tandfonline.com.

Vishnu Padayachee (2015) Central Bank Independence: The debate revisited. *Transformation: Critical Perspectives on Southern Africa*, 89: 1–25. Reprinted by permission of the editor, *Transformation*.

1

The Context of Economic and Social Policy-Making in the ANC

Talks about the transition to democracy in South Africa began fitfully and largely in secret in the mid-1980s. But President FW de Klerk's announcement on 2 February 1990 that the apartheid regime was unbanning the African National Congress (ANC) and other liberation movements, and the release of Nelson Mandela nine days later, took the transition onto a much higher plane and at a rapid rate. That South Africa remained the only fully capitalist economy on the continent at that time is not in doubt. While we do not subscribe to the notion of 'South African exceptionalism', we maintain that its capitalism was an extreme, stunted and distorted one. All of these characteristics, in different ways, had a bearing on the very nature of the transition, including on economic and social policy options and choices. Two such features are worth noting here. Firstly, South African capital represented by white-owned conglomerates such as Anglo American Corporation and Sanlam, both established around the end of the Second World War, remained powerful, globally connected and influential as the twentieth century wound to a close. Secondly, the apartheid regime's economic institutions remained well-resourced and internationally connected, despite decades of sanctions and the crisis of the apartheid state. These state institutions included the Ministry of Finance, the South African Reserve Bank, the Central Economic Advisory Services, a number of regional, national and provincial development finance institutions, and the national statistics agency (Central Statistical Services).

The real power among the constituencies engaged in negotiations lay in the hands of white business and in the institutions of the late apartheid state, as journalist and author Martin Plaut argues: 'The men who had run South Africa for decades also embarked on a process designed to incorporate senior members of the ANC. Radical economic policies were dropped in favour of more conventional macro-economic prescriptions' (2012: 31). As Plaut suggests, this was no accident; it had been thought through by the old regime and it was to prove decisive in many economic policy battles, including, as we show, the crucial issue of the independence of the South African Reserve Bank (see chapter 6).

Against these factors, most components of the liberation movement, including the Tripartite Alliance consisting of the ANC, the South African Communist Party (SACP) and the Congress of South African Trade Unions (Cosatu), were fragmented, under-resourced and under-capacitated. But its moral and political standing among its own people and in the international community was never higher than it was around 1990 when formal negotiations were poised to begin. These were undoubtedly major assets that ultimately enabled the ANC to prevail at the formal negotiations for a democratic, non-racial, non-sexist and unitary South Africa. As we will attempt to show in our discussion of the economic and social policy debate inside and outside formal constitutional negotiations, it is precisely this goodwill and trust that the ANC rapidly threw away in the search to win the support of international finance capital. This perceived necessity was based on the view that foreign investors would come to support the post-apartheid economy provided that the country played by the rules of the international game.

Keith Hart and Vishnu Padayachee have characterised South African capital in the following way:

> The durable features of South African capitalism since its modern inception are mining, racial domination, and an uneven relationship between the state, finance and industry. Although the national economy went through long swings between an external and internal orientation, each of the main periods we have highlighted (1870s–1914, 1914–45, 1945–79, 1980s–2008) was marked by both. South African capitalism has a markedly 'neo-feudal' character, distinguished by a cult of alpha-male leadership, cronyism between firms, banks and government, a relative absence of competition, weak democracy in the workplace, [an absence] of a flourishing culture of small and medium enterprises; in other words, a tendency towards absolute rather than relative surplus value … which has its roots in British colonialism, rural Afrikanerdom and a history of racial oppression by a small white minority (2013a: 80).

Hart and Padayachee question the extent to which any of this has changed since the advent of democracy. Of course, 25 years into South Africa's democracy, few can deny that notable progress has been made in addressing some of the economic and social legacies of the apartheid regime. Yet, progress has not been as widespread, rapid or sustainable as may have been hoped for. The 'triple challenge' of unemployment, inequality and poverty, as the ANC government of today defines it, as well as the challenges related to economic growth itself, remain stubbornly intractable. At the time of writing, the economy has slipped into a recession, the second in ten years, the country's investment grade has been reduced to junk by two international credit-rating agencies, and, despite attempts at their restructuring in this yet early stage of the post-Zuma era, the governance of state-owned enterprises still remains nothing short of shambolic. The much-anticipated inflows of capital, which the ANC bent over backwards to achieve have not materialised; instead both legal and illegal capital outflows have reached obscene proportions.

Together with a serious crisis of service delivery (water, sanitation, electrification, health) in many parts of the country and a concomitant rise in service delivery protests and labour action, as well as weak performance by firms, both big and small, a double whammy of macroeconomic disequilibria and microeconomic stagnation faces the country today. Corruption, personal accumulation projects and governance challenges add to the woes of the still relatively new democracy. A serious, sober and critically reflective analysis of how South Africa has reached this point is necessary and perhaps overdue.

Part (and we stress *part*) of the explanation for the current malaise, we maintain, may lie in the historic neglect of economic and social policy thinking in ANC political strategy since its formation in 1912 and the relative weakness and lack of creativity of its economic capabilities and thinking in the 1990s, which impacted negatively on the quality and creativity of its policy formulation in the crucial years of the transition to democracy and beyond. In our view, the decisions taken in that period of the transition (*c*.1990–1996) continue to constrain the scope to rethink and reimagine an economic and social dispensation of the kind that is needed to escape the current economic and social impasse. The question of how this came to pass lies at the heart of this book.

Our title comes from the ANC's 'Strategy and Tactics' document adopted at a landmark strategic conference in Morogoro, Tanzania, in 1969: 'To allow existing economic forces to retain their interests intact, is to feed the root of racial supremacy, and does not represent even the *shadow of liberation*. Our drive towards national emancipation is, therefore, in a very real way bound up with economic emancipation' (ANC 1997: 391–392, emphasis added).

The important point made here is about the imperative that political freedom is accompanied by an appropriate set of economic and social policies that would serve fundamentally to transform the lives of the people whom the liberation movement represented. Anything short of such a fundamental economic emancipation would, therefore, represent a 'shadow of liberation'.

This book represents an attempt to critically assess the economic and social policy theorising, thinking and choices made by the ANC – in alliance with the SACP and its various trade union partners – in the transition era to democracy (c.1990–1996). However, it is consciously located in a longer historical context – a periodisation we have chosen to start with is the African Claims document produced under the leadership of ANC President AB Xuma in 1943, and which ends in the publication of the Growth, Employment and Redistribution document produced by the ANC-led government of Nelson Mandela in 1996.

In elucidating our arguments on the character of the ANC and its foundational policy orientation, we refer extensively to a fully recognisable 'social democratic' basis to the policies advocated by the modern ANC (from 1940 on). While we locate social democracy as a strand of socialist thought (a 'variety of socialism' if you will), our reference to social democracy is not meant in its strictly ideological sense of a commitment to a parliamentary road to achieving socialism on the basis of working-class participation through political parties in a constitutional democracy. Rather, what is meant by social democracy is in terms of its substantive economic and social content: the provision of universally provided public goods (such as health, education and welfare services) by the state as an entitlement of social citizenship with a commitment to achieving equity (as opposed to merely ameliorating poverty). This would be achieved through redistributive economic policies that enable social solidarity among all citizens across social strata and thereby ensure a common sharing of the social heritage by all citizens collectively. Additionally, this would be best achieved through deliberative, democratic practices in the context of a constitutional democracy.

While the reasons for a fully fledged social democratic tradition of socialist thought not flourishing are complex, it is our view that the polarisation of intellectual life in South Africa within the left performed a seminal role in preventing social democratic ideas from developing in the country, within which the various positions of the Communist Party of South Africa (CPSA) (and then the SACP after 1950) was most significant. The CPSA/SACP drew on a Stalinist interpretation of social democracy in the 1930s that bizarrely equated 'social democracy' to fascism in its corporatist underpinnings (described as 'social fascism'). This interpretation prevented the dictatorship of the proletariat, which was the orthodox communist movement's favoured political strategy to achieve class power. This hostile ideological attitude to social democracy historically informed the political approach of orthodox communist parties, including the SACP, to 'non-communist' varieties of socialist thought. It is worth noting that celebrated Marxist theoretician Leon Trotsky did not share this orthodox view and argued for an anti-fascist front, including social democrats who would 'March separately, but strike together!' against fascism (Trotsky 1931: n.p.).

THE ANC AND THE POST-APARTHEID ALTERNATIVE

Most accounts suggest that the ANC paid little or no attention to economic (or social) policy during much of its history, including in the exile years. Its overall approach to politics could be described as 'liberal reformist'. This is best captured in its 1923 African Bill of Rights document, which demanded civil liberties for blacks equal to those enjoyed by whites under the 1910 Union Constitution. As Pallo Jordan has observed, 'as for the idea of radically restructuring the economy, that was not even a part of their political vocabulary' (1988: 149). Even though, under the presidency of Josiah Gumede, the ANC's political strategy was briefly radicalised, democratised and internationalised, Gumede's radicalism cost him the presidency. An old-guard leadership under Pixley ka Isaka Seme and Zacharias Richard Mahabane not only ousted Gumede, but drove out his working-class supporters in what Jordan (1988: 149) has described as a kind of McCarthy-style witch-hunt.

Attention to economic and social policy remained absent until Xuma's African Claims in South Africa was adopted (ANC 1943). African Claims was a document with a recognisably social democratic impetus in the proposals it put forward for a post-segregation society. It argued for state intervention to secure social rights to systems of health, education and welfare for all on the basis of universal political and social citizenship. While this social democratic impetus was sustained in the Freedom Charter of 1955, the banning of the ANC in 1961 led to the subsuming, if not near abandonment, of economic and social policy theorising in favour of a primary imperative to secure a unitary, non-racial, democratic state established on the basis of a universal franchise (Van Niekerk 2013; 2017).

But it is also undeniable, as Laurence Hamilton puts it, that

> *if not always completely worked out*, its focus on freedom from alien rule, colonialism and apartheid consistently involved a sense of what might be necessary for the real, concrete, everyday freedom of all South Africans within a democratic South Africa. This is evident in nearly every strategy

and policy document or publication ever since its founding in 1912 and in particular: the 1943 *African Claims in South Africa* document: the 1955 Freedom Charter … and the Reconstruction and Development Programme (2014: 17, emphasis added).

Though African Claims was lacking in specific substance and detail, we would agree that the ANC was therefore the carrier of important values and principles about the kind of post-apartheid society that was needed. We describe those values as being broadly 'social democratic' even though the movement rarely used this concept, which was traditionally associated with European left politics.

What needs to be borne in mind was that the ANC since its formation was faced with a well-resourced, Western-backed and brutally repressive regime, which consumed its attention and resources, in particular in establishing the conditions for a democratic society through revolutionary armed struggle. As late as 1987, the venerated leader of the ANC, Oliver Tambo, declared in a speech to international business that 'the African National Congress is committed to bringing about fundamental change to the entire socio-economic and political formation which constitutes the South Africa of today' (Tambo 1987: n.p.).

Tambo went further to say that on questions of relevance to economic policy the ANC 'has its perspectives, deriving from the people, which are embodied in the Freedom Charter adopted in 1955 … In the context of its parameters, we believe that the issues as to how the wealth of our country is redistributed for the benefit of all our people, how the economy of our country is remoulded in order that all South Africans may thrive and prosper, are of prime importance and should find their solutions in the *context of democracy*' (1987: n.p., emphasis added).

He then concluded his speech by saying that the primacy of establishing a non-racial democracy meant that 'the *preoccupation* of the African National Congress is, and should be, the relentless prosecution of the all-round struggle to achieve freedom and democracy in our country' (Tambo 1987: n.p., emphasis added).

In such a context, in which the ANC was fully preoccupied with establishing a non-racial democracy under severe conditions of political repression, the postponement of developing economic policy alternatives until democracy was achieved is understandable. Yet, from Tambo, it is also clear that when that time for economic and social policy development arrived, those policies had to be determined under the ideological umbrella of the Freedom Charter. Laurence Harris, the left-wing British economist and one of the ANC's foremost thinkers on economic matters in the 1980s and 1990s, concedes the point about the ANC's underdeveloped thinking on economic policy: '[T]he ANC did not give a high priority to research on economic policy' (1990: 25).[1] At the same time, this void in economic and social policy thinking was to impact negatively on the organisation's ability to think about economic and social policy at the time negotiations for democracy and freedom arrived in 1990.

Jeremy Cronin, then SACP deputy general secretary, has conceded that 'we were not well positioned, intellectually, theoretically in terms of policy formation, in terms of socio-economic transformation. It was understandable. We had been very focused on the political tasks, democratisation, mobilisation, fighting a guerrilla struggle' (in Gumede 2007: 84). Cronin makes a series of insightful observations on the ideological character of the SACP and the ANC on the eve of negotiations:

> The 1990s for the SACP was a paradoxical moment. The 'Soviet' legacy we were part of collapsed. The Party was unbanned in 1990 and half of the Party Central Committee resigns … *So the ANC does not [undertake] a profound reflection on the collapse of the Soviet Union and so forth, it just soldiers on … does not reflect on new global realities. And the new democracy is emerging with all kinds of economic policy mistakes and miscalculations and so forth* (Cronin interview, 14 March 2016, emphasis added).

We partially share Cronin's position that what happened was 'understandable', arguably a function of the balance of forces and the messy outcome characteristic of most negotiated settlements (see also chapter 4). Yet, after 1990, the ANC, seen through a balance-of-power lens, had some not inconsiderable moral and political power. At the international level, the ANC, and Mandela in particular, had virtually unqualified support from some Western governments. Bill Clinton, who was very close to Mandela, became president of the United States (US) in 1992. There was also significant support from Western civil society solidarity organisations, such as the Anti-Apartheid Movement based in the United Kingdom (UK) and the Black Caucus in the US. Locally, the ANC was unchallenged in its support through organisations such as the United Democratic Front, Cosatu and the South African National Civic Organisation, as well as the churches and other social movements. Never were South Africans more united in their stand to bring about a non-racial, non-sexist and unitary democratic South Africa. That this power was not used effectively to secure the left social democratic trajectory, which was historically embedded in the ANC, is something akin to a tragedy. This is a point that Ronnie Kasrils, too, makes powerfully (Interview, 30 March 2017).

At the same time, we do not, on the basis of our research, share the views of those who claim that the ANC leadership sold out in one form or other; we do not accept that those in positions of leadership in the ANC's economics team set out deliberately and solely for personal benefit or glory to sell out the ANC's historical commitment to social and economic justice; and we do not accept that the 'sell-out' occurred as a result of some kind of conspiracy and secret late-night meetings that involved international financial institutions and local capital.

Our research reveals many weaknesses in the ANC economics team, in its capabilities and experience, and in the processes and practices involved in the debate and negotiations around forging a post-apartheid economic strategy. It is also clear that some important progressive economic policy alternatives were ignored and then unceremoniously discarded. There are many complex and overlapping explanations for this, as we suggest in chapters 4 and 5.

We accept the existence of multiple influences – both economic and political, and both internal and external – on ANC economic thinking in the 1990s. While we point to such multiple influences and stress some that may have been underestimated or downplayed to date, we would like to emphasise upfront that it is not our intention in this book to offer any kind of mathematical or sociological 'weighting' of these multiple influences or indeed to 'finger' anyone or any group within or outside the ANC for what happened. We plan to provide the narrative of economic and social policy debates and thinking within the ANC Alliance in the 1990s as we saw it, warts and all,[2] as trained social science and economic researchers, admittedly with the benefit of hindsight, but also from our own perspectives as participants in some of these events.

It must also be stressed at the outset that we do not claim that we have mastered the whole story in every respect. This exercise has proven to be extremely difficult to research. Some participants in the drama of the 1990s with whom we were keen to speak were reluctant to grant us interviews; records, even those at some official archives, are still not complete or easy to access systematically; and there are likely to be records and personal recollections scattered across the nation and internationally that we were not even aware of. So all in all, if there are gaps and some misinterpretations, as there undoubtedly will be, we hope that this is understandable. Our aspiration is that we have begun to pave the way for later researchers to pick up and develop these threads more fully, until one day a more robust and sustainable record of these globally celebrated, yet complex, times is achieved.

2

African Claims, the Freedom Charter and Social Democracy, 1943–1960

THE ORIGIN OF SOCIAL DEMOCRATIC IDEAS IN THE STRUGGLE AGAINST FASCISM IN THE 1940S

The period between 1939 and 1945 was a significant one for the development of inclusive social policies that created the possibility of a social democratic option for a post-war, post-segregation South Africa. The war against fascism led to many white workers enlisting in the army. This meant that the United Party government under Jan Smuts was forced to depend on black economic and political support for the Allied war effort, of which South Africa was a part. The need to maintain 'industrial peace' in Smuts' phrase (Hansard, vol. 43, 1942, col. 5) and fearing Japanese invasion after the collapse of Singapore in February 1942, the United Party established a series of commissions on a post-war 'people's charter'. This included examination of the social needs of urban Africans, who were the bedrock of industrial growth and thus the war effort. These social policy reviews in health, education and welfare represented the most extensive examination of the effects of poverty and lack of social service provision in South African history, only surpassed by the democratic government of Nelson Mandela in 1994. The reviews identified the need for direct government intervention to overcome the failure of the policy of segregation to stem the tide of black urbanisation in the 1940s, and to ameliorate the health and welfare conditions of Africans in the urban areas. They also showed that the system of capitalism neglected to remunerate African workers at a level adequate to sustain their livelihood in urban areas.

A number of detailed social development proposals consistent with a broadly social democratic impetus emerged between 1940 and 1944. They recommended a national health service under state control; the extension of state housing and welfare provision for Africans; the eradication of the pass laws, which forcibly controlled the movement of Africans; the extension of social security into a national system incorporating urban Africans; central government control of African education; and specific measures around the extension of milk provision and feeding schemes for Africans. The political circumstances of the war against fascism induced this search on the part of the Smuts government for more inclusive social policies that could relieve the poverty of urban Africans, and was led by liberal reformers in the government. The unstated 'diswelfares' caused by segregation and capitalism were thus not allowed to remain undealt with, but were seen by these government commissions as the responsibility of the state.

The reformist proposals emerging in South Africa were broadly comparable to the more inclusive social policy proposals in the UK in the 1940s, based on state protected social rights of citizenship that were spearheaded by the Beveridge Report. These proposals eventually led to the establishment of the welfare state following a landslide Labour Party victory in 1945. In the colonies, the strategic consequences of the 'self-determination' provisions of the 1941 anti-fascist Atlantic Charter were also taken up by anti-colonial radicals (United Nations 2018). For example, as early as 1942, the African-independence political activist George Padmore identified the strategic importance of the call by the Atlantic Charter to make global democratisation and extension of welfare part of the struggle against colonialism (Padmore and Cunard 1942). This position was consolidated at the 5th Pan Africanist Congress in Manchester in 1945, where the resolution of the West Indies delegation was adopted. It called for the 'immediate introduction of all forms of modern social legislation in existence in metropolitan areas, e.g., old age pensions, family allowances, national health and unemployment insurances ...' (Padmore 1963: 60).

The anti-fascist 'war years' thus created a global climate for the investigation of radical social reform ideas of a social democratic character. These ideas were seized upon by intellectuals in the black opposition movements in South Africa, such as AB Xuma, a public health doctor and president general of the ANC between 1940 and 1949. The convergence on the need for fundamental social reforms in South Africa between the Xuma-led ANC and the segregationist, liberal, white ruling United Party of Smuts was made possible by the acceptance of the Atlantic Charter's provision for post-war democratisation and the extension of social security to all nations under nazi and fascist occupation. The United Party supported this objective globally and joined the war on the Allied side in 1940, while the ANC produced a citizenship charter in 1943, African Claims, which related the Atlantic Charter to the lack of democracy and social rights for blacks in South Africa. Both groups, for very different strategic reasons, hoped the implementation of the Atlantic Charter would be beneficial for post-war South Africa.

AFRICAN CLAIMS IN SOUTH AFRICA, 1943

The impact of the international rights-based Atlantic Charter of 1941, which established the political foundations for a post-war settlement, had a major influence on South African opposition political movements. In particular, its call to 'respect the right of all peoples to choose the form of government under which they will live; … and self-government restored to those who have been forcibly deprived of them', as well as its advocacy of inclusive social policy aimed at 'securing, for all, improved labour standards, economic advancement and social security' (Borgwardt 2002: 46), was applied to South Africa in the ANC's 1943 document, African Claims in South Africa. Leaders of the ANC, such as Xuma and ZK Matthews, were already exposed to a social rights discourse through their educational activities at liberal universities and intellectual engagements with liberals and civil rights activists in the US and Britain in the 1930s. For example, following the completion of his medical studies, Xuma gave a speech entitled 'Bridging the Gap between White and Black', which compared the position of blacks and whites in South Africa against an American ideal, and which gave 'hope and citizenship rights to all alike' (in Walshe 1970: 60). They were thus acutely interested in the implications for blacks in South Africa of the advocacy of global democratisation and social citizenship by Allied leaders, the US in particular, in opposition to fascism and nazism.

The African Claims policy framework for a social democratic future was firmly rooted in the intellectual traditions of the ANC. This was reflected in the Atlantic Charter Committee of 1943, assembled by Xuma to prepare the provisions of the African Claims document. The committee included leading figures of the African intelligentsia, such as the chairperson, ZK Matthews (executive member of the ANC); James Calata (secretary general of the ANC); Moses Kotane (general secretary of the Communist Party of South Africa [CPSA][1] and member of the ANC); Govan Mbeki (trade secretary of the Federation of Organised Bodies in Transkei); Edwin Mofutsanyana (member of the National Executive Committee of the ANC and member of the CPSA); Gana Makabeni, trade unionist and president of the

Council of Non-European Trade Unions); Pixley ka Isaka Seme (attorney and member of the ANC National Executive Committee); RV Selope Thema (editor of *Bantu World*, member of the Native Representative Council and speaker of the ANC); and AB Xuma (president general of the ANC). The thinking of the Atlantic Charter Committee was distilled in African Claims in South Africa, the most significant statement by the ANC in the war years on the new post-war 'good society', based on black enfranchisement and social rights of citizenship. Its strategic political intervention was to apply political, civil and social rights, which were advocated in the Atlantic Charter and endorsed by the ruling United Party, to the disenfranchised black people in South Africa.

The section on a Bill of Rights in African Claims echoed the American Declaration of Independence. It set out the most unequivocal statement of African expectations for full, unqualified rights to citizenship: 'We, the African people in the Union of South Africa, urgently demand the granting of full citizenship rights such as are enjoyed by all Europeans in South Africa' (ANC 1943: 217). The Bill of Rights then stipulated in greater detail the content of such citizenship, its specificity worth citing in some detail:

- **civil rights**: 'To equal justice in courts of law, including nominations to juries and appointment as judges, magistrates and other court officials'; 'Freedom of movement, and the repeal of the pass laws'. 'The right to own, buy, hire or lease and occupy land and all other forms of … property.'
- **political rights**, based on: 'Abolition of political discrimination based on race … and the extension to all adults, regardless of race, of the right to vote and be elected to parliament, provincial councils and other representative institutions'; 'The right to be appointed to and hold office in the civil service and in all branches of public employment.'
- **social rights,** based on: 'The establishment of free medical and health services for all sections of the population'; 'The right of every child to free and compulsory education and of admission to technical schools, universities and other institutions of higher education'; 'Equality of treatment with any other section of the population in the State social services, and the inclusion on an equal basis with Europeans in any scheme of social security'; 'That the African worker … be insured against sickness unemployment, accidents, old age and for all other physical disabilities arising from the nature of their work; the contributions to such insurance should be borne entirely by the government and the employers'; 'The extension of all industrial welfare legislation to Africans engaged in Agriculture, Domestic Service and in Public institutions or bodies' (ANC 1943: 217–221).

The ANC's 1943 Bill of Rights started from civil rights. These, in turn, led directly to political rights and finally to recognition of social rights. These claims prefigured TH Marshall's famous 1950 essay on citizenship and social class and the political evolution of civil, political and social rights through three consecutive stages (Marshall 1950). It represented the most significant statement on non-racial, universal rights of citizenship in the period of the 1940s, and, in its universality and focus on state-provided 'public goods', unambiguously represented the origins of inclusive social democratic thinking and a concomitant social democratic development path for post-segregation South African society.

However, for the ANC, led by Xuma, the absence of political enfranchisement of blacks revealed the limits of liberalisation and the possibilities for a broadly social democratic reform agenda suggested in the early war years. The authors of African Claims were not naive in their belief that the radical claims made would be acceded to. In the document's preface, Xuma states: 'As African leaders we are not so foolish as to believe that because we have made these declarations that our government will grant us our claims for the mere asking. We realise that for the African this is only a beginning of a long struggle entailing great sacrifices of them, means and even life itself. To the African people the declaration is a challenge to organise and unite themselves under the mass liberation movement, the African National Congress' (ANC 1943: 210).

After repeated failed attempts to secure a meeting with Smuts to discuss the implications of the Atlantic Charter, Xuma sent him a copy of African Claims and its Bill of Rights (Gish 2000). After reading the document, Smuts sent a reply to Xuma through his private secretary, Henry Cooper, in September 1944, rejecting African Claims as a 'propagandistic document intended to propagate the views of your Congress … [The prime minister] … does not agree with your effort to stretch its meaning so as to make it apply to all sorts of African problems and conditions. That is an academic affair which does not call for any intervention on his part …' (in Gish 2000: 129). The failure to implement inclusive social policies demonstrated the limits of social citizenship based on social democratic ideas in the absence of civil and political rights.

By 1945, the possibility of developing and implementing progressive social policies of a social democratic character was eclipsed by the right-wing drift of the white electorate, who voted the United Party back into power on a 110-seat majority in July 1943. The ANC, meanwhile, underwent a radicalisation following the confluence of a new militant Africanist nationalism under the stewardship of Anton Lembede and AP Mda, along with the increasing influence of trade unionism, the rise of civil disobedient squatter movements and boycotts of bus services.

SOCIAL DEMOCRACY AND THE FREEDOM CHARTER

The account of how the Freedom Charter came to be conceived, how a 'thoroughly bourgeois activist' (Bernstein 1999: 145), ZK Matthews, came to propose this 'radical' charter in Stanger, how the document came to be assembled from scraps of paper and the backs of envelopes are all well known. In his account of it, Rusty Bernstein (1999), one of its drafters, along with Ben Turok and many others, makes two important points. The first relates to the way in which the charter had to reconcile what appeared to be quite irreconcilable demands, reflecting the different strands within the ANC Alliance at the time. Thus, on economic policy, there were, among the scraps of paper in the tin trunk where they had been collected, demands for the nationalisation of mines and banks, alongside demands to end barriers to black private ownership and shareholding. Phraseology had to be employed creatively in an attempt to keep all sides happy, not always with success. Claims were made that the Communist Party influence ensured that the document had a socialist flavour and substance.

The reflections of Turok, a leading South African Communist Party (SACP) activist, on a 1953 clandestine meeting held at the factory of Julius First (a senior Party member) seems to support a non-interventionist Party influence in the strategic discussions on the Freedom Charter. The meeting was convened by Yusuf Dadoo, chairperson of the Central Committee of the SACP, with a group of seasoned communist activists, including Fred Carneson, Joe Slovo and Ruth First.

> We met in the factory, in the shed. And there were fires – coal burners – around the table, because it was freezing cold. And Yusuf opened up with a sort of international perspective. And then Michael Harmel led and so on. Now, we [the SACP] had a document called the 'Minimum Programme'.[2] When I was asked to speak, I thought, what am I going to say? I think I was told that, well, the Party programme, the Minimum Programme, should be somehow a basis for the Freedom Charter. Now it's not an instruction and I don't remember how that happened. I'm not sure that I consciously said to myself or anybody else that the Freedom Charter must reflect the Minimum Programme of the Party. But I think that in my mind there was that, you see. So when I came up to the meeting, the meeting the day before, when I was presented with this reformist economic clause [of the Freedom Charter], I looked at it and I thought, no no no. This is not what I'm about. Now, whether that was in my head ... or whether it was reflecting all the stuff I'd learnt in Europe, in England, in the Labour Party and all that, I can't recall. And who knows how one's consciousness works ... But there's no doubt that

the independent policy-making of the Party influenced all of us. How much, and to what degree, what the mechanisms were, I don't think I'm able to say. But it was there (Turok interview, 31 May 2014).

Bernstein (1999: 159) points out that 'nationalisation is not necessarily a gateway to socialism', making the example of the then nationalised railways and electricty supply, embedded within a system of white supremacy and gross economic injustice.

Bernstein's second point, either missed or little appreciated by most commentators, including ourselves until now, is that, contrary to general belief among Congress activists, 'debates over economic policy and the relative merits of capitalism and socialism were everyday stuff … The debate over the economic clauses of the Charter was not much more than an additional element in an ongoing debate' (Bernstein 1999: 160).

In a revealing response to Niël Barnard (the apartheid-era head of South Africa's National Intelligence Service) and others who visited Mandela in prison, when asked about the nationalisation policy of the ANC, Mandela's reply was that: 'Nationalisation might occur for certain "monopoly" industries but that he had always considered [the Freedom Charter] a blueprint for African-style capitalism' (Harvey 2001: 143). Of course, one has to remember his audience on this occasion. However, while some may stress the 'capitalism', we would point to the 'African' style; surely he had in mind a more collective, socialised form of economic organisation?

In *Season of Hope*, Alan Hirsch (2005) has pointed to a line in a 1956 article by Mandela, apparently supportive of the development of a black bourgeois class, in which he proposes that the ANC has always been a party of private enterprise, black business development and a market-oriented party. Rather than shifting to the right as some have suggested, the ANC was simply reverting to its pro-market, pro-private enterprise roots. We do not accept this argument. In our interpretation, Mandela's 1956 article, published in the journal *Liberation* and reproduced by Thomas Karis and Gwendolen Carter (1977), explicitly legitimates nationalisation of the wealth of the country, consistent with the provisions of the Freedom Charter. His arguments for a multi-class alliance led by working people to establish democratic governance in the interests of the whole society is perfectly consistent with a social democratic approach. Indeed, the stress on democracy is a characteristic feature of such an approach. Here are the relevant sections quoted in full:

> The workers are the principal force upon which the democratic movement should rely, but to repel the savage onslaughts of the Nationalist Government and to develop the fight for democratic rights it is necessary that the other

classes and groupings be joined … The cruel and inhuman manner with which they are treated, their dreadful poverty and economic misery, make them potential allies of the democratic movement. The Non-European traders and businessmen are also potential allies, for in hardly any other country in the world has the ruling class made conditions so extremely difficult for the rise of a Non-European middle class as in South Africa. The law of the country prohibits Non-Europeans from owning or possessing minerals. Their right to own and occupy land is very much restricted and circumscribed and it is virtually impossible for them to own factories and mills. Therefore, they are vitally interested in the liberation of the Non-European people for it is only by destroying white supremacy and through the emancipation of the Non-Europeans that they can prosper and develop as a class. To each of these classes and groups the struggle for democratic rights offers definite advantages. To every one of them the realisation of the demands embodied in the Charter would open a new career and vast opportunities for development and prosperity. These are the social forces whose alliance and unity will enable the democratic movement to vanquish the forces of reaction and win the democratic changes envisaged in the Charter (Mandela 1956: 7–8).

Turok responds to Hirsch by insisting that, while the ANC held some contradictory positions on this issue, it is wrong to claim that the ANC wanted 'free rein' for a bourgeois struggle. We will return to this point in chapter 4.

MASS-BASED POLITICAL MOBILISATION, NON-RACIALISM AND THE EMERGENCE OF THE FREEDOM CHARTER IN THE 1950S

This exclusionary Africanist position was to change with the 1952 Defiance Campaign against Unjust Laws and the development of a non-racial political tradition under the newly emerging political leadership of Oliver Tambo and Mandela.

The mass politics of defiance in the 1950s increasingly brought into focus the dialectic of race and class – that is, the struggle to overcome national oppression was not reducible to a struggle against apartheid racism but had to confront the class relationships that reproduced inequality and underpinned racism. By implication, it had to confront the nature of the post-apartheid state and the post-apartheid society offered as an alternative to capitalism, as well as the repressive social exclusion associated with draconian apartheid legislation.

The ANC's campaigning around rights of political citizenship became a primary focus of its political activities in the 1950s, with the specific concerns of social policy gradually subsumed under this primary political objective.

Andrew Mlangeni, last surviving member of the Robben Island group of Rivonia Trialists and a member of the CPSA and the ANC in the 1950s, was based in Dube, Soweto. His reflection on the ANC's preoccupation with national liberation objectives to the virtual exclusion of deliberations on economic policy is telling:

> You know in the 1950s, especially after the Defiance Campaign, the ANC was emphasising freedom, freedom for the people of South Africa, but in particular, the black people. There wasn't so much talk about the economic position of the country, what the policy of the ANC was on the economy of the country. What was being emphasised was largely freedom, that we must be free to elect a government of our own like the white people at the time. So that we can live as the white people of South Africa lived at the time. In the branches of the African National Congress not much was being discussed about the economy of the country. Things only changed after the Freedom Charter was adopted (Mlangeni interview, 6 October 2015).

In 1952, Albert Luthuli became the president general, and he was to lead the ANC until his death in 1967. Luthuli commented in 1952 on the shift to militant opposition around citizenship demands as follows:

> In so far as gaining citizenship rights and opportunities for the unfettered development of the African people, who will deny that thirty years of my life have been spent knocking in vain, patiently, moderately and modestly at a closed and barred door? What have been the fruits of my many years of moderation? Has there been any reciprocal tolerance or moderation from the Government, be it Nationalist or United Party? No! On the contrary, the past thirty years have seen the greatest number of laws restricting our rights and progress until today we have reached a stage where we have almost no rights at all: no adequate land for our occupation, our only asset, cattle, dwindling, no security of homes, no decent and remunerative employment, more restriction to freedom of movement through passes, curfew regulations, influx control measures; in short we have witnessed in these years an intensification of our subjection to ensure and protect white supremacy.

It is with this background and with a full sense of responsibility that, under the auspices of the African National Congress (Natal), I have joined my people in the new spirit that moves them today, the spirit that revolts openly and boldly against injustice and expresses itself in a determined and non-violent manner (in Pillay 1993: 47).

What accounts for this displacement in the ANC from a concerted attempt to develop economic and social policies under Xuma in the 1940s, leading to the social democratic formulations of African Claims, to the relative policy barrenness of the 1950s, leading up to the Freedom Charter of 1955? A telling reason could be the combination of increased repression under the apartheid regime and weariness with constitutionally bound protests, with a more militant political leadership emerging in the ANC. Turok explained it as follows:

Now you see, a leadership is sensitive to the mood of the people. My guess ... is that the masses were tired of a respectable ANC, and Mandela and Tambo and company reflected this tiredness. We want to go all out. Don't forget, the regime was more and more repressive. Things were getting rougher and rougher, and pass laws were tougher and so on. What you've got to do is also look at the social protest period, and see under this policy thing was there a different dimension, subterranean? And I suspect you'll find that. The Miners' Strike [of 1946] certainly shows that all this talk about nation-building representivity, inclusiveness and all this, underneath all that there were miners who were saying, 'To hell with this' ... Underneath these statements there was a kind of fatigue. The Fort Hare protests[3] shows you that they [the ANC Youth League members such as Mandela and Tambo] were willing to be sacked from Fort Hare and they were ... all that stuff shows that they were not at all impressed by this nation-building and representivity and the African Claims language. There was an undercurrent of fatigue, I suspect (Turok interview, 31 May 2014).

This period of militant opposition was met with a repressive response from the National Party and the introduction of legislation that curbed civil and political rights. These included the Suppression of Communism Act No. 44 of 1950; the Criminal Law Amendment Act No. 8 of 1953, which was aimed at anyone who protested against the repeal or modification of any law; and the Riotous Assemblies Act No. 17 of 1956, which prohibited public gatherings in open spaces if they threatened the public peace (SAIRR 1978: 418, 431).

In this climate of repression, social policy, the public good, was subordinated to the political objective of achieving an unqualified franchise. Nevertheless, in the period of the mass-based political activism of the 1950s, the ANC was moving to formalise its position on the place of democracy, social policy and the public good in relation to the state in a post-apartheid nation. This took the form of a public Congress of the People in 1955 in Kliptown, which inaugurated the Freedom Charter and which the ANC, with the SACP, were instrumental in organising. The Freedom Charter gave expression to the increasingly militant civil disobedience campaigns in favour of civil and political rights, such as the Defiance Campaign against Unjust Laws of 1952. The Freedom Charter contained a series of demands framed by the primary citizenship demand – 'The People Shall Govern'. In addition to civil and political rights, it contained demands for social rights consistent with social democracy, including rights related to income; state-provided education, which would be free; universal housing; and free state-provided medical care.

These were framed specifically as follows:

- The state shall recognise the right and duty of all to work, and to draw full unemployment benefits; Men and women of all races shall receive equal pay for equal work; There shall be a forty-hour working week, a national minimum wage, paid annual leave, and sick leave for all workers, and maternity leave on full pay for all working mothers.
- Education shall be free, compulsory, universal and equal for all children; Higher education and technical training shall be opened to all by means of state allowances and scholarships awarded on the basis of merit.
- All people shall have the right to live where they choose, be decently housed, and to bring up their families in comfort and security; Unused housing space to be made available to the people; Rent and prices shall be lowered, food plentiful and no-one shall go hungry; A preventive health scheme shall be run by the state (Freedom Charter 1955 in Karis and Carter 1987: 205–208).

The Freedom Charter contained demands about the control of wealth, which were predicated on public ownership and nationalisation as the mechanism to achieve it: 'The national wealth of our country, the heritage of South Africans, shall be restored to the people; the mineral wealth beneath the soil, the Banks and monopoly industry shall be transferred to the ownership of the people as a whole' (Freedom Charter 1955 in Karis and Carter 1987: 206).

Gavin Williams (1988: 81) argues convincingly that there are important continuities between the Freedom Charter and previous ANC statements, such as the Bill of Rights of African Claims, in that they both represented the interests of working people who were 'unified by the structures of racial discrimination and oppression'. Williams further makes the point that 'the Freedom Charter was distinctive in explicitly claiming South Africa for all its people, in its concern for the rights of all "nationalities" among the people and in taking up demands of women … and it puts forward a cogent series of declarations which resonate with a wide range of people's experiences and aspirations in a way that no previous documents ever did' (1988: 80).

The Freedom Charter represented a programme for a future post-apartheid society, but did not specify how this was to be achieved. Its declamatory tone suggested that it would involve a protracted political struggle, and its ideals would not be the subject of negotiation. Substantively, the goals of the Freedom Charter could not be achieved without a redistribution of wealth and resources between the white minority and the black majority. However, this does not imply that the major beneficiaries would necessarily be the working class and the poor, as the Freedom Charter was not a class-based, socialist programme; it incorporated demands on individual rights to land and property that were compatible with a liberal democracy. Mandela argued in 1956 that 'whilst the Charter proclaims democratic changes of a far-reaching nature it is by no means a blue-print for a socialist state but a programme for the unification of various classes and groupings amongst the people on a democratic basis' (1956: 5–6). In the same article, however, Mandela asserted: 'The Charter is more than a mere list of demands for democratic reforms. It is a revolutionary document precisely because the changes it envisages cannot be won without breaking up the economic and political set-up of present South Africa' (1956: 5). The demands of the Freedom Charter were not socialist but rather a confluence of revolutionary nationalist and social democratic approaches. This was reflected in demands for nationalisation of mineral wealth, banks and monopoly industry, which at a minimum implied an actively interventionist state. It would be in the emphasis placed on the implementation of economic and social policies that the limits of the Freedom Charter's objectives would be revealed, as they presupposed the establishment of a democratic government sympathetic to its implementation. Luthuli's comments to the 44th Annual Meeting of the ANC in December 1955 are instructive as to the interpretation of the Freedom Charter within the leadership of the ANC. Arguing that the Freedom Charter should be ratified (which it was eventually at a Special Conference of the ANC in April 1956), Luthuli asked:

> What is the implication of the charter? The charter definitely and unequivocally visualises the establishment of a socialistic state. It therefore brings up

sharply the ideological question of the kind of state the African National Congress would like to see established in the Union of South Africa.

...

My own personal leanings are towards the modified socialistic state, patterned on the present-day Great Britain, a middle-of-the-road state between the extreme ultra-capitalistic state as we see it in the United States, and the ultra-socialistic state as we see it in Communist Russia ... My advice to the conference would be to accept the charter with the qualification that it does not commit itself at present until further discussion on the principle of nationalisation, of means of production, as visualised in Section 3 of the charter (in Pillay 1993: 84–85).

Luthuli explicitly identified with the social democracy of Fabian socialism as found in the post-war British Labour Party, which ushered in the welfare state. Reflecting the plurality of thinking in the ANC, he considered himself a 'Christian socialist' (in Pillay 1993: 32). In an interview in *Drum* magazine in 1953, Luthuli was asked whether he considered communism a 'serious menace to South Africa', to which he answered:

No, I do not. The nature of our own movement at present is Nationalist rather than Communist. There should be room for all political parties among us. At the moment we are only concerned with rescuing ourselves out of the mire, and we cannot yet say which direction we shall follow after that. For myself, I would wish for Socialism, in the British sense – if I were in England I would vote for [Clement] Attlee. But in Congress we have people of many different political beliefs – Capitalists, Socialists, and the rest ... (Luthuli 1953: n.p.).

The key issue is that Luthuli identified himself as a non-communist socialist, rather than as anti-communist. In a response to an article in 1956 by prominent ANC Youth League intellectual and later member of the Liberal Party and Pan Africanist Congress (PAC), Jordan K Ngubane, on the communist influences on the ANC as reflected in the Freedom Charter, Luthuli distinguished the Freedom Charter from Soviet-style communism as follows:

Mr. Ngubane poses as an expert on the Communistic doctrines of Marx, Lenin and Engels and finds the Freedom Charter a Congress implemen-tation of these doctrines. I do not claim to be such an expert, but I deny categorically Mr. Ngubane's charges and I dare him to prove them. The most that could be said about the Freedom Charter is that it breathes in some of its clauses a socialistic and welfare state outlook, and certainly not a Moscow communistic outlook. Mr. Ngubane is concerned that the Charter calls for the nationalisation of certain branches of commerce and industry – in actual fact the number of such industries and commercial undertakings so mentioned is very limited; the Charter in this regard reads: 'The national wealth of our country, the heritage of all South Africans, shall be restored to the people; the mineral wealth beneath the soil, the banks and monopoly industry shall be transferred to the ownership of the people as a whole; all other industry and trade shall be controlled to assist the well-being of the people; all people shall have equal rights to trade where they choose, to manufacture and to enter all trades, crafts and professions.' 'The Land shall be shared among those who work it.' Mr. Ngubane would like the world to believe that this is a document preaching the Moscow communistic creed. In modern society, even amongst the so-called capitalistic countries, nationalisation of certain industries and commercial undertakings has become an accepted and established fact (Luthuli 1956: n.p.).

Even though the comments of Mandela and Luthuli suggest that there was contestation within the ANC over the redistributive emphasis of the Freedom Charter, it was ratified at the Annual Conference of 1955. Its strong advocacy of social rights and state intervention in securing such rights made it compatible with the development of a Keynesian, social democratic welfare state, based on the social rights of citizenship. This represented an unequivocal continuity with the social democratic agenda established in the 1940s by the ANC. Far from being a 'minimum programme', the Freedom Charter suggested such a far-reaching transformation of South Africa that it would take a social revolution to achieve the goals of the 'good society' implied in the realisation of its demands. Seen from the lens of a democratic South Africa, the realisation of these demands implies a radical transformation in the organisation of political and economic power in the country.

The National Party under Hendrik Verwoerd viewed the Freedom Charter as a direct challenge to its state authority, and the charter was met with a hostile response. The National Party arrested the leadership of all the major political groups that had been involved in the Freedom Charter campaign, foremost of which was the ANC. Over a period of four years, during the Treason Trial, it attempted to prove that the citizenship demands of the Freedom Charter could be achieved only by a violent overthrow of the ruling government. The attempt to do so failed, and the case was dropped in March 1961 when the court ruled there was no case to answer.

The ANC was committed to civil disobedience campaigning, which, it hoped, would lead to the ruling party agreeing to a national convention. Such a national convention would allow for meaningful negotiations on a future constitutional order, based on the universal extension of the franchise. The National Party regime rejected the proposal for a national convention and resorted to increased violent repression of political protest, culminating in the indiscriminate shooting of unarmed anti-pass law protesters in Sharpeville on 21 March 1960. A state of emergency was declared nine days later, effectively outlawing all opposition political activity. The ANC and the PAC were banned following the promulgation of the Unlawful Organisations Act No. 34 of 1960.

The ANC's response to the banning was contained in a statement by an Emergency Committee of the ANC on 1 April 1960. Recording that the ANC had historically attempted a non-violent, peaceful solution to resolving South Africa's political problems, the statement indicated that such a solution was not possible under the current government of Verwoerd: 'The first essential towards resolving the crisis is that the Verwoerd administration must make way for one less completely unacceptable to the people, of all races, for a Government which sets out to take the path, rejected by Verwoerd, of conciliation, concessions and negotiation' (in Karis and Carter 1987: 573).

It reiterated political citizenship as its primary demand: 'We cannot and never shall compromise on our fundamental demands, as set forth in the Freedom Charter, for the full and unqualified rights of all our people as equal citizens of our country. We do not ask for more than that; but we shall never be satisfied with anything less' (in Karis and Carter 1987: 573).

Finally, the statement listed a set of proposals calling for the end of the state of emergency and the release of political prisoners, scrapping the system of pass laws, and doing away with laws curbing civil and political rights, concluding with the demand for a 'new National Convention representing all people on a fully democratic basis, [which] must be called to lay the foundations of a new union, a non-racial democracy, belonging to all South Africans, and in line with the United Nations Charter and the views of all enlightened people everywhere in the world' (in Karis and Carter 1987: 573).

The banning of the ANC in 1960 put an end to the possibility of dialogue between the opposition movement and the government on a democratic constitutional order, based on a universal franchise. The banned ANC was left with no alternative but to rely on mass mobilisation and underground forms of struggle as a means of overthrowing the apartheid regime, including the use of armed struggle.

By 1962, Luthuli was more categorical about the form of interventions that the state should support to realise the post-apartheid good society. In an article entitled 'If I were Prime Minister', published in the United States in *Ebony* magazine in February 1962, he offered economic and social policy proposals that unambiguously reflected his intention to establish a social democratic welfare state in South Africa if he was made prime minister:

> The solution to the South African problem will call for radical reforms, some of them of a really revolutionary nature. The basic reform will be in the form of the government. At present, there is a government by whites only. This should be replaced by a government which is truly a government of all the people, for the people, and by the people. This can only be so in a state where all adults – regardless of race, colour or belief – are voters. Nothing but such a democratic form of government, based on the parliamentary system, will satisfy (Luthuli 1962: 21).

Indicating his own preference for a state based on social democracy, Luthuli argued that to address the 'man-made inequality' of apartheid 'will demand what will appear to whites in South Africa to be revolutionary changes. Some form of a system such as is found in Great Britain and Sweden might meet the case' (Luthuli 1962: 22).

Luthuli then expressed the mechanisms that the state would employ to achieve its social democratic policy goals of free education, affordable municipal housing and state-provided employment for 'the bulk of people', who would also enjoy unqualified rights to unionisation:

> It is inevitable that nationalization and control – even on a larger scale than now – would be carried out by the government of the day after freedom, if justice is to be done to all, and the state enabled to carry out effectively its uplift work … State control will be extended to cover the nationalization of some sectors of what at present is private enterprise. It will embrace specifically monopoly industries, the mines and banks, but excluding such institutions as building societies (Luthuli 1962: 23).

Luthuli then advocated that the new government should have as its objective the creation of a 'democratic social welfare state': 'I realize that a state such as

I visualize – a *democratic social welfare state* – cannot be born in one day. But it will be the paramount task of the government to bring it about and advance it without crippling industry, commerce, farming and education' (1962: 26, emphasis added).

Most tellingly the article reveals that Luthuli had given some thought to the actual policies that the state would employ in order to achieve its goals that were consistent with social democracy. These included government regulation and nationalisation of the private sector; redistributive rates of taxation; and protection of workers' right to strike, concomitant with the entitlements associated with 'social compacting'-type accords between labour, the state and enterprise as found in Scandinavian social democracies and the post-war British Labour Party under Clement Attlee, which ushered in the welfare state:

- Private enterprises, commerce and industry *would be under government control as now, and probably stricter. Supertax on all high incomes should be levied on a higher percentage than now to meet the needs of uplifting the oppressed of former days.*
- *State control should be extended to cover the nationalisation of some sectors of what at present is private enterprise.*
- Human rights as declared by the United Nations would be entrenched in the State Constitution.
- All workers would enjoy unqualified trade union rights *with a charter laying down minimum wages and conditions.* There would be no discrimination on grounds of colour or race. Merit would be the qualifying factor.
- The present framework of industrial legislation in so far as it applies to Whites would form the basis of industrial legislation. *Workers would have the right to strike, for even if strikes might be costly and wasteful, it gives the individual a greater security if he knows he has the right, and it makes him feel a partner in the undertaking* (Luthuli 1962: 23, emphasis added).

The discourse within the ANC between 1940 and 1962 as reflected in its key policy documents and the thinking of its presidents on a future state that could overcome the legacies of segregation and apartheid were premised on a state form that was democratic and would intervene in the economy to secure redistributive social policies in health, education and welfare. The substantive form of such a state was a social democratic welfare state. This is reflected in the policy formulations of the 1955 Freedom Charter, which demonstrated a reconnection with the inclusive discourse of the 1943 African Claims, and unequivocally in social policy with a social democratic idea of the post-apartheid 'good society'.

The evidence from ANC policy literature and the reflections of key ANC thinkers and leaders such as Xuma and Luthuli (neither of whom were members of the CPSA) reveal that the ANC had an unmistakably social democratic view of the post-segregation and post-apartheid 'good society'. Veterans such as Turok, Ahmed Kathrada and Mlangeni, whom we interviewed, confirm this picture of an ANC that was strongly committed to a society and an economy where the interests of the poor, marginalised, oppressed and exploited were to be the main focus of its work in any future democratic government, where it would rest with the state to drive this process through redistributive economic and social policies. Whether they articulated this as social democracy or socialism or something else matters less than the essential substance of the thinking and ideas.

The debate on ANC economic and social policies for a post-apartheid society, such as they were before 1994, were to evolve in three distinctive locales: Robben Island, the exile community and, in the latter part of the 1980s and 1990s, within South Africa. The following chapter reveals some telling observations from Mlangeni on the narrowing interpretations of the 'nationalisation' clause of the Freedom Charter as discussed among the imprisoned ANC comrades. It suggests that the more radical social democratic impetus, advocated by Luthuli up until and shortly following the banning of the ANC in 1961, would not be developed much further. The primary imperative of national liberation, based on a multi-class alliance of the oppressed, dominated the discourse of the ANC and eclipsed the clearly articulated policy proposals developed by Xuma and Luthuli.

3

Incarceration, Exile and Homecoming, *c.*1960–*c.*1991

In 1961, the ANC was declared a banned organisation. Many of its leaders were arrested; others had to go underground or flee the country for Lusaka, London and other parts of the world sympathetic to their cause. The years that followed required a whosesale reorganistion of the movement in a difficult global context dominated by Cold War considerations. The West provided little support for the ANC, while offering considerable financial and political support to the apartheid regime. The role of the American Central Intelligence Agency (CIA) in tipping off the South African authorites about Nelson Mandela's whereabouts, which led to his arrest near Howick, Natal, in August 1962, has been well documented. The US Consul in Durban, Donald Rickard, was the CIA operative who provided the information. The arrest had the effect of seriously setting back the struggle against the apartheid regime (Garcia 2016: n.d.). In London, Oliver Tambo secured a base for the ANC, from which it could begin the massive task of raising funds, developing new political strategies and growing international support under Cold War conditions. And in Lusaka, the ANC began, with limited resources, to establish a rudimentary living and working base, as well as the elaborate machinery and structures, to wage the military and propaganda campaign against the apartheid state (Macmillan 2013). In all this, the role of its (acting) president, Tambo, loomed large. But we begin this chapter on an island within view of Cape Town's Table Mountain, which used to be a leper colony and is today one of the wonders of the new world.

ROBBEN ISLAND

The winter of 1964 on Robben Island, when Mandela and six other Rivonia prisoners arrived there, was the coldest that anyone could remember. So fierce were the Atlantic winds sweeping across the island that prisoners working in the quarries were numbed to the bone, hardly able to raise their picks … [The cell of the man who would forever be remembered as the world's most famous prisoner] was so cold he slept fully dressed in prison garb. Outside the cell was fixed a white card giving his name and identification number: 466/64 (Meredith 1997: 281).

While robust, organised discussions occurred on matters of political economy and strategies of political liberation, very little of what we could describe as economic and social policy debates occurred within ANC or other circles on Robben Island. Here, as compared to the more policy-oriented, evidential and analytical chapters that follow, we can only offer some anecdotal and personalised glimpses into issues that are tangentially linked to economics and social policy. This is partly because, as Pallo Jordan has noted (see chapter 1), little such policy debate took place on the Island for understandable reasons, but also because so few reliable or consistent sources exist about those aspects of life on Robben Island. Ahmed Kathrada and Andrew Mlangeni (among the most senior ANC leaders who were imprisoned on the island from the mid-1960s), whom we interviewed for this study, confirm these impressions obtained from the secondary literature.

Education and economics on the Island

Robben Island lies off the coast of Cape Town and is the site where political prisoners were incarcerated by the National Party government. It was often referred to as 'the university' because a lot of learning took place there. Less well-educated prisoners took high school courses through Rapid Results College, and more formally educated comrades registered for degrees and diplomas at the University of South Africa (Unisa) – both were correspondence-based institutions. Mandela and the Pan Africanist Congress (PAC) leader Robert Smangiliso Sobukwe both studied at the University of London by correspondence, the latter for a degree in economics (Pogrund 1990: 195). One of the biggest problems faced by prisoners in relation to their studies was the restriction and censorship of books and other study material. All books bearing in the title the words Marx, Marxism, Lenin,

Leninism, Russia, China, Cuba, socialism, communism, revolution, civil war, violence, Africa, anti-apartheid and all books of any kind written by black authors were routinely banned. Although most academic journals were also subject to draconian censorship, the *South African Journal of Economics* and *African Studies* were not proscribed. Most issues of the *Financial Mail* were stopped; the few let through were extensively redacted, apart from the advertisements. The British *Economist* somehow got through but only in a mutilated state until it, too, was banned in 1968. *Farmer's Weekly, Huisgenoot, Readers Digest, South African Panorama* and *Lantern* were allowed in, although often heavily censored (Alexander 1994: 60–65).

Around 1966, Sobukwe was allowed to read the British economics magazine *Economica*, which had suddenly and without explanation been made available to him (Pogrund 1990: 241). Later, when formal studying was allowed, Sobukwe read, among other 'heavyweight titles' (as Benjamin Pogrund puts it), *Capitalism, Socialism and Democracy* (presumably by Joseph Schumpeter). Sobukwe comments, 'I never dreamt I would come to enjoy Economics like this … [though] some articles, while interesting, contain so much maths that they leave huge gaps in my understanding' (Pogrund 1990: 250).

Few would contest the view that Govan Mbeki was the most educated and well-read of the Robben Island prisoners in matters related to the study of economics. We rely mainly here on Colin Bundy's (2012) excellent biography of Mbeki. Mbeki took formal courses in business economics through correspondence study at Unisa and other tertiary institutions; he successfully read for an Honours degree in economics and began coursework towards a Master's in economics. His essays, some for formal study, were many and varied and showed a highly sophisticated grasp of both economic theory and economic history. His three-part essay on 'The Rise and Growth of Afrikaner Capital' demonstrates his skills as an analyst of the economics and politics of the growth of this racially defined fraction of South African capital; significantly, it predates Dan O'Meara's (1983) classic study of the same subject (*Volkskapitalisme*) by two years. Mbeki also wrote a theoretical essay entitled 'Notes on the Business Cycle, Unemployment, Inflation and Gold', making the point that Afrikaner economists favoured a certain amount of inflation for economic growth, as rising prices would lead to rising profits and business development. He wrote an insightful essay entitled 'Economic History: South Africa' as well as one on a subject once again very topical in South Africa today, entitled 'Monopoly Capitalism in South Africa: Its Role and Extent'. One final example of the essays he wrote was entitled 'Movements in African Real Wages: 1939–1969' (Mbeki 2015).

Given the time, context and prevailing restrictions, it is not surprising that Mbeki did not turn his undoubted intellect to matters of economic policy. Nevertheless, his work suggests that he understood the Freedom Charter as a policy document of the National Liberation Movement, and not just as a political programme. Among other arguments Mbeki made was one against the proposition that the Freedom Charter would permit a flowering of African capitalists, making a case instead of the Freedom Charter as a vision of a 'national democratic republic' and as a 'transitional phase towards a socialist society' (Mbeki 2015: 37). We learn from Bundy's afterword to the book that Mbeki settled for the 'modest revolution' of 1994 and voiced no public criticism of the neo-liberal Growth, Employment and Redistribution programme, championed by his son, Thabo (Mbeki 2015: afterword).

Despite restrictions on reading, there were often robust and sometimes tense debates and clashes among ANC comrades over a range of political and social issues, some of which have only come to light after 1990. Mandela and Govan Mbeki clashed over the latter's attempts to get the ANC to mobilise and organise to link worker and peasant struggle, as well as over Mandela's apparent willingness to open talks with Bantustan leaders.

Although both men have denied it, Govan Mbeki's relationship with Mandela was particularly complicated. They disagreed strongly over Operation Mayibuye – the swashbuckling programme for armed insurrection which Mbeki wrote with Joe Slovo in the early 1960s – and then, in prison, over Mandela's willingness to entertain alliances with Bantustan collaborators. So serious was the conflict between the two men at one point that, in 1975, a group of nine ANC leaders on Robben Island convened to try to find a solution; a report smuggled out to ANC leadership in Lusaka contended that 'the two who represented polar opposites in attitudes and opinions were Madiba and Govan' (ANC 2001: n.p.).

In the midst of such titanic clashes over political tactics and strategy, some further evidence of matters related to economic and social issues could be found. Thus, for example, in *Long Walk to Freedom* Mandela remarks:

> For a number of years, I taught a course in political economy. In it, I attempted to trace the evolution of economic man from the earliest times up to the present, sketching out the path from ancient communal societies to feudalism to capitalism and socialism. I am by no means a scholar and not much of a teacher, and I would generally prefer to be asked questions than to lecture. My approach was not ideological, but it was biased in favour of socialism, which I saw as the most advanced stage of economic life then evolved by man (Mandela 1994d: 455).

This sense that socialism was the end goal of the struggle, as expressed here by Mandela, was shared by most of the leadership of the anti-colonial struggle in Africa and Asia in the post-war era. Largely based on a broad allegiance to the communist ideology of the Second International and Third International, this approach was rarely debated. The nature of the economic transformation was mostly taken as obvious, flowing from the expected collapse of capitalism under its inherent contradictions and a more or less seamless transition to socialism. ANC comrades on Robben Island, in South Africa generally and in exile benefited from reading Maurice Cornforth, Maurice Dobb, George Padmore and Eric Williams, among others, writers whose works revolved around anti-colonial and anti-segregationist struggles in various parts of the world (Maharaj interview, 16 August 2016).[1] As Mac Maharaj observes:

> I can only speak from my recollection of what the kinds of issues were that we were living in the 50s when I became active, and the 60s. And I think that the mood in the 1950s, not only in the left movement but in the broad anti-colonial movement, was that the question of the transformation of society, particularly the economic transformation, had certain easy answers. And those easy answers were largely based on the experience of the Second and Third Internationals. Even the debate from the Fourth International assumed that that transformation is an easy thing to achieve (Maharaj interview, 16 August 2016).

According to Mlangeni, discussions on the Island among ANC prisoners were 'based purely on the Freedom Charter'. They seemed largely to be restatements of the intentions of the Freedom Charter and the non-racial society based on equality it sought to create with little attention to the policies, programmes or mechanisms by which this was to be achieved:

> We said, if we achieve what is said in the Freedom Charter, we'll have achieved the kind of South Africa, a society in South Africa that we'd like to see emerge, a society where people are equal … We want the land which was largely owned by white people, to be owned by all the people of South Africa, there must be equal distribution of the land among all the people of South Africa, for example. People must be equal before the law, something which did not happen before, the judiciary, the judges, the magistrates must treat black people the same way they treat white people in court, you must be treated as a human being (Mlangeni interview, 6 October 2015).

Mlangeni revealingly indicates that when the Freedom Charter clause on nationalisation was debated on Robben Island, his original view that it represented a socialist proposal was disavowed during the discussion.

> At first I also had the same view that nationalisation of the mineral resources, etc., is socialism but further discussions, more discussions on the Island proved to us that no, it doesn't mean that we are introducing socialism in South Africa. It simply means that banks and mineral resources must be shared among those who work it; it doesn't mean introducing socialism … I also had that interpretation that it meant that the resources must be shared among the people of South Africa (Mlangeni interview, 6 October 2015).

It is a moot point whether discussions of the Freedom Charter on the Island, in which Mandela was a key figure, opened up or closed down the powerful social democratic impetus in the thinking of Albert Luthuli over the period of the mid-1950s to the early 1960s, as discussed in chapter 2. It would seem from the available evidence (including from *Long Walk to Freedom*) that Mandela was politically cautious and privileged the multi-class alliance politics of the ANC in the context of the imperatives of national liberation. Luthuli went much further to engage with the implications of the social democratic path he advocated, unequivocally locating a central role for labour in such a social democratic agenda of social compacting.

Of course, the conditions for any such open debate among comrades on Robben Island were very constrained for many obvious reasons. Among other factors were that the ANC leadership (the High Organ) was physically separated from other political prisoners and because of the limitations of prison life in South Africa under grand apartheid (Kathrada interview, 9 October 2015). This is how Maharaj describes the conditions:

> Look at it from the point of view of the prisoners in those circumstances. I left in 1976; by 1978 they had stopped taking them to the quarry to work. You're now roaming around in the single cells fairly freely, you can play sports, you've got a dining room, you can sit down and discuss and slowly more newspapers are becoming available, but that's only what you're getting. So, your information is extremely patchy. It is not sufficient to make any solid study of any problem. There is no in-depth debate, there is no continuity in your reading (Maharaj interview, 16 August 2016).

'Inqindi and Marxism'

Kathrada, who admitted to knowing little about economics, pointed out that little or no economic or social policy debates occurred on Robben Island in the first ten to twelve years after 1964. The Freedom Charter, including its economic clauses as approved by the ANC in 1956, was accepted without question. However, in the later 1970s, after the Soweto student protests, many young ANC cadres arrived on the Island. After they fled South Africa, they had been trained in countries such as the German Democratic Republic. These young comrades contributed to a revival in discussions about both political strategy and (to some extent and indirectly) economic policy. The meaning and value of the Freedom Charter in changing circumstances became a subject of intense debate (Kathrada interview, 9 October 2015).

It seems that the coming to power of 'Marxist' parties in both Angola and Mozambique in the mid-1970s was also a powerful lever to reopen these debates. While the two-stage theory of revolution and internal colonialism was not directly raised, the question that arose was: if the Angolans and Mozambicans could take the great leap from essentially peasant societies to Marxism-Leninism, why not South Africa? Could South Africa, too, not take one big step to socialism? (Maharaj interview, 16 August 2016).

It was in that context that the document that came to be called 'Inqindi and Marxism' was drafted. *Inqindi* is an isiZulu and isiXhosa word meaning 'fist'. Little has been written about this milestone document that was produced and circulated on Robben Island after 1978. It is not even certain who wrote the first draft, or who edited it. Kathrada tells us that he acted as something of a go-between among prisoners in the drafting of the document (Kathrada interview, 9 October 2015).

According to Kathrada, Mandela and his comrades in B section had a first stab at it, and later, after comments were received from comrades in other sections, he was tasked with liaising with as many comrades as he could and writing the final version, incorporating all comments. There were two main aims of producing the document. The first was to encourage all comrades, whether from the ANC or the South African Communist Party (SACP), to study Marxism. The second aim was to remind comrades of the difference between a national struggle and class struggle (Gerhart and Glaser 2010: 492–497). The core of the arguments in 'Inqindi' relate to the role of the working class in the struggle, and from there about whether the struggle was for a nationalist or a socialist future. There was a debate about the use and meaning of the phrases such as a 'national bourgeoisie', 'national democracy' and 'bourgeois democratic republic', which were used in drafts.

33

For us here it is important to realise that one element of the debate was to under-stand the economic basis of class conflict through 'scientific knowledge'. However, there was no elaboration on this point and we are no wiser from studying the document about how far forward it took the understanding about the nature and character of the struggle. On one point, however, it is clearer and more interesting: 'Unlike Marxism which guides a CP [communist party] before and after the taking of power, the role of African nationalism is limited to the pre-liberation phase of the struggle. It cannot be used to reshape society after liberation, nor for the purpose of developing a new mode of production different from capitalism or socialism, as some political organisations claim' (Gerhart and Glaser 2010: 497).

In the end, it could only be claimed that the document asserts the dynamic nature and flexibility of the Freedom Charter and its value to the struggle over two decades after Kliptown – in short, a 'progressive nationalism' (Gerhart and Glaser 2010: 497).[2]

Maharaj, who was no longer in prison when 'Inqindi' was being drafted, recalls the mood and thinking around 1978:

> But I know a number of comrades, who were the leading voices in our internal discussions on the Island, raised the question on whether the time had not arrived for the ANC and the Congress movement to proclaim its objective of socialism. Because we were looking at what was happening in Angola and Mozambique with a sense of excitement … So, whatever was happening was in a very strange way being taken and put into a theoretical box that you created … You were not looking (sic) that the reality was chan-ging your theoretical outlook … So, when I got out of prison [1976] and I got to Mozambique, I was there for just a few days, but I remember my shock when I learned that the barber shops had become nationalised. And I said, my God, is this what I was saying is a great development, right, what is this about? (Maharaj interview, 16 August 2016).

In summary, within the limits of the strict censorship of literature, some reading around questions of the economy took place but these readings and discussion did not lead to any direct consideration of economic or social policy. Some debates over the Freedom Charter's clauses did occur but there appears to have been con-sensus about the correctness of the Freedom Charter's broad-church approach. The question of whether a direct (one-stage) struggle for a socialist goal should be waged only comes up after the arrival on Robben Island of the young post-Soweto generation of prisoners. 'Inqindi' represents an attempt to come to grips with their concerns, but in the end it does not resolve the matter one way or the other.

IN EXILE: LUSAKA, THE ECONOMICS UNIT AND THE DEPARTMENT OF ECONOMIC PLANNING

The nature of life in exile

> Physically, it's like being in South Africa again. I feel at home and elated. The climate is mild, unlike the enervating humidity of Dar es Salaam and Luanda … jacarandas are in bloom. Then there are the images: Asian shops with Coca-Cola and Vaseline adverts in so-called 'second class' business districts; the crowded townships abuzz with hawkers selling everything from boot polish to bananas and single cigarettes; the suburban houses with 'Beware of the Dogs' signs; walls with jagged glass along the tops to deter 'kabalalas' (burglars); South African railway wagons with the SAR–SAS logo in English and Afrikaans; school kids in neat European-style uniforms … (Kasrils in Macmillan 2013: 6–7).

Hugh Macmillan also reminds us, however, that 'any study of the ANC in exile has to begin by stressing the homesickness, loneliness, pain, alienation, sense of loss and the waste of energy and time that were essential features of life for most exiles and for much of the time' (2013: 1). There can be no doubting this sense of pain and loss.

The 'semi-detached member of the ANC', Ez'kia Mphahlele, observed in an interview:

> When I was abroad I felt that the ANC in exile was quite something else. The leaders were there all right, but the things that they were doing just didn't seem to me to be important at all. Trivialities like attending conferences of one kind or another, tearing across the world, you know, and getting international money. Also, tribalism was pretty rampant in the exile movement. Xhosa against Zulu against Sotho. I kept saying to myself: back home there had been so much cohesion among us. I mean nobody ever bothered about these ethnic groupings at all. But in exile, man, the thing just emerged in bold relief (in Macmillan 2013: 3–4).

A second contextual point to note concerns the well-documented narratives of corruption, greed and personal wealth accumulation that pervaded the ANC in Lusaka, at the expense of the movement's foot soldiers. There are accounts of smuggling donated goods across borders for private gain, of foreign funds being diverted to buy luxurious cars for top ANC officials and more. Terry Bell reminds us: 'Hani and six of his comrades penned a memorandum complaining of the nepotism, rot and corruption in the ANC after the shambles of the Wankie and Sipolilo campaigns of 1967/8. For Hani's pains a hearing was held, and he was sentenced to death, a sentence later overturned by then acting ANC president OR Tambo. Hani left the ANC for a time before being persuaded to return' (Bell 2016: n.p.).

One final point on the Lusaka context was made by Jeremy Cronin, and that relates to the splits and divisions among the ANC membership based there:

> I was now in the underground structures in Cape Town, in the UDF [United Democratic Front], and from the underground structure we sent out a request to Lusaka through complicated couriers and all kinds of dangerous things for ourselves and the couriers, what to do about one of the trade unions. I think it was in the clothing sector. We were looking for advice. And eventually we did not get a response … So eventually we just did what we, through our native intelligence, we could see needed to be done. And then about a year later, through again a complicated channel a thing came back telling us to do something which completely misunderstood the reality … Remember, in our time, how people would say, Lusaka says,
>
> …
>
> And when I got to Lusaka I realised, okay, this particular grouping, the so-called cabal, they are not aligning to Lusaka's Mac Maharaj … This particular grouping, they are not aligning to Lusaka's Chris Hani. But we got a warning a bit from Jack and Ray Simons when they came home, at their famous 1990 UWC [University of the Western Cape] welcoming home, and they said, you guys are kind of getting it wrong here, you know. It is we guys who must kind of learn from you guys (Cronin interview, 14 March 2016).

In summary, the general conditions of exile life in Lusaka do not appear to have been conducive to serious attention to and debate about matters of economic and social policy. Instead, much attention appears to have been directed at other, sometimes more basic, struggles, tensions and divisions within the movement. Yet, evidence does exist that the ANC began more seriously than ever before to consider the establishment of structures to analyse economic conditions and the nature of South African capitalism, and it is to these matters that we now turn our attention.

The Morogoro Conference of 1969

Arguably the most interesting and important statement of the ANC's stance on 'economic policy' before the 1980s, alongside that of the 1962 statement by Luthuli (see chapter 2), is to be found in the 1969 'Strategy and Tactics' document (ANC 1997). The national consultative conference in Morogoro came at a time when the ANC was at a crossroads over several major issues: addressing the memorandum of grievances prepared by Hani and some of his colleagues following the Wankie campaign; palpable tensions between communists and nationalists within the movement; and the debate over the question of admitting Indians, coloureds and whites as full members of the ANC itself. All this was happening at a time when Tambo, who had assumed the ANC leadership in 1967 after Luthuli had died under mysterious circumstances outside Groutville in Natal, was grappling with a number of major strategic matters. For instance, he was trying to establish the ANC's political footprint and credibility as the leading component of the liberation movement both internationally and within South Africa, while at the same time securing its financial sustainability and its global diplomatic stature.

These issues and the way they were addressed are mainly outside the scope of this book. The 1969 'Strategy and Tactics' document, however, is important for the vision that it developed for the movement going forward, a vision that touched on matters social and economic. In a clear reference to the programme of nationalising the commanding heights of the economy, it stated:

> In our country – more than in any other part of the oppressed world – it is inconceivable for liberation to have meaning without a return of the wealth of the land to the people as a whole. It is therefore a fundamental feature of our strategy that victory must embrace more than formal political democracy. To allow the existing economic forces to retain their interests intact is to feed the root of racial supremacy and does not represent even the *shadow of liberation*.[3] Our drive towards national emancipation is therefore in a very real way bound up with economic emancipation (ANC 1997: 17, emphasis added).

While not going all the way to endorse an advance to a communist or socialist future, as does 'The Road to South African Freedom', the SACP's 1962 programme, this is nevertheless very close to that without using those exact words. Thomas Karis and Gail Gerhart make the following comment on this point: '*Strategy and Tactics* essentially reiterated the analysis of the SACP's program of 1962, that the South African system was a "colonialism of a special type". These words did not appear in the ANC document, but in virtually identical language, *Strategy and Tactics* declared that the "main content of the present stage of the South African revolution is the national liberation of ... the African people"' (1997: 36).

While recognising various tendencies within the broad church of the ANC, a more progressive (arguably, left social democratic) policy agenda emerges out of Morogoro's 'Strategy and Tactics' document, and not a narrow African nationalist agenda. Even Stephen Ellis, a fierce critic of the ANC and SACP, has argued that the document 'clearly reflected the influence of the Communist Party's manifesto published in 1962 ... It marked the ascendancy of the SACP's theoretical and practical vision of struggle within the ANC' (2015: 77). Ellis may have meant this in a pejorative and cynical sense, but there is every reason to believe that he was right. 'Strategy and Tactics' clearly lays down a strong marker about where the ANC stood at that moment in its history as far as economic emancipation was concerned.

The Economics Unit

In 1980, the ANC in Lusaka approached the Regional Economic Commission for Africa (ECA) for assistance in conducting a socio-economic survey of South Africa. In order not to lose control of the project, the ANC decided to mobilise and organise its own in-house capacity to contribute to and shape the outcomes of the ECA-led survey. In that way, the Economics Unit of the ANC, headquartered in Lusaka, came into being in February 1982. It brought together 'politicised economists' from different existing departments, since one of its aims was to support other departments, such as the Treasury, Information and Publicity, Research and the International Department, in their work. More generally, its work was to be focused on 'interpreting economic issues for the movement and preparing briefings and fact papers for the National Executive Committee of the ANC' (ANC Lusaka Mission Archives, Box 84, Folder 9).

Pallo Jordan, who was head of ANC Research in Lusaka, informs us that the Unit did not do economic policy work in any direct sense. It was set up to analyse selected aspects of the South African economy, including issues around monopoly capital and South African conglomerates. It commissioned or co-ordinated a variety of projects. Norman Levy, then based in Amsterdam, conducted a skills audit of the African labour force in South Africa. Jordan himself wrote a paper on the National African Federated Chamber of Commerce and Industry (Nafcoc) as part of a project on the African bourgeoisie. Victor Matlou wrote a paper entitled 'South African Monopoly Capitalism, Social Deprivation and Social Emancipation' for a Council for the Development of Social Science Research in Africa (Codesria) conference. Laurence Harris – a leading member of the Economic Research on South Africa (EROSA) group of progressive academic economists in London and a member of uMkhonto we Sizwe (MK) (see chapter 4) – prepared a paper for the unit on the mixed economy model, but Jordan does not remember Harris presenting the paper in Lusaka (Jordan interview, 4 August 2017).

About 50 such political economists were brought together in the Economics Unit; they were based in both Zambia and Tanzania. Various fields of responsibility were identified and individuals were assigned to these. Thus, for example, Thabo Mbeki (then recently back from his postgraduate studies at the University of Sussex) was responsible for development strategy; Selebano Matlape was delegated to mining; Conny Dlinges and Tony Seedat to industry; Barney Pitso and Jacob Chiloane to agriculture (policy and practice); and Sizakele Sigxashe and [M] Medupe to the financial and monetary system.

Others involved in the work of the Unit from early on, some since its establishment, included Max Sisulu (later its head), former student leader Jeff Marishane and Patrick Magapatona (its long-standing secretary). Thabo Mbeki, Jaya Josie and Neva Makgetla also served in the Unit at various times in the early 1980s.

The academic qualifications of those economists based in Tanzania are provided, while those of economists based in Lusaka are not given. Of the eight based in Tanzania, six are listed as having a Master of Arts in Economics, one a Bachelor of Arts in Economics and one a Bachelor of Arts in Accountancy. It is not stated where they obtained these qualifications.

Neither the Economics Unit nor the later Department of Economic Planning (DEP, discussed below) was really an economic *policy* unit; rather, they were more study groups on the economy (Sisulu interview, 25 August 2016). Like-minded comrades were invited from the Soviet Union, Cuba and neighbouring African countries to give seminars on their experiences in economic transformation, and the Lusaka comrades travelled to these countries for seminars on a regular basis.

Although Lusaka organised and raised funds for many comrades to study abroad, much of this was in medicine and engineering and not economics. Bheki Langa, who did his PhD in economics in Moscow, was a rare exception. One thing Sisulu recalls was the eagerness of many younger comrades to join MK and fight rather than study. Thandika Mkandawire supports this contention when he makes the point that many of the post-1976 generation who reached Lusaka 'were relatively ignorant of the struggle and its objectives and had a militarist inclination' (2005: 134). And they were eager, too, to pursue a leap into socialism without any consideration of the realities of the South African situation. 'We had to work very hard to try to convince them otherwise,' Sisulu argues (Interview, 25 August 2016).

When Josie arrived in Lusaka in 1983, the Economics Unit was not very strong at all. Its members included Sindiso Mfenyana, Joe Nhlanhla and Max Sisulu. According to Josie: 'Thabo was ostensibly the head as the Unit fell into the Department of Information and Publicity. Pallo Jordan was head of Research and as such was an integral part of the Unit. I was deployed as an economic researcher under Pallo in a place called Makeni [a suburb of Lusaka] – that's where the whole library was – and so on and we had to do research' (Josie interview, 30 January 2015).

Josie argues that London-based economists and members of the Communist Party of Great Britain (CPGB), Laurence Harris and Ben Fine, were influential figures in the Lusaka debates (such as they were) on economic issues.

Josie also recalls that a meeting on the economy took place in 1985 in Lusaka, where the notion of the mixed economy came to the fore. But he remembers the conference for one other reason as well:

> The most significant thing that happened at that 1985 meeting which stands out for me quite clearly was that while we were sitting in that plenary, Pallo or Max who was chairing said, Thabo is coming, and he is bringing some South African from Stellenbosch, a guy called Van der Merwe [likely to be Hendrik van der Merwe]. He came there and talked to all, sitting and looking there and discussing issues, very cynical, very kind of patronising – we got this all covered, guys – you know that kind of attitude, and I sat there. It only later dawned on me, in fact these guys were the forerunners of the negotiations that were taking place, because later on Wimpie [de Klerk] and all these guys came over. In fact, he [Van der Merwe] was part of the delegation with Wimpie that came and he was the economic person (Josie interview, 30 January 2015).

For Josie, it was Hani who had the vision to raise more practical economic policy issues linked to the struggles of ordinary South Africans in the townships as opposed to mouthing this or that theoretical line:

> Chris was very seldom in Lusaka, but when he did come he played a very key role, because he was more on the frontline, he was inside the country, he was

training people, he was in MK, he was the real revolutionary, and I worked closely with Chris and even with [Joe] Slovo. When Slovo was in London, he would talk to Laurence [Harris] and people like that, but in Zambia I would be the one they would discuss with. You could see Chris's view. He was not verbose, he was very reflective but he would raise some clear issues, and he was the only one in my view that came across very strongly on the issue of redistribution. Chris Hani was very clear; even Slovo did not raise it as sharply as Chris Hani raised the issue of redistribution and inequality as opposed to just poverty. And for Chris Hani this was one of the key areas that needed to be addressed, because none of the others raised the issue. And I think for many of us who came from the townships, that was a key issue, because we could see what was driving the problems in the townships on the ground, and all indicators that came through were showing that levels of inequality, levels of poverty, education, all those strikes and things, were about inequality (Josie interview, 30 January 2015).

Gail Gerhart and Clive Glaser sum up the Freedom Charter debate and the broad economic stance in the 1980s, on the eve of the many 'meet the ANC' gatherings across Africa and Europe, as follows: 'Had numbers and high position counted, the communists in the NEC [National Executive Committee], who made up at least three-quarters of its members after Kabwe, might have been expected to swing their weight to ensure that the ANC's vision of a future South Africa conformed to socialist principles. But this did not occur; instead, the ANC's blueprints emerged with a clear social democratic stamp' (2010: 150).

In January 1986, a report appeared in the *Star* newspaper that the South African Nafcoc had held informal discussions with the ANC after it had drafted a business charter of social, economic and political rights and an accompanying action programme. While reluctant to disclose which members of the ANC they met, the *Star* report notes that Nafcoc had held prior discussions with various members of the Cabinet, including the minister of constitutional planning, Chris Heunis (*Star*, 22 January 1986). We know that David Willers, the London director of the South Africa Foundation, sent the Federated Chamber of Industries charter to the ANC's Solly Smith. The ANC in Lusaka received the charter on 6 February 1986. Key aspects of the charter included the following: 'South Africa must publicly remain committed to market-related policies in an essentially open economy', and there is a need to 'implement an integrated programme for growth-oriented adjustment based on supply-side economic considerations' (ANC Lusaka Mission Archives, Box 126, Folder 60).

It is interesting to note that a major purpose of the Economics Unit was to ensure that the movement had trained economists thinking about the future economic emancipation of a democratic South Africa. 'Our drive towards national emancipation is therefore in a real way bound up with economic emancipation. Preparations for the attainment of genuine economic independence cannot be postponed until freedom day' (ANC Lusaka Mission Archives, Box 24, Folder 5).

Sadly, there is no evidence that this noble objective was met, and after 1990 the ANC scrambled to develop such a policy-making capacity.

The Department of Economic Planning

Following its second National Consultative Conference in Kabwe in 1985, the ANC decided to upgrade the Economics Unit by establishing the Department of Economic Planning (DEP). This was done in June 1987. Among those joining the DEP at this time were Bheki Langa, who had just completed his PhD in the Soviet Union. Max Sisulu was appointed the head.

The objectives of the DEP were to develop economic strategy and policy options for an 'independent South Africa' based on the 'aspirations of our people as expressed in the Freedom Charter' (ANC Lusaka Mission Archives, Box 24, Folder 4). Research on policy and strategy is added for the first time to the rather less ambitious goals set for the Economics Unit. Areas added at this stage were the macroeconomy, energy and power, public finance, the role of women in development, wildlife and tourism, as well as income distribution – all policy areas absent from the list of responsibilities developed for the Economic Unit (ANC Lusaka Mission Archives, Box 24, Folder 4).

The Research Unit of the Department of Information and the DEP had extensive contacts and formal relations with a number of organisations in both the non-governmental organisation and academic sectors in many parts of the world. These included the Economic Commission for Africa (members attended the 14th session in Niamey, Niger, in April 1988), the United Nations Environment Programme (members attended the 1st session of its Governing Council in Nairobi in March 1988) and the United Nations Conference on Trade and Development (two delegates attended the 35th session on debt and development in Geneva in September 1988). Soon it developed a productive relationship with the Department of Economics at the School of Oriental and African Studies (SOAS), University of London, through its contacts with Laurence Harris, who had long been involved in intelligence work for the movement along the Botswana border (Keable 2012).

Harris, with later support from Ben Fine and Peter Robbins, established EROSA, which worked closely with the movement in London and Lusaka (see chapter 4). It also worked closely with the Transnational Institute in Holland (ANC Lusaka Mission Archives, Box 24, Folder 4).

From early on in its existence, the DEP was tasked with gathering relevant material from and contacting (sympathetic) progressive economists working within South Africa. The proposal for the DEP's establishment makes the point that 'it is important to note that information written inside South Africa will be obtained as much research and economic analysis is going on there which is extremely useful' (ANC Lusaka Mission Archives, Box 84, Folder 9).

Another of the DEP's tasks was to build up its internal library in Lusaka, with newspapers 'from home' and journals. Among the 20 journals identified for purchase were the *South African Journal of Economics*, *Zimbabwe Journal of Economics*, *Journal of Southern African Studies*, *Third World Quarterly*, *Review of African Political Economy*, *Journal of Development Studies*, *Journal of Development Economics*, *Farmer's Weekly* and the *Financial Mail*. The *South African Labour Bulletin* (the Economist Intelligence Unit's journal), *Monthly Review* (New York), *Work in Progress*, Codesria's *African Development* and the *Oxford Bulletin of Economics and Statistics* were also ordered. All in all, if these were received and subscriptions maintained, a reasonable balance of progressive and mainstream journals were available to the ANC's researchers in Lusaka (ANC Lusaka Mission Archives, Box 84, Folder 9).

Though our archival research reveals little about the day-to-day work of the DEP in Lusaka, we do learn that the department organised some seminars on the economy in Lusaka and other parts of the world.

In Amsterdam in December 1986, a conference entitled 'Research Priorities for Socio-Economic Planning in Post-Apartheid South Africa' was held. At that conference a paper on 'Income Distribution and Poverty' was presented by Francis Wilson and Mamphela Ramphele, both senior researchers from the University of Cape Town (UCT). Another paper on South African industrialisation was presented by UCT's Anthony Black. It is of interest to note that the distinguished proponent of dependency theory, Andre Gunder Frank, was in the audience. In responding to these papers, Frank argued that the 'South African economic crisis was a direct result of the world economic crisis with internal factors playing a very minor role'. He also argued that 'redistributive pressures would make a future South Africa less able to compete in the capitalist world market' (Oliver Tambo Papers, Box 040, Folder 357).

At another one of these workshops, between 14–17 August 1989, at the First In-House Seminar of ANC Economists in Lusaka, a paper by Laurence Harris

(1989) entitled 'The Mixed Economy of a Democratic South Africa', read by Helena Dolny in his absence, appears to have been much discussed. Harris set out alternative visions of the mix of the private and public sector and suggested that one that leans towards socialism would be most appropriate in South African conditions. He favoured some degree of nationalisation, especially in certain sectors, such as those that are fundamental inputs for industrial development. But he also warned that nationalisation comes with costs. In the end, he argued that the 'roles of the market, regulation and planning are much more important than the degree of state ownership' (Harris 1989).

A paper in response to Harris by Vella Pillay, dated 9 October 1989 and penned in London, also addresses these issues. Pillay's paper distinguishes between the long-term goals of the Freedom Charter and short-term interventions that appear to be left social democratic in nature. The latter include 'enough food, shelter, social security, medical facilities, unemployment benefits, free and equal education and an improvement in the working conditions and power of workers'. He favoured anti-monopoly and anti-trust policies in respect of the powerful local conglomerates, being fully cognisant of the power of the conglomerates to undermine a democratic state. At the Lusaka in-house seminar, Rob Davies' paper set out an economic vision of a mixed economy in which there will be a 'considerable role for private capital'; he also set out a list of immediate goals, such as meeting basic needs and improvements in the conditions of working people (Oliver Tambo Papers, Box 039, Folder 0354). Though these are not policies but ideas put forwarded by qualified and trusted comrades, they do represent core aspects of a left social democratic programme rather than either African nationalism or Soviet-type socialism.

Phineas Malinga informs us that despite some scepticism the 'question of economic policy had [indeed] received the attention of the broad liberation movement' (1990: 21). He reminds us that the ANC's Constitutional Guidelines commissioned by Tambo and approved by the NEC in August 1988 contained a section on the economy. It argued for a state that would ensure 'that the entire economy serves the interests and well-being of all sections of the population … the economy shall be a mixed one … co-operative forms of economic enterprise, village industries and small-scale family activities shall be supported by the state …' (Malinga 1990: 22). Yet, Malinga concedes that the Guidelines are 'more cautious than the Charter about the role of the state in the economy' (1990: 22), given the very changed economic circumstances all over the world, including in the management of the Soviet economy.

Gerhart and Glaser express this same position, as follows: 'Without repudiating anything in the 1955 Freedom Charter, the [Constitutional] Guidelines positioned the ANC as a social democratic party strongly protective of individual rights while also committed to "corrective action which guarantees a rapid and irreversible redistribution of wealth and opening up of facilities to all'" (2010: 181).

It is worth remembering this in the context of the discussion that we have had in chapter 2 over AB Xuma and Albert Luthuli, both ANC presidents, and in what follows in chapter 4, especially the position articulated by Alan Hirsch to explain shifts and changes in the 1990s. Clearly, there were many positions in the spectrum between Soviet-style socialism and petty bourgeois African nationalism that were held by leadership figures in the Congress Alliance over the period of our study. To focus on any one view as representative of that of the ANC as a whole would be a serious mistake, in our judgement.

In July 1989, 115 representatives of the Five Freedoms Forum[4] travelled to Lusaka to meet and hold talks with senior ANC leaders. A conference was held at the Intercontinental Hotel in Lusaka from 29 June to 2 July 1989, where a number of important exchanges about the post-apartheid economy took place. The issue of nationalisation and the meaning of a 'mixed economy' were among the matters under discussion. There was agreement across the floor about the need for a mixed economy with private-sector and public-sector ownership and control (see chapter 5 on the role of business for more on this). While holding the Freedom Charter line on nationalisation, ANC delegates accepted that under some conditions 'a premature nationalisation can result in impeding social control by the destruction or downgrading of industry'. The case of Mozambique was cited by the ANC as an example of such 'premature nationalisation'. Towards the end of the conference, a South African business person, Ronnie Bethlehem, asked if the ANC had a policy position on the floating of the rand and whether the rand would be linked to gold or any specific international currency. It is hard to say if he was being serious or just trying to embarrass the ANC. The ANC responded that it was not able to answer this question because it had to be recognised that 'a struggle for liberation did not necessarily guarantee experience in issues such as economics' (Louw 1989: 86). This speaks to the issue of experience, which we raise at various times in this book.

The leadership of the Economics Unit and the DEP in Lusaka may have been involved in many important events and exchanges over policy and strategy during the 1980s, but they were also drawn into some totally mundane and bureaucratic issues that may well have detracted from their core work. Some of the things that senior ANC and DEP members had to deal with were nothing short of mind-boggling. Jordan speaks of these matters as 'absurd bureaucratic controls' (Jordan interview, 4 August 2017). Here is one of many examples we unearthed at the University of Fort Hare archives. Late in 1989, a DEP staffer wrote to Henry

Makgothi, assistant secretary general of the ANC, requesting leave and support to travel to Harare to marry his fiancée. He was asked by Makgothi to get a written recommendation from his head, Max Sisulu. Sisulu then wrote (somewhat tongue in cheek) to Makgothi as follows:

> Since Cde Mandla Tshabalala is an adult he does not need the permission of the Department to get married, but our department, however, wishes to vouch for his good character and honourable intentions. And request the movement to give him and his fiancée every possible support and assistance. The DEP for its part will give Cde Mandla a leave of one month in December, to give him time to prepare for and enjoy his marriage and new status.
>
> In the year of Mass Action for People's Power!!!
> Amandla! Maatla!
> (ANC Lusaka Mission Archives, Box 84, Folder 9)

IN EXILE: VELLA PILLAY, ECONOMIC RESEARCH AND THE LONDON COMRADES

> Yes, the empire was collapsing: Ghana had become free; Malaysia and [Tanzania] were getting independence. In London there were people from all over the world, little groupings supporting the liberation struggles in their different countries: Nigerians, Kenyans, Tanganyikans, Burmese, Indonesians, Sri Lankans, Indians, South Americans, West Indians, Irish. It was a very cosmopolitan environment, and we were bound by a unity we felt when we met one another. There was a commonality in our struggles, so I didn't feel lonely, in spite of the insularity of the British (Maharaj in O'Malley 2007: 82–83).[5]

In a recently published paper, Vishnu Padayachee and John Sender (2018) deal at length with the role that radical economist Vella Pillay played for over half a century in economic policy analysis, both in exile and on his temporary return to South Africa in the early 1990s. While we draw significantly from that paper, we try here to provide a glimpse of policy debates in the years of exile by focusing on developments in London, building the story around the key figure of Pillay. Even his detractors – of which there were many, including in the SACP in the 1960s and some of the 'neo-liberals' in the ANC and in academia in the 1990s – would not be able to contest the claim that Pillay was the foremost ANC economist in London from the late 1940s until his return to South Africa in 1991. There were very few, if any, in the movement more qualified and experienced in economic analysis and policy than Pillay. His story is inextricably bound into the narrative of ANC exile politics and economics in the British capital for all those long and difficult decades. In fact, we would contend that to the extent that any significant discussion of economic matters and economic policy for South Africa occurred over this period within exiled ANC circles, Pillay likely would have been central to it.

Pillay was without any doubt a figure of very significant influence in the ANC–SACP in exile. When Oliver Tambo left South Africa in March 1960, he found a house in Muswell Hill, North London, close to the home of Vella and Patsy Pillay, and they struck up a political and family connection that lasted until Tambo's passing in South Africa in 1993. By that time, Vella had returned to Johannesburg with Patsy to head up the Macroeconomic Research Group (MERG) project (see chapter 4). As Ellis notes, 'Vella Pillay, *although rarely mentioned in ANC histories,* was one of the main intermediaries between the SACP and Moscow …' (2015: 40, emphasis added). In the 1950s and early 1960s, Vella and Max Joffe were the leading SACP figures in exile. There may have been a reason for this 'omission' as we will see soon. This may, however, be a necessary moment to draw attention to and make a small contribution to correcting this egregious Stalinist-style side-lining from history of such a significant intellectual and senior policy thinker of the South African liberation movement.

The front cover of Ellis's book on the ANC in exile features a photograph of three key figures sitting around a low table covered in documents and deep in discussion. The occasion is the first visit by South African communists to an official meeting of communist and workers' parties in Moscow on 3 November 1960. They were Yusuf Dadoo, the chairperson of the SACP since 1972, Mao Zedong, the head of the Chinese Communist Party, and Vella Pillay, the SACP representative in London at that time (Ellis 2015: 12–13, fn. 43). In 1962, Pillay accompanied Arthur Goldreich to a four-hour meeting with Deng Xiaoping in Peking (Frankel 2016: 77). But his story begins long before these early 1960s experiences.

Pillay was born in Johannesburg on 8 October 1923. After matriculation, he attended the University of the Witwatersrand (Wits) where he studied part-time and graduated with a BCom degree. Like many others of his generation, he became politicised at university. He joined the Federation of Progressive Students at Wits and became deeply involved in the activities of the Transvaal Indian Congress. He soon joined the Communist Party of South Africa. In the mid-1940s, he became involved in resistance to the Pegging Act – a forerunner to later apartheid legislation, such as the Group Areas Act, which attempted to segregate and discriminate against Indians on matters of land, property, trade and residence. In June 1948, he married Patsy, another activist, in the Cape where racially mixed marriages were then still legal. But the looming National Party plans for stricter policing of racial boundaries and his acceptance by the London School of Economics (LSE) to study there for an Honours degree in international economics led the couple to move to the UK in January 1949. While studying at the LSE, again part-time, he relied on Patsy to keep them going financially; she had found a job as the secretary to Krishna Menon, the world-renowned first Indian high commissioner in London after independence.

Vella found a job as a research officer at the State Bank of China in London. There he remained a loyal member of staff for the rest of his working life, rising to the position of assistant general manager (the second in charge) by retirement. He remained an active member of the ANC in exile, writing for, distributing and smuggling copies of the *African Communist* and *International Bulletin* (which he helped to produce) into South Africa, ably supported by Patsy.

Soon after Mac Maharaj arrived in London in 1957, Pillay set about the task of building a cell of the SACP. Maharaj found this strange as he had thought that the Party had long ceased to function or even exist (Maharaj interview, 16 August 2016). The unit consisted of Vella, Patsy and Mac. A few years later, Vella became the SACP Central Committee representative in the UK (O'Malley 2007: 82). He became the key link between the SACP in South Africa and the rest of Europe. When he visited London in May 1962, Mandela visited Pillay and Dadoo as the leaders of the SACP there, and laid out the view that the ANC had to be given greater pre-eminence on the international stage: 'Mandela later met Yusuf Dadoo and Vella Pillay and informed them that the ANC had to project itself as an inde-pendent force, represented by Africans at international conferences. Firmly, he told Dadoo, this was not a departure from ANC policy, rather, an unbundling of being stuck in a nebulous image that appeared to represent everyone, in effect a break with recent ANC policy – and cross-Congress cooperation' (Benneyworth 2011: 90).

Aside from such ethnic politics at play in exile, Pillay soon became a victim of both personal infighting and rivalries within the Party, which had little to do with ideology and was to some extent a result of the growing Sino–Soviet tensions in the early 1960s. It is not easy to untangle these. The SACP, arguably the Communist Party most steeped internationally in the repressive political practices historically associated with Stalinism, regarded Pillay's employment at the State Bank of China with some suspicion. He had to be a Maoist, they believed, to work there. There was no small irony in their conclusion, given that the Chinese Communist Party, in fact, broke with the Soviet Communist Party in 1956 in a Sino–Soviet split. This came after the public revelations of Nikita Khrushchev condemning Stalinism, to the practices of which the SACP (and the Chinese Communist Party) remained slavishly committed throughout, and notwithstanding the formal distancing of the Soviet Union's Communist Party from such political practices. But this was not all, far from it. For all of the 1950s, Pillay, as the SACP representative in Europe, was the key that unlocked ANC–SACP access to both Moscow and Beijing. However, when the generation of Dadoo's communists (including Michael Harmel) arrived in London in around 1960, they resented this influence and apparently set about undermining Pillay. Maharaj recalls that in 1960 or 1961, on a boat on a Moscow river, Harmel or someone of that seniority in the Party presented Vella with a choice: either remain with the State Bank of China or face expulsion from the SACP. We know from Irina Filatova (2012: 528) that Pillay, Dadoo, Harmel and Joe Matthews were all in Moscow in late 1960, the second visit by Pillay and Dadoo in that year.

Vella refused to quit the Bank of China even when he was offered a 'sweetener' in the form of a job at an equivalent proposed Russian state bank in London. These key developments are captured by Maharaj as follows:

> … the party had been dominated by white members and there was a need for many white members to stand down. But within that context all sorts of personal issues arose and I think that therefore what I am saying about Vella is that the conflict that opened up, and according to him … he described to me the occasion where on a boat in Moscow, while they were having a meeting in Moscow, on the boat trip he was approached. He didn't tell me who; I don't know if it was Michael Harmel, who put the issue to him that he had to choose between working at the Bank of China and his representing the party. He thought this was an unreasonable proposition and he thought it was a cruel proposition but already there was enough unhappiness in his relationship with many of them. It was one thing for comrades that had gone to London fleeing from post-Rivonia … it was another thing for [people like] Vella who had family and everything settled in London to start to say I will give up my job. Where do you go? I know that before that the Soviets were courting Vella to come to help set up a Russian Bank, the equivalent of the State Bank of China, and therefore approached Vella and offered him a higher formal position than what he occupied at the Bank of China. And his response was to say to the Soviets, after he thought it through, to say, no, look chaps, I will stay with the Bank of China … I know my position, I know they will not take a Chinese and replace me. So my future is more

secure with the Bank of China. That had little to do at that stage with any ideological issue (Maharaj interview, 16 August 2016).

Pillay's widow, Patsy, also a former Party member and friend of Ruth First, now in her early nineties, recalls that Joe Slovo visited Vella and her at their London flat. It was there (after asking Patsy to leave the room) that he informed Vella that he could not continue to serve as the party representative in Europe or on the Central Committee as long as he continued to work at the State Bank of China (Patsy Pillay to John Sender, email correspondence with Padayachee, 29 June 2017).

As Vella observed to his friend and comrade Ronald Segal: 'The SACP then decided to side-line me, and since then I ceased to have any connection with them. But my relations with Oliver Tambo and the ANC remained close and undisturbed' (Segal's biographical notes on Vella, in Vella Pillay private archives).[6]

With growing calls for sanctions against South Africa at the United Nations after Sharpeville and in the wake of the UN arms embargo in 1962, Pillay became deeply involved in the campaign to boycott South African exports to the UK. He spoke on the same platform as Julius Nyerere (then president of the Tanganyika African National Union), Trevor Huddlestone and others on 26 June 1959 when the campaign to launch the Boycott South African Goods campaign was launched in Holborn Hall in London. This was a campaign that led to the formation to the British Anti-Apartheid Movement, a key branch of the global Anti-Apartheid Movement (Gurney 2000: 123). Pillay would serve with great distinction as its treasurer and then vice chairperson for many years. On the occasion of his eight-ieth birthday in 2003, then President Thabo Mbeki sent Pillay a message, which read in part: 'Your outstanding contribution to the liberation of our people will always be remembered with fondness, particularly your role in establishing one of the greatest solidarity movements of our times – the British Anti-Apartheid Movement.' In his tribute to Pillay on that occasion, Ahmed Kathrada observed, 'Many of us knew you as a brilliant economist and a dedicated freedom fighter.' Kader Asmal, whom Pillay had taken under his wing and mentored, noted that 'the only honour that Vella would want is a commitment from all of us to ensure that we consolidate and deepen the democratic gains which so many freedom-loving South Africans fought and died for' (Letters in Vella Pillay private archives). While involved in all this South African struggle work, Pillay was invited by Ken Livingstone to join the Greater London Enterprise Board, with the special task of assisting the Greater London Council to promote the local economy and enhance opportunities for blacks in London. All this while he remained an employee of the State Bank of China.

After he arrived in London, Maharaj quickly joined up with Pillay in the boycott campaign, including via the Africa Committee of the Communist Party of Great Britain (Gurney 2000: 133). Maharaj recalls that Pillay was the SACP contact person in London, a representative of the Central Committee, and the underground conduit for *New Age*, the banned ANC-supporting South African newspaper. 'Exiled students from South Africa – Kader Asmal, Steve Naidoo, Manna Chetty, Essop and Aziz Pahad, Thabo Mbeki – found the Pillay household [in Muswell Hill] a home away from home' (O'Malley 2007: 80). Maharaj recalls a meeting of the Africa Committee at the Marx Memorial Library, at which the agrarian question in Africa was debated. Jack Woddiss, one of the participants, questioned the view that the transfer of land to the state (on behalf of the people) under socialism would automatically raise productivity, a view that Maharaj had until that time taken for granted. It was one of the few real debates over economic and development policy that Maharaj had witnessed at that time.

By 1978, Pillay had completed his MSc in economics at Birkbeck College, University of London, obtaining First Class marks for his quantitative and econometric work and a Merit pass overall. There were very few South African Congress Movement activists who received comparably rigorous training in economics, although a few were trained in the rigidly orthodox economics of the former Soviet bloc (Padayachee and Sender 2018).

Pillay researched and published widely on the South African economy and related subjects throughout the 40 or so years he lived and worked in London. He often used the pseudonym 'P. Tlale', especially when he wrote for the *African Communist*. In the January–March 1964 edition, he wrote 'Sanctions against Apartheid' under that pseudonym; in the July–September issue of that same year he wrote 'The Apartheid Economy Today', and in the September–December 1965 edition he wrote 'The Imperialist State in Apartheid'. 'The Apartheid Economy Today' was written well before the revisionists Harold Wolpe and Martin Legassick published their seminal work in around 1972; it placed a Marxist imprint on South African economic historiography, and demonstrated a sharp appreciation of the complex interrelationships between race, class and the apartheid state in South African capitalist accumulation. He understood clearly that the much-celebrated 'economic boom' that South Africa was experiencing at the time was based on class exploitation and racial oppression and that it would not be sustained because of that fact alone. In fact, he predicted that the repressive state controls needed to keep it going would prove to be its ultimate undoing:

> Subjected to intense exchange controls and attracted by the demands created through the growing volume of overseas investment as well as of

the war economy, South Africa's ruling capitalists have again joined with the Verwoerd regime to intensify the rate of African exploitation with all its explosive political and other consequences. But not even the employment of Hitler's techniques of economic control and organization can stop the explosion of the South African crisis. On the contrary, it will hasten it (Pillay 1964: 59).

Pillay wrote many monographs for the Anti-Apartheid Movement, for the United Nations Centre Against Apartheid (where he was good friends with Enuga S Reddy, the renowned head of the Centre). For the latter organisation and in his capacity as vice chairman of the British Anti-Apartheid Movement, he wrote 'The Role of Transnational Corporations in Apartheid South Africa' (August 1981) and 'The Role of Gold in the Economy of Apartheid South Africa' (March 1981). Demonstrating his close familiarity with European economic affairs, he published articles in *Africa South*, including 'The Belgian Treasury' (1960) and 'The European Economic Community and Africa' (1958).

In the early 1980s, Pillay joined with sympathetic Marxist economist and activist Laurence Harris and later with Ben Fine in establishing an economic research capacity for the ANC in London. Harris had a long-standing and active engagement with the ANC, which is respected in South Africa to this day, and he had been closely associated with the ANC–SACP's armed wing, MK. He is reported as assisting in running guns and other weapons for MK along the Botswana border (Keable 2012), and as being involved in an attempt to travel by boat down the eastern coast of Africa from Mombasa to the Transkei coast on an MK assignment (Jordan interview, 4 August 2017). Together with members of the Research Unit of the ANC's Department of Information (and from the late 1980s with the DEP), Harris formed a research consortium called Economic Research on South Africa. EROSA was set up on the model already established by the Research on Education for South Africa (RESA) project, organised by another South African exile academic and activist, Harold Wolpe, famous for his work on the articulation of modes of production and colonialism of a special type (Fine 2010: 26). An unswerving commitment to the struggle against the heinous system of apartheid primarily drove these British economists. Working with the ANC they made it their task to study and better understand the complexities of the racialised South African economy and how it could be transformed equitably and democratically. Fine recalls that his first task for the ANC through EROSA was to assess the prospects of South African mining, based principally on his knowledge of coal mining in Britain rather than of South Africa (2010: 26). EROSA produced a number of papers on the South African economy, which (according to Ngoasheng

1992: 121) went beyond a critique into areas of policy recommendations. This included work on the minerals-energy complex, the savings-investment constraint and the nature of the South African financial system. The group related to the ANC in exile through Pillay, Sisulu and Jordan (IDRC 1991: 7).

At the ANC economic policy conference in Harare in April–May 1990, Pillay presented a detailed paper on the essential steps in economic policy immediately upon the seizure of state power. He recommended a day-to-day agenda of the key steps that needed to be taken upon assumption of power. He was a strong opponent of the idea of granting the South African Reserve Bank (SARB) independence from the new government, arguing that this would seriously compromise the democratic state's power to influence and shape a co-ordinated policy response to the economic legacy of apartheid.

In a letter to his friend and comrade Lionel (Rusty) Bernstein, Pillay expressed grave concerns about the way the debate over economic policy was proceeding (we develop this point in chapter 4). He predicted that if the movement allowed itself to be seduced by South African and international capital to compromise on its economic policies, it would pay a high price one day. This long quote from that letter is worth setting out in full:

> What I find outrageous is the invidious position in which poor Nelson [Mandela] has been placed (by some of his colleagues) in having to frequently shift the movement's economic goal posts. I know who is responsible for this: it found its most telling expression in Nelson's unfortunate speech to businessmen on May 23 [1990]. I also feel that our friend JS [Joe Slovo] is perhaps showing a willingness to skate on very thin ice on these matters. I fear that the people in the townships, the rural areas and the unemployed – all of them may at some point react pretty strongly to what appear as deliberate ambiguities in the movement's economic policies and programme. This is a serious worry for me. I had a long chat with Jay Naidoo of Cosatu [Congress of South African Trade Unions) last month: he expressed fears even more grave than I have had: he declared that the trade union movement will not allow any foot dragging on any of the key issues of economic policy (Letter from Vella Pillay to Rusty Bernstein, 14 June 1990, in Vella Pillay private archives).

In the early 1990s, Vella was appointed director of the ANC's Macroeconomic Research Group (MERG). Although he was the director and not an author or editor, he played a powerful role in shaping the ideas and policy framework behind the 1993 MERG report. Fine insists that the ANC could not have done better at that time than appoint him to that post:

> Well, for me, it seemed a very natural choice and I was very pleased. First of all, Vella had been in London in exile for many years and was a very accomplished and experienced economist. He was head of Foreign Exchange Reserves for the Bank of China and so there was probably no one better in the progressive movement who knew about how to manage foreign exchange reserves and issues involved in that. Laurence [Harris] and I also knew him very well because he'd done the MSc (Economics) of Birkbeck where we both taught, which was a university or a college of the University of London, specialising in teaching people at work, and so he did that part-time. He was also treasurer of the Anti-Apartheid Movement. He'd also been on the board of the Industrial Wing of the Greater London Council ... so his credentials for leading MERG were very strong. It probably also coincided with his ability to come back to South Africa, where of course he had very strong connections with the ANC leadership and he was a respected figure. I know he had a very close relationship with Mac Maharaj, but he seemed to have good connections with Mandela as well (Fine interview, 30 June 2015).

Pillay continued to write and publish well into his eighties, including an important piece on monetary and exchange rate policy in the volume edited by Jonathan Michie and Vishnu Padayachee (1997: 101–124).

Other developments in exile

But Vella Pillay and his comrades at SOAS were not the only active members of the ANC in exile in London, when it came to matters of policy. Harold Wolpe and Norman Levy were deeply engaged in thinking about education policy through their work in London for the Solomon Mahlangu Freedom College in Tanzania, though differences and tensions between London and Tanzania over educational policy were evident. Levy (2011) recalls that in the late 1980s the ANC held internal discussions in London on the 'economy, health, the constitution and the agrarian situation' and began to draw up 'concrete policy documents' on these topics. He himself undertook a profile of population, education, manpower distribution and skills training in South Africa, at the request of the ANC Research Unit headed by Pallo Jordan. 'The report was intended to provide an overview of the labour market and an accurate picture of the racially skewed economy. This it did. But I am not sure that the study ever received the attention we expected once Mandela took office or whether a similar survey has since been undertaken' (Levy 2011: 401).

And as things began 'stirring' in the 1980s, what may be termed policy discussions also took place elsewhere in the world involving South African exiles from the ANC and the SACP. In March 1987, a conference devoted to stimulating long-term work on post-apartheid South Africa was held in Moscow, following a meeting between Oliver Tambo and Mikhail Gorbachev in November 1986. Representatives from both the Soviet and ANC–SACP sides were impressive and included Moscow State University historians Apollon Davidson and Irina Filatova, and Jordan, Zola Skewyiya, Ivy Matsepe-Casaburri, Tessa Marcus, Levy, as well as Soviet-trained economist and DEP head Max Sisulu, among others. Sisulu gave a paper on the theme of nationalisation and restructuring of the economy, which Levy recalls 'made it clear that the chances of the implementation of the Freedom Charter were small if the grip of the monopolies on the economy was not loosened' (Levy 2011: 497).

Bethuel Setai, who passed away in May 2015, was one of the most qualified, albeit conservative, economists in the broad ANC camp. Setai's influence on ANC economic policy is not clear, but he was well respected, judging from his role after his return to South Africa in 1991. In the exile era, Setai was one of the very few ANC-aligned cadres with a PhD in economics from a Western university, as compared to those with economics degrees from the former Soviet Union or its satellites. He received his PhD from New York University in 1973, after leaving South Africa to join the ANC. He taught economics in a number of Western universities, including at Lincoln University in Pennsylvania, which had been founded in 1854 by the Quakers for people of African descent. He rose to become head of the Economics Department there, no mean feat. In 1987, he taught at Yale University, where he appears to have been part of a 'South African economic policy unit', of which we know little or nothing. In between Lincoln and Yale, he taught at the National University of Lesotho, where his students included Tito Mboweni, who later became the SARB governor. As is evident from Setai's book, *The Political Economy of South Africa* (1977), his views were very orthodox and neo-classical. As pointed out by Chris Barron in the *Sunday Times* (31 May 2015) obituary: 'The command economy had no place in his thinking', and 'he blamed the disaster he saw unfolding in South Africa on a limited understanding of basic economics'. On his return to South Africa in 1991, Setai worked at the Development Bank of Southern Africa and served on the Transitional Executive Council, later assuming several positions in the civil service after 1994. Nonetheless, it is worth noting that this highly educated, neo-classical economist with strong ANC credentials was effectively side-lined (whether by design or accident) from the economic debate and any major policy role after 1990 by the new ANC economic leadership, who ironically were themselves busy taking their first steps in the direction of economic orthodoxy.

IN EXILE: THE SACP AND THE STRUGGLE FOR SOCIALISM

The SACP played a critical role in shaping all aspects of ANC thinking throughout this period (1960–1990), but it is also clear that the ANC did not simply succumb to an SACP line on all matters at all times, even when communists were in a majority in structures such as the National Executive Committee (NEC). Neither did the SACP have an appetite for pushing the ANC nationalists to their way of thinking. It is hard to imagine, says Ben Turok, how ANC leaders of the calibre of Tambo, Mandela, Sisulu and others (even if they were simultaneously SACP members) would take instructions from the SACP (Turok interview, 29 January 2015). That much is clear, for example, in the debate about the turn to armed struggle in the early 1960s. While ANC President Albert Luthuli and some leaders of components of the movement (Yusuf Cachalia, Monty Naicker and JN Singh, even the SACP's Moses Kotane initially) had reservations and were lukewarm and tentative in their acceptance of it, the SACP 'had already moved some way towards armed struggle' (Levy 2011: 264).

Ours is not to undertake a comprehensive review of the role and place of the SACP in the struggle, especially in exile. That has been done by others (see, for example, Ellis and Sechaba 1992; Maloka 2002). Here we offer some basic understanding of SACP politics in order to better assess its role in the economics debate in this period and beyond.

A new programme of the SACP, 'The Road to South African Freedom', appeared in 1962, and this document helps us understand how the Party read the Freedom Charter in relation to its ultimate socialist objectives. Filatova expresses this approach as follows:

> The document stated that the ANC was a national-liberation organisa-
> tion and that, together with the SACP, it was part of the national-liberation
> alliance. It also pledged the party's 'unqualified support for the Freedom
> Charter' which it considered to be 'suitable as a general statement of the
> aims of a state of national democracy'. The Charter, the document ran, 'is

not a programme for socialism', but it necessarily and realistically calls for profound economic changes … which will answer the pressing and immediate needs of the people and lay the indispensable basis for the advance of our country along non-capitalist lines to a communist and socialist future (2012: 526).

An uncritical acceptance of the Soviet model of the transition to socialism was the central pillar of the SACP's approach to the struggle in South Africa. As Jeremy Cronin observes, the Party in the 1970s and 1980s appeared to accept that, given its own limited capacity on economic matters, a future economic dispensation for South Africa would be worked out in accordance with a line supplied by the Communist Party of the Soviet Union (CPSU) in Moscow or the Communist Party of Great Britain in London, with key figures such as Laurence Harris and Ben Fine, both CPGB members, in the lead (Cronin interview, 25 July 2017). Whether he meant this literally or otherwise is not entirely clear. Neither developments in Hungary (1956) nor Czechoslovakia (1968) shifted that dogmatic SACP support of the Moscow line. Turok is critical of the SACP's dogged commitment to the Soviet line, where little consideration was taken of the particular dynamics of South African economic and social reality:

> And I would argue that what held the [Communist] Party back for so long was that the dogma of the Comintern was imposed mechanically without taking account of the dynamics of South Africa. That's what the Comintern did. They imposed. And it led to stasis from which it took years to recover.
> …
> I think the Morogoro 'Strategy and Tactics' was a very important document, a brilliant piece of work. Whereas the 'No Middle Road' was not. I've read 'No Middle Road' many times, and Slovo was wrong. He said that there's going to be a steady transition from democracy to socialism and he based it on class forces and the working class and look where we are. It was wrong. The transition in South Africa has not followed that at all. Where's our October? We've had our February. So I've read 'No Middle Road' more than once, and I felt that he was being Leninist. The single phase. Where's a single phase today? Good God. We're reversing, rather than going forward (Turok interview, 29 January 2015).

While many accounts suggest that the SACP remained a fierce adherent of a Soviet, Stalinist orthodoxy at least until the early 1990s, Max Sisulu points to some important cleavages within the Party – almost as if there were, in his words, 'two parties' (Sisulu interview, 25 August 2016). Chris Hani and Moses Mabhida, he argues, represented two very different traditions within the Party. Hani, keen to engage in open, robust debate on all matters, including the future of the economy, was very analytical, pragmatic and democratic in his approach to the debates that happened in Lusaka and Tanzania. Mabhida, on the other hand, was an orthodox Stalinist who had no time to listen to alternative views and who remained convinced of the correctness of the Soviet model and line to the end. While the SACP was gripped by orthodoxy, it also contained in its ranks extraordinary younger minds who were communists in the bold, imaginative tradition of Chris Hani. A striking theorist and strategist of the SACP in this Marxist-Leninist tradition was Jabulani 'Nobleman' Nxumalo (popularly known as Comrade Mzala), perhaps the most incisive young revolutionary intellectual associated with the SACP in the post-1976 period of exile. A revered MK veteran of the Soweto generation, Mzala voraciously read the Marxist classics with intense, near-scholastic enthusiasm, and avidly debated and published on revolutionary strategy and the national question, subjecting commonly-held political shibboleths in the Party to intense scrutiny. This often landed him in deep trouble with the avowed Stalinists, but their grudging respect for his irrepressible intellectual enthusiasm and political commitment, combined with his immense popularity amongst the rank-and-file soldiers of MK, always proved his saving grace. He authored a critically incisive biography on Gatsha Buthulezi (1988) published by Zed Press, and was asked by no less than venerated ANC president OR Tambo to write his biography, such was the esteem in which he was held. Mzala was preparing for this biographical writing task to be undertaken at Yale University as well as finalising his doctorate on the 'national question' at the Open University in the UK at the time of his premature death in London in 1991 at the age of 35, a tragic loss to the liberation movement of a great mind. Robert van Niekerk recalls meeting Mzala in late 1990 after an ANC memorial event in London, months after the unbanning of the ANC with a tide of cautious optimism sweeping through the mass democratic movement in South Africa, and with preparations underway for negotiations with the apartheid regime. After thanking Mzala for the penetrating insights on revolutionary strategy provided through his writings and circulated clandestinely (in the UDF youth structures of which the author was then a member), he was left perplexed by Mzala's parting observation. Mzala said, 'Comrade, we must be vigilant, though, that we do not create *neo-apartheid* in South Africa'. That the structures of white domination could take some new, non-statutory form in the democratic South Africa still to be negotiated was entirely unthinkable at that stage in the ranks of the ANC-aligned mass democratic movement. A clue to Mzala's vigilant observation is perhaps to be found though in his writing in the ANC journal *Sechaba* as early as 1982. His arguments echoed those of the 1969 Morogoro 'Strategy and Tactics' document on the inextricable link between political and economic emancipation, including a prescient observation on the role of international capital: 'For our revolution, therefore, no neo-colonial solution can be contemplated. The national democratic revolution in South Africa rests on the twin pillars of political and economic emancipation. And because the South African economy is inextricably bound up with international capitalism, because the South African economy is deeply penetrated by international multi-national corporations, our revolution has a deep-going anti-imperialist content (Mzala 1982: 16). These are (in the context of our research) rare analytical qualities displayed by a young comrade at that stage, when most in the ANC/SACP had barely begun to think about economic policy matters.

Tension between the ANC and the SACP over strategy and tactics and about the means to pursue the struggle, as well as over its ultimate objective, was always evident, but largely suppressed. The Party, even when it had the numbers in the ANC's NEC, chose not to use its power. The debate over 'Inqindi and Marxism' on Robben Island is one example of this. But 'Inqindi' was a document that appeared to gloss over major differences and resolved nothing. Such differences and tensions came out more openly as one moved into the late 1980s and the real prospect of power came into play.

By the mid-1980s in Lusaka, Harris introduced the notion of a 'mixed economy'. In a paper prepared for a workshop in Lusaka on the theme 'The Debate about a Mixed Economy' and summarised by David Lazar on his behalf, Harris observes that 'there are different types of mixed economy. The ANC wishes to move from one oriented towards capitalism to one oriented towards socialism. This policy must take account of the international economic environment'. Harris, Lazar notes, lists three criteria for distinguishing these broad types of mixed economy: 'which classes hold economic power; how investible surplus is used; the extent of the economy's independence of [*sic*] the world market'. He then considers the merits and problems with nationalisation, and the roles of the private sector in such a mixed economy. Harris insisted that the 'state should attempt to control particular key prices: the price of maize, the exchange rate of the currency and interest rates. Foreign exchange controls and flexible regulation of the exchange rate provide the state with an important lever to direct the economy' (Oliver Tambo Papers, Box 039, Folder 0354). So, for Harris, in the mid-1980s, a mixed economy had a clear socialist orientation and a strong role for the state in key areas. Not surprising then that by the time he came to write a 1993 paper for the *Review of African Political*

Economy, he appeared livid at the direction that the South African left, including the SACP and Cosatu, were taking the policy debate – reforms without any prospect of socialism, is how he put it (Harris 1993: 97). For this he appears to lay the blame squarely on Slovo's shifts, comparing post-1990 developments in Party strategy to Slovo's iconic 1976 paper 'No Middle Road'.

> Clearly that is a long way from 'the complete destruction of the state that serves the capitalist class' that he [Slovo] wrote about in 1976, and it contains no prospect of socialist struggle. Slovo's rationale for it is that South Africa is not even at the stage of a national democratic revolution; the ANC has not won the liberation struggle. In this bleak situation, his vision for the next decade is a historic compromise under which the machinery of state will remain in the hands of the conservative Afrikaners that have held it since 1948 ... The 'big issues' that were for so long the touchstones of socialists in South Africa – nationalisation of banks, mines and factories; nationalisation and redistribution of the land; universal health care and universal, equal education – have effectively been abandoned (Harris 1993: 98).

But let us return to the chronology of events. The Seventh Congress of the SACP held in Cuba in April 1989 was attended for the first time in exile by South African-based communists, including Cronin. According to Cronin, the entire congress was 'brilliantly' chaired by Thabo Mbeki, one of his last official party roles before he quit the Party on his return to South Africa (Cronin interview, 25 July 2017). There, the issue of the path to power, the two-stage theory to eventual socialism and related themes dominated discussion. 'The programme adopted by the SACP at this congress was more explicit than the Party had ever been on the tasks of the national democratic state – its role was to root out domination by foreign capital and create the industrial and technical base for Socialism through democratic ownership and control of the economy ... [including] ... mining, heavy industry, banks and other monopoly industries' (Levy 2011: 410).

As an aside, Levy observes that the congress ended with a rousing rendition of the ANC national anthem, *Nkosi Sikelel' iAfrica*, but a less robust singing of the Communist anthem *Internationale*, 'which fewer people knew' (Levy 2011: 411).

Although it believed that an insurrectionary uprising was the likeliest outcome to the developing crisis in South Africa, the SACP did not rule out the possibility of a negotiated settlement. But it issued the following cautionary warning in its 1989 strategic assessment, 'The Path to Power': 'We should be on our guard against the clear objective of our ruling class and their imperialist allies who see negotiation as a way of pre-empting a revolutionary transformation' (SACP 1989: n.p.). It then continued with a most prescient judgement: 'The imperialists seek their own kind of transformation which goes beyond the reform limits of the present regime but which will, at the same time, frustrate the basic objectives of the struggling masses. And they hope to achieve this by pushing the liberation movement into negotiation before it is strong enough to back its basic demands with sufficient power on the ground' (SACP 1989: n.p.).

As evidenced in recent books by Willie Esterhuyse (2012) and Sampie Terreblanche (2012), the ANC in exile, under the leadership of Thabo Mbeki (who was also a Party member at the time), had conceded at the 'talks about talks' that the ANC was not, had never been and would not become a socialist party. Recall Mbeki's stinging response to Canadian academic Robert Fatton in 1984: 'The ANC is not a socialist party. It has never pretended to be one, has never said it was, and is not trying to be one' (Mbeki 1984: 609).

This attitude was not shared by some ANC comrades who were also SACP members. In the early 1980s, some heterodox anti-apartheid economists, then working at the Department of Applied Economics at Cambridge University, offered their professional economic policy advice to the ANC. The message was conveyed by one of the department's senior academic staff, South African born economist John Sender, to a SOAS colleague known to be very close to the ANC, Laurence Harris. Harris, according to Sender (Interview, 10 September 2015), passed on this offer to Harold Wolpe. Wolpe apparently turned down the offer, arguing that the ANC was not interested in what he termed 'Keynesian compromises' (Sender interview, 10 September 2015). Their sights were apparently firmly set on a struggle for socialism in terms of the movement's two-stage theory of revolution. So here were two very different interpretations of the ANC/SACP line.

Whatever Mbeki's views, the leading exiled members of the SACP appeared to lead discussions about economic policy in the 1980s to the extent that these issues were debated publicly. When the very first of the post-apartheid economic policy conferences was organised by the Centre for Southern African Studies at York University in the UK, from 29 September to 2 October 1986, the leading exiled ANC members present were all senior SACP members. They included Essop Pahad, Harold Wolpe, Mongane Wally Serote, Helena Dolny, Norman Levy, Selebano Zacharia Matlhape and Rob Davies – none of whom were trained economists. A young Tito Mboweni is also on the list of participants; it is not clear if Mboweni was then or ever a member of the SACP. Of these participants, only Davies presented a formal paper, entitled 'Nationalisation, Socialisation and the Freedom Charter'. He argued for a socialist transformation led by the state, and complemented by worker action at the point of production (Suckling and White 1988: 173ff.).

Despite the strength of the SACP presence at such gatherings, we agree with Bill Freund when he questions the real influence of the SACP on economic policy from a Soviet planning angle, despite their success in pushing left positions at Morogoro. We would maintain that much of this left SACP influence had to do with form rather than content. How a Soviet planning model would be imposed on and work in a modern capitalist economy, such as South Africa, despite all its inequities, does not appear to have been a subject debated within SACP circles: 'Virtually no one in the ANC or the SACP had more than limited knowledge about Soviet economic planning or Soviet economic institutions. The influence of the SACP was more important in terms of the structure of a disciplined political party and in propagandising against the power of the West internationally than in any coherent diffusion of socialist ideology' (Freund 2013: 520).

In his diary, SACP theoretician and activist Jack Simons describes in great deal his classes with Party activists at Novo Catengue Camp held from January to March 1979 (in Karis and Gerhart 1997: 707ff.). Simons was responsible for a 'special group' (former Moscow-based activists and departmental heads), who he claims did not 'obtain new knowledge or insight into the SA struggle' (in Karis and Gerhart 1997: 708). He lectured on Cuba, Isandlwana, matters of discipline, the Freedom Charter, the ANC constitution, national and class struggles, colonialism and so on. He comments favourably on a class held on 6 February 1979, observing that 'many good Marxists are coming up – not concerned with hair splitting or abstractions – and able to apply concepts – also to SA' (in Karis and Gerhart 1997: 710).

The SACP appeared bereft of ideas on economic policy even after 1990. SACP stalwart Pahad told an interviewer in that year that the SACP 'doesn't have concrete economic policies as yet' (Butler 2007: 286). Not surprising then that DEP head Trevor Manuel was confidently able to pronounce that 'the South African Communist Party would accept the existence of a "mixed economy"' (Butler 2007: 286–287).

Many South African-based members of the ANC Alliance did not appear to share this interpretation. For example, Alec Erwin, then a key figure in Cosatu and later a leading figure in the National Economic Forum,[7] and later still a Cabinet minister under Mandela and Mbeki, sent the following message to the 'capitalists' at a conference organised by the Institute for Democratic Alternatives in South Africa held in Paris in 1989: 'You fat cats have had your chance. When we take over there will be no private property: industry will be fully nationalised, and the state will be the only real instrument of social development' (in Giliomee 2003: 675). In our interview with Erwin, he challenged the authenticity of this statement attributed to him. If it was portrayed by Giliomee as a direct quote, it was wrong, he claimed (Erwin interview, 23 October 2015).

In exile into the 1980s, the SACP appears to have developed different strands, as Cronin explains:

> Partly related then to the disjuncture that happens in exile between the kind of flowering of a new left Marxism … but the *African Communist* Marxism is just chugging along in a different space … kind of regurgitating that kind of stuff, very dry stuff, which Slovo recognises in the mid-80s, okay. Suddenly there is a trade union movement, a powerful one. By the mid-80s, Cosatu [emerges] and it is saying it is a socialist organisation … So the party suddenly realises, woops, there is a kind of anti-capitalist socialist welling; we have been so focused on helping the ANC … and on the MK front and so on, and we are kind of losing the ideological battle. So at that stage *Umsebenzi* comes out. And it is very much Slovo's intervention, who is now, he has now just become the general secretary of the party as well …
>
> …
>
> But again, if you look at *Umsebenzi* it is all about how to break a tail, how to conduct clandestine work, written by Ronnie Kasrils at this stage. It is … very political and very little if anything on trade unions and trade union organisation and so forth … intervening into the debates around workers and populism, but not social or economic policy. It is kind of side-lined. And we carry that into the early 1990s, so we focus on Codesa, basically, and on building the party with Hani doing that and … Slovo being focused on Codesa and someone like myself also being focused on Codesa. So it is very much the political and constitutional side of things that we are focused on as a party rather than on economic policy, and we were quite weak on that front. We had not developed an organic capacity (Cronin interview, 14 March 2016).

By the early 1990s, the SACP had opened up a debate about the implications of global political developments after the fall of the Berlin Wall and Soviet-style socialism for the Party's position. Slovo was at the forefront of this. Here is how Cronin puts it:

> We lived in this very paradoxical moment, as the Communist Party in South Africa, so the very moment that the very significant South African breakthrough was clearly on the cards, the legacy of which we were undeniably a part, was collapsing. And so then Slovo entered into the debate with his 'has

socialism failed?' He always regretted not [adding] the second part to that, which was 'has capitalism succeeded?' And the answer to both he intended to be *no*. So there was an attempt led by Slovo really to think profoundly about perestroika and glasnost and to engage with it. In the case of Slovo, a little bit over-enthusiastically, I think, in retrospect … Gorbachev became materially a bit more of a hero than I think the party would want to make him. But what it did do was open up an important belated debate inside of the Communist Party. A reflective thing. And Slovo was trying, in 'Has Socialism Failed?', unlike Gorbachev, to have glasnost and perhaps perestroika in terms of thinking, particularly in paradigms on the one hand, but on the other hand not become anti-socialist but to maintain it. And it is an uneven document but nonetheless I think important; it kind of created a space for a debate (Cronin interview, 14 March 2016).

But according to Cronin, the ANC did not engage in a similar debate, as we have noted already: 'So the ANC never does that profound reflection on the collapse of the Soviet Union and the lessons to be learned and so on. It kind of just soldiers on. And therefore … does not reflect on the new global reality in which this new democracy is emerging. Okay. With all kinds of economic policy mistakes and miscalculations …' (Cronin interview, 14 March 2016).

In a speech to an invited audience at investment managers Davis Borkum Hare on the eve of the publication for debate of the seventh draft of the Reconstruction and Development Programme, Slovo carefully threaded his way towards some explanation of the SACP's economic policy stance. He began with a classic hedge: 'There has to be a certain open-endedness in the process of policy formation and implementation. That open-endedness must not be construed as a weakness. On the contrary' (Slovo 1994: 1).

While insisting that the SACP had not given up on its long-term goal of socialising the means of production, and of nationalisation, Slovo put forward the idea of a mixed economy 'for the foreseeable future' and nationalisation only on the balance of evidence. He insisted, too, on the need for a strong state to drive development, citing the successful examples of Japan, Taiwan and South Korea. Slovo also reminded his audience of a key resolution taken at the 1991 SACP Congress, the first inside the country since it's unbanning: 'While state involvement is considered necessary for effective planning, it can take a multitude of forms, from fiscal policies, joint projects with the private sector, state enterprises, to affirmative action and certainly direct state involvement to ensure the provision of public utilities and social services. We reject old style statist and commandist control. Our draft constitution commits us to respect and protect private property as may be necessary for effective economic development and growth' (Slovo 1994: 2–3).

HOMECOMING

Accounts of homecoming by leading exiles vary considerably. Thabo Mbeki's narrative of returning, as related to Mark Gevisser, is one of 'seamlessness'. Yet, Gevisser captures something much more complex, something much more fluid and conjunctural about the figure that Mbeki cut at Vergelegen, the wine estate near Somerset West above False Bay in the Cape, owned by the Anglo American Corporation, where the ANC NEC gathered soon after its members returned:

> Mbeki seems slightly uncomfortable in the photograph [taken on the lawns of the estate] in a too-tight suit over a pullover, an outfit conjuring the threadbare revolutionary rather than the urbane statesman-in-waiting. He is no longer in the broad paisley ties and floral shirts of the fashionable young Sussex-trained freedom fighter, but nor, yet, has he appropriated the stockbroker's style of broad-striped shirts, or the comfy middle-age of black cardigan over gold shirt. The photo seemed to me to capture its subject, uncomfortably, in some interregnum of style – Gramsci's old not-yet-dead and new struggling-to-be-born rendered sartorially – as he negotiates the space between exile and home, the transition between being in opposition and being in power (Gevisser 2007: 573).

Soon matters of economic policy for a democratic South Africa required his attention.

The Department of Economic Planning relocates

Though it crosses our periodisation into the early 1990s, it makes more thematic sense to cover the relocation of the Department of Economic Planning (DEP) from Lusaka to Johannesburg in this chapter.

Most commentators writing after 1990 point to the weakness of the movement's external economics capability, a weakness that, despite the existence of the Economics Unit from 1982 and the DEP from 1987, may have constrained its policy-making role as it settled into South African realities in a very different and challenging global economic environment. Trevor Manuel was explicit in admitting to this weakness, the (understandable) result of the failure throughout the ANC's history to address issues of economic policy directly. So he observes correctly that when the DEP left Lusaka there was not much by way of economic policy ideas. Part of the problem in Zambia, Manuel notes, was the varied quality of economic education and training – what we have consistently referred to as its uneven training capability in economics – and the lack of policy ideas:

> People go off to Bulgaria, and the education you get in Bulgaria would be different to those who went to the Soviet Union, and that would be different from people who went to the UK. Tito went to East Anglia, some of the people went to the LSE, there were people around Oxbridge ... but there was no way in which this would be articulated together, so the way in which I used to describe it then was the ANC didn't leave Lusaka with truckloads of filing cabinets with policy in (Manuel interview, 4 July 2016).

This much is clear in an early report by the DEP to ANC headquarters: 'Because of the smallness of our personnel and other problems of growth, it has as yet not been possible for the department [DEP] to implement its planned specialisation and division of labour and draw clear cut job descriptions for all members ... the main problem confronting the [DEP] presently is uncertainty and lack of clarity on the new structural changes introduced in the movement following the July session of the meeting of the NEC' (ANC Lusaka Mission Archives, Part 11, DEP, Box 24, Folder 5).

It is also noticeable that with few exceptions – Jaya Josie, Max Sisulu, Tito Mboweni and, of course, Thabo Mbeki – none of the many comrades who worked in the Economics Unit and the DEP, and whom we name above, reappear in South Africa after the unbanning of the ANC in February 1990. Josie chose or was pushed out of the DEP – recall he was the co-ordinating secretary of MERG from 1991 and was replaced by Vella Pillay – and returned to complete his PhD in London under the supervision of Laurence Harris (Josie interview, 30 January 2015). Sisulu appears to have been side-lined somewhat from the leadership, though he remained part of the DEP team even in late 1993, as our discussion in chapter 4 shows.

Curiously, Sisulu is frequently referred to in official documents as 'Head of DEP' in 1992 and 1993 – that is, after Manuel took over from him in August 1991 (Nelson Mandela Papers, University of Fort Hare). For Manuel, this was simply because no one told Sisulu that he had been replaced, so he continued believing that he was still the head. Manuel himself felt it difficult to inform Sisulu of this change because of the latter's seniority in all respects, including age and experience in the ANC: 'Max was at the Kennedy School at the time, if I remember, and it was a very difficult issue. I arrive with a kind of instruction from the officials and as a NEC member I am now head of DEP. Max had been looking after this area of work since exile. Nobody said to Max you are no longer head of DEP …' (Manuel interview, 4 July 2016).

However, we now know from Sisulu directly that it was only later, in fact around 1995, that he accepted a World Bank scholarship at the Kennedy School of Government. Manuel (Interview, 9 September 2016) disputes this.

In our interview with him, Sisulu appeared outwardly pragmatic and resigned about the fact that he lost out to Manuel as head of the DEP. Manuel was a member of the NEC and the National Working Committee (NWC), so his political senior, Sisulu points out, and it was thus not surprising that Manuel took over as head of the DEP, despite his lack of training in economics. But we did get the distinct sense in our interview that this was not the whole story. Clearly, even for this loyal (arguably aristocratic) son of the South African struggle, that decision could not have been an easy pill for Sisulu to swallow.

Sisulu makes the valuable observation that when he returned to South Africa to work in the DEP he found it strange that it was the South African comrades who were least keen to engage in debates over economic policy. This was odd, he thought, because he had been led to believe that democratic practice was a key feature of the internal struggle. This internal group consisted of Manuel, Alec Erwin, Maria Ramos, Neil Morrison, Moss Ngoasheng, Leslie Maasdorp and others. Mbeki gave them his protection and it was not easy, Sisulu maintains, to challenge people like Manuel, who was the head of the DEP and an NEC/NWC member, but also, in part, because of Mbeki's protection. This internal grouping had become convinced that there was no alternative to their interpretation of the balance of forces and economic ideas globally; in other words, they believed there was no alternative to neo-liberal globalisation. Few dared challenge Mbeki and this largely internal ANC team because of his seniority and his intellect, and in the fraught political climate of the time when the stakes were so high no one wanted to engage in open warfare with their own comrades (Sisulu interview, 25 August 2016).

Even as late as the early 1990s, many of the most senior ANC political leadership did not fully appreciate the importance of economic issues in the transition, Sisulu maintains. Nor did they fully appreciate the role of the global, progressive economics community that had come willingly, selflessly and enthusiastically to support the ANC in shaping economic policy through structures such as MERG. In fact, Sisulu claims, there was in Lusaka a much greater appreciation of the importance of the economy in the transition to democracy. Having lived in many African countries and in the Soviet Union, Sisulu understood that South Africa was very different from these countries and that, given its entrenched capitalist class, a more pragmatic and cautious approach to economic transformation was necessary (Sisulu interview, 25 August 2016).

At the July 1991 ANC conference in Durban, the first since its unbanning, Manuel was elected to the NEC. Later, he was elected onto the NWC. At that point, he was telephoned by Cyril Ramaphosa and informed that it was Mandela's wish that he (Manuel) take over the headship of the DEP. He protested his ignorance of economics, but claims he was faced with no option; it had been so ordered (Manuel interview, 4 July 2016). He arrived at his Shell House office in August 1991. Already there were some 'talented but inexperienced' economists – and note here Manual's use of the term 'inexperienced' (Green 2008: 338). Among them were Sisulu (a Soviet-trained economist), Ramos (an economist trained in South Africa and the UK), Vivian McMenamin (an economist from Natal, trained at London University), and Mboweni (a development economist trained in Lesotho and at the University of East Anglia in the UK). There were many others who were not formally trained in economics but attempting, with the aid of short courses at various overseas finance houses, to come to terms with the modern world of economics, finance and budgets. Among this group were Ketso Gordhan and Ismail Momoniat. Among now well-known figures in the South African business world such as Maasdorp, Ngoasheng and Lesetja Kganyago (currently SARB governor) were others who were based at the DEP for varying periods in the early to mid-1990s.

Freund also reminds us of the unevenness in the economics training of the DEP members. Some had a Soviet or Eastern European economics training; many others in the DEP, arguably the majority, had some local or Western training in economics but had only a superficial or no interest in a socialist or radical transformation of the economy. These latter cadres included (according to Freund) Ketso Gordhan, Mboweni, McMenamin, Morrison, Ramos and Colin Coleman. They 'began to be pushed into rapid training'. Freund points out that most of this group are now prominent figures in the private sector and many are in the banking and financial sector (2013: 521). Others had no training in economics of any kind but were social scientists of one kind or other.

Manuel was not initially received with much enthusiasm. Mboweni reportedly felt that 'it was a political appointment', and Momoniat was 'lukewarm'. Manuel himself admits that there 'was some measure of disaffection' (Green 2008: 334–336). His first task was to restructure and focus the DEP on economic policy and training. After all, what he inherited was not in great shape: the fluidity of ANC economic policy in the late 1980s and early 1990s was precisely a reflection of its vagueness during the organisation's exile years (see above). Here is how Manuel himself describes the challenge he faced:

> Look, my understanding of it is that essentially the ANC as a liberation movement does liberation stuff in particular areas. There may have been a better impetus [in some areas], so when Oliver Tambo convenes people like Zola Skweyiya and Albie Sachs and Kader Asmal and he says I want you to craft constitutional principles, that is a direct mandate to get involved in constitutional policies. Draw on your experience, go back to African Claims, go back to the Freedom Charter, draw on our experiences, draw on the best of what you know from the world and fashion the principles that are a direct mandate for policy formulation … there was never any way in which these matters would articulate with any precision (Manuel interview, 4 July 2016).

On relocation to Johannesburg, the DEP initially consisted of two departments: economics, headed by Sisulu, and a land commission, headed by Derek Hanekom. It covered a wide range of policy areas, including finance, trade and industry, minerals and energy, agriculture, land affairs, science and technology, the environment and development planning. In September 1990, it co-ordinated (rather than researched) the publication of a Discussion Document on Economic Policy, which was based, in part, on the policy document published in May in Harare (see chapter 4 for more on this). Its substantive work covered a bewildering range of responsibilities, including liaison with multilateral organisations, regional work, training, internal service for the ANC, outward communication, campaigns and, of course, policy work. The May 1992 policy conference, which led to the 'Ready to Govern' document was a highlight of the latter. A number of workshops were also convened. They related to the national budget, trade policy, and investment, mining and anti-trust policy. Some papers, it is claimed, were produced or were intended on issues such as environmental policy, rural finance and credit, and agriculture, but we have not been able to locate these in the archives at the University of Fort Hare or in any of the major university libraries. The DEP played a key role in the establishment of both MERG and the Land and Agricultural Policy Centre in 1991–1992.

A number of training courses were held for DEP in-house staff and, in addition, DEP staff were sent to various courses overseas. These included a World Bank course in public expenditure management in Washington, DC, placement with the Central Bank of Pakistan, an International Monetary Fund (IMF) course on financial planning and a course at Georgetown University in Washington on international trade. DEP delegations also visited the following countries for courses related to economic management: the US, France, Germany, Malaysia, Australia and Canada. Of course, interactions with existing state institutions (such as the SARB), state corporations (such as Eskom, South African Airways and the Post Office) and government departments (finance, state expenditure) were common in the early 1990s.

Manuel provides richer details on the training organised via the DEP, apart from the training that occurred via MERG. The one major problem in this regard, he concedes, was that DEP staff had such a wide variety of training in economics – from the former Soviet Union, the UK, China and elsewhere. Mandela, he recalls, was very keen on training, and often raised this with visiting delegations. For example, he persuaded the Bundesbank governor to invite a group of DEP economists to Germany (see chapter 5 for more on this). He also persuaded New York mayor David Dinkins to organise the placement of about 20 young black economists in leading New York banks. Through the efforts of Judd Sumner at Goldman Sachs, Mboweni organised for a group, including Ramos, Kganyago, Morrison, Bongi Kunene and others to visit the Goldman Sachs trading floor and be shown around the company for two weeks. An Alliance delegation, including Jayendra Naidoo, Cheryl Carolus, Thozamile Botha, Mboweni and Manuel, visited the World Bank around 1992 and spent two weeks there, living in rather austere conditions at an IMF hostel in Washington. Mbeki apparently joined the delegation towards the end. It was there, Manuel observes, after he heard World Bank Africa President Edward (Kim) Jaycox promise 'by hell, we will teach you how to budget' that he was determined never to fall into the Bank's clutches. Nazir Alli (later CEO of the South African National Roads Agency) spent six months learning about infrastructural development at the World Bank, and then another three months in North Africa under the World Bank's auspices. Manuel himself attended a modelling course for a week at the Indian Statistical Institute in New Delhi (Manuel interview, 9 September 2016).

A crucial task was, of course, policy formulation and co-ordination, and a DEP report to the ANC secretary general dated March 1992 and signed by Manuel addresses some of the challenges in this area: 'Undoubtedly, a substantial amount of ground has been covered, a fair amount remains. What is difficult is ensuring that decisions are taken on aspects of policy. The report refers to a series of papers written or in the drafting process; there is no understanding of how these documents will be adopted by the ANC as its policies … Hence a tendency for the perception that policy is made on the hoof' (Nelson Mandela Papers, Box 237, Folder 17).

A table in the above report on the state of the DEP in the regions is revealing. Regional associations on economics, land, and science and technology were planned in each of 14 ANC regions. Using a scale of 1 to 5, with 1 being very good and 5 being very bad, the report points out that only the Western Cape is given a 1 for its economics associations; six regions are rated a 2, and five are rated very bad (the last including the Pretoria–Witwatersrand area, northern Natal, the Midlands, Northern Cape and southern Free State). So, all in all, this was not a totally satisfactory state of affairs on economic matters. 'The track record of the DEP [in the regions] leaves much to be desired', the March 1992 report observes (Nelson Mandela Papers, Box 237, Folder 17).

The report proposes for ANC approval a revised structure for the DEP, with a head, deputy head and policy portfolios. In some cases, the first names of proposed heads are pencilled in – Max for macroeconomic policy; Tito for trade and industry; Ketso [Gordhan] for development; for agriculture, Derek [Hanekom]. No recommendations were pencilled in for land, mining and energy, environment or regional integration. The report also mentions the need for an administrative secretary, receptionist, typist/filing clerk and librarian/data person. Crucially, the report calls for a 'closer relationship to the negotiations process than has been the practice' and a 'closer and ongoing relationship to the leadership'. These last points are important because they hinted that such closer relationships to the Convention for a Democratic South Africa (Codesa) negotiations and the ANC leadership did not exist to any satisfactory degree by March 1992 (the date of the report). If this situation did not improve, this would surely have negatively impacted on the economic policy-making and approval process. To some extent, as we will see in chapter 5, this may have impacted on issues such as the debate over SARB independence at Codesa.

As we note again later (see chapter 4), the DEP clearly understood the importance of 'democratic participation': 'If the DEP does not relate to the movement in a democratic way, it will likely become alienated from its original aims, as has happened with research organisations in some independent African countries. Moreover, only democratic structures permit the DEP to undertake participatory research and popular education in a systematic manner' (Nelson Mandela Papers, Box 237, Folder 17).[8]

CONCLUSION

Yet, this is precisely what did happen, and the DEP did become alienated from its original aims. Its members simply ignored all that was going around them within the movement itself and turned elsewhere for their economic ideas.

Here is how Gevisser, a sympathetic commentator, summarises the DEP's approach over the period we assess in the next chapter: 'But Manuel's DEP paid little attention to MERG and – all but ignored during the whirlwind of negotiations in the early 1990s – quietly set about writing an economic policy in accordance with the international financial institutions. The DEP's approach was by no means secret, but their report-backs were ill-attended, and the only senior leader with the intellectual background to be able to follow the complex macro-economic debates they presented was Mbeki himself' (2007: 668).

We turn now in chapter 4 to institutional economic policy developments in what we term the decade of liberation (1985–1996). We explore the more substantial economic policy debates within the broad movement from the formation of Cosatu in 1985 to economic policy-making during the first few years of the democratic government led by the ANC. Thereafter, in chapter 5 we try to interpret and make sense of these institutional developments.

4

Economic Policy Debates during a Decade of Liberation, 1985–1993

This chapter and the next lie at the heart of our project in so far as they relate to the key economic debates during the transition to democracy. Drawing on the long history of policy debates that we have traced in previous chapters, we try to make sense of what transpired in the economic policy debate in the crucial first half of the 1990s. For something did unfold, but what exactly, and why? Was the policy shift away from the ANC's traditional values the result of some grand conspiracy by a small elite in the ANC bent on selling out the legacy of African Claims and the Freedom Charter? Or was it the outcome of a rather chaotic, messy and haphazard unfolding of events under conditions of pressure, where an underprepared ANC leadership was outmanoeuvred by the still well-resourced economic institutions of the apartheid state and by the local big business sector? Were the international financial institutions and Western governments the key influence? Or was it something else?

It would be naive to try to advance some kind of 'mathematical weighting' to all the factors that may explain what unfolded in the economic policy debate within the democratic movement in the 1990s. This book is not a 'who done it' mystery. Rather, our aim is to rely on our training as academics, our political instincts and our judgement to lay it all out before our readership, as we understand it and based on the available evidence we were able to secure. We use evidence from various public and private archives, from the growing number of recently published memoirs of leading ANC politicians, from other secondary sources and documents, and most importantly from dozens of in-depth interviews with key actors from across the political spectrum that have not been aired before in any coherent and systematic way.

Firstly, discussion of the evolution of ANC economic policy thinking in the 1990s and the perceived radical shift from the Reconstruction and Development Programme (RDP) to Growth, Employment and Redistribution (GEAR) cannot really be understood without some recognition of the economic policy changes that the National Party government had been instituting since the late 1970s. Secondly, we need to understand economic policy developments within the ANC Alliance as a whole, including in the Congress of South African Trade Unions (Cosatu) and the Economic Trends Research Group set up by Cosatu in the mid-1980s. Thirdly, we need to review some of the early economic policy conferences that fed into and informed the 1990s debate. We do break a little with chronology here to dip into some developments as early as the late 1970s so as to create the essential context for and flow of our main narrative.

THE NATIONAL PARTY'S PROGRAMME OF ECONOMIC POLICY REFORM

With regard to the policy shifts in the National Party, it must be pointed out that commission after commission, report after report, white paper after white paper was produced to re-examine the National Party's policies. For decades following its decisive 1948 electoral victory, state-interventionist economic policies were developed that favoured poor white Afrikaners and Afrikaner business development. Later, by the 1960s and 1970s, policies shifted to support a more inclusive white South Africanism. These changes in the direction of economic reform, aimed at reducing the heavy engagement of the state in support of Afrikaners and whites in general, were led by Prime Minister (later President) PW Botha, who, according to Hermann Giliomee was a 'reformer in the socio-economic field way ahead of de Klerk' (2012: 291). On becoming prime minister in 1978, Botha set about with steely purpose and a clear vision to develop his white South African nation. That meant expelling or neutralising all those so-called *verkrampte* (ultra-conservative) elements in the state bureaucracy, mainly concentrated in the Transvaal National Party, whom he saw as potential obstacles. By the time 'his man', Gerhard de Kock, took over as governor of the South African Reserve Bank (SARB) in 1981, this first 'cleansing' task was more or less complete.

As argued by Mike Morris and Vishnu Padayachee (1989: 95ff.), the first phase of these reforms, beginning in the late 1970s, represented the triumph of a market-oriented group of state reformers, including De Kock, Jan Lombard (monetary policy), Sebastian Kleu (industry and trade policy) and Simon Brand (regional strategy and agriculture) over the group of classic apartheid hardliners.

Lombard, a very senior economic bureaucrat with 50 years of government service, was an influential figure in the drive towards what he himself termed 'economic liberalism'. His book *Freedom, Welfare and Order* (1978), which owed much to his mentor Friedrich Hayek, became very influential inside and outside government circles. Here, in an extract from a private memoir with very restricted circulation written in about 2012, is what he had argued:

> Because of my noise about 'economic liberalism' as the way out of our political dilemmas I was even invited to become President of the Free Market Foundation, a newly established movement in South Africa monitoring excessive government intervention in the market economy and driven by the energies of Michael O'Dowd (from Anglo American) as Chairman and Leon Louw as its full-time Director. We invited the famous herald of these ideas, Friedrich Hayek, to visit South Africa, after which a few of us were invited to become members of the 'Mont Pelerin Society', an international forum with the same aims consisting of mostly prominent academics like the famous Chicago economist Milton Friedman. During my tenure as President of the Economic Society *in 1980–81, I called for a system of much greater independence for the Reserve Bank.* Following Milton Friedman, I believed that there is no lasting social benefit to be derived from the creation of money for the government of any country by its central bank (Lombard n.d.: n.p., emphasis added).

His remark *at that time* about greater central bank independence is worth noting, and we will return to this debate in chapter 6. Since 1961 and after the Sharpeville political crisis, the apartheid regime tightened exchange controls to stem capital outflows and introduced the 'blocked rand', which in 1979 was replaced by the financial rand. However, following the report of the De Kock Commission on Exchange Controls tabled in November 1978, there was a gradual easing of exchange controls. The financial rand itself was abolished in 1983, and non-residents could repatriate the majority of their South African investments via the commercial rand.

This easing was short-lived, however, and the financial rand system was reintroduced on 1 September 1985 as sanctions pressure tightened and the country introduced a unilateral standstill on foreign debt. The financial rand was eventually abolished by the democratic ANC-led government of national unity in 1995, though some exchange controls remained in place. However, it is important to recall that the apartheid regime had itself (as early as 1978) begun gradually to implement the market-oriented reforms in respect of exchange controls, so pre-dating the ANC reforms. Reform in many other areas, including in the labour market and industrial and trade policy, mirrored moves in exchange control policy. Thus, by the time political negotiations began in 1990, the economic policy stance of the late apartheid government was unambiguously market-oriented. Lombard's dream of 'economic liberalism' had by then largely been realised.

So, in many areas of economic policy, the National Party and the government just had to hold their market-friendly position when formal negotiations commenced in the early 1990s, rather than moving left or right. The ANC appears to have been either acquiescent or powerless to challenge these existing National Party economic policy proposals, which were developed by its well-capacitated economic institutions, including the Central Economic Advisory Services, the SARB, the Central Statistical Services, the Treasury, and agencies such as the Development Bank and the Land Bank.

We return to these issues related to the role of the apartheid regime and its key figures later in this chapter when our narrative reaches the early 1990s.

PROGRESSIVE ECONOMIC POLICY DEBATES IN THE MID TO LATE 1980S

The mid-1980s was a period of feverish excitement for the progressive, anti-apartheid academic community in general. Labour, civic and political mobilisation and activity, led by the United Democratic Front, reached new heights following the Johannesburg-based township revolt, which began in November 1984. The independent, non-racial trade union federation, Cosatu, was formed in December 1985. Internationally, the sanctions campaign had intensified, culminating in the US Comprehensive Anti-Apartheid Act of 1986. In mid-1985, a partial state of emergency was declared, and this was made total one year later. These and other developments combined to stimulate the establishment of new research networks and organisations, which focused on providing support to progressive labour, social and political movements and formations that were beginning to take the anti-apartheid struggle to new heights.

These networks, which were frequently harassed by the state security police and were forced to work under conditions of secrecy, were led by young, progressive social scientists and economists, predominantly white and male at this time. Many had returned to South Africa from studies overseas in the 1970s, where they were influenced by an eclectic mix of dependency theory, Third World studies, and the theories of neo-colonialism and Marxism popular at places such as the University of Sussex at the time. Some worked from within universities at a time when even the liberal South African universities were invariably unsympathetic to this kind of work, and they linked up with non-university-based research networks; others set up and worked within externally funded research and service centres. These groups, which were formed in the second half of the 1980s, included the Labour and Economic Research Centre, the Community Agency for Social Enquiry, the Community Research and Information Centre, the Economic Trends Research Group, the Community Research Unit, the Labour Research Service, the Labour and Economic Research Project, the Sociology of Work Programme, Planact, the Centre for Health Policy Studies, the Centre for Development Studies and various regional Education Policy Units.

In the mid-1980s in the UK, a small group of progressive economists, including the Marxist economists Ben Fine (then at Birkbeck College), Laurence Harris (then at the Open University) and the well-known South African émigré banker Vella Pillay (then a senior manager at the State Bank of China in the City of London), together with some members of the ANC's Department of Economic Planning (DEP), formed a research consortium called Economic Research on South Africa. EROSA produced a number of papers on the South African economy, which, according to Moss Ngoasheng (1992: 121), went beyond a critique into areas of policy recommendations. This included work on the minerals-energy complex, the savings-investment constraint and the nature of the South African financial system. The group related to the ANC in exile through Pillay, Max Sisulu and Pallo Jordan (IDRC 1991: 7; Fine, personal communication, 1997).

The development of academic-led think tanks focusing on economic analysis and policy issues was boosted by a number of milestone international conferences in the second half of the 1980s. The first of these was held at York University in September/October 1986 and its theme was 'The South African Economy after Apartheid'. The conference brought together a group of liberal and left-wing economists opposed to the apartheid state, and participants were closely vetted by the ANC. Off-agenda meetings between the ANC delegation (which included Essop Pahad, Harold Wolpe, Rob Davies and Wally Serote) and South African academics were held under conditions of secrecy. The sharp debate between Pahad and Alex Callinicos over the interpretation of some point made by Marx and Lenin is still vivid. While the conference did not come up with any significant policy positions, it did bring together for the first time some of the key academics and activists who over the next decade would play an important role in the economic policy debate in

South Africa. Selected papers from the York conference were published in a book edited by John Suckling and Landeg White (1988).

A veritable flood of economic, social policy and other anti-apartheid conferences followed. These were held in Beijing (1986), Amsterdam (1986), Boston (1987), Freiburg (1987), Harare (1988, 1990), Paris (1989) and Lausanne (1989). At these conferences, progressive South African social scientists and economists were able to meet, some for the first time, with high-ranking members of the still-banned ANC, South African Communist Party (SACP) and the South African Congress of Trade Unions.

Also in 1986, South-African-born economist, John Sender, then at the Department of Applied Economics at Cambridge University, organised a conference on South Africa. John Lonsdale edited a book titled *South Africa in Question* (1988), which was a product of this conference. Though not narrowly focused on the economy, economic issues were integral to it, and participants (including Merle Lipton, Frene Ginwala, Colin Murray, William Beinhart, Shula Marks and Harold Wolpe) addressed a number of issues linked to economic policy. As Sender informed us, it was sometime after that conference that Wolpe and Harris decided that what young ANC economists really needed was further training in Moscow, rejecting the offer of training in macroeconomics by the 'sell-out Keynesians' at Cambridge's Department of Applied Economics (Sender, personal email communication, 15 July 2016).

The 1986 York conference had essentially been an internal gathering of ANC–SACP politicians and ANC-aligned economists from South Africa and elsewhere, plus a few sympathetic liberal South African economists. The 1989 Lausanne conference, on the other hand, took place against the backdrop of the 'talks about talks', which were sponsored by Consolidated Goldfields. Reflecting those developments, Lausanne was an occasion that brought together politicians, economists and business people aligned with the apartheid state and their ANC–SACP counterparts, also in politics, business and academia. Pieter le Roux, a development economist from the University of the Western Cape (UWC) with a social-democratic orientation, who worked closely with Jakes Gerwel, a co-organiser of the conference (subsequently vice chancellor of UWC and later the first director general in President Mandela's office), informs us of the rather relaxed atmosphere that prevailed, and the ease with which participants from both sides related and exchanged political and economic ideas. At one point, a cross-section from all sides even retreated to watch some rugby on TV.

Altogether there were 57 delegates, 26 from within South Africa (including Pieter le Roux, Simon Brand, Stephen Gelb, Rudolf Gouws, David Kaplan, David Lewis, Jan Lombard, Lieb Loots, Colin McCarthy, Philip Mohr, Terence Moll, Moss

Ngoasheng, Pundy Pillay, Maria Ramos, André Roux, Conrad Strauss, Servaas van der Berg and Lourens van Wyk) with about 20 from the external ANC (including Tito Mboweni, Bheki Langa, Raymond Mokoena, Bontle Modise and Manto Tshabalala). This conference was preceded by two planning meetings that Le Roux had with the ANC – one in a safe house in London and one at Harare Airport.[1]

It is not without interest to point to the career trajectories of some of the ANC-aligned participants at Lausanne. Those who ended up in big business (finance) include: Maria Ramos (Wits to DEP to Treasury to Absa/Barclays); Moss Ngoasheng (Natal University to DEP to the Presidency to his own BEE company); André Roux (UWC, Development Bank to Treasury to Investec Bank); Tito Mboweni (DEP to Cabinet to SARB to Goldman Sachs). Others became state ministers or bureaucrats: Manto Tshabalala (Cabinet); David Kaplan (University of Cape Town to Department of Trade and Industry to UCT); Pundy Pillay (UWC to the Presidency to Wits); Bheki Langa (KwaZulu-Natal government to ambassador); Fuad Cassim (Wits to the Public Investment Corporation to Treasury to Banking Association of South Africa).

It is useful here to set out Le Roux's full, largely unedited, take on how the Lausanne conference came about, Gerwel's role, and about some of the participants:

> Jakes Gerwel said [to me], you know the big question when we have the transition will be where will the economic policy go. In fact, that is the reason why we didn't have a settlement until the Soviet Union collapsed, the [apartheid] establishment was no way going to settle for that, but I think [there] must be debate and I'm sure Simon Brand will be positive about a dialogue, how do you feel? Then he spoke to Thabo, I think. Then he got back to me and said, well, see what you can get together. Then I went to the Swiss ambassador because Simon said, 'Look, we cannot have a meeting with the ANC, PW won't allow it, but if we can have a conference organised where we can have ANC people'. And he suggested Switzerland because it was a neutral place.
>
> …
>
> So I went to see the Swiss ambassador and he said – 'ag [sic], another thing about this', because there was a lot of debates and [he was] not interested at all … and then he had a young bright guy in his office who said after-wards, 'This is a brilliant idea', and he made direct contact with the head of fiscal development in Switzerland … Then I met Thabo in Zimbabwe for the first … no, I first met him in London where I also met Harold [Wolpe] and so we spoke about the idea. I spoke to Simon Brand, he came back to me. I assumed later on I thought they were doing it behind PW's back but I think

PW was quite happy to organise something as long as he can pretend that this was not negotiations …

…

What happened then is, from the establishment [side] the only one that I dropped, when he spoke about speaking to PW, he was the guy that was in charge of Eskom at that stage, Jan Nacht; he was a heavyweight Afrikaner, but Jan Lombard was vice president, Frans Barker was head of the Manpower Commission, Simon Brand … the guys at the Afrikaans universities, Potch, Stellenbosch, that were close to the Afrikaans establishment, we invited them.

…

In the meantime, the ANC, I heard in the background, there was a big thing, 'should we have this conference at all?' Ben Fine and those guys said, no, we should organise it, we don't know exactly where we stand. But then eventually Tambo came down in favour of the conference. But what it did mean is, the people from the ANC side were [then younger and] all lower-profile people. Thabo himself didn't come. In fact at that time the political negotiations were going on; I didn't realise that …

…

A lot of people, like Maria Ramos … Fuad Cassim, a lot of the internal ANC people were there. Of the external people the highest was Tito Mboweni. Quite a few of the other guys that were relatively important, Max [Sisulu] wouldn't come. Max was against it; I'm very sorry now because I got to like Max much more than Thabo later on, when I got to know him. But I think Max and Thabo had a bit of rivalry, also in politics. It's also these personalities … (Le Roux interview, 29 January 2015).

The reference to the collapse of the Soviet Union, Gerwel's role, the presence of senior apartheid bureaucrats such as Brand, Barker and Estian Calitz is significant, as was the mention of Mboweni, clearly rising in the ranks of the ANC in exile. Also of interest is the opposition to the conference of Sisulu, then head of the ANC's DEP in Lusaka. Nowhere on the scene at that time was Trevor Manuel who was to assume the position of head of the DEP in Johannesburg within 18 months.

COSATU AND THE ECONOMIC TRENDS RESEARCH GROUP

The Economic Trends Research Group (ET) was initiated at the request of Cosatu in late 1986, following on earlier efforts within the new union federation to educate workers and shop stewards in economics. In the following quotation, note Alec Erwin's stress on left social democracy:

> I always marvel at how much work we actually did in Cosatu. We start in 1985. Before that you had the St Peter's courses, where we did shop stewards' courses over weeks in economics. Those courses were left social democracy, quite a far-left social democracy, socialism we called it, but it was fairly tempered with some reality. It had a lot more to do with the history of capitalism in South Africa with respect to racism. Then in 1985 we started Cosatu education, following on a very similar approach, and then in 1986 we start ET because we realise we are going to get more research that way. So we start to prepare ourselves quite well, and I think the thing Cosatu did well is top worker leadership; we took them through a lot of economic courses, and they became really good at this (Erwin interview, 23 October 2015).

ET was initially located within the auspices of the Labour and Economic Research Centre in Johannesburg and was co-ordinated by Stephen Gelb, a Canadian-trained South African economist. The project was funded mainly by Canadian, British and German foundations, and locally by the South African Council of Churches. ET began its work with eight researchers based in Johannesburg, Durban and Cape Town. By late 1990, membership had grown to 21 (Gelb 1991: xi).

ET's initial work was to examine the likely impact of sanctions on the economy and on Cosatu membership. However, it soon became necessary to broaden the scope of ET's work to examine the structure of the South African economy, and to begin to understand the nature and origins of the crisis that had beset the economy since the early 1970s. That work (Phase One) culminated in the publication of a major report to Cosatu and a book, *South Africa's Economic Crisis* (1991), edited by Gelb, which provided both a macroeconomic overview of the economy and a detailed analysis of some key sectors. The theoretical foundations of the research were located in terms of an adaptation of the French Regulation School to South African conditions, what Gelb called racial Fordism (1991: 13).

One of ET's main claims to fame was that, despite initial difficulties, it did manage to forge an effective, productive working relationship, linking mainly university-based researchers to a major national labour movement – perhaps the first such relationship on this scale in the history of this country. However, the links between ET and Cosatu, even in its most developed phase, were neither highly structured nor as strong as many believe. Key to the success of its operations were the mainly white, male 'organic intellectuals' of the union movement. Most of them were from its metal affiliate, the National Union of Metalworkers of South Africa (Numsa), including Alec Erwin, Jay Naidoo, Bernie Fanaroff and Geoff Schreiner. Even as late as September 1989, there was an intense debate within ET about whether to extend its reach more formally into the union federation, and, if so, how. Erwin argued passionately for ET members to relate more closely to the new structures that some of the unions had set up to deal with economic policy issues: 'This is a time of acute political change. Organisations and intellectuals need to engage. Let's not establish a broad bank of knowledge first, then intervene, but get into research and policy formulation, learn from other experiences and press on' (Original hand-written minutes, ET meeting, Cape Town, September 1989, Vishnu Padayachee private archives).

But this plea met with resistance from some of the researchers.

Weak links with the ANC can of course be explained by the fact that in the early years of ET's existence, the ANC was still banned from operating in South Africa. However, there was little or no attempt by the ANC in exile to forge closer links with ET researchers. In fact, we would argue that the ANC in London was suspicious of the motives of the local ET leadership. Furthermore, as a report by the International Development Research Centre (IDRC) notes, the absence of a closer relationship with ANC structures could also be explained, in part, 'by the reticence of some members of ET to have their research associated directly with the political movement' (IDRC 1991: 11).

There were also concerns within and outside the group about the appropriateness of the theoretical approach employed by the ET leadership. A few years later, Ben Fine and Zavareh Rustomjee noted: 'Gelb's ... notion of racist Fordism ... quite clearly reflects the imposition of a questionable regulation theory originally developed for other purposes with limited purchase on the peculiar features of the South African economy. It is quite incapable of dealing with its complexities and differences at the level of detail ...' (1996: 242).

Let us examine a broader assessment of ET through the observations of some leading commentators and critics.

In a prescient article dealing with the post-1985 era, Mike Morris referred, among other issues, to ET and its relationship with Cosatu. He warned then that the failure to deal adequately with the legacy of the past could lead intellectuals and political activists in two dangerous and contradictory ways: one to return to a totalising framework – romantic, appealing, yet unrealisable, slogans of the past; the other to slide into the 'technicist logic' of apartheid-era state policymakers, which these same progressive economists had so vociferously opposed in the past. This was dangerous, he argued, 'because if social problems are reduced to technical ones in the tense and fraught transition currently under way in South Africa, it is a short step to authoritarian repression to ensure the implementation of unpopular technical solutions' (Morris 1996: 270–271).

Michael Neocosmos (1997) has examined the role and response of left intellectuals in South Africa through a review of two key left debates – the civil society debate and the workerism versus populism debate. He argues that opposition debates during the decade (1985–1995) were largely located within a statist framework, regardless of the ideological leanings (nationalist, liberal or socialist), and that by the early 1990s the discourse of left intellectuals contributed to the eventual domination of statism and the defeat of the mass popular movement. Left intellectuals who emerged out of earlier popular struggles largely followed the current into what Neocosmos calls the 'corporatist statism' of the 1990s; they now conform, he contends, to Mahmood Mamdani's characterisation of African intellectuals as 'state fetishists' (Neocosmos 1997: 53). Those committed to popular forms of democracy have been side-lined or silenced. He concludes: 'All indications are that the left in particular, will remain irrevelant in South African politics unless and until it finds something to say regarding democracy' (Neocosmos 1997: 54).

Turning specifically to progressive economists, Neocosmos charges that they placed too much faith in the new state to resolve the problems of development, ignoring totally the organisations of the people. By the early 1990s, the responsibility for South African transformation was, through the process of marginalising people and their mass organisations, left entirely to the state. 'As a result,' Neocosmos concludes, 'it became much more difficult for the Left to withstand the critique of statism by economic liberalism for example, when the latter made itself felt on the issue of "development" in particular' (1997: 52).

In a blistering polemic, Ashwin Desai and Heinrich Bohmke (1997) trace what they term the current 'retreat' in the thinking and practice of the small group of progressive South African social scientists and economists from the mid-1980s. The mainly white, male economists in ET, they observe with approval, were closely allied to the non-racial trade union movement, and distinguished themselves by being unafraid to criticise the tactics and strategies of the ANC-led liberation movement when they felt this necessary. An anti-apartheid, 'Bohemian-style' sub-culture, they assert, knit this exclusive group together. However, with the demise of apartheid, beginning around 1990, the 'bottom fell out of their market'. As the 'new government moved to the right', these critics contend, so the research work and theoretical disposition of progressive economists 'moved in tandem' (Desai and Bohmke 1997: 30–31). Most of the ET group, they contend, tossed their main weapon – critique – into the sea and sought their political rehabilitation as the balance of power shifted to the ANC by quickly becoming consultants to the ANC and then by providing academic rationalisation for the neo-liberal economic philosophy of the new ANC-led government. 'Because this same set had so dominated left-thinking in South Africa, their betrayal has all but crushed a critique of the transition' (Desai and Bohmke 1997: 32).

In a response to Numsa's Bobby Marie, an unnamed Cosatu member, in a paper entitled 'Lunch at the Carlton with Bobby and the Boys', makes this telling observation some time in 1992: 'The failure of the Economic Trends Group … to produce any original thinking for a socialist Way Forward is similarly an indictment of the progressive intelligentsia. The tragedy is that Cosatu seems to have remained mired in their thinking – captive to discredited assumptions: discredited by the reality of increasing poverty and deprivation all over the Third World' (Anon. *c.*1992: n.p., Vishnu Padayachee private archives).

We note these criticisms from various quarters, but we would not want readers to be left with a view that ET was an ineffective and detached group of ivory-tower academic economists, who somehow failed to lay down the foundations of a socialist future for South Africa. It would be grossly unfair to set ET against such an unrealistic benchmark. The quality of research produced both for the ET book (Gelb 1991) and in other working papers, the incredible effort that went into understanding the nature and theory of the crisis in the South African economy (however contestable that theory may be today), and the intense and regular engagements between ET researchers and ever-widening numbers of Cosatu shop stewards and members, in our view represent an invaluable and lasting contribution and foundation for the economic policy debate that was to follow, even if a direct line cannot be readily drawn between them. The fact that the intensity and character of those engagements between ET researchers and Cosatu did not continue into the post-1990 era is another matter altogether.

ECONOMICS ABSENT FROM THE LATE 1980S 'TALKS ABOUT TALKS'

A number of books have recently addressed the issue of the talks about talks between the ANC in exile and various groupings of South Africans, notably Afrikaner academics and business people, many of them 'reformers' still close to the National Party (Barnard and Wiese 2017; Esterhuyse 2012; Terreblanche 2012). Thus, for example, secret pre-negotiation discussions were held between ANC exiled leaders, led by Thabo Mbeki, and a group of Afrikaner professors and business people based at Stellenbosch University. The latter were tasked by Niël Barnard, then head of the apartheid-era National Intelligence Agency, to initiate these talks at various locations around the world, but mostly in the UK. The costs for these meetings (which covered the period 1987 to 1989) were carried by Consolidated Goldfields, a major British gold mining company, which had been deeply invested in South African mining for over 100 years.

From Willie Esterhuyse's (2012) book and interview (10 March 2015), we know that issues relating to the economy were raised from time to time, but the economy was not Esterhuyse's terrain of expertise, nor did it appear to be of much interest to him. Though many Afrikaner business people attended these talks about talks, the question of the future direction of the country's economic policy did not come up, apart from the issue of the ANC's avowed policy of nationalisation. Stellenbosch economist Sampie Terreblanche (who attended all the early meetings) did try to move beyond this to raise issues related to addressing the apartheid legacies of poverty and inequality, but he did not make much headway and was eventually excluded from later meetings (Esterhuyse 2012; Terreblanche 2012).

But these were not the only talks about talks. In 1986, Frederik van Zyl Slabbert led a group of prominent Afrikaner academics and business people to a meeting with the ANC in Dakar. One of the delegates was André du Pisani, a research fellow at the South African Institute of International Affairs. While highly impressed by the ANC leaders he met, Du Pisani was disturbed by their lack of ideas on economic policy. According to Graham Leach, Du Pisani believed:

> ANC economic policy was its weakest point, that they had little understanding of the workings of a modern sophisticated economy. He was disappointed by their views on issues like the role of the state in the economy, the position of private enterprise and the redistribution of wealth; on the latter point the ANC had not been able to suggest any mechanism for achieving this objective, saying that they had not given economic policy much thought and that the party which eventually governed South Africa would decide upon economic matters (Leach 1989: 160).

Ben Turok also makes the point about the strange 'absence' of any consideration of socio-economic issues at these talks: 'There is now abundant evidence of a slippage on economic issues in the discussions that Thabo Mbeki and others held with representatives of the apartheid regime in the 1980s. I recall a meeting of the ANC branch in London where we were briefed on a proposed bill of rights for the Constitutional Guidelines [presumably around 1991]. The omission of socio-economic rights was obvious' (Turok 2015: 46).

The mainly Afrikaner business people who participated in these talks about talks were quick to size up the balance of forces and react with their own set of economic ideas. Here is Giliomee, an Afrikaner historian and participant at the Dakar talks, on the issue of the economy, which also reveals that the ANC did, in fact, try *initially* to stick to their historic interventionist economic policy stance:

> In the discussion on a post-apartheid economy, Leon Louw, an office-bearer of the Free Market Foundation, entered a plea for massive decentralisation and privatisation, to which the ANC delegates replied with a strong insistence on state intervention to 'democratise' the economy. Some expressed the view that the system ultimately had to culminate in socialism. Appealing to the Freedom Charter, they demanded the nationalisation of the mining and banking sectors, the redistribution of the land and collectivised agriculture. The new South Africa would have to guarantee 'the masses of the people freedom from hunger, disease, ignorance, homelessness and poverty.' [Sociologist Laurence] Schlemmer warned that all-or-nothing strategies could actually strengthen the [apartheid] regime … The few businessmen who attended the Dakar conference took home the ANC's radical criticism of the economic policy. *The business community in South Africa would soon embark on initiatives to win the movement over to market-oriented policies* (Giliomee 2009: 37, emphasis added).

FROM TALKS ABOUT TALKS TO NEGOTIATIONS

On 11 February 1990, Nelson Mandela walked out of Victor Verster Prison as a free man after almost 27 years of incarceration. With the scene now set for negotiations over a future democratic South Africa, it was made clear to Mandela and other ANC leaders that consideration of post-apartheid economic policy could not be delayed much longer.

A number of policy documents were prepared, with varying degrees of sophistication, in the very early 1990s. The Economic Manifesto emerged from a March 1991 ANC economic workshop in preparation for the July 1991 ANC national conference in Durban. The manifesto was a moderate document, lacking the previous (mainly SACP-inspired) revolutionary language. There is no reference to terms such as capitalism, socialism or communism, nor of Cosatu's call for 'workers' control', or even the language of the Freedom Charter. It referred only to a major inquiry into monopoly capital. Juxtaposed to this is an early signal of the conservative approach to fiscal and monetary policy that became bolder later. The manifesto speaks of 'responsible' policy on government spending and inflation, but also speaks about women's oppression, rural poverty and land dispossession (Bond 1991: 17). Altogether, the manifesto appears to be of uneven quality in terms of policy focus and coherence; it reflects the understandable confusion of the time as the ANC struggled to cope with competing demands and pressures, as the inevitability of full-blown negotiations with the regime neared and democratic governance loomed ever closer.

Moss Ngoasheng[2] provides a candid account, written in 1992, of the very limited capacity of the DEP (of which he was a part) to undertake any substantive research on economic policy, while also admitting that the DEP was clearly (though understandably) outgunned by the economic policy capacity of the apartheid state:

> The DEP, and indeed the whole movement, has had no experience in formulating concrete economic (technical) policy not to say anything about implementation.
>
> …
>
> The experience within the DEP is that it is not always possible to undertake such in-depth research work. Firstly, the resources (material and human) required are not available within the DEP. Secondly, the DEP is expected to respond to a myriad of demands from the organisation's heterogeneous constituencies – political leadership, workers, rural people, the unemployed, squatter communities, black business, etc. These demands, which are not always reconcilable, made it difficult if not impossible for the DEP to develop and sustain a well-structured research programme. The point, however, is that there is no way that a group of five people can undertake research in a whole range of economic issues that needed to be covered. The state for example has a number of departments and utilises specialist commissions to deal with all the issues that the DEP is expected to deal with. The DEP sought to resolve the capacity issue by farming out work to outside researchers, that is to its associate members and sympathetic economists located in other institutions (Ngoasheng 1992: 116, 118).

It is worth providing some evidence for the important point that Ngoasheng makes about the competing demands on the time of the DEP staff, which left little time for real policy work. In a report to the ANC secretary general dated March 1992, Trevor Manuel bemoans the fact that communication and liaison takes up 'so much of the energy of DEP professional staff'. This communication, he notes, includes publication of articles in newspapers, journals and periodicals, delivery of papers to conferences and seminars, speaking at ANC mass meetings, briefing foreign diplomats, addressing various corporations at different levels, meeting prospective investors to set out policy, visiting major installations like factories and mines, addressing fundraising breakfasts and dinners, and giving radio and television interviews. He concludes, 'whilst it would be useful to quantify this area of work, the examples are too numerous' (Nelson Mandela Papers, Box 237, Folders 12–17).

THE MACROECONOMIC RESEARCH GROUP

Nelson Mandela and the origins of MERG

During a visit to Canada in June 1990, Mandela argued for the 'urgent need for a better understanding of economic policy issues in South Africa within the anti-apartheid movement as it prepares for forthcoming negotiations' (Van Ameringen 1995: 6). The Canadian government offered tangible support. A team of Canadian and African economists (headed by Gerry Helleiner, and including John Loxley and Benno Ndulu) was appointed to make recommendations to the political leadership about how to improve the movement's capacity to formulate economic policy. Their work was co-ordinated by the progressive Canadian development agency, the IDRC.

The IDRC found that the economic policy capacity of the movement was both underdeveloped and uncoordinated. Even where capacity existed – for example, among local university-based economists who were sympathetic to the movement – their research often duplicated other work, was not sufficiently focused on policy, and was poorly linked to the ANC's DEP. The DEP, in turn, was understaffed, poorly organised, and its leadership appeared to have made little or no effort to mobilise the relevant experience available at some of the universities.

The team made two major recommendations for immediate action. The first suggested an enhancement of the movement's capacity to monitor developments in the economics arena, arising from the actions and policies of the (then) apartheid state and the private sector. The second called for the establishment of a Macroeconomic Research Group (MERG) – based on local and international networks – to 'stimulate and co-ordinate policy research and training in the identified priority areas' (Van Ameringen 1995: 41).

Ben Fine reminds us that the training element initially was seen as more important, but that at some point Vella Pillay was approached to lead a process that looked more specifically at economic policy options. As Fine recalls:

> [Early in 1991] Vella Pillay came to see me and said, 'I have this request from the highest level', I think he meant Mandela, to propose an alternative set of economic policy-makings and he wants MERG to do it. I was reluctant because it seemed to me that this was reproducing exactly the syndrome we were facing, that every time there was a request for policy, it was always urgent and it was always being done by outside people such as myself, which I was willing to do, but it was a question of building capacity, so if we did it again, it would just reinforce that lack of … but nevertheless, Vella prevailed and we basically set about trying to bring together the research into a coherent set of policymakers. We also had some more funding to do some macroeconomic modelling and so on (Fine interview, 30 June 2015).

None of our informants could tell us definitely how Pillay came to be appointed as MERG director. While it was rarely spoken about openly, there were certainly whispers at the time within left academic circles that Pillay was some sort of economic dinosaur, who was not an appropriate person to lead the MERG process. Trevor Manuel informs us that Pillay appears to have been supported and encouraged to head MERG by ANC heavyweights Mac Maharaj and Max Sisulu, who was the long-standing head of the DEP in Lusaka (Manuel interview, 4 July 2016). Maharaj denies that he had any direct role in Pillay's nomination, claiming that he was not even in the ANC's National Working Committee at the time when such decisions would have been made or ratified (Maharaj interview, 16 August 2016).

Sisulu recalls that it was the DEP that nominated Pillay for the MERG position, a decision approved by the MERG Steering Committee (Sisulu interview, 25 August 2016). In fact, in a letter on a MERG letterhead from Manuel to Mandela, dated 24 January 1992, Manuel notes, 'We are happy to inform you that the MERG Steering Committee is now in the process of appointing a co-ordinator for the programme.' Manuel signs as Interim Chairperson of the Steering Committee (Nelson Mandela Papers, Box 237, Folders 12–17). Perhaps even to this day, given subsequent developments, some people do not want to be seen to have had a hand in the appointment of Pillay. In any event, Pallo Jordan informs us that Pillay's appointment was announced at the National Executive Committee (NEC) by Mandela, and that there was general support for this, given Pillay's qualifications and wide experience as an economist. Jordan also tells us that he was personally pleased as it went some small way to making up for Pillay's shabby treatment at the hands of the ANC–SACP in the mid-1960s (Jordan interview, 4 August 2017).

Sisulu knew Pillay from the early days of his exile and interacted with him over many decades in Lusaka, London and Moscow. He came to respect Pillay very much. In the very early 1990s, before MERG was fully established, Pillay was invited and made frequent visits to the DEP in downtown Johannesburg, coming from London at his own expense and engaging vigorously with DEP comrades. His knowledge, seniority and ideas were initially welcomed by everyone at the DEP and he often joined the team in meetings with apartheid regime economists, the SARB, local capital and international agencies. It was natural, Sisulu argues, that when the time came in 1992 to nominate a full-time director for MERG the DEP would turn to Pillay. 'Vella fitted the bill', is the way he describes the reasoning behind the decision (Sisulu interview, 25 August 2016).

So back to the chronology of events around the establishment and work of MERG. Mandela's statement of intent to set up MERG in November 1991 is noteworthy for three main reasons. Firstly, he begins with a comment that is clearly a misrepresentation by claiming: 'The economy of this country always has and will continue to remain central to our struggle for national liberation.' No one who is even vaguely aware of this country's history will accept this contention. Secondly, he recognised that the apartheid 'government is implementing economic strategies that go well into the future and might even tie the hands of a democratically elected government'. In hindsight, this was indeed a prescient observation. Thirdly, despite some radical rhetoric,[3] the address was considered and even cautious. Our economic programme 'will be based on realistic policy objectives and implemented through acceptable policy instruments', he stated, though he does not say acceptable for whom.[4]

MERG was led by a Steering Committee, which consisted of representatives of the ANC, Cosatu and the South African National Civic Organisation, although Sanco was hardly a presence at any level of the MERG process for reasons that remain unclear. The Steering Committee was chaired by Manuel. Various other committees intended to liaise with the researchers or the movement were set up, including the Economics Research Committee.

There was also a Donors Steering Committee Forum to co-ordinate funding efforts. Research funding came mainly from several international development agencies, including from Canada and Sweden. The US, the UK and Germany met the expenses of some of their economists, who participated as international advisers to MERG. Pillay played a key role in co-ordinating and distributing funds. There is some evidence that these Western governments did try to use their funding to influence developments in MERG. John Sender recalls that some MERG staff experienced interventions (and bullying) by senior diplomats working at the British and other Western embassies who wanted to reduce the influence of Marxist economists on the research output. We now know that British diplomats have gone on record to boast about their success in influencing ANC economic policy debates – and about the role of their 'spooks' (FCO 2013: 34; see also Padayachee and Sender 2018). We characterise these claims of influence as gross exaggerations.

The DEP-led task force, which was asked to give effect to these recommendations, decided to locate the MERG research projects (wherever feasible) at the historically black universities (HBUs) of the Western Cape, Durban-Westville, Fort Hare and the University of the North. The MERG secretariat was based at the Department of Economics, headed then by Merton Dagut, at the University of the Witwatersrand. It was felt that the development of capacity on the economic front was best co-ordinated through the HBUs, which would benefit in various ways (funds, new human resources, etc.) as part of their own efforts at institutional transformation. The objective of MERG's training and capacity-building programme was to train a core of some 200 to 300 black economists by the end of April 1994.

Eleven research projects were initially identified. These included projects on a macroeconomic framework and a model of the South African economy. The research programme was launched at an academic conference in Johannesburg in January 1991.

Apart from the research, leading international economists were brought in for lengthy periods to train South African researchers, especially in areas such as macroeconomic modelling, where South African expertise was deficient. These included the New School's Lance Taylor and his one-time student and Vermont University colleague Bill Gibson. Another who made a notable contribution was the respected Canadian economist Gerry Helleiner. Benno Ndulu (now governor of the Tanzanian Central Bank), John Loxley from Canada and Bruce MacFarlane, who was brought in to teach Kaleckian macro-modelling, also offered support at various stages of the MERG project.

Training and capacity-building workshops were held at various centres, and funding was obtained to send selected young black South African economists abroad for varying periods to complete short courses, or to begin formal post-graduate diplomas or degrees. Some leading bureaucrats in the National Treasury and other state departments over the past 20 years or so were beneficiaries of this scheme. Sender reminds us that these beneficiaries included Lesetja Kganyago (SARB governor), Steven Hannival (chief economist at the Department of Trade and Industry), Leslie Maasdorp (former director general of public enterprises, now vice-president and CFO of the BRICS New Development Bank) and Maria Ramos (former director general of the National Treasury and later CEO of Absa) (Sender, personal email communication, 15 July 2016). MERG also offerred workshops for trade unions to prepare new training material, designed to encourage trade unionists to debate macroeconomic policy issues. These highly successful workshops were led by a mix of local and international economists.

MERG's interactions with the ANC leadership

In order to undertake the task of producing a macroeconomic framework, a Reference Team and Editorial Committee, consisting of both local and international economists who would work alongside the research teams, were set up by the MERG Steering Committee in March 1993. Workshops were convened at which the research teams and key ANC policymakers met with the Reference Team and Editorial Committee to discuss their research findings and recommendations.

These meetings and workshops were particularly tense affairs, but ideological or other differences about the substantive content of the MERG proposal were hardly ever expressed. The already poor interpersonal relations between the MERG administration, some local researchers and the DEP deteriorated further. The DEP argued that the MERG leadership appeared to ignore the official policy positions of the ANC and to arrogate to themselves the role of policymaker. Some local research team leaders felt that they were being marginalised in the compilation of the Framework Vision; some local economists complained to the DEP behind the backs of the MERG leadership that their contributions were being misrepresented in the MERG chapter drafts and that the process was being taken over by radical 'foreign' economists.

MERG research director John Sender has a different view on all these issues. He argues that *some* local researchers, who were generously funded by MERG to produce specific papers, failed to write a single word throughout the course of the project; others produced poor drafts and were offended when the editorial team made critical comments on their drafts. Cosetted by apartheid, and used to believing that they were pre-ordained to take over the running of key economic institutions after apartheid, they were simply not used to being treated in this way by 'foreigners'. It was thus not surprising that they complained about Vella Pillay and Sender to those they saw as holding their destiny in their hands (Sender interview, 10 September 2015).

Sender also points out that at least four major workshops were held during the course of the project, at which both DEP and Cosatu leadership were present. But, as we note below, the ANC at executive level (and even the DEP) appears to have been only perfunctorily engaged in the debates about drafting MERG policy proposals, choosing instead to spend time with World Bank officials and local business leaders. Drafts of MERG chapters were circulated in advance of these workshops, but Sender does not recall that the ANC Alliance members present raised any substantial policy issues at the workshops or at the regular Steering Committee meetings. It did not appear, he argues, as if they had read or absorbed any of the policy content of these drafts (Sender interview, 10 September 2015).

Some of the MERG researchers, including Lance Taylor, had an opportunity (through a meeting organised by the DEP) to brief the ANC leadership on matters of the economy. However, as the following quote from John Matisonn makes very clear, even by April 1992, the ANC leadership appeared to have very little interest in engaging with these internationally acclaimed economists:

> It was April 1992 and, for the African National Congress, economic policy was on the back-burner. The ANC politicians who were in the headlines, like Nelson Mandela, Cyril Ramaphosa and Joe Slovo, were intensely involved in the political negotiations with the government. Thabo Mbeki was dealing with the right wing. Trevor Manuel, Tito Mboweni and Maria Ramos, of the ANC's then still obscure department of economic planning (DEP), wanted to expose the ANC leadership to current economic thinking in preparation for the ANC's role in the government. About 40 members of the ANC's national executive committee (NEC) trooped over from Shell House to the shabby Holiday Inn on De Villiers Street in Johannesburg for a workshop. Lance Taylor, Massachusetts Institute of Technology professor of economics and Latin America expert, wanted to focus on macro-economic policy, in particular macro-economic constraints – in other words, on how government policy options are limited by a drop in foreign currency reserves, by high interest rates, by how much they cause inflation, or by a negative balance of payments (Matisonn 1998).

At question time, the subject evinced so little interest that it was left to the ever-courteous Mandela to ask the only question. Yet within two years, the issues Taylor had raised would dominate not only the ANC's economic thinking in the government, but would determine the parameters of government policy in every department of state (Matisonn 1998).

Ronnie Kasrils, relying on his recollection of a discussion with Moeletsi Mbeki, informs us that the MERG administration regularly sent reports and working papers to the DEP, and that these were re-packaged and sent up to ANC headquarters. However, Kasrils, who was elected to the NEC in 1991 and was also on the Central Committee and Politburo of the SACP, insists that none of these reports from MERG were discussed in these decision-making organs. As a result, MERG was, in his words, the 'invisible man' to the broader ANC Alliance leadership (Kasrils interview, 30 March 2017; Kasrils 2017: 232). For this, Kasrils believes collective blame should be accepted by the ANC Alliance leadership. The SACP, he argues, given its history and its mandate as the leading revolutionary formation, should have insisted on playing a bigger role in driving an economic programme appropriate to addressing the needs of the working class and the poor in this early period. Kasrils believes that it failed in this revolutionary duty. Here is how he puts it in his recent book: 'Those were dangerous and exciting challenges, and we turned our backs on the dismal science of economics as we contested for the prize of political power. It needs to be said, that lack of economic focus represents the Faustian pact of a collective leadership to which I belonged ... We should have put up a fight. Instead, we allowed the ANC to succumb to the neo-liberal, free-market economic embrace because some of us were fast asleep' (Kasrils 2017: 238–239).

Some would argue that the young and relatively inexperienced DEP leadership held no strong ideological policy positions on the economy in this early phase (1990–1994). Ben Fine is adamant that, though broadly opposed to the emerging MERG line, the DEP was bereft of any strongly argued ideological positions on economic policy.

> There was a political decision to disown and ostracise basically the whole MERG process and report and so on. That was really indicative of the huge changes that had taken place in the policy arena in the previous six months, so that the MERG report was perceived and the process was seen as an embarrassment to the direction the ANC leadership then wanted to go. But in many ways, I don't think the issue was one of what was the substance of the reply or the response. It's not clear they had alternative policies that they had to put forward. It's just that they disagreed ... But to be blunt and also reflecting my naivety, I actually felt sorry for Tito and Trevor because I felt that I had no reason to believe until that point [that] they weren't supportive of us. I felt 'poor bastards', they have to spend all this time mollycoddling and soothing the fears of the big bourgeoisie and so on. They were

just involved in a public relations exercise. I think Tito would say otherwise; I don't know about Trevor (Fine interview, 30 June 2015).

Later, Fine notes: 'Alec Erwin was different, but Alec wasn't really involved in these debates by that time. I am not sure what he was doing then, but he wasn't closely involved with the DEP, that I can remember. But as I said, I saw them much more as figureheads. I had no reason to believe [they] had opinions of their own, which was silly, actually, possibly patronising, or that they disagreed with the general line that was being taken' (Fine interview, 30 June 2015).

But there was one central policy issue on which the DEP did appear to have a clear position, though not one that was openly argued or debated. This was about the Reserve Bank (see also chapter 6). Fine recalls this as follows from what happened at the MERG launch in December 1993: 'The only thing I remember was that Trevor Manuel said, not only must we not put forward government retaining control of the Reserve Bank, we must not even discuss the matter because the concern was about the stability of the rand ... I suppose that's quite interesting; it's indicative they actually thought we might be influential, and so they felt it was important to contain and control what was coming out of MERG' (Fine interview, 30 June 2015).

Bill Freund's (2013: 527) interpretation is that before Manuel's arrival at the DEP in August 1992, DEP pronouncements were fairly progressive, being against low wages, and in favour of capital being raised locally, raising corporate taxes and unbundling of conglomerates. Later under Manuel, Freund argues, they may have been guided to believe that there was no alternative to a market-friendly approach to post-apartheid reconstruction and development. Any ideas that involved state action in economic life may have been seen as 'socialism' (a failed model), and would therefore be ruled out without any need for debate. The rest of the story may well have unfolded as a direct consequence of perceptions of the prevailing 'balance of power'. Those constituencies that shared this general market-friendly approach – the international community, international institutions, local and international big capital – and who clearly wielded 'power' were going to be taken more seriously by the ANC than those such as Vella Pillay, Ben Fine, Laurence Harris and John Sender, widely perceived to be old-style British left-wing economists. The marginalised (mainly black) citizenry may also have demanded greater intervention to end their poverty and improve their employment prospects and service delivery, but theirs was a weakened constituency, whose interests could be ignored, at least for some time, given the ANC's uncontested position among the black electorate. As Adam Habib notes: 'The power relations that prevailed in the early to mid-1990s, as defined by the balance of class power, the nature of state-society relationships and global power configurations, put pressure on ANC leaders, configured their choices and prompted them to adopt and implement GEAR' (2013: 84).

MERG held one of its major workshops, involving many international researchers and local researchers in Johannesburg in the second week of April 1993. On Easter Saturday, we all heard of the assassination of Chris Hani – revolutionary, soldier and intellectual, one of the most popular leaders of the ANC Alliance, revered by millions, especially the poor, the young and the more militant wing of the Alliance. The country stood on the very edge of a precipice and Mandela made a powerful TV speech to quell the anger and restore some calm. Many members of the MERG research team who were in Johannesburg attended the funeral and memorial service at FNB Stadium in Soweto on 19 April. These included professors Gerry Helleiner, John Loxley, Ben Fine, Laurence Harris, John Sender and Vishnu Padayachee. We were collected from the Devonshire Hotel on Jorissen Street and driven to Soweto through flames and barricades, with the sounds of gunshots and explosions echoing all around us. The upper stands of the stadium literally shook under the power of thousands of toyi-toying feet. Driving the VW combi was none other than Tito Mboweni, future governor of the SARB, and in the front passenger seat was Maria Ramos, future director general of finance.

In their biography of Hani, Janet Smith and Beauregard Tromp inform us that just two weeks before his assassination Hani was talking about the 'critical need for a conference of the left, to try to redefine the nature of socialism' (2009: 268). Moeletsi Mbeki was 'emphatic' (according to Smith and Tromp) that Hani no longer saw the SACP as the vanguard party of the working class, though he was equally disdainful of Thabo Mbeki and others who were critical of the SACP. British journalist John Carlin wrote that, at the time of his death, Hani's political vision had 'mellowed into something more closely resembling [Labour Party leader] John Smith than Fidel Castro' (in Smith and Tromp 2009: 268–269).

The MERG Editorial Committee presented its final report to the democratic movement at a formal media launch in Rosebank on 3 December 1993. At that meeting, the head of the DEP introduced the MERG report, and then promptly and publicly rejected it in its entirety. Mandela withdrew the foreword that he had agreed to write, and he did not even attend the launch (Freund 2013: 531). It was, in fact, almost impossible to find anyone to write the foreword, until ANC stalwart and the University of Fort Hare Vice Chancellor Sibusiso Bengu agreed.

So what has our research revealed about the sequence of events leading up to 3 December 1993?

Our archival research at the University of Fort Hare has revealed that Jessie Duarte (then a senior staffer and Mandela's PA) wrote a fax to Mandela dated 23 September 1993, which said:

Dear Comrade President
1. The meeting in Newclare was an excellent event.
2. I'm sending you the foreword of the MERG policy booklet [*sic*].
3. Cde Max Sisulu requests that you provide the foreword.
4. Please let me know your instruction in this regard.

Note the date of 23 September, and note, too, that the request was initiated by Max Sisulu, former head of the DEP, and not by Trevor Manuel, then the DEP's head.

The draft foreword (whose 'author' is unknown to us) accompanying the fax is just over a page long and includes the following important concluding paragraph, suggestive of support for MERG from at least some quarters of the ANC at that late stage:

In such a critical phase in the country's development, the MERG initiative to produce an economic framework to address these issues is to be heartily welcomed. The framework represents not only a crucial contribution to the democratic government's understanding of the various problems, but also offers a serious and well reasoned economic strategy to resolve the multitude of problems. In this document a viable, coherent and consistent set of policies are presented, capable of ensuring sustainable growth and an improvement in the quality of life for the majority of the population and, at the same time, address the severe deprivation of those people in greatest need. The future government will pay very close attention to the proposals contained in the Macroeconomic Framework. On behalf of the African National Congress, I wish to express my gratitude to MERG, its staff, researchers and various committee members for their unstinting efforts in producing this comprehensive framework in such a short period of time. Finally, let me sincerely thank the donors to the MERG initiative for their most generous support (Nelson Mandela Papers, Box 66, Folder 678).

On 14 October, a memo by Manuel to Duarte requested that the president of the ANC not write the foreword. Here is what Manuel wrote:

Tito Mboweni reported to me that Cde President has been requested to write a foreword for the MERG macro-economic framework document. Whilst the principle of a foreword by the President is sound, the problem which arises is that he may be writing a foreword for a document which may be in conflict with ANC policy as adopted at the National Policy Conference [May 1992]. Tito and I serve on the Steering Committee, in fact I am the elected Chairperson; yet we have not seen the framework to date. We are attempting to correct the matter. COSATU and the ANC are the policy-makers in the MERG since we own the process, yet we have not seen the document which will soon be public and which we will be expected to defend (Nelson Mandela Papers, Box 66, Folder 678).

It is not yet clear to us how Manuel came to the view that the final MERG framework 'may' be in conflict with ANC policy if he had not had sight of or read the report, or what policy proposals he was most concerned about. One such policy that may have been contentious for the DEP was the issue of the SARB independence (see chapter 6).

In a fax to Pillay, the MERG director, on the very same day and stamped URGENT twice, Manuel requested an extended breakfast meeting (to include Erwin, Mboweni, Sisulu, Pillay and himself) to address this issue, on or before 20 October 1993 (Nelson Mandela Papers, Box 66, Folder 678).

That meeting, which Pillay refers to as the Executive of the MERG Steering Committee, took place on 19 October 1993. A few days later, on 25 October, Pillay distributed the final draft of the Macroeconomic Policy Framework, with a cover letter to the MERG Steering Committee, the Economic Policy Advisory Group, the Economics Research Committee, the MERG Reference Team members and the heads of the MERG Research Teams. He called for comments to be addressed to him by 15 November 'to be confined to what may appear as glaring inconsistencies in the text and not to textual or terminological issues' (Letter from Vella Pillay to MERG Steering Committee and others, in Vella Pillay private archives). So what we have is Manuel's view that neither the ANC (via the DEP) nor Cosatu had sight of the MERG draft report. But the MERG research director, Sender, vehemently denies this, arguing that all draft versions were distributed to the key policymakers in the ANC and Cosatu. Perhaps the explanation is that no one had bothered to read it: '[Manuel's] verbal responses suggested to me that neither he nor Tito ever read drafts of the substantive [MERG] chapters in any detail. Trevor bullied and pressured us to complete the Final Draft at breakneck speed. My impression was that, up to the last minute, he wanted a book to wave at critics of the ANC and did not much care about its content' (John Sender, personal communication via email, 15 July 2016).

In a fax to Mboweni dated 11 November, Pillay observes that 'we have had no comments of substance so far on the [MERG] document'. And in a return fax on the same day, Mboweni asks, following a meeting with Erwin and Jay Naidoo, for an extension for the deadline for comments, arguing that the document was a week late in reaching the desks of many comrades in the ANC and Cosatu (Correspondence in Vishnu Padayachee private archives). We are not sure if Pillay acceded to this or indeed if he received any comments. In any event, on 5 November 1993, Pillay, in introducing the main speaker Archbishop Trevor Huddlestone, took the opportunity to present the core policy proposals of the MERG framework at the inaugural Oliver Tambo Memorial Lecture that was given by the archbishop in the presence of Mandela, Adelaide Tambo and hundreds of others. Pillay reminded the audience that Oliver Tambo had been the patron of MERG since its inception in 1991 and that he had retained a close interest in the work of MERG. He then set out the major areas that MERG researchers had investigated. He pointed out, among other policy recommendations, that MERG research had proposed: 'The South African Reserve Bank should be subordinate to the government such as to allow monetary, interest and exchange rate policies and the flow and direction of credit in the economy to be consistent with the democratic state's policies in the areas of public sector expenditure and taxation, in trade, industrial diversification and development, employment generation and social and economic infrastructural investments' (Speech at OR Tambo Memorial Lecture, in Vella Pillay private archives).

This was without doubt the key MERG recommendation, which was at variance with the proposals adopted at the May 1992 ANC consultative policy conference, as Manuel may have had in mind in his fax to Mandela's office on 14 October. Pillay's speech of 5 November 1993 anticipated that the MERG document would be presented to the ANC, Cosatu, Sanco and others.

On 3 December 1993, the MERG policy framework was presented to the world at the Rosebank Hotel (now the Crown Plaza Hotel), where it was effectively disavowed by the DEP members present. One after another, members of key economic divisions within the DEP took to the podium to denounce MERG's stance in what could only have been an orchestrated move (see later in this chapter). As Fine, who was one of the MERG report's co-authors noted, looking back at all this:

> A long sequence of witnesses for the prosecution (i.e. department heads) uniformly marched into the discussion of the document and routinely and ridiculously rubbished it in what could only have been a badge of loyalty. I must have mentioned that I was simply bewildered at the time ... these people one after another, rubbishing my work on housing,

electricity, schooling and health when I had merely given intellectual support to what were their policies. This is why I talk about conspiracy although without evidence as such. To me, though, in retrospect, they must have been told to turn up and rubbish it (Fine, email correspondence, 10 February 2017).

Among the senior DEP and ANC members who participated in this ritual were Billy Cobbett (on housing), Cheryl Carolus (on social welfare), Max Price (on health) and Trevor Manuel (on SARB independence).

Fine recalls these developments more than two decades later:

[Cheryl Carolus] basically said, 'Welfare has nothing to do with economics; why are you even commenting on it?' This came as a great shock and I didn't feel it so much at the time, but in retrospect relatively quickly, I felt it was quite personally aggressive against me, and of course at that time, we didn't know anything about what was going on in negotiations, and suddenly some 20 years later, I sort of look back upon this and came to the conclusion or hypothesis, that actually there was … a political decision to disown and ostracise basically the whole MERG process and report and so on. That was really indicative of the huge changes that had taken place in the policy arena in the previous six months, so that the MERG report was perceived and the process was seen as an embarrassment to the direction the ANC leadership then wanted to go.

…

Billy Cobbett was there, and the World Bank – strange, the World Bank in the early 1990s had itself gone through a big change in its own housing policy, where previously state intervention to build housing was abandoned, and the whole emphasis was on creating opportunities for individuals to enter into home ownership through access to housing finance and so on. Whereas my argument was very much that providing housing finance is not going to build any houses – for example, it might even go into speculative housing. So really it was the provision of housing, actually creating the institutional capacity to deliver housing, that was important, not how you finance it. In fact, that was the general argument that I used, which was that the major constraint on the delivery of public services in South Africa was the institutional capacity to deliver, given the history, the fragmented administrations and so on. And it wasn't necessarily finance, but if you treat it as being a financial issue, then what would happen is you would worsen the institutional capacities to deliver. So there was basically a rejection of the notion that there should be a big public-sector-led housing building programme.

…

On health, to my astonishment, I think Max Price gave the response on behalf of the department and it was very much one of 'we are short of resources, therefore it is better to keep the private health system going for those who can afford it and then that would mean that we'll have lesser charges on what we can provide' and so on. So these positions came as a great surprise to me, in part because in doing the research for those sections of the MERG report, I travelled around the country, talking to policymakers and activists to see what they saw as the way forward, in part on the basis of their experiences and struggles. But in many ways, I don't think the issue was one of what was the substance of the reply or the response. It's not clear they had alternative policies that they had to put forward. It's that they disagreed …

…

The only thing I remember was that Trevor Manuel said, not only must we not put forward arguments for government retaining control of the Reserve Bank, we must not even discuss the matter because the concern was about the stability of the rand (Fine interview, 30 June 2015).

No one stood up and said in so many words that 'MERG was being dumped'. However, MERG researchers present, including Fine and Pillay, knew that this was so. The shock at the rejection of the MERG economic policy recommendations and the manner of it was acutely felt by the drafters of the MERG report, especially as they had all at various times since the 1980s (in some cases earlier) been so warmly held within the embrace of the senior ANC leadership. Pillay never really recovered from this rejection and expressed his sentiments and hostility openly. In his fare-well address to the SOAS alumni, Fine tells his audience that they are the first to hear that 'I turned down the chance to take [SA] citizenship and become economic adviser to Mandela' (Fine 2019: 11) and 'I was also offered South African citizen-ship by Joe Slovo, indicative of the height of appreciation prior to the MERG fall from grace' (2019: 11, fn. 28). Though anecdotal in nature, this is further evidence of what many perceived as the 'unexpected' turn of events in so far as the ANC's economic policy stance is concerned. MERG's recommendations were not again raised in the economic policy that followed (though the National Party did refer to MERG as we shall see), and Pillay was shut out of all future discussions of economic policy. As Kasrils puts it: 'Manuel formally thanked them and then imperiously consigned them to a footnote in history. He virtually told them to go to hell' (2017: 233).

It was not until ten years later, and after his death, that the ANC paid its respects and said thank you to Pillay.

So what do other commentators say about why MERG was dumped?

Habib (2013: 85) argues that 'my contention with MERG is not that its policy recommendations were problematic, but that it lacked an understanding of the politics required to turn its recommendations into state policy'. But clearly its recommendations were problematic to some people in the ANC, and it is difficult to imagine how MERG's research leadership, tasked by the ANC to recommend a macroeconomic framework for post-apartheid South Africa, was in any position to turn their recommendations into state policy on their own. There is a presumption in Habib's comment that MERG operated totally independently of the ANC, that it had the power and capacity to neutralise big business. This argument elides over the fact that the MERG Steering Committee (and its Executive Committee) was chaired by Manuel, and that it included Mboweni, Naidoo and Erwin, all key members of the ANC and the Alliance. That MERG's policy recommendations were regularly presented to the Alliance leadership through the DEP in Shell House over two years is now evident. What more could have been done by MERG after December 1993, when not even the ANC had state power (apart from its role in the Transitional Executive Council), is hard to conceptualise.

Political philosopher Laurence Hamilton's explanation lies in the nature of the 'elite economic compromise':

> The quick and sorry demise of the ANC's 'Making Democracy Work' policy [MERG] is a case in point, indicative of the way in which the elite economic compromose sacrificed many of the ANC's previously stated goals for the perceived absolute priority to secure monetary and fiscal policy that was attractive to international investors ... As an attempt to turn the general promises of the Freedom Charter – for housing and health care – into practical policies, it was the most important research base for the ANC in the early stages of its unbanning (2014: 102).

Jeremy Cronin has argued that with the effective expulsion of the 'outstanding British economists' after the stillborn MERG report launch, the economic policy debate in South Africa was dealt a serious blow (Cronin 1997). The MERG project and its successor, the National Institute for Economic Policy, became marginalised despite the sterling efforts of scholars such as Asghar Adelzadeh, Renfrew Christie,

Morley Nkosi and Trevor Bell. It is evident that for some time after December 1993, Pillay, Fine, Harris and Sender were not invited to participate in the local economic policy debate. Fine speaks of being 'cold-shouldered' for some time, until suprisingly the minister of labour, Tito Mboweni, invited him to become a member of the Labour Market Commission. Harris later became a frequent adviser to both the SARB and the National Treasury. Pillay and Sender, who headed the MERG office in Johannesburg, soon returned to London.

The failure of Cosatu to get fully involved in MERG may have been a factor, too. According to Erwin:

> I said right at the beginning, Cosatu didn't take ownership of MERG; we didn't see it as MERG. We were involved in MERG because Jay [Naidoo] and I had been seconded to the steering committee from September 1993 or something, so we got in through that way, but MERG was never seen as a Cosatu project in any way at all. We were not hostile to it; we knew a lot of the people – you [Vishnu Padayachee] were involved, John Sender, a lot of people, everyone (Erwin interview, 23 October 2015).

As intriguing as it may be to unravel some of the mystique surrounding the dumping of the MERG report, what is critical is to understand that this dumping and the nature of it created the momentum for agents in the ANC, politics, business, civil society and the academy to abandon independent and critical thought, and to fall behind a 'default' market-friendly economic policy position that could be summarised as 'there is no alternative'.

This paved a path that led in mid-1996 to the production of the Growth, Employment and Redistribution strategy, with the announcement that it was 'not negotiable' (see more below).

No one in the MERG administration office or among its leading researchers was naive enough to believe that MERG's recommendations would simply become official ANC economic policy. What would reasonably have been expected was a debate within the ANC–SACP–Cosatu Alliance in some appropriate forum, where these recommendations and others from the DEP, the SACP and Cosatu would be thoroughly debated by representatives of the mass democratic movement, including progressive academic economists. From there, the NEC of the ANC would have had been expected to agree on some policy package. Something along these lines was done under far more difficult circumstances in 1955 and 1956 with the ANC's adoption of the Freedom Charter, and those processes are rightly celebrated to this day, but none of that was done in 1993.

MERG's economic policy recommendations

Despite all the drama, the MERG report was later published by the Centre for Development Studies, a progressive policy research centre at UWC, as a book, *Making Democracy Work: A Framework for Macroeconomic Policy in South Africa* (MERG 1993).[5] In addition, 45 research papers and reports were produced by the MERG research teams over two years and dozens of young economists were trained.

The theoretical foundations of the MERG economic policy framework lie in what we would characterise as a broadly Cambridge or Post-Keynesian approach – in the tradition of Keynes, Robinson, Kaldor and Kalecki – where effective demand failures and the possibility of under-full-employment equilibrium are recognised as key problems. MERG envisioned a two-phase, 'crowding-in' approach to South Africa's development – a state-led social and physical infrastructural investment programme focusing on housing, education, health and physical infrastructure investment as the growth drivers in the first phase, followed by a more sustainable growth phase that would see private-sector investment kick in more forcefully as growth picked up (MERG 1993: chap. 1). In the light of post-1994 developments, it is worth spelling out some of the proposals made then in respect of the crucial state-led first phase:

1. In education, MERG proposes a minimum of R5 billion (in 1992 prices) in annual recurrent and teacher training expenditures and a lifting of annual education expenditures from the current R0.5 billion to R5 billion …

2. In adult basic education, MERG proposes a four-year programme for persons already in the workforce, at the rate of 50 000 new trainees per year; and a programme for unemployed persons who will be engaged on physical infrastructural projects, and who will receive training similar to that for employed workers, at the rate of 100 000 new programme entrants per year …

3. In health, MERG proposes a programme to provide 2 000 clinics at a capital cost of R300 million (in 1992 prices) and a recurrent cost of R1.5 billion per year; and a basic health care and nutrition programme which will be implemented at a cost of R1 billion per year.

4. In housing, MERG proposes that the government triples the number of housing sites from the current 100 000 to 300 000 per year. The number of formal houses completed should rise, step by step, from the current levels of approximately 38 000 per year to 350 000 per year by the early part of the next century.

5. MERG proposes the establishment of a realistic statutory minimum wage, set initially at about two-thirds of the Minimum Living Level (MLL). Such a policy will have positive macroeconomic and microeconomic consequences (MERG 1993: 3).

And then the proposals focus on industrialisation, trade, exports and so on.

As the MERG modelling showed, the approach was fully consistent with the required macroeconomic balances. 'The realisation of MERG objectives will be impossible unless policy is characterised by prudent and risk averse fiscal, monetary and balance of payments management' (MERG 1993: 4). So much for the charge that MERG was advocating populist macroeconomic policy.

Economist Nicoli Nattrass made the point in the heat of the 1990s debates: 'Although it can be argued that MERG's more aggressive interventions are likely to deter rather than encourage investment, and that certain labour market policies might increase rather than reduce unemployment, the MERG report has a commendable focus on supply-side measures. In particular, training, education and technological advance are seen as necessary to boost productivity. This focus is evident also in the RDP. However, whereas the key MERG proposals are carefully costed, the RDP measures are not' (1994: 359).

In a 2016 opinion piece, the 'very market-friendly' commentator Peter Bruce rightly criticises the ANC government for failing to prioritise or concentrate on any one priority; he goes on to observe that 'just imagine how far we would have come in 21 years had the top priorities been education, health, housing and infrastructure, and they had been attended to and resourced with money and expertise in that order' (Bruce 2016).

SUMMING UP

So what problems and lessons did the MERG exercise reveal vis-à-vis the relationship between progressive academic economists and the policy process?

Firstly, a very poor and antagonistic relationship existed between some local research team leaders and the mainly British academics in the MERG administration, which reflected different cultures and histories of policy engagement. Secondly, the urgent need for policy options tended in practice to conflict with the much longer-term task of training and capacity-building, creating tensions throughout the programme. Thirdly, the role of international economists in the MERG process was unnecessarily controversial. The 'disproportionate' number of foreigners in the Reference Team and Editorial Committee, it was argued, had the effect of wrenching the policy process out of the hands of South African nationals and of making the process more of a top-down one than was originally envisaged. Matthew Kentridge points out that Stellenbosch economist Servaas van der Berg 'made his disquiet on this matter known to DEP head Trevor Manuel, complaining that not since colonial days had South Africa's economic policy been drawn up by foreign economists' (Kentridge 1993: 56), though his 'distaste' for foreign economists may have been confined only to those with heterodox views. In contrast, Manuel described the engagment of the international economists, who were interacting with young ANC economists from local universities in formulating policy, as a 'fascinating experience' – a view he confirmed in our interview with him (Green 2008: 351–352; Manuel interview, 4 July 2016).

Despite all the organisational, political and ideological difficulties and differences that beset MERG, and the dumping of its report by the ANC leadership, the MERG report was widely acknowledged as being an important academic and policy contribution and a challenge to the previous government's Normative Economic Model (NEM). Moses Mayekiso, speaking on behalf of Sanco, observed that 'even opponents of MERG will have to concede that this document is among the most rigorous, even-handed and stimulating ever produced about the South African economy'. Referring to the MERG recommendation that the SARB be nationalised, Mayekiso observed:

> Indeed MERG director Vella Pillay has earned the gratitude of many future generations by putting the issue of [the] Reserve Bank onto the public agenda. The MERG recommendation for a nationalised Reserve Bank is by no means out of step with international thinking. From my own dealings with the banking industry I certainly believe that the most powerful bank in our country, with responsibility for monetary policy and exchange controls [sic] must be controlled by the government of the people, not by an anonymous crowd of money mandarins (Moses Mayekiso, speaking about the Sanco Press Release, 3 December 1993, in Vishnu Padayachee private archives).

The SACP's Jeremy Cronin referred to the MERG report as 'a perfectly reasonable and coherent approach' and 'a broad macroeconomic framework that demonstrates that we [on the left] can reconstruct without resorting to voodoo economics' (Correspondence with MERG co-ordinator, Vella Pillay, in Vishnu Padayachee private archives).

Langa Zita, at the time a senior member of the SACP and later to be a director general in the national Department of Agriculture, had the following recollection of MERG:

> I can still remember the first MERG draft. It was a very important and well thought out framework for the country. It was not radical, okay, but it was progressive. It was what I would call a social democratic, third-world framework ... It was a useful point of departure, and it was far more scientific than the RDP. There had been processes of economic modelling done around it. There was serious work done by economists on it. I thought it was a very decent piece of work (Zita interview, 10 August 2017).

Dale McKinley, an independent, progressive writer and researcher, succinctly captured the situation as follows:

> While the [MERG] report did not set out the kind of more radically anti-capitalist development path that many in the broad liberation movement desired, it was designed to directly address the historical, systemic inequalities of the apartheid era and create the conditions for the redistributive path to economic growth through a particiatory and democratically accountable interventionist state ... its fundamentals were brushed aside as 'idealistic' and effectively ignored. Instead the ANC chose to join the liberal chorus of corporate capital, the National Party as well as powerful western countries and international financial institutions ... (2017: 75).

Even *Business Day*, which was very critical of Pillay and the MERG project in general, on the eve of the MERG launch noted in a leader-page article that 'the MERG framework, for all its faults, presents a serious challenge to the [previous] government's approach [the NEM]' (Steyn 1993). Furthermore, numerous positive academic reviews of the MERG book were published in international journals. In the *International Review of Applied Economics*, Chris Edwards argues: '... it is hard to see a peaceful or prosperous society emerging from the application of the "orthodox economics" of the NEM. In comparing MERG and the NEM in the light of the appalling legacy of apartheid, it seems clear that there is no alternative to an approach modelled on that of the MERG' (1995: 108).

Freund lays some of the blame for the rejection of 'the bold effort of the MERG team to move in a different direction' on global corporates such as Morgan Stanley:

'To a large extent, the return to orthodoxy brought about an extended reproduction of a given developed economy with modest growth, mass unemployment, unprecedented levels of inequality and continuing lack of the tools required for building a more skills-based economy albeit benefitting the middle class' (Freund 2013: 533).

Clearly, the process of organising MERG was more complicated than some had anticipated. Mboweni ruefully observed to Pillay as MERG was close to the end of its work: 'I would like to preface my reply to your letter by saying that the MERG process, as you are well aware, has been a big challenge for all of us. We have never had the opportunity to do anything of the scale and character of this project before' (Mboweni to Pillay, fax dated 1 November 1993, in Vishnu Padayachee private archives).

But back to an assessment of MERG's value. The significance and value of the MERG report was surprisingly affirmed by senior ANC leaders at a dinner on 23 November 2006, organised by the then deputy vice chancellor of Wits University, Yunus Ballim, and the Wits Economics Department, then headed by Harry Zarenda, and financially supported by the Presidency. The dinner was in honour of MERG co-ordinator, Vella Pillay, who had passed away in London on 29 July 2004. Cabinet ministers Essop Pahad and Alec Erwin argued that although the ANC and the democratic government chose another development path, MERG's contribution was highly valuable, with some of its key recommendations – especially in respect of the role of state infrastructure spending – finding their way into the current policy debate. Minister Pahad noted that 'MERG was not marginalised. Work of that magnitude cannot be ignored and it continues to influence the economic thinking of the broad revolutionary movement in South Africa even now' (Padayachee's notes from the dinner in private archives).

Journalist Terry Bell, writing in the context of an increasingly strident debate within the Alliance over the direction of economic policy, notes: 'Behind the latest series of spats between senior members of the governing Tripartite Alliance is the spirit and legacy of the late Vella Pillay. Pillay headed the first alliance economics think-tank, the Macroeconomic Research Group (MERG) which drafted the first – and controversially discarded – post-apartheid macroeconomic statement' (2007: n.p.).

5

On the Way to GEAR, 1994–1996

READY TO GOVERN

Surprisingly little is known about an important and official ANC document that addressed economic policy. This was the Ready to Govern (RTG) document approved at the ANC's May 1992 policy conference. In order to make more sense of the path to the ANC-led government's Growth, Employment and Redistribution (GEAR) programme in 1996, we need to backtrack a little in time to the 1992 policy document. Tito Mboweni makes no reference to RTG in his paper on formulating policy for a democratic South Africa, though he does observe that 'formulating economic policy has been one of the most difficult and challenging tasks confronting the democratic forces' (Mboweni 1994: 69). This echoes a comment he made in a letter to the Macroeconomic Research Group (MERG) director, Vella Pillay, in November 1993 (Letter in Vishnu Padayachee private archive).

In late May 1992, the document that came to be titled Ready to Govern was debated and adopted by the ANC. A section of the document was labelled 'Economic Policy'. An economics commission attended by about 100 delegates (including Mboweni, Alec Erwin and Ben Turok) gave careful attention to a draft document entitled 'The Growth Path for the New South Africa', prepared by Mboweni. A vigorous debate ensued about matters centred around the absence of the word 'development' in the title of the paper (Turok 2003: 261) and about nationalisation and privatisation. Nelson Mandela himself entered the debate, warning the conference that nationalisation would meet much opposition in the West. Turok claims he opposed any attempts to rule out the option of public ownership, and the matter was only resolved after the conference ended with a watered-down commitment to the public sector's role within a mixed economy (Turok 2003: 262). Nevertheless, it would appear as if RTG was the first official policy document adopted at a full conference by the ANC since the adoption of the Freedom Charter in 1956. For this reason, its significance cannot be underestimated, though its contents were rather vague and its line somewhat populist. RTG was essentially an ANC document, driven by the Department of Economic Planning (DEP), and in which the Congress of South African Trade Unions (Cosatu), the South African Communist Party (SACP) and South African National Civic Organisation (Sanco) were more minor players.[1]

We turn to RTG's main prescriptions on economic matters. To achieve the goals of eliminating poverty and inequality, promoting growth and employment, and democratising the economy, among other issues, RTG proposed two components as part of its national development strategy:

> Redistribution programmes to meet the basic needs of our people. A priority in this regard will be the provision of basic services, affordable housing and infrastructure. In addition, legal, practical and psychological barriers created by apartheid and patriarchy will be broken down, so as to open up the economy to give opportunities to those who have historically been excluded. The restructuring of the South African economy on the basis of new, comprehensive and sustainable growth and development strategies in all sectors of the economy.
>
> The democratic state will have ultimate responsibility – in cooperation with the trade union movement, business and other organs of civil society – for coordinating, planning and guiding the development of the economy towards a sustainable economic growth pattern. Emphasis will be placed on macroeconomic balance, including price stability and balance of payments equilibrium. The policy surroundings will be characterised by the principles of transparency, consistency, predictability and accountability (ANC 1992: sec. D).

By 1992, commitments to macroeconomic balance and price stability had become a routine part of the ANC's lexicon in matters of economic policy, reflecting the need to maintain in delicate balance so many differents parts of the movement, South African society as a whole, and the international economic and political community. But the South African Reserve Bank – this important policy institution whose role and mandate was to become a matter of contention later – is not even mentioned.

Trevor Manuel informs us that Mandela called a meeting of the top ANC economists during the RTG May policy conference. Also present was Joe Slovo. Mandela apparently argued that Slovo would not support the use of the word 'privatisation' in any ANC policy document, and that any role for the state in the economy had to be based on the 'body of evidence' (Manuel interview, 4 July 2016). Manuel further states:

> There was also a crafting of the role of the state in the economy that was first used in Ready to Govern. I think it would be referred to as the body of evidence, which at the time was thought to be a very smart move because we were saying that we wouldn't just take a knee-jerk ideological view on the role of the state in the economy. It may be one of those hinge clauses to think about it in policy terms because it doesn't have a precedent; it is crafted for the Ready to Govern conference and then it finds its way into the RDP [Reconstruction and Development Programme] document and it may have shaped some of these. But when we present the document at some point on the first day [of the RTG conference], over a break Madiba convenes those of us from the DEP who were there – say Tito, Moss Ngoasheng, maybe Viv [McMenamin], I think Maria [Ramos] was at the LSE [London School of Economics], Ketso Gordhan. It's a grouping like that – you know, could be some people added some people subtracted, but it's a grouping like that sitting in the room with Madiba, Alfred Nzo, Walter Sisulu, Joe Slovo and one or two others. And Madiba says, 'You chaps have done very well in convening this conference and I think in broad terms we are supportive of what you want to do and there are some parts that begin to shape the debate in a way that can take us forward'. And he then comes to this body of evidence clause, as I call it, which says 'the role of the state in the economy shall be … guided by the body of evidence' – that's broadly the clause. Shoot me for getting this thing a little bit wrong, but that was broadly it. Madiba suggests to us that this is correct. 'There is only one problem with it,' he says; 'Joe [Slovo] here says that if you have that word privatisation then it's going to be very difficult for the Communist Party to support it. I want Joe to speak because he must say what he said to us, that the party can support the entire document provided that one word is changed'. So Joe motivates exactly what Madiba said so we don't even need a time-out; we look at each other and we say, 'That's fine'. So that becomes I think the pivot of Ready to Govern (Manuel interview, 4 July 2016).

RTG makes no mention of another policy matter that Mboweni has been associated with. In 1993, when he was deputy head of the DEP, Mboweni had proposed the idea of a one-off statutory contribution called a reconstruction levy. He expressed this in an article in the Johannesburg *Star* newspaper, with the disclaimer that it was written in his personal capacity and did not reflect official ANC policy (see Nelson Mandela Papers, Box 66, Folder 683). His idea was that the levy would go into a special fund, not the general budget, and be used for development programmes, including housing, infrastructure development, rural development, land reform and so on. Mboweni had prepared a briefing document on his idea of a reconstruction levy, dated 3 August 1993, in which he set out to explain this notion more fully to the ANC leadership in the context of the media controversy in which the levy was being emotively viewed as a 'wealth tax'. He has elsewhere claimed that the campaign by the media scuttled his proposal. 'The media's success in my case is clearly illustrated by the unwillingness of the ANC leadership to touch the issue of a reconstruction levy' (Mboweni 1994: 72). Elsewhere, Mboweni refers to the policies in RTG as 'too general and too broad. Some people have criticised them for containing what they call *motherhood issues*. In other words, it is far too easy for everybody to agree on them' (Nelson Mandela Papers, Box 66, Folder 684, emphasis in original).

So the progressive policy idea of a reconstruction levy did not see the light of day, even though Slovo made a jocular reference to it at an investment seminar organised by the brokerage firm Davis Borkum Hare (Nelson Mandela Papers, Box 203, Folder 049).

THE RECONSTRUCTION AND DEVELOPMENT PROGRAMME

Formulation of the programme

In contrast to MERG, academic economists had almost no role in the drafting of most versions of the Reconstruction and Development Programme (RDP), which was launched as a book and ANC economic manifesto just before the April 1994 elections. Instead, as Patrick Bond has observed, 'several dozen praxis intellectuals from the NGOs and labour drafted the document, partly I think because they had close working relationships with the democratic movement social forces who mandated the drafters to move in this or that direction' (Personal communication, July 1997).

Manuel notes that the idea of something like an RDP followed the end of the May 1992 policy conference and was initiated at a meeting involving himself,

Erwin and Jeremy Cronin. Manuel confirms the role that Bond played in the technical committee finalising the document around February 1994, especially as more and more of the Alliance heavyweights were forced to turn their attention to the elections that were looming in April 1994 (Manuel interview, 4 July 2016).

> Let me come back to that because it may be a small issue in the greater scheme of things but quite important in understanding dynamics. So the guy left holding the pen [in the RDP process] was Patrick Bond who was working at Planact, and then people would whisper in the corridors asking who is this Canadian [sic]? … He was in Nicaragua, he was in Zimbabwe, what is he doing here now? And so on, but you know, but he was left holding the pen, which is why there are curiosities in the crafting. Almost anybody who has looked at the South African economy will talk about the GDP. Anybody trained in North America will talk about a GNP. That's how the GNP comes into the RDP document. It is used repeatedly …
>
> …
>
> Now you see if you look at it, and this is where incomplete issues sometimes create enormous difficulty, if you look at the RDP and go back and look at the financing, the RDP chapter makes broad sweeping statements, which were premised I think on some idea that the post-apartheid dividend would be so large that it would fund all of the changes. And there are statements about the tax-to-GNP ratio, the deficit-to-GNP ratio and the debt-to-GNP ratio would not be increased. You find those things in the Financing the RDP chapter. The long and the short of it is that you couldn't survive with that in the real world (Manuel interview, 4 July 2016).

Cronin points out the SACP's support for the idea of something like an RDP:

> The idea of reconstruction and development – I think we introduced the notion of programme – is good but it cannot just be. Let us develop it into a Charterist-type elaborated perspective for preparing for the decade in which we are living, for the end of the twentieth century going into the twenty-first century. So it was the Party that grabbed the idea of a reconstruction and development programme and welcomed union involvement in its elaboration … and so forth. But we called for it to be an elaborate programme, which we did not necessarily have the capacity to fill the empty spaces with (Cronin interview, 14 March 2016).

Part of the process of finalising the RDP involved holding four or five workshops, each of which were attended by about 100 members from democratic movement structures. Yet, as Turok has observed, the RDP was largely driven by the Cosatu secretary general, Jay Naidoo, with support from the ANC deputy secretary general, Cheryl Carolus. Carolus 'smoothed the path within the ANC' (Turok 2003: 260). John Sender confirms that the final RDP draft was largely put together by Naidoo himself. Sender recalls that he and several others from MERG's Wits office worked solidly at Naidoo's request, sitting at Cosatu's Braamfontein offices. 'We made it a lot more focused, clearer and better. All our proposals were ignored in the final document' (Personal communication, 15 July 2016). Because of his research interest in international financial institutions, Vishnu Padayachee commented (at the request of Erwin) on those sections of the RDP document that dealt with post-apartheid South Africa's relationship with the International Monetary Fund (IMF) and the World Bank. His comments and redrafting were totally ignored.

Despite Carolus's efforts to smooth things within the ANC as the process was approaching its culmination, some ANC members expressed serious reservations about the lack of reference to 'fiscal discipline' and the importance of a stable macro-economic policy environment, which was to become Mandela's central, overriding policy message during numerous speeches in the immediate post-1994 era of democracy (see Chapter 8). The national RDP conference convened at the Nasrec exhibition centre was attended by over 1 000 delegates. At the final plenary, chaired by Manuel, an attempt was made to defer adoption to engage in further consultations, but Turok and Erwin successfully opposed this (Turok 2003: 260ff.). However, as Erwin has observed, the production of the RDP was essentially a Cosatu initiative from start to finish; it was only the final version that was fiercely debated and became part of the ANC election manifesto after February 1994.

Equally, the RDP process did not involve the participation of many academics in any organised sense. Why was this?

The answer appears to be that the grassroots leadership of the movement, who were charged with driving the RDP, either did not trust or have much faith in what they may have perceived to be endless theoretical and intellectual debates by academics at a time when the need for decisive policy positions appeared most crucial. Bond, who was a crucial figure in the RDP process, and later served in President Mandela's RDP office, has observed that the ANC leadership was not entirely comfortable with the RDP, and their acceptance of it as a basis for post-apartheid reconstruction was a political act. The RDP was to become little more than a discursive symbol around the time of elections and immediately thereafter (Bond, personal communication, July 1997).

By the time the final version of the RDP was accepted, it was not a radical document. Its recommendations in respect of trade, monetary policy and exchange rate policy, and the independence of the Reserve Bank, among others, closely tracked Washington Consensus thinking. As Bond noted, it was, in the course of its formulation, impacted by 'status quo' forces, both South African and international, who had made great efforts since 1990 to influence the political leadership of the ANC. In the end, the RDP reflected an uneasy compromise between 'the feasibility of combining a social welfare state in the developmental sphere with neoliberalism in the economic sphere' (Bond 2000: 54).

It is important to understand that the RDP and the Interim Constitution were being finalised at a time when campaigning for the 27 April elections was gaining momentum, leaving little time for careful drafting. Manuel describes what it was like then:

> On the RDP ... we were already campaigning in the fields because this was February '94 and the elections were looming and you couldn't sit around drafting when you needed to be on the ground running around – leadership coming into places, preparations necessary, follow-up necessary, getting systems in place. So you didn't have the luxury of sitting down and drafting as you may have been able to do two years earlier because the political dynamic and momentum have shifted ... But within those discussions there would be negotiations and I was, you know, I wasn't personally ever involved. The only negotiations I was ever taken into was on the public service, when it was Mac Maharaj and Niël Barnard ... I wasn't involved in the negotiation, but the key issue in the negotiations coming out of DEP people was you've got to give the Reserve Bank independence ... there was an NEC [National Executive Committee] meeting and this [independence] was one of those issues. And not Mac but Kader Asmal actually said that Vella disagrees with this clause on independence, and then there was a very intense debate around Kader's point and he was joined by Mac in the process. But it [their argument] didn't hold up (Manuel interview, 4 July 2016).

Erwin maintains that by the end of the RDP process 'all key economic thinkers or players [as he refers to them] were largely at one' except for some like Bond and a 'few ultra-left academics'. The importance of inflation was discussed there, he claims, and 'we had pretty much reached agreement on that ... The independence of the central bank had been extensively debated and we reached agreement on that, too,' he asserts (Erwin interview, 23 October 2015).

Mandela, whose support was crucial in the end, 'embraced the RDP with enthusiasm', according to Simon Barber (2004: 77). Mandela saw its contribution to a more just society because it combined the virtues of a centralised economy and the free market. Both the SACP and Cosatu emphasised the importance of the RDP's commitment to state-led development, while Finance Minister Derek Keys was pleased that it represented the best of both worlds – fiscal conservatism and aggressive growth, coupled with social justice. And the document was sufficiently cleansed over various iterations of its 'radical' elements to please local capital. Anglo American Corporation executive Michael Spicer stated that he was pleased by the balance between its people-centred aims and the requirements of economic growth and foreign investment (Barber 2004: 77).

While there is little doubt that the broad developmental thrust of the RDP had support from many people and groups in the ANC Alliance at the time, some like Mac Maharaj stressed the need for the ANC to democratise the process among its branches and its membership:

> In the coming months the struggle around the economic future of our country will certainly intensify. From the side of the ANC-led alliance, the task is not to invent a whole new set of policies. We need, rather, to defend and advance the RDP mandate of our government. We need, also, to once more anchor economic issues amongst the majority of our people. If the pressures on economic policy-making are confined to those who are most articulate, to those who own and control much of the media, then we will always be at the mercy of market 'sentiments' and 'concerns'. The great majority of our people couldn't give a hoot if Trevor Manuel is black or white. They want to see delivery, and policies that make delivery possible. The great majority of our people don't get into a panic because COSATU is calling for a stay-away or because the NP [National Party] is leaving the Cabinet … We need to ensure that it is the feelings, concerns and fears of the great majority of working people in our country that impact on economic policy-making – and not the privileged prejudices of the yuppies on the Johannesburg Stock Exchange (O'Malley interview archive, Maharaj, 12 December 2002).

That this process of democraticising the economic policy debate across society did not happen is now a well-known fact. Regrettably, this non-consultative approach carried over into the 'democratic' era. This failure to subject economic policy to democratic debate within the movement is, in our assessment, one of the greatest mistakes that occurred during the transition to democracy.

The RDP White Paper

In September 1994, less than six months into the new government, the RDP White Paper was released. Asghar Adelzadeh and Vishnu Padayachee (1994) were quick to publish a paper that noted sharp changes in its content compared to the widely debated and Cosatu-driven RDP Base Document. They pointed out that to argue that the RDP Base Document and the RDP White Paper should be read as complementary suggests a continuity of economic strategy and policy that simply does not exist. The emphasis on fiscal discipline, the dropping of nationalisation as a policy option and the fact that privatisation creeps in in many places – albeit in disguise as 'the sale of state assets' – are just a few of the discontinuities between the two documents. The changes in principle, detail and emphasis go well beyond these examples (Adelzadeh and Padayachee 1994: 3).

The White Paper represented 'a very significant compromise to the neo-liberal, "trickle-down" economic policy preferences of the old regime', despite assurances from ANC ministers that only the language of the old RDP had been changed to suit the new demands of governance, argue Adelzadeh and Padayachee (1994: 2). Their rather prescient conclusion is worth quoting:

> An essentially neo-liberal RDP strategy, which is what we are left with, may well generate some level of economic growth; should this happen, the existing mainly white and Indian bourgeoisie will be consolidated and strengthened; the black bourgeoisie will grow rapidly; a black middle class and some members of the black urban working class will become incorporated into the magic circle of insiders; but *for the remaining 60–70 per cent of our society this growth path, we venture to predict, will deliver little or nothing for many years to come* (Adelzadeh and Padayachee 1994: 16, emphasis added).

There is an interesting footnote to the RDP story that the former statistician general, Pali Lehohla, tells, which testifies to the tactics and residual power of the old apartheid bureaucrats to thwart progressive ideas. In early 1995, Lehohla and his colleague, Benny Mokaba, came to the view that 'statistics based on the RDP paper must be a constitutional entity'. Presumably this meant that the mandate and powers of the office should be enshrined in the Constitution, which was then being finalised by the Constituent Assembly. The head of the Central Statistical Service (CSS), an apartheid-era appointee named Treurnicht du Toit, was apparently vehemently opposed to their ideas. Lehohla states that 'we were embroiled in a fight that had too many fronts. Our documents failed to reach the drafters of the

Constitution.' Lehohla, who had argued further that the post of statistician general had to be advertised in the new era, was opposed by Du Toit, and was declared *persona non grata* in the CSS (Lehohla 2017: n.p.) even though he won that battle in the end. In November 2000, after Mark Orkin resigned, Lehohla finally became statistician general of South Africa and remained in that post until November 2017.

THE SUB-COUNCIL ON FINANCE

As part of the reconvened negotiations process, a Transitional Executive Council (TEC) was formed in order to ensure that a fair and level playing field existed in the run-up to the democratic elections in April 1994. No legislation or policy would be passed by the old regime unless it was approved by the TEC. In addition, the TEC would debate and prepare other pressing strategic matters related to politics, the economy and espe-cially the forthcoming democratic elections in the same spirit. The TEC held its first meeting in Cape Town on 7 December 1993. It consisted of many chambers, and here we consider briefly the work of the TEC's Sub-Council on Finance.

For a brief period after 7 December 1993, Padayachee served on a sub-committee of the Sub-Council of Finance, which was charged with preparing the ground for South Africa's re-entry into international capital markets. Much useful work was done by key ANC economists (Mboweni, Maria Ramos and Neil Morrison, among others), state economic bureaucrats (James Cross, Theo Alant, CJ Roets) and the lone Democratic Party member, Geoff Engel. They worked together to pave the way for the country's pending entry into capital markets, through the mechanism of the many road shows that were held around the world and in South Africa. The establishment of the TEC opened the path to formal discussions with the IMF and the World Bank. We address the application for an IMF loan facility that needed the TEC's approval in chapter 6.

THE NATIONAL PARTY'S RESPONSE TO MERG AND THE RDP

The National Party (NP) clearly gave more attention to economic policy than the ANC. But Chris Stals, for one, believes that both parties should have directly addressed the matter of macroeconomic policy in the process of formulating the new Constitution. In his view, the Constitution should have included an explicit commitment to a market economy (Telephonic exchange with Padayachee, 23 November 2017).

Democratic elections were held on 27 April 1994. The ANC won 62.7 per cent of the popular vote and realised a sizeable majority in parliament. On 10 May, a Government of National Unity (GNU) was formed, with the ANC controlling most of the Cabinet positions. The NP won 20.4 per cent of the popular vote and was entitled to six Cabinet posts. Nelson Mandela was elected president, with the NP's FW de Klerk and the ANC's Thabo Mbeki as deputy presidents.

A week before he assumed office (on 2 May 1994 to be exact), in a speech at the Carlton Hotel in central Johannesburg, Mandela affirmed the ANC's commitment to the RDP. He stated categorically 'that the ANC would put the RDP into effect. He warned that parties opposing the RDP would create tension in the GNU' (Roelf Meyer Papers, PV 912, 1/12/1/1).

Despite this, the NP, in line with its commitment to influence the economic policy of the democratic government, began a strategic campaign to discredit and undermine ANC economic policy positions, including MERG and the RDP. The ANC may have barely read the MERG report before dumping it, but key NP sympathisers in and outside the GNU had clearly read both MERG and the RDP Base Document carefully and decided they would use these to pressurise and 'embarrass' the ANC for its apparent 'populism'. In a media release on 19 April 1994, as part of its election campaign, the NP publicised the results of what it called an 'independent' report on the cost of the RDP. They argued that implementing the RDP would cost R70.63 billion and that this would be fiscally imprudent and irresponsible. Dawie de Villiers, a senior NP member and soon to be the minister of environmental affairs and tourism in the GNU, argued in the same media release that 'people need a strong NP to act as a brake on the ANC. The ANC's [economic] policies would be disastrous for South Africa and the NP will fight against them all the way.'

The 'independent' report being cited here was prepared for the NP by Roelof Botha, the eldest son of then Foreign Minister Pik Botha (Papenfus 2010: 799) and a senior lecturer in economics at Rand Afrikaans University, as well as a certain Tony Kerpel, a former British government special adviser, who is styled in an NP media release as 'an adviser to F.W. de Klerk'. The fact that a former adviser to the British Conservative Party government had assumed a role as an adviser to De Klerk at that crucial stage of the transition is not without significance. Yet, when asked about Kerpel, the former president claimed that he could not recall that name (Interview, 28 January 2019). These authors observe in their report: 'If people are amazed by the high cost of the ANC's promises then that is because these promises are so extravagant. We have simply costed them. We did not invent them' (Roelf Meyer Papers, PV 912, 1/12/1/1).

The Japie Jacobs memos

As we know, the GNU then developed the RDP White Paper with wide inputs from the different parties. The White Paper was released in early September 1994; we have commented on its rightward drift earlier on in this chapter. On 27 September 1994, a memo on the RDP (with restricted circulation) was prepared for De Klerk by AS (Japie) Jacobs. It was entitled 'An Appraisal of the White Paper on Reconstruction and Development: A Strategy for the Renewal of our Society'. Jacobs had been senior deputy governor of the South African Reserve Bank until his term ended in 1990, after which he became economic adviser to the minister of finance (first Barend du Plessis, then Derek Keys, and by the time this memo was prepared, Chris Liebenberg). Though broadly supportive of the RDP White Paper (in whose drafting the NP had a role), the memo, prepared by an adviser to a minister of the GNU, was clearly written as a strategy to guide the NP's approach to and critique of the White Paper. This abuse of an official government position for party political purposes is remarkable to say the least.

Jacobs argues that the NP needed to take a strategic approach to the RDP:

> It is therefore essential that the NP should support the RDP and assist with its implementation – particularly in the Ministries managed by NP Ministers; in the Western Cape (where the NP has to take the initiative for its implementation) and at [the] third tier level of government ... The temptation will be great (as occurred in Namibia) to present the programmes as a bonanza from the ANC for which only the ANC supporters benefit. The point must be stressed that the programme is funded by the State and that the previous government had already during its term of office started to allocate more resources for socio-economic programmes (Roelf Meyer Papers, PV 912, 1/12/1/1).

The memo then goes on to look at specific aspects of the White Paper. In reviewing the document's proposal to form a broadly based, multi-stakeholder economic policy advisory body to be called the National Economic Development and Labour Council (Nedlac), Jacobs notes that a chamber devoted to macroeconomic policy 'is not contemplated' for Nedlac:

> The underlying reason is that the ANC Ministers are reluctant to admit that the MERG model (of which the RDP forms an integral part) is not a suitable vehicle for the formulation of a macroeconomic growth strategy

for South Africa. The only alternative is the Normative Economic Model, which was at its release rejected by the ANC and COSATU in particular. The ANC Ministries should hence be questioned on the standing of the MERG document and the structures to be established and the procedures to be implemented to construct a fully integrated longer term macroeconomic strategy for South Africa (Roelf Meyer Papers, PV 912, 1/12/1/1).

Jacobs is full of praise for the White Paper's endorsement of fiscal discipline, noting that 'this is a precondition for the successful implementation of the programme and enables the NP to give it its full support'. He is critical of the 'failure' of the White Paper to advocate for 'a more flexible and efficient labour market', and he warns against the 'interventionist and targeted (selective)' industrial policy proposed.

On 11 November 1994, Jacobs drafted another memo, on the letterhead of the Office of the Executive Deputy President, FW de Klerk, and addressed to the administrative secretary of the NP minister of provincial affairs and constitutional development, Chris Fismer. This memo is marked *Vertroulik* (Confidential) and written in Afrikaans, and it was faxed from the South African Reserve Bank. Here Jacobs again advises about the excessive spending underlying the RDP Base Document, somewhat scarcastically pointing out that the latter was *not* a policy document of the GNU.

Here is what he says:

> COSATU en NIEP[2] (die vader van die MERG model wat die oorspronlike HOP[3] strategie ingesluit het) het in hulle getuienis vir die Gekose Komitee[4] gemor oor die feit dat die Witskrif afwyk van die sogenaamde [HOP] basisdokument. Dit gaan veral oor die *markstruktuur en fiskale dissipline* … NIEP se standpunt is dat die Staat 50 persent van die land se jaarlikse besparings vir HOP moet aanwend. Dit is natuurlike oordadig … Die oorspronlike *Reconstruction and Development Programme – a Policy Framework (1994) was 'n politieke manifesto en is nie 'n beliedsdokument wat deur die Regering van Nationale Eenheid aanvaar nie* (Roelf Meyer Papers, PV 912, 1/12/1/1, emphasis in the original).

Translation:[5]

> COSATU and the NIEP (the originator of the MERG model, which included the original RDP strategy) complained in their evidence to the Select Committee about the fact that the White Paper diverges from the so-called [RDP] Base Document – this matter is not at all clear in this context. The criticism is mainly about the issues of the market structure and

fiscal discipline. NIEP holds the view that the Government should apply 50% of the country's annual savings to the RDP. This is naturally excessive. The original *Reconstruction and Development Programme – A Policy Framework (1994) was a political manifesto and is not a policy document that was accepted by the Government of National Unity.*

In his autobiography, De Klerk is openly self-congratulatory about the success that the NP achieved in respect of economic policy. 'I felt that we exercised a positive influence in ensuring that the Government's Reconstruction and Development Programme ... would be funded in a responsible manner ... and that the ANC would not be able to claim sole ownership of the RDP' (De Klerk 1998: 344). This quiet satisfaction also came across in an interview he granted to Jannie Rossouw and Vishnu Padayachee (28 January 2019).

It appears that Mandela had come to learn of the NP's attempts at undermining the ANC's economic policy positions, especially that of the RDP. In her biography of former NP Foreign Minister Roloef (Pik) Botha, Theresa Papenfus writes about this. She refers to a Cabinet meeting held on 18 January 1995, at which Mandela expressed his frustration at De Klerk's lack of support for the RDP (Papenfus 2010: 758). These tensions around the RDP, as well as De Klerk's uninvited intervention in the deteriorating relations between the ANC and the Inkatha Freedom Party and other government matters, simmered throughout 1995. They became public at a clash between Mandela and De Klerk, which took place on the occasion of mining giant Gencor's centenary anniversary function. Pik Botha points out that in their official speeches at the event, each had made strong criticisms of the other and Mandela abruptly left the hall as a consequence. Mandela was followed by De Klerk, and the two appeared to have had a heated exchange on the street as they approached Mandela's car.

That infamous exchange occurred on 29 September 1995.

In April 1996, President Mandela closed the RDP office and transferred the balance of its funds to the National Treasury. On 8 May, the NP, its work apparently done, quit the GNU to pursue a life on the opposition benches (Mandela and Langa 2017: 88–89; 212–213).

On 14 June 1996, within a few months of the closure of the RDP office, the National Treasury of the ANC-dominated GNU published its Growth, Employment and Redistribution (GEAR) programme, with the shocking announcement that this essentially neo-liberal policy – which appeared more aligned to the NP's and Margaret Thatcher's contemporary economic thinking than anything in the ANC's toolkit of economic ideas – was 'non-negotiable'.

Manuel strongly denies the causal links that the left has made between the closure of the RDP office and the publication of the GEAR document (in Green 2008: 425). Naidoo, in contrast, is clear that these policy developments were intrinsically connected (2017: 107). We invite you to join the dots yourself.

Derek Keys and the Normative Economic Model

But we need now to backtrack to more fully appreciate the NP's role in respect of economic policy.

At the time he was elected leader of the NP in 1989, De Klerk did not have the same command of the economic reform agenda as PW Botha. He had apparently turned down an earlier proposal of the post of minister of finance, offered to him by Botha, as he felt that he was not the best qualified person for the job, which went to Barend du Plessis (De Klerk interview, 28 January 2019). But that shortcoming quickly changed. Between February and September of that year, De Klerk appears to have undergone something of an 'internship' on economic matters. Hermann Giliomee quotes the Broederbond chairperson, Pieter de Lange, to the effect that De Klerk first underwent 'economic instruction' led by Gencor chairperson Wim de Villiers and then Gencor CEO Derek Keys, who tutored De Klerk over weekends on the way the economy works. This 'economics training' by Keys was confirmed by De Klerk to us (28 January 2019). Keys is quoted as observing that De Klerk 'grasped at once what the issue was when I had to raise something … his sense of judgement [about economic matters] was top rate' (Giliomee 2012: 292).

Central to the NP strategy on the economy was its 1993 Normative Economic Model (NEM) and the role played in its development and marketing by Keys. Keys had been plucked carefully from his post as CEO of Gencor, while on a trip to China, to become De Klerk's 'technocratic' trade and industry minister in 1992, to which the finance portfolio was soon added. In a political masterstroke, Keys accepted the 1992 post on condition that he was an 'independent' minister appointed to Cabinet in consultation with the ANC (Naidoo 2010: 190). That would allow him to secure the credibility and perceived neutrality needed to speak to the ANC. De Klerk later observed proudly: 'The NEM had provided the framework for the economic and financial policy during the rest of my administration [i.e. the crucial years before the 1994 elections]. I was deeply aware of the fact that our challenge was not only to negotiate a new constitution, but also to ensure that, after the election, the ANC would implement the right economic and financial policies' (1998: 334–335).

It is significant that the NEM was tabled at the multi-party talks for a democratic South Africa in March 1993 as one of the 'Basic Documents' of the negotiations. No other party tabled an equivalent economic policy framework as far we could ascertain (Leon Wessels Papers, PV 883, 1/02/2/1/1).

The prime minister's Economic Advisory Council and its professional economic secretariat, the Central Economic Advisory Services (CEAS), had played an important, though changing, role in economic policy debates and formulation since it was established under Hendrik Verwoerd in the early 1960s. Among other things, it produced an Economic Development Plan (EDP), an indicative planning framework based on growth model designs typical of that era. By 1987, under PW Botha, it had produced its ninth EDP. Under President de Klerk and Finance Minister Keys, the CEAS, then headed by Jan Dreyer with Estian Calitz as his deputy, was commissioned to produce a tenth EDP as the De Klerk government's economic model in preparation for negotiations. Keys proposed that it be called the Normative Economic Model (Calitz interview, 12 January 2017).

The NEM, as argued in the MERG report (MERG 1993: 5–6), focused narrowly on the alleged constraints faced by the economy. It suggested that growth rates could only be raised via the supply side, including lower personal and corporate taxes to increase savings. It encouraged privatisation, deregulation and competition, and high positive real interest rates – a package aimed at stimulating private sector investment – arguing that any other strategy would crowd out the potential of the private sector (dominated by old South African capital) and lead to pressure on the balance of payments. Altogether, its policy prescriptions differed little from the avowedly market-dominated policy platforms favoured by Western conservative political parties and the Washington institutions in the 1980s. In addition, its appropriateness for the challenges for post-apartheid economic reconstruction was highly questionable.

According to the private memoir of Jan Lombard (n.d.), after the new government was in power, the World Bank had asked Mandela to inform them of the government's economic priorities. Lombard claims that it would have been natural to send the World Bank the NEM, but Jacobs, Keys' special adviser at the time, asked a small team of economists to 'revamp' the NEM for the World Bank without 'its underlying analytical foundations' (Lombard n.d.: 78). This 'revamping' exercise took place at the South African Reserve Bank with the support of the governor and some of its economists, including the senior deputy governor, Jan Lombard. The Development Bank of Southern Africa (DBSA) also provided a few economists to the team, and there were some unnamed 'outside' economists. Later, many of this team of insiders and outsiders were to formulate and design the GEAR document, working in secret at the DBSA. The revised document was apparently approved by Keys and the deputy finance minister, Alec Erwin, as well as by the DBSA chairperson, Wiseman Nkuhlu. When Keys went to Washington with the plan, Jay Naidoo, who was part of the South African government team, refused to support its submission on the grounds that Cosatu had not been involved in its production (Lombard n.d.).

An early 1990s document emphasised the need for De Klerk and Keys to hold the economic line, while ensuring that they held onto their positions. Here is how it reads:

> The dilemma can be simply and starkly stated: how does a democratic South Africa resolve the massive problems of social injustice and inequity without destroying the fragile economic structure which ultimately provides the only hope for achieving the goals? The most prudent course to follow will be to stretch out the timing of many of the ANC policies relating to housing, education and other social expenditures. Clearly there will be much political tension and disagreement regarding priorities and timetables, *and de Klerk as Deputy President and Keys as Finance Minister will have to play a very delicate role in this area to maintain Mandela's confidence and remain key figures in the government.* The social science literature dealing with the feasibility of combining political and social reform with policies of economic redistribution provides many more warnings of disaster than positive case models. The prospects for democracy over the next decade are inextricably linked to the resolution of this central problem (emphasis added).[6]

Ronnie Kasrils makes the following acute observation about how he saw De Klerk's role across the crucial years of the transition: 'Everything he did was aimed at ensuring that the final journey out of apartheid would not entail the dreaded farewell to an economic system from which the Afrikaners in particular and whites in general had benefited so much' (2017: 235).

In order to understand from an insider how these early engagements unfolded, here is Erwin's recollection of the events of the early 1990s:

> So by 1992 the extent of engagement and interaction with the [apartheid] state was pretty extensive … What had happened was that you had the unions now heavily engaged in government, especially after Derek Keys came in. So by 1992 we had the National Economic Forum, that gave us access to the top of [the apartheid] government, [people like] Estian Calitz, Japie Jacobs, [and

from] the central bank, Chris Stals … and then from the DEP side by 1992 [Trevor Manuel] was starting the internal ETC [Economic Transformation Committee] and we kept in touch with them … in 1993 Jay [Naidoo] and I used to spend a lot of time at Shell House (Erwin interview, 23 October 2015).

Erwin's account of his first major encounter with Keys is fascinating, almost political theatre, and it shows the amazing astuteness and tactical skills of Keys (and to some extent the naivety of the ANC) in bringing key struggle figures around to his point of view:

> By then Mandela and Mbeki and others were saying, look, this is what we can sustain on the international front, this is what we can't, and we would engage. Then in 1992 we were sitting with this team of Keys … Keys summons me and Jay Naidoo one night, and he says I will buy you dinner, I am sorry it is at the Rand Club but I just want to talk to you guys. By then we had the National Economic Forum going.
>
> …
>
> So three of us sat. Jay will remember it; it was a lovely dinner …
>
> …
>
> So he says, guys, you guys are going to take power and I admire what Cosatu has done. *Your sense of the economy is far better than anything of the ANC.* In order to help our country, I am prepared to open the books to you, I want you guys to understand what's working. Not just Cosatu, I am going to do this for the ANC but I thought you guys would be the most troublesome, so I am talking to you first. So that's what I want to do. I want you to come look at anything we have. I will not hold back; you can have anything you want. *So that's the first meeting; that's what started all of us thinking …* (Erwin interview, 23 October 2015, emphasis added).

Naidoo, the second key insider in our narrative, was clearly impressed by Keys and referred to him as the 'eminent and respected Head of Gencor' (2010: 189). He goes on to say:

> Derek Keys was an experienced businessman who was firmly committed to South Africa. He had an open and engaging personality and none of the ego of achievement. Within weeks of taking office, and in our first meeting, he presented his famous 'golden triangle', a partnership between government, labour and business. It converged our thinking that we should have a

binding reconstruction pact that would form a new democratic government. Our discussions led to an agreement to set up the National Economic Forum (NEF) to begin negotiating the economic transition (Naidoo 2010: 190).

Let us get back to the Normative Economic Model. Academic Wessel Visser emphasises the importance of the NEM in the economic policy debate:

> The NP government published its Normative Economic Model (NEM) in March 1993, which was heavily influenced by the IMF's neo-liberal dogma. When the ANC, together with other liberation organisations, started to negotiate with the NP for a new democratic political dispensation in 1990, it had little economic experience. The South African left prepared itself for a revolutionary take-over of both the state and the economy, and was therefore unprepared for an evolutionary reform process. Prior to 1994 the ANC was beguiled by a plethora of neo-liberalist corporate scenario-planning exercises and ANC leaders were fêted with private 'orientation' sessions and confabs at exclusive game resorts (Visser 2004: 10).

The choice of words like 'beguiled' and 'feted' are instructive, as we will note again in the conclusion.

That this multi-pronged bombardment upon a young, unevenly trained and inexperienced ANC economics leadership succeeded beyond 1994 is clear from the similarity between the NP's NEM and the ANC's GEAR programme on the major policy issues, including fiscal restraint. Here is De Klerk again: 'We ... supported GEAR. In my opinion, the National Party's greatest contribution in the Government of National Unity was to promote the adoption of a balanced economic policy which would assure growth and progress and which would steer a course away from the socialist tendencies which the ANC had espoused for the whole of its existence ...' (1998: 345).

POST-1994 ECONOMIC POLICY-MAKING: GEAR

Trevor Manuel moved to the Treasury in April 1996. He describes his entry as follows (and the subsequent resignation of the Treasury director general, Estian Calitz):

> When Madiba asked me to move from trade and industry to finance, he asked me with Thabo in the room – it's about August 1995– he said, as Chris

Liebenberg [is leaving] … the one thing that I want to ask you is to move in very close to what Chris is doing so you can smooth that entire transition. So we do that indeed, and Gill Marcus was only told late in March that this thing is going to happen because she was chairing the Portfolio Committee [on Finance]. So Madiba announced it on the 28th of March that there would be a series of changes. Now, one of the changes was that Jay Naidoo is moving to telecommunications and the RDP office was being shut down. I would move from trade and industry to finance, Theo Alant would be my deputy, Alec who was deputy minister of finance would become minister of trade and industry. Madiba announced all of that together. So I went to the house. I knew what was coming, and the only other person in the house was Chris Liebenberg and Chris said to me, so it's happening today, but he said, you owe me one, *boetie*. I said, what do I owe you? He said, you know this morning I had to tell Estian Calitz, because you must tell your DG, so I said to Estian that Madiba was announcing, the president was announcing, this and he said, so minister, do you know who is taking over, and I couldn't lie and I said, Minister Manuel is moving across. And he said to me, well then minister, I must ask you that I would like to renegotiate my conditions of service. That was public sector speak for 'I would like to resign'. So Chris said, that's what you owe me; you don't have the problem of having to deal with Estian Calitz. So now I move across to finance (Manuel interview, 9 September 2016).

Soon after the April 1994 elections, and preceding GEAR, something occurred that provided further early signs of where the democratic government was going with economic policy. A little-known policy package was developed by Keys, which Erwin, his deputy, referred to as the 'six pack'.

We had accepted that what macro-balance meant was a degree of currency and price stability; therefore, we will accept attempts to discipline the deficit and discipline expenditure. There was a little document in Cabinet called the six pack, which precedes all of these. It's a precursor to GEAR. I can't remember all the six, but it's exactly that, so it is to stabilise the price, stabilise the deficit, curb excessive consumption expenditure, make space for capital … but that was the six pack that myself and Derek formulated and put before Cabinet. There is a way of trying to get Cabinet to realise, look, this is not business as usual, we must pull in, and this is why we're pulling in (Erwin interview, 23 October 2015).

Sometime late in March 1996, it became known that a team of economists had been secretly assembled to draw up a macroeconomic framework. At the time, Nedlac was debating the development of a shared economic vision that was expected to go through a broad consultative process. The most lucid and credible account to date for what followed is Jay Naidoo, then minister without portfolio, whom Mandela had asked to lead the implementation of the RDP (Naidoo 2010: chap. 34).

The account that follows relies heavily on Naidoo's autobiography. He observes that 'unknown to most of the political leadership in the country, another process exploring how the economy could be stabilised was being written up in the back rooms by a think tank. This was later to morph into GEAR' (Naidoo 2010: 253). Naidoo makes it clear that a highly secret series of meetings had been taking place at the DBSA since late 1995, convened by Erwin, as deputy minister of finance. Key people included (we undertand from Naidoo's book) a number of unnamed 'business-oriented economists', many of whom had not been involved in any of the Alliance's economic policy-making processes. The ANC's Economic Transformation Committee (then headed by Labour Minister Tito Mboweni) was not represented.

Naidoo names as an expert participant Stephen Gelb, an economist closely associated with the labour movement and who had headed the Economic Trends Research Group in the late 1980s (see chapter 4). Naidoo claims that although Gelb had been 'sworn to silence' about these secret developments, as a democrat Gelb had felt obliged to report on these processes to the ANC Economic Transformation Committee, which he did in March 1996. Naidoo claims that there was 'absolute outrage' at the Economic Transformation Committee at such a process that excluded all the relevant structures of the movement. As Mac Maharaj points out, GEAR was neither initiated nor approved by the Economic Transformation Committee, on which he served as transport minister nor by the Cabinet (Maharaj interview, 16 August 2016).

A few days later, a meeting was convened at Mandela's home, where the president had to quell growing disquiet and rising tension among those present. Mandela (who must have been briefed by someone prior to the meeting) attempted to assuage sentiment by speaking about '*our home-grown structural adjustment policy*' (Naidoo 2010: 254, emphasis added). The leaders of the Alliance who were present were, according to Naidoo, 'aghast that there was no room for consultation' (2010: 254). A few days later, another meeting was convened at Shell House, with both Erwin and Manuel present. The latter two hurriedly presented their report, and there was very little time for discussion (as the two had to catch a plane to Cape Town). The Alliance partners were 'incensed', especially as this came on the back of the closure of the RDP office earlier that month. 'The greatest setback was that there had been no real attempt to canvass such a major policy shift in our ranks' (Naidoo 2010: 254).

Naidoo refers to the closure of the RDP office in April 1996 and the announcement of the GEAR programme in June of that year in strong terms:

> A new statist narrative emerged which made our people mere bystanders in the development process and pitted 'pragmatists and realists' on the one side against so-called utopian idealists on the other. In complete secrecy, a plot was devised by a cabal that operated outside traditional ANC structures, the Tripartite Alliance and even the Cabinet and parliament in order to terminate the RDP initiative. The RDP office was closed within weeks and a new strategy known as GEAR became the programme for advancing development in South Africa. In one Stalinist process, the entire social consensus between the alliance partners and the majority of citizens which we had been building for decades, was destroyed (Naidoo 2017: 107).

Cabinet was presented with GEAR for the first time on the following day; again, there was 'no room for any discussion or changes'. Manuel then presented GEAR to parliament that same afternoon as a fait accompli. Very little of the parliamentary debate is new or revealing and so we note only a few points from that debate. The deputy minister of finance, Gill Marcus, confirmed in parliament that work on developing the GEAR package had been 'going on for some time, and goes well beyond a quick-fix response to the currency crisis'. She indicated that neither continuing along the existing macroeconomic path, especially in respect of the fiscal stance, nor using fiscal expansion as a basis for a growth strategy was sustainable. The latter approach, she noted, had been 'considerered' ... '(b)ut our analysis demonstrated that increased spending drives up interest rates, crowding out private investment' (Hansard, vol. 10, 1996: 3092–3093). Marcus summarised the core logic of GEAR as follows:

> [The] package establishes a solid macroeconomic foundation from which we will generate growth and jobs. It recognises that income inequality works against achieving growth and that the surest way to effect redistribution is through job creation. Different components are linked into an integrated package that seeks to control inflation while meeting the objectives of generating employment-creating growth and reducing poverty. We need to bear in mind that it is an integrated package, and the combination of all

the elements is essential for it to have the desired effect (Hansard, vol. 10, 1996: 3092).

For his part, Trevor Manuel in his position as Finance Minister, in response to a question from an NP member, ruled out privatisation as a 'panacea for all ills' arguing that 'it is one instrument amongst others, and unless one looks at economic instruments in that way, one makes major mistakes' (Hansard, vol. 10, 1996: 3096).

According to Jeremy Cronin, Manuel hurriedly presented the GEAR document to some members of the SACP on the eve of its official announcement. The meeting at Shell House was attended on the SACP side by Charles Ngqulaka (SACP chairperson), Cronin and possibly by Geraldine Fraser-Moleketi. Cronin recalls that Manuel 'briskly' presented five slides, which purported to demonstrate the volatility of the rand and why a modelled macroeconomic programme was necessary to appease disquiet among the international investor community. The SACP, in response, issued a three-line statement welcoming GEAR. A similar engagement with Cosatu may have happened. The point is that Manuel is right to claim that some consultation over GEAR did occur among Alliance partners, but the nature and character of these consultations needs to be taken into account (Cronin interview, 25 July 2017).

On 14 June 1996, Manuel unveiled GEAR, with the announcement that it was 'non-negotiable'. On 17 June, the full GEAR document was sent to Mandela with a note (in an unidentified hand) that read, 'Tata. This is the final product' (Nelson Mandela Papers, Box 66, Folder 678). In an effort at damage control after the fallout within the Alliance structures over the development and imposition of GEAR, Mandela said the following to the 1997 Cosatu National Congress:

> It is in the nature of an alliance that its partners will not agree on all matters that fall within the broad vision that binds them. What is important is the readiness to discuss disagreements when they do arise and the shared commitment to find solutions. It is therefore not in keeping with the character of our Alliance when Cosatu declares that positions it holds that differ from those of the ANC or government are non-negotiable. By the same token it is wrong for the ANC to present its own positions as non-negotiable, even while exercising its broader responsibilities in government (Mandela 1997: n.p.).

Mandela's inconsistency between this public position on debating policy within the movement and the actual 'non-negotiable' policy positions he came to support provided critical political cover for those bent on pushing GEAR through, and has thus far been neglected or underestimated. Indeed, his role in economic policy in the 1990s has not yet been opened up for debate, and much of the perceived change in policy direction has been attributed to Thabo Mbeki and his young economic guns. As Bill Freund observes: 'Mbeki and Mboweni were important players but Nelson Mandela himself, easily converted to the need to work with dominant global forces and with South African business (notably through the influence of Harry Oppenheimer whom he systematically consulted), was hardly innocent in this regard' (2015: 59).

THE 'NON-NEGOTIABILITY' OF GEAR AND RESPONSES TO IT

Opinions differ about the nature and degree of consultations over GEAR within the Alliance. Manuel called it 'sour grapes', arguing that the proposals were presented to the Alliance, which agreed with aspects of it but not with the fiscal stance (Gevisser 2007: 665). In our interview with him, Manuel claimed that there was no possibility of negotiating the GEAR document with the unions, given prevailing conditions. Erwin agrees, claiming that 'we could not have a public debate about GEAR because if you do that the capital markets respond to everything you say. In hindsight we were too cautious' (2016: 145). Maharaj recalls that GEAR was presented to the Cabinet, where he was minister of transport and part of the economics cluster, as a 'done deal'. The Economic Transformation Committee had neither initiated nor approved of GEAR. He maintains that, aside from its content, the process of producing GEAR was the 'most significant departure from ANC culture' in its entire history (Maharaj interview, 16 August 2016).

Despite his position as head of the ANC's Economic Transformation Committee, Labour Minister Tito Mboweni, it has been pointed out, 'was not a central player in its formulation' (*Sunday Independent*, 1 June 1997, cited in Michie and Padayachee 1998). Mark Gevisser quotes Mboweni as having argued that 'he thought that they made the wrong decision. If GEAR had come through the ANC rather than having been imposed by the executive, Cosatu would have been more comfortable with the process even if they disagreed with aspects of it' (Gevisser 2007: 665).

In an interview with Padraig O'Malley, Mboweni is careful to signal his full agreement with the policy stance of the GEAR approach, especially on the imperative to reduce the budget deficit, and he claimed that support from a 'left-wing' angle:

> I'm an economist and I consider myself a left-wing economist. It's wrong to say that continue the status quo, just continue expanding the deficit [and] that makes left-wing sense. It doesn't, that's actually right-wing because very

soon you …. enter into a position where you can't sustain your deficit any more. If you can't sustain your deficit any more what happens? You go for structural adjustment so you end up with an extremely right-wing position and yet you thought you were pursuing left-wing positions. There is every sense in left-wing economic policy to be very strict with your budget deficit in order for you not to fall into structural adjustment (O'Malley interview archive, Mboweni, 18 August 1992).

Mboweni goes on to justify the need to reduce the budget deficit, contrasting his position to that of the National Institute for Economic Policy (the successor to MERG):

So, you can't have that situation, you can't have a left-wing movement that argues that just keep on borrowing, somebody one day will sort it out. No that's wrong. They say it's a breed of new economists who are clustered around the National Institute for Economic Policy who argue that you should just keep on raising the deficit and I don't know what kind of research they have done to say that. So, the approach is, yes, let's reduce the deficit (O'Malley interview archive, Mboweni, 18 August 1992).

Yet, Mboweni distanced himself from Manuel in the manner in which GEAR was debated and presented as 'non-negotiable'.

In response to O'Malley (POM), on this point, Mboweni (TM) responds as follows:

TM: Well that you must raise with Trevor, the non-negotiable. I don't want to get involved in that.
POM: But the markets took that as …
TM: I know but you must raise that with Trevor Manuel not with me. The issue I am raising is the technicalities of the economic policy. That's the one that I'm raising. That's just lousy politics.
POM: Well it is lousy politics because if the markets see you going back and negotiating with COSATU and modifying the macro-economic programme it will be seen as a sign of weakness.
TM: I know, that's why I'm saying, raise it with Trevor, not with me (O'Malley interview archive, Mboweni, 18 August 1992).

Maharaj recalls that in December 1995 (while GEAR was being developed in secret at the DBSA), a Cabinet meeting at the Union Buildings debated and approved

133

a major infrastructural roll-out plan. Transport infrastructure development, including the Maputo Corridor development project, would form a key element of a state-led investment programme aimed at promoting employment and growth. It was rendered a 'dead letter', he notes, in a context where another very different approach to economic policy [GEAR] was being hatched (Maharaj interview, 16 August 2016).

GEAR was withheld even from Nedlac, the policy advisory forum of business, labour, the government and the community, as the chair of the business group, Raymond Parsons, points out, and even from the ANC itself. According to Parsons and Ali Parry, Mandela apparently admitted that 'a decision was taken at the highest level that the implementation of GEAR as a "stability pact" was non-negotiable and urgent and that consultation would be kept to a minimum'. Mandela went on to say that 'even the ANC learnt of GEAR far too late – when it was almost complete' (in Parsons and Parry 2018: 74–75). Whatever the reason, Parsons and Parry admit that GEAR 'did put considerable strain on the Nedlac processes' (Parsons and Parry 2018: 74–75).

Erwin argues that the GEAR approach was unavoidable, that it was not much different from MERG and that there was really no alternative to it:

> So as I look back I don't see anything massively that could have been very different. I know Vella and others thought MERG was different, I must say you have to take me through that. I can't see anything that was massively different in MERG, I think they [GEAR team] were fine-tuning issues that MERG had. The MERG things didn't take into account what was already on the negotiating table; *we didn't have time to absorb them* and then decided to proceed because we didn't see anything that was massively different (Erwin interview, 23 October 2015, emphasis added).

Pippa Green's (2008) biography of Manuel is somewhat disparaging of those who expressed any reservations about the process or the contents of what became GEAR, and effusively laudatory of those who drove it. Yet, curiously, she presents Manuel as someone who was (even at that stage) not entirely sure about the correctness of the programme's policy stance. In her account, it was Mbeki who pushed what became GEAR from late 1995, with Erwin (then deputy finance minister) initially taking political responsibility. Manuel is characterised as having 'immense courage', but also as one who 'had to be persuaded that it [GEAR] was the correct route to take' (Green 2008: 439). It was presented to Mbeki in mid-May at the Presidential Guest House in Pretoria by Manuel, who according to Green's unnamed source, was a 'little unsure of parts of it'; 'there wasn't a great deal of conviction in his pres-entation'. But, she observes that he had obviously cleared the details beforehand with Mbeki. Mbeki's body language apparently made it clear that the policy was 'going to go' (Green 2008: 440). Mbeki's role as the mentor of this group is clear from Gevisser's account of these dramatic developments, though we should not dis-count the support and cover that Mandela gave the process and its leaders.

According to Green (2008: 437), closer to the ground in the production and marketing of GEAR were Treasury officials Maria Ramos, André Roux, Iraj Abedian, some unnamed officials from the Reserve Bank, and some 'funnies from the Labour Department' (arguably an indirect dig at Labour Minister Mboweni who had expressed some concerns about the process). University of Stellenbosch econo-mist Servaas van der Berg was also part of the technical team that prepared GEAR.

What is clear here is that a few people – Mbeki, Manuel and Erwin politically; Ramos, Roux and Abedian technically – drove this process, which began well before the rand's fall became alarming. It is also clear that this occurred in secret at the DBSA; and that the entire process was hurriedly forced through the structures of the ANC, government, Cabinet and parliament, with little or no democratic discus-sion and debate. After he took over the Finance Ministry in February 1996, Manuel drove this team, described by Gevisser as having 'a rogue pioneering status … They were a Camelot; comrades brave enough to take on the foreboding highground of international capital; trailblazing cowboys of reason and modernity: And their quiet guru was Thabo Mbeki' (Gevisser 2007: 668).

We reject, as mythology and hyperbole, Gevisser's characterisation of the team in these terms as the 'knights in shining armour'. Rather, we see the ANC eco-nomics team as being caught off guard by the speed of events, unevenly trained in modern economic theory and policy, somewhat poorly prepared, inexperienced, possibly daunted by the mathematics, the budgeting process and the accounting, as some infomants admitted to us without wishing to be identified by name.[7]

In the end, this led to them being intellectually seduced in comfortable surroundings and eventually outmanoeuvred by the well-resourced apartheid state and by international and local pro-market-friendly actors. These actors included NP members with whom they had to deal during the negotiations and in the early years of the GNU, as well as the South African conglomerates and Western governments and agencies. Cosatu may have been better prepared in some ways, but their power was severely limited by the secretive and closed nature of economic policy debates.

And for some reason, the SACP, which one would have expected to be a more influential player on the economy, was all but absent, as Kasrils ruefully admits

(Interview, 30 March 2017). They simply went along with the ANC leadership as if 'sleepwalking into the future' (Kasrils 2017: 235). As discussed in chapter 4, Kasrils is on record as saying that the SACP allowed the ANC 'to succumb to the neo-liberal, free market economic embrace because some of us were fast asleep' (2017: 238–239).

In a letter to Rusty Bernstein dated 14 June 1990, Vella Pillay makes the following observation, which illustrates this point: 'I have attended several meetings arranged with business groups as part of the ANC's delegation. On several occasions I found myself repeatedly surprised by the extraordinary "flexibility" of several of our leading comrades – *a flexibility almost bordering on a fawning and cringing position in the presence of the South African conglomerates* ... I also feel that our friend JS [Joe Slovo] is perhaps showing a willingness to skate on very thin ice on these matters' (Vella Pillay private archives, emphasis added).

We asked Cronin why he thought a new hegemony around GEAR consolidated so quickly, given that the SACP and Cosatu, even some in the ANC, may have had different economic ideas by the mid-1990s.

> I think there are a number of things at play. So I think there, firstly, there is the weakness of the Communist Party, in particular in terms of social and economic policy. So we are, you know, we kind of almost defer to Cosatu to develop economic labour market and other policies. Or [we defer] to progressive NGOs. Our [communist] models have clearly failed. And we were off balance in that space. So we were confident about the political, to some extent, and confident in our role in helping to defeat white minority rule. But, so we were not, we were kind of absent to a considerable degree in that [economic policy] space.
>
> ...
>
> Secondly, I think that the Cosatu think tanks[8] were social democratic. So there is a bit of suspicion. So we were kind of fairly close to Alec Erwin and some people like that, you know, are working with us and we are working with them, supporting them and so on. But we are coming out of quite different legacies. So he would be coming out of a progressive, left-leaning social democratic tradition and studied the auto sector in Australia and, you know. A lot of interest in Sweden and so on. From those quarters, whereas we had dismissed all of that as yellow unionism, whatever. So there is not a strong bloc and a coherent bloc. But the point was, where I need to come to is, you see, I think also we were not in a social democratic moment, globally. Which I think we thought we were (Cronin interview, 14 March 2016).

THE LACK OF A DEMOCRATIC CULTURE OF ACCOUNTABILITY

The fact that the culture of political accountability – such a feature of the mass-based politics of Cosatu and United Democratic Front structures in the 1980s – was displaced behind an ironclad veil of 'non-negotiable' economic policy positions isolated the Mbeki-mentored economics group from the critical feedback of progressives in the mass democratic movement. In the end, they cannot claim, then or now, that they had the informed support of the mass democratic movement for a policy stance such as GEAR, which deviated so much from the ANC's previous positions. But the roots of this elite and autocratic approach to policy formulation can be found earlier in the transition.

Both authors of this book were themselves active members of ANC branches in Cape Town and Durban. Neither recalls any discussion of the ANC's September 1990 discussion document on the economy. In Durban, Padayachee (together with comrades such as Cyrus Rustomjee, a qualified and trained economist) led seminars on the economy in a number of branches. It would appear that the discussion document did not come to branch level there for discussion or feedback. We raised this issue with Leslie Watson, an experienced activist in the ANC's Athlone branch; David Abrahams, a senior youth activist in the ANC-aligned mass democratic movement in the 1990s; and Shepi Mati, a highly experienced ANC-aligned political activist and one-time president of the Congress of South African Students, who was the secretary of the Guguletu branch of the ANC in the early 1990s. Enver Motala, a member of the executive of the Western Areas branch in Durban, has no recollection of any discussions around ANC-produced economic policy documents, but is quick to recall the many ANC and Cosatu meetings at which versions of the RDP were discussed, led by Cosatu comrades (Motala, in conversation with Padayachee, 20 April 2016).

They all confirm on the record the lack of discussion and consultation on the DEP's economic policies. Watson recalls her ANC branch discussions focusing mainly on building ANC organisational structures and popularising the ANC, with economic, social and other policies presented as a fait accompli. Abrahams vividly recalls discussions on the various iterations of the RDP and plans to establish RDP councils to deepen participation at local level, until this initiative was summarily shut down sometime in 1993 or 1994. Mati, similarly, recalls that while there was engagement with a range of issues, including on the RDP, there was no discussion in the branch about ANC economic policy (Robert van Niekerk, in conversation variously with Abrahams, Mati and Watson, 16–18 April 2016). We cannot and do not, of course, claim that these views are 'representative' of the body of ANC opinion, but they do provide some anecdotal insight on the absence of consultation and democratic policy debates in ANC grassroots structures, although further research will be required to confirm the representivity of these observations.

Yet, such democracy was precisely what the DEP understood as key to the policy debate. In an undated memo to the ANC headquarters, the importance of democratic participation in policy-making is strongly emphasised: 'If the DEP does not relate to the movement in a democratic way, it will likely become alienated from its original aims, as has happened with research organisations in some independent African countries. Moreover, only democratic structures permit the DEP to undertake participatory research and popular education in a systematic manner' (Nelson Mandela Papers, Box 237, Folder 17).

It is ironic then, and even bizarre, that Mbeki 'safeguarded, even relished, the DEPs obscurity' (Gevisser 2016: 149).

One final point on the lack of democratic culture relates to Mandela's approach to debate over economic policy. Returning from Davos in 1992, Mandela informed the NEC that global captains of industry and world leaders would shun and isolate South Africa (like they did Cuba) if it pursued 'socialist' policies. As Kasrils puts it: 'Even Joe Slovo and Chris Hani, the foremost communists, have been prepared to swallow the Davos narrative out of deference to the man' (2017: 32). Elsewhere, and referring to a different context, Kasrils observes that 'all in the entire movement were wise enough – or cowardly enough – to silently endure the old man's [Mandela's] scolding' (2017: 31–32).

Of relevance here on Mandela's demeanour are accounts by both Pallo Jordan and Kasrils. Sometime in 1992 Manuel and Saki Macozoma led a presentation of the Mount Fleur scenarios (an exercise in future-forging) at a meeting of the ANC's National Working Committee, itself an unusual matter, as economic policy was rarely discussed at such a level in the ANC during that period. The scenarios used terms such as Icarus, borrowed from Greek mythology, to describe projected economic possibilities. A sombre-looking Mandela chaired the meeting; Mbeki and Hani were among the ANC heavyweights not present. Slovo was present but was silent throughout the debate – hardly surprising, given that he had shown no interest at all in MERG or the economic policy debate in the 1990s. In the discussion that followed, Jordan and Kasrils challenged the analysis underlying these scenarios as being superficial and simplistic, a public relations exercise. They were both dismissive of it on ideological grounds as well. Jordan spoke to us of his total rage about these scenarios, a view he presented at the meeting with some anger. Jordan believed that the presenters did not appear to be aware of the full version of the Greek myths they were so eagerly and loosely employing (Jordan interview, 4 August 2017). According to Kasrils, Mandela grew visibly impatient, then angry at these critical interventions. He sharply reminded them and the meeting of the fragility of the South African economy and the very changed global environment post-1989 within which the ANC needed to articulate policy, arguing against any talk of a more radical economic policy stance. He then stalked out, bringing the debate to a sudden end (Kasrils interview, 17 May 2017).

Elias Masilela (2007) recounts a somewhat similar (though less formal) event. On Mandela's first visit to Swaziland in November 1990, he called for all South Africans living there to meet him at Manzana Guest House. Mandela was accompanied by Mboweni, Macozoma, Tokyo Sexwale and Colin Coleman, among others. Mandela addressed the gathering on a broad range of issues and invited questions. A then very young Masilela (later the CEO of the Public Investment Corporation) asked him about the feasibility of nationalisation given the 'extremely fragile economy'. It did not go down well. According to Masilela, Mandela was visibly irritated by the question, to the extent that he clearly felt it did not warrant a response. 'Not only that, he suddenly lost his appetite for the meeting and immediately stood up and walked out of the room' (Masilela 2007: xviii).

In the second event (late 1990), Mandela clearly did not want to entertain any challenge to nationalisation, then an avowed part of ANC economic policy according to the Freedom Charter; in the first event (late 1992), he clearly did not want to entertain any perceived criticism of an emerging pro-market, corporate economic policy stance.

It is important that we are aware of the impact of such interventions by this most influential political figure on open debate, including on economic policy options. The culture of the ANC – hierarchy, respect, Ubuntu – often precluded such open debate as may have been expected and required within the liberation movement at that critical juncture. Then there is the matter of the overriding need to maintain unity within the broad church of the movement, especially in conditions of exile. Mandela's generation was totally preoccupied with this objective, so entertaining open debate on the economy may well have created internal divisions that the ANC could not afford, especially immediately post-1990.

ROUNDING UP THE DISCUSSION TO DATE

The key point here is that the DEP and the ANC in government, in failing to hold themselves accountable, opened themselves decisively to intellectual seduction by big business, international financial institutions, Western governments and, most significantly and fatally, the NP, their direct political competitor and the government until 27 April 1994. This represented a rupture from a democratic political culture of engagement within the mass democratic movement and a strategic policy rupture from the recognisably social democratic trajectory of the ANC since the war years. The process of producing both MERG's programme (with representative governing structures of the Alliance partners and regular workshops) and the RDP (with its remarkable commitment to accountability to its base) was the most consistent expression of this latter trajectory. Cronin's recollection of the development of the content of economic policy contained in the RDP Base Document contrasts decisively with that of the 'market-friendly' thinking in the DEP: 'In the RDP we were essentially arguing a strong Keynesian (approach), which was that growth was important but that it would be growth through redistribution, and that was kind of a redline that Trevor and Tito and Mbeki declined to (think beyond) ... In their minds it was 'grow the cake', which would enable us to do the just things that the Freedom Charter calls for' (Cronin interview, 14 March 2016).

As Cronin recalls:

> The whole GEAR argument was, in effect, let's use neo-liberal (largely macroeconomic) tools to 'grow the cake' and then we can do redistribution. This was what lay at the heart of the 1993–1994 debate around the RDP – was it about 'growth through redistribution', or 'growth then redistribution'. The compromise became 'growth *and* redistribution' but with a 'growing the cake' assumption prevailing. Did we all get it wrong back then by assuming that development = redistribution? (email exchange with Cronin, 16 August 2017).

By the end of 1993, when the Keynesian recommendations in favour of a state-led public investment programme – especially focusing on housing, education and health delivery – was unceremoniously dumped by the ANC leadership, a choice had been made. The RDP that was finally approved in early 1994 by the ANC's NEC, was then turned into an RDP Discussion Document and White Paper in September 1994 by the GNU in a process that watered down and exorcised all radical, interventionist ideas (Van Niekerk 2013: 130–139). In six short years, the ANC had made the shift from the social democracy and nationalisation of African Claims and the Freedom Charter and latterly the RDP, to a market-driven and top-down Growth, Employment and Redistribution programme, hardly pausing to catch breath on the way.

That some comrades to this day feel a deep sense of betrayal about these events in the 1990s is undoubtedly true. Here, for example, is how Ineke van Kessel expresses this: 'Among various former activists, Mrs Thatcher's TINA (There Is No Alternative – to the free market and liberal orthodoxy) has become received wisdom. Others do indeed speak of betrayal but more often than not they feel betrayed by former comrades rather than by more abstract ANC policies. Some critics of the neo-liberal order seem genuinely committed to their belief in a more just society but others just want a share of the riches' (2009: 217).

Kasrils, who is otherwise fiercely self-critical of the choices made on economic policy, nevertheless rejects the 'betrayal' critique of people like Manuel:

> I do not believe that the pact that was made involved a 'sell-out' akin to that of the Faustian Zuma to the Mephistophelian Guptas.[9] The belief of Mandela and the other negotiators of the settlement that there was no option, no other possibility, but to agree to the compromises arrived at may well constitute an error of judgement but it was not a conscious betrayal. Nonetheless, it was a monumental trade-off that many critics have come to regard as a catastrophic chain of errors (Kasrils 2017: 225).

6

Making Sense of the Economic Policy Debates

OPPOSING INTERPRETATIONS

A number of analysts have attempted to explain how all the developments in policy-making discussed in chapter 4 happened, in particular why the ANC made the choices it did regarding social and economic policy from the late 1980s to the mid-1990s.

To date, two broad approaches to the explanation of these events can be discerned: one best articulated by Patrick Bond (2000) in *Elite Transition: From Apartheid to Neo-Liberalism in South Africa*; the other advanced by Alan Hirsch (2005) in *Season of Hope: Economic Reform under Mandela and Mbeki*. Our analysis departs from both, though we do share some elements of Bond's argument.

Bond is correct when he notes that there is yet 'no conclusive statement about what is happening and how we should confront it until more arguments are tested against time and opposing view points' (2000: 2–3). We began our project 15 years after Bond made this statement and 26 years since the unbanning of the ANC. We believe that this distance from those heady and hotly contested events does offer some advantages, especially as we have interviewed many of the actors in that unfolding drama, from opposing sides, hopefully satisfying the point made by Bond of the need to seek and understand opposing viewpoints. But we do not expect that everyone will agree with our interpretation. We are especially sensitive to the fact that our own colleagues and comrades in the Alliance[1] may find our interpretation difficult to accept, but this is how we see it based on our analysis of the evidence secured and our understanding. We fully expect future commentators to cover similar terrain, and who knows if they will come to similar conclusions to us or to very different views.

Bond's view is neatly summed up as follows: 'A large part of the drought experienced in the realm of macroeconomic policy – which would, by 1996, decisively rule out the implementation of RDP [Reconstruction and Development Programme] social promises – stemmed from intellectual retreat by select ANC leaders' (2000: 54). Such a retreat, it would appear, arose out of the nature of South Africa's capitalism and its integration into global circuits of 'uneven and combined' development, which locked in the policy options open to the ANC leadership during the transition to democracy. Bond's theoretical explanations are supported by John Saul, a respected and long-serving socialist scholar, who describes the ANC's choice of the neo-liberal option as ideological, a 'wholesale capitulation to the market' (2005: 208). He observes that a wave of business-friendly scenarios grew to force out earlier more progressive ideas, such as that of the 'dirigiste neo-Keynesianism' of the Macroeconomic Research Group (MERG) and the 'growth through redistribution' approach of some within the Alliance itself (Saul 2005: 205).

Bond's sell-out/betrayal view has also been supported by Stellenbosch academic Sampie Terreblanche. Terreblanche (2012: 3) speaks of the 'secret negotiations' that took place in the early 1990s over the future economic system for South Africa, between some members of the ANC leadership, powerful white South African capitalist interests, including the Oppenheimer empire of the Anglo American Corporation, and Western financial and political interests as represented by, among others, the Bretton Woods institutions and Western embassies. As a result, Terreblanche argues, the 'ANC leadership core was co-opted and bribed by black economic empowerment (BEE) deals so long as it would maintain fiscal austerity, deficit reduction and would keep taxation and expenditure as fixed proportions of the GDP' (2012: 69).

In an article in the British *Guardian* newspaper in 2013 headed 'How the ANC's Faustian pact sold out South Africa's poorest', former minister, Ronnie Kasrils, notes:

> From 1991 to 1996 the battle for the ANC's soul was under way, and was eventually lost to corporate power: we were entrapped by the neoliberal economy – or, as some today cry out we 'sold our people down the river' ... the ANC leadership needed to remain true to its commitment of serving the people ... [it] needed to remain determined, united and free of corruption, and above all, to hold on to its revolutionary will. Instead, we chickened out (Kasrils 2013b: n.p.).

In a new introduction to the fourth edition of his book *Armed and Dangerous*, Kasrils, quoting Terreblanche, speaks of 'secret late-night discussions' involving the leaders of American and British companies. They faced a team of 'young ANC economists schooled in Western economics', who were reporting to Nelson Mandela and who were 'either outwitted or gradually frightened into submission by hints pertaining to the dire consequences for the South African economy should the ANC government prevail with what were considered ruinous, unworkable and flawed Soviet-era forms of economic development' (Kasrils 2013a: xxv). He goes on:

> Agreement at the level of secret negotiating and endorsement in very broad terms later by an ANC–SACP leadership eager to assume political office (myself no less than others) sealed our Faustian moment. Those late-night deliberations were never revealed to the ANC's collective leadership at NEC [National Executive Committee] level nor to the SACP for that matter. Joe Slovo, SACP chairman and leading theoretician, engrossed with the 'sunset clause' golden-handshake pension pay-off for the racist old guard, knew nothing to my knowledge of the night-time shenanigans and certainly did not raise any alarm bells. We readily accepted that devil's pact and are damned in the process. It has bequeathed to our country an economy so tied into the neo-liberal global formula and market fundamentalism that there is very little room to alleviate the dire plight of the masses of our people (Kasrils 2013a: xxvi).

At one level, we share some of these sentiments, but the problem with these versions is that they remain trapped in a conspiratorial world view – powerful men in smoke-filled rooms in Washington and London pulling the strings in far-flung neo-colonies of a contemporary Western empire, with the active support of greedy local politicians. All of this is argued without offering any hard evidence, though of course by its nature such evidence is hard to come by. There is little doubt that Washington Consensus ideas and policy prescriptions did influence some of the key players in the ANC's economics boiler room (the Department of Economic Planning [DEP]) and in the academy. The 'high life' that came with cosying up to organisations such as the International Monetary Fund (IMF) cannot fail to have made an impact. But does this amount to consciously betraying the people's struggle in the interests of private accumulation and global capitalism, all led and forced through by a small team around the DEP during late negotiations and early democratic government? We think not. In fact, as we argue in this book, to contend this is to concede too much power to the DEP. In our view, the DEP team seriously lacked the kind of training in complex economics at a critical point in the trajectory of the discipline – the Soviet economic model had died and the old Washington Consensus was losing ground in the debates around the Asian miracle. Short executive courses in debt management at selected New York investment houses could never have been an adequate substitute. The 'end of history' had not happened as Francis Fukuyama (1992) had suggested, yet the ANC leadership seemed to think it had. It fell headlong into the hypothesis that there was no alternative to a narrow market-led economics model. As a result, we failed to create our own bit of history, to create our own distinctive mark on the kind of economic model that was needed to put an end to the appalling legacy of apartheid.

To be fair, we need to point out that Kasrils appears to have changed his argument somewhat. In our interviews with him, he admitted that after further reflection he no longer concurred with Terreblanche's narrative based on 'secret late-night trysts', while maintaining that the eventual neo-liberal outcomes did arise out of some degree of Western influence on the 'outwitted or frightened' local policymakers in the ANC at that time (Kasrils interviews, 30 March and 17 May 2017).

Hirsch was a researcher in the Economic Trends Research Group and the Industrial Policy Project, and later chief director for policy in the Thabo Mbeki Presidency. He argues that by taking the path it did in the 1990s, the ANC was, in fact, returning to its 1950s anti-colonial roots, an approach and economic programme following from a (black nationalist) bourgeois struggle against feudalism. Hirsch explains that 'the ANC approach is sometimes summarised as elements of a northern European approach to social development combined with Asian approaches to economic growth, within conservative macroeconomic parameters. This remains the intellectual paradigm within which the ANC operates' (2005: 4). He cites an article written by Mandela in 1956, in which the latter heralded 'the charter as a manifesto for, of all things, private enterprise' (Hirsch 2005: 34). Hirsch quotes Mandela as follows: 'For the first time in the history of this country, the non-European bourgeoisie will have the opportunity to own in their own name and right, the mills and factories, and trade and private enterprise will boom as never before' (Hirsch 2005: 34). He observes that 'interestingly, the passage on the "non-European bourgeoisie" was excluded from the version of the article included in the Ruth First collection of Mandela's writings published in 1965' (Hirsch 2005: 63).

For Hirsch, then, the ANC's flirtation with socialism in its exile years was simply a 'three-decade aberration, a consequence of the romance of the *uhuru* moment, the pull of Moscow and the power of the South African Communist Party (SACP), before Mbeki and others shifted things back to the centre in the mid-1980s (in

Gevisser 2007: 667). ANC activist and intellectual Khulu Mbatha shares this view, arguing that the Freedom Charter is a 'pro-capitalist document' and that '[t]he ANC has never at any period of its history advocated a revolutionary change in the economic structure of the country, nor has it, to the best of my recollection, ever condemned capitalist society' (Mbatha 2017: 132–133).

Gail Gerhart (1978) captures the thinking of the ANC at that time in a far more contextualised way. She reminds us that the mid-1950s was the period in which the ANC was most under attack from the apartheid regime for its supposed 'communist' links. In a lengthy submission to the Treason Trial, ANC President Albert Luthuli makes point similar to that of Mandela. 'The African business community has a full place in Congress and I personally regard African business enterprise as something to be encouraged' (Luthuli in Gerhart 1978: 119). But, as Gerhart points out, as far as future social and economic order commitments were concerned,

> the ANC remained firmly wedded to the liberal ideals for which it had always stood. It visualised a redistribution of wealth to blacks, but not an attack on class differences as such. It stood for a reallocation of land to give Africans their just share, but would never have countenanced the abolition of private land ownership. A controversial clause of the Freedom Charter called for the nationalization of mines, banks and monopoly industries, but this was seen as taking place within the framework of a predominantly capitalist system. 'It is certainly not Congress policy to do away with private ownership of the means of production,' Luthuli declared in the same statement to the Treason Trial (1978: 118–119).

This position is more social democratic than liberal, we would argue, but certainly not a narrow black (African) nationalism nor fully pro-capitalist.

Here is ANC/SACP veteran Ben Turok's response to Hirsch's argument:

> There can be no doubt that there were conflicting strands in the ANC, then and now. The CPSA [Communist Party of South Africa] view was reflected in Slovo's 'No Middle Road'. And the two Joes [Slovo and Matthews] certainly influenced the formulations in Morogoro. Also Mandela had strong nationalist views in his early days. But I think it is wrong to say the ANC wanted free reign for a bourgeois struggle. Indeed there was no thought of bourgeois leadership of the national movement. There were contradictions, yes, as in Prof Matthews' response to the economic clause in the Freedom Charter, but it was never class specific. Of course, we supported opening of the economy to Africans – trade, etc. But this was not overtly to block a later

advance to socialism which many took as given. What Thabo advocated was a kind of BEE to open the way for a bourgeois class. But it was never intended that that class should be hegemonic (Email exchange with Padayachee, 20 May 2015).

In similar vein, as late as 1988, Harold Wolpe, one of the movement's most critically incisive and influential intellectuals, who had chosen to remain firmly within the ANC–SACP fold despite reservations, noted: 'What is absolutely clear in the contemporary period is that no section of the national liberation movement is committed to, or struggles for, what may be termed a "bourgeois national democratic revolution"' (Wolpe 1990: 33).

Here is Alec Erwin on this point:

> Cosatu leadership met with Thabo Mbeki in 1987 or 1988. We were pleased to find that there was quite a lot of left thinking there, then quite important. We had meetings with Thabo Mbeki and Aziz Pahad, and Steve Tshwete and others, where we went into economics much more, and it became very clear that Mbeki's vision for the economy was also fairly clearly left social democratic, and his appreciation of international balance of power and capital was far better than ours. So we were feeling very comfortable with that (Erwin interview, 23 October 2015).

And the SACP deputy secretary general, Jeremy Cronin, expressed this as follows in our interview with him:

> The understanding of the ANC, I think – I suppose what the Freedom Charter for me would represent would be the crystallisation of a kind of radical democratic vision, let us call it that, within the ANC, which had been there potentially. But I think it is consolidated and it gets consolidated at the same time that the ANC becomes for the first time really a mass movement with, you know, a popular movement in the broader sense of the word (Cronin interview, 14 March 2016).

For Pallo Jordan, the Freedom Charter is not a socialist programme, but neither is it a conventional bourgeois democratic programme. For the petty bourgeoisie it may have been a maximum programme, which secured their class aspirations. For the SACP and the proletariat, it represents a minimum programme, which creates the conditions for a second phase of the revolution (Jordan 1984: n.p.).

It is, therefore, our view that it is unfair of Hirsch to dredge out a single obscure comment from Mandela to make a point (out of context) about the ANC's support for private enterprise in the 1950s. All the evidence suggests that the situation was far more complex, contingent and fluid than the simple picture of policy continuity that Hirsch presents. Furthermore, how does Hirsch reconcile this position with the view Mandela expressed in *Long Walk to Freedom* on the reasons for his attraction to Marxism: 'I found myself strongly drawn to the idea of a classless society which, to my mind, was similar to traditional African culture where life was shared and communal. I subscribed to Marx's basic dictum, which has the simplicity and generosity of the Golden Rule: "From each according to his ability, to each according to his needs"' (1994d: 120).

The point here is that the complexity, even ambiguity, of Mandela's position is not revealed by a crude and selective extraction of his views in particular political contexts. Hirsch's (2005: 5) argument, supported by some leading ANC comrades, including Trevor Manuel, was that there was no real alternative to a market-friendly approach in that context. He points out that the ANC leadership was acutely aware of prevailing domestic and international conditions, and was preoccupied with not giving up sovereignty to international financial capital, private or multilateral.

Hirsch places great store on the wisdom of the post-1990 ANC leadership, in particular Thabo Mbeki (later his boss) and Manuel, for making the correct policy choices, and for the conservatism and caution with which it approached economic policy formulation. So two things lie at the core of Hirsch's interpretation: firstly, that there was no alternative to a Washington Consensus approach to the economy in the 1990s, and secondly, that this approach coincided rather neatly with the ANC's historical commitment to private property, private enterprise, free trade and the growth of a black bourgeoisie.

THE ROLE OF SOUTH AFRICAN BUSINESS

In his paper on MERG, Bill Freund (2013: 527) emphasises the role of South African business and, in particular, stresses the meetings between Mandela and Harry Oppenheimer, the 'doyen of South African business'. As we shall see, there are differing views on the real content of business's role and its influence on ANC economic policy.

Freund also stresses the complementary role of a series of corporate scenarios: one from Old Mutual/Nedcor, a second from Sanlam, and the Mont Fleur bird-flight simulations of August 1992 (more about this later). Then there was the role of the Consultative Business Forum, a pressure group set up by 'liberal' and progressive local business leaders, whose aim was to engage the ANC on the economy.

But before we turn to these developments, it is worth commenting briefly on Anglo American Corporation CEO Gavin Relly's meeting with Oliver Tambo and the ANC in Lusaka in 1985. Relly apparently defied Oppenheimer,

> … who had ordered him to cancel the trip, and [Relly] led a delegation of seven Whites, including Tony Bloom of the Premier Group; Harald Pakendorf, editor of *Die Vaderland*; Tertius Myburgh, editor of the *Sunday Times*; Hugh Murray, editor of *Leadership SA*; and some opposition leaders. The ANC delegation included Oliver Tambo, Thabo Mbeki, Chris Hani, Mac Maharaj, Pallo Jordan and James Stuart. The meeting, hosted by Zambian President Kenneth Kaunda, took place at Mfuwe, Kaunda's presidential game lodge (South African History Online 2012: n.p.).

Former Anglo American chief economist Gavin Keeton recalls the scenario-planning work undertaken by Clem Sunter and others. Apparently not everyone at Anglo was happy with this 'diversion' from normal duties, but Relly was. The scenario-planning exercise, according to Keeton, was influential among the white population by giving them a sense of hope for a post-apartheid future (Keeton interview, 12 June 2015). Sunter (1987) even went so far as to present a copy of his book, *The World and South Africa in the 1990s*, to Mandela at Victor Verster Prison. He also presented it to the ANC leaders in Maputo sometime in the late 1980s.

In 1986, Relly visited the ANC in Lusaka. He is reported to have said: 'We accept the likelihood of some form of mixed economy with a measure of state planning and intervention … because there is a quite justifiable emphasis on the part of black South Africans on a more equitable distribution of wealth to compensate for the errors of omission and commission of the apartheid era' (Relly in Louw 1989: 80).

This is without doubt a very significant statement coming from someone who at the time was the head of the leading and most globalised capitalist corporate entity in the country. This view is picked up by Keeton, also a senior Anglo American executive at that time. Of significance and worth noting, as a precursor to Keeton's comments, is that in 1990, Anglo American placed an advertisement in a UK newspaper quoting clauses of the Freedom Charter on job creation, food, housing and education, asking how politicians could expect to deliver on these clauses if the (post-apartheid) economy could not. This was positively observed and picked up by Mandela himself in a major keynote speech he made to the Consultative Business Forum in May 1990 (Mandela 1990).

Keeton informs us that Anglo American leadership in the early 1990s began to explore various fiscal policy options to support some degree of post-apartheid redistribution. Briefing papers for the Anglo leadership were produced along these lines, until they realised, much to their surprise, that the ANC leadership was not interested in such options. This is a crucial point and it is worth quoting our exchange with Keeton on this:

> GK [Gavin Keeton]: I was involved in writing some briefing papers for our people involved in it … there was the talk at the time that … a percentage of the market capitalisation, the JSE [Johannesburg Stock Exchange], should be taken and put into a fund to help, you know, restructure South Africa. And then basically we were told, well … you must stop writing these things; the ANC is not interested … That is not what they want to do. So quite how that happened, I do not know.
> VP [Vishnu Padayachee]: Did you get a sense of what people thought the ANC wanted to talk about?
> GK: Well, I mean, I think already they began to think the ANC actually wants a very conservative fiscal policy. They do not want this sort of expenditure-type thing which people were looking to the capital market to fund (Keeton interview, 12 June 2015).

This significant observation by Keeton on the ANC's disinterest in redistributive options in the transition era (and no doubt welcomed by Anglo American) seemed to reflect a wider uncertainty in sections of Big Business about the policy direction of the ANC. Michael Spicer, a leading strategist in Anglo American and personal assistant to Relly when Mandela was released, expressed this view of ANC policy-making in the period leading up to and following the 1994 elections:

> The policy trajectory of the ANC was subject to multiple internal and external influences – the most celebrated was of course the Chinese and Vietnamese strong warnings to Mandela on nationalisation at Davos in the early 90s. Then there was the secondment of various ANC economic officials to Wall Street by Richard Gnodde of Goldman Sachs, and of course the impact of the fall of the Berlin Wall. The discussions at the Brenthurst Group were counterposed by the many groupings like MERG arguing for a much more socialist orientation [sic]. You will recall the interminable debates on whether the ANC should adopt a strong Anti-Trust policy, with Trevor Manuel threatening to tear Anglo apart 'limb from limb' …
> ANC policy evolved in a confused way, with lots of backwards and forwards, RDP being replaced by GEAR, and then reversing back in 2004 towards

the Developmental State. We in Anglo remained concerned about ANC economic policy throughout the period and had difficulty understanding where it was headed (Michael Spicer, email communication 14 April 2019).

Nevertheless, it would appear that Mandela often took the lead in cultivating close relationships with major international and local business people. He spent holidays with Clive Menell, the powerful head of one of the country's leading mining empires, and 'he entertained at the home of one of Johannesburg's most ostentatious business people, insurance magnate Douw Steyn, where guests were met in the driveway with champagne on silver salvers' (Waldmeir 1997: 255–256). Steyn, in fact, bought a luxurious home for Mandela (and Graça Machel) after his divorce from Winnie Mandela. We know little about any influence that Steyn might have had on Mandela on matters of economic policy. Perhaps not unexpectedly, key players in the business sector tend now to downplay their influence and that of big business on ANC economic policy thinking.

Bobby Godsell, a long-standing former executive director of Anglo American, responding to a question about this issue at a Wits workshop to launch a new project on the role of business in South Africa's transition, argued strongly against the view of big business's influence on Mandela and the ANC on economic policy. It was 'bullshit', he claimed, to argue that either the Brenthurst meetings (which he often attended) or the scenario-planning exercises directly impacted economic policy issues such as nationalisation (Wits University Seminar 2016).

Kalim Rajab (2017: 36–38), one-time personal assistant to Oppenheimer, points out that these meetings were set up at Mandela's suggestion. Initially one-on-one meetings between Mandela and Oppenheimer, they were soon extended to include other key players from both sides. They were chaired by Conrad Strauss, with Godsell part of the organising secretariat and Menell a key player from the side of business. ANC participants over time included Cyril Ramaphosa, Trevor Manuel, Tito Mboweni, Popo Molefe, Mosiuoa Lekota and Tokyo Sexwale. Godsell insists that these were no more than 'getting to know you' meetings, and that issues such as nationalisation and macroeconomic policy never featured. He makes the observation that neither Mandela nor Oppenheimer had much to say in these expanded meetings (Godsell interview, 5 April 2017). According to Erwin, these meetings were mostly about 'building confidence and preventing panic' (Email communication, 13 June 2017). Yet, Rajab maintains that the discussions were 'wide-ranging' and included labour issues and discussions on the role of free markets, globalisation and macroeconomic policy (2017: 38). Rajab argues that a much-debated aspect of Oppenheimer's contribution 'was in persuading the ANC on the merits of macroeconomic stewardship' (2017: 36).

The South African Foundation, an association of South Africa's largest corporations and multinational companies with a significant presence in South Africa, makes the point that 'one might have expected business in South Africa to exert a higher level of influence on economic policy than it has: in some respects, the diminutive business sector in Mauritius outplays us' (South African Foundation 2002: 10).

Spicer has a somewhat different take:

> The major point to make about this transitional period was that leading businesses invested heavily in influencing the transition because they believed it was necessary for their short, medium and long term interests. Organised business was populated by senior representatives of the leading companies who employed a significant range of specialists in the fields of public affairs, labour relations, economics and social investment. The relative coherence of corporate South Africa was therefore mirrored in organised business institutions ... Business too engaged intensively with all the parties in a myriad of consultations, conferences and seminars on prospective economic policy and, indeed, a wide range of other policy matters. A number of scenario planning exercises were carried out, building on the Anglo-American scenarios of the mid/late 1980s which had helped shape thinking of some elites (including senior National Party leaders) about the need for a negotiated future and an economy that was geared to the changing world environment (Spicer 2016: n.p.).

It is worth visiting the Mont Fleur scenario-planning exercise and understanding its impact on economic policy. The Mont Fleur Group, in which Pieter le Roux was a key figure and Manuel, then head of the ANC's DEP, a member, presented four scenarios about political options and the future of the South African economy. The first was the 'ostrich in the sand', a status quo option with the National Party government rejecting negotiations and going it alone. The second was the 'lame duck' option, a prolonged transition under a weak compromise government, in which no side was satisfied. The third was the 'Icarus', the bird that flew briefly, described by Hermann Giliomee (2012: 351) as 'a black government, unhampered by constitutional checks, embarking on a huge and unsustainable public spending programme that crashes the economy'. The fourth option was the 'flight of the flamingos', where 'everyone rises together' (Giliomee 2012: 351). Finance minister Derek Keys adapted these scenarios with fresh, in-depth data, reputedly provided by Rudolf Gouws, chief economist of Rand Merchant Bank, and presented it to FW de Klerk's Cabinet and to the ANC, among others. Manuel later relates the impact of the scenarios: 'It was very important because we were trying to understand the Icarus scenario and the dangers of macro-economic populism' (in Giliomee 2012: 351). A few years later, at the presentation of the Growth, Employment and Redistribution (GEAR) programme, Manuel stated: 'It's not a straight line [from Mont Fleur to GEAR]. It meanders through, but there's a fair amount in all of that going back to Mont Fleur … I could close my eyes now and give you those scenarios: then you probably carry it for life' (in Green 2008: 368). See below for more on the Mont Fleur scenarios.

On balance, our view is that South African business did play a significant role in influencing ANC thought on economic policy through moral suasion and efforts, such as the scenario-planning exercises – they punted a market-friendly approach to post-apartheid economic policy. The Mont Fleur exercise and the Brenthurst meetings appear to be significant, though to what extent remains debatable. However, if Keeton is right, by the early 1990s, the ANC leadership was already dismissive of some of the redistributive options that corporates such as Anglo American were prepared to consider.

THE ROLE OF THE LATE APARTHEID STATE

We argue throughout this book that the role of late apartheid economic leaders in the government and the civil service, as well as the well-resourced economic institutions of the late apartheid state, were more significant in the shaping of ANC economic policy in the 1990s than was big local business. As we have said, we cannot give this any mathematical weight, but it is clear that this influence has not been given much attention.

Derek Keys' role during the transition was central in our judgement, even though he left government after presenting the first democratic-era budget a few months after 27 April 1994 for personal reasons unrelated to any political or policy differences (Erwin, email communication, 13 June 2017).[2] His knowledge, institutional memory, seductive charm, inclusiveness and closeness to both De Klerk and Mandela, and his international and business networks, allowed this Johannesburg-born chartered accountant to rise to the status of a veritable institution all by himself. Keys' influence began (according to De Klerk, interview, 28 January 2019) when Keys met the ANC leadership for the first time at Fleur du Cap, the wine estate of business person Anton Rupert sometime in 1991, where he briefed them on the 'fiscal crisis' facing the state. He appears to have charmed Manuel, Mboweni and Erwin, and they, in turn, appear to have revered him. Here is Patti Waldmeir's interpretation of these relationships in the lead-up to 1994, as she speaks about the internal ANC ructions on the policy of nationalisation:

> Mandela would get some help in the struggle to bring his colleagues round to reality – from De Klerk's new Finance Minister, Derek Keys, a former businessman who became a great favourite with some top economic thinkers in the ANC. He had the clarity of vision to see what needed to be done, *and the political skill to persuade the ANC and the trade unions that they saw it first themselves.* He spent endless hours listening to the ANC and stroking its leaders. 'Alec Erwin was sent by God; Jay Naidoo, I embrace him', Keys used to tell everyone who would listen. After the adversarial relations of the past, the ANC welcomed his positive approach (1997: 256–257, emphasis added).

We concur with this judgement, and with Waldmeir's (1997: 257–258) assertion that out of Keys's crash courses in fiscal reality, an ANC team emerged 'with as powerful a commitment to budgetary discipline and fiscal conservatism as white South Africa could have wished for'. Keys also made sure to warn his old National Party colleagues not to 'crow about' their successes in this regard (Waldmeir 1997: 258).

But what even Waldmeir fails to point out is that Keys was not alone in this effort. On taking office in mid-1992, he quickly assembled a formidable economics capacity from the late apartheid economics institutions, including his Ministry of Finance, the South African Reserve Bank (SARB) and the Central Economic Advisory Services (CEAS). It was CEAS that led the research behind what became the government's market-friendly Normative Economic Model, published in 1993 at the height of the negotiations. And he then had the great tactical sense to draw the young and inexperienced ANC economics team into that market-friendly world with skill and grace, first in the multi-party Economics Technical Committee, which was established in the run-up to the formation of the cross-party Transitional Executive Council (TEC) in December 1993, and later in the Government of National Unity.

Jaya Josie, who, because of his public finance training in Britain, was involved in the drafting of the democratic government's first budget, stresses the domineering role of the CEAS economists Jan Lombard, Jan Dreyer and Hannes Smith, and of Estian Calitz, then the director general of finance and a former senior economist at CEAS, in this process. It was through this budgeting exercise, according to Josie, that the ANC comrades first came to really learn of the degree to which the apartheid government was indebted (mostly to the local banks) and to the reality that there would be no apartheid dividend (Josie interview, 30 January 2015).

It would appear that the issue of debt was central to the coming together of the old and the new guard. Calitz explains that both the National Party and the ANC feared debt, though for different reasons and that this common fear drove the bonding that occurred. This fear of debt surprised even the IMF's Michael Bruno, according to Calitz.

> Bruno said was that he was so surprised when he came to South Africa, because he has never observed a country going through the sort of dramatic political change that South Africa was going through, where he found people so wary of debt. And I was wondering, why is this so, because I experienced it before the change and after the change. So what is the common denominator in this? I am not sure that I know the answer, but something that occurred to me at the time was, both before and after 1994, the incumbents were wary of foreign intervention but for different reasons. Before 1994, the National Party in government was dead scared of being prescribed to. You can look at speeches by P.W. Botha [which insist that] 'we will not let the outside world prescribe or dictate to us'. After 1994, there was another wariness of the new government – that is, of conditionalities by the IMF and the World Bank, which is one of the reasons why they wouldn't want an IMF loan (Calitz interview, 1 March 2015).

Both parties also had an interest in securing foreign investment flows to South Africa and were prepared to adjust positions to facilitate this, both before and after 1994. Here is Calitz again on this:

> There was this meeting in London after Mandela was released; it must have been early 1991 then, after Davos. He addressed investors in London and they were very wary about the nationalisation policy of the ANC, and he was quoted as saying that 'nationalisation is the policy of the ANC, but if that is going to prevent South Africa from getting foreign investment', he himself will try and persuade the ANC to change that. So I think the leadership of Mandela very often comes as a very important factor, but of course he had to be convinced as well (Calitz interview, 1 March 2015).

Although he would not be drawn on any one person who did the 'convincing', it is clear to us that someone like Keys, whom Mandela respected, would have been a major player in this process.

To sum up: most interpretations of the economics of the South African transition note, but then either misunderstand or underestimate, the role of the late apartheid state and its key economic institutions and personnel such as Keys and Chris Stals and their respective economics teams. It was so much more romantic for progressive commentators, such as Pippa Green and Mark Gevisser, to exaggerate the credentials and role of the 'trailblazing cowboys' of Shell House (see chapter 3).

Yet, unlike some other colleagues (Bond, Saul, Terreblanche), we do not interpret the actions of the DEP members at Shell House as some sort of purposive 'betrayal' or 'sell-out'. However, in our view, they did fail the democratic movement in some crucial ways: by too easily embracing a Washington Consensus world view and arguing that 'there was no alternative'; by believing naively in the face of sound international evidence that there was a linear connection between the embrace of (old) Washington Consensus prescriptions (liberalisation) and future flows of foreign investment and from there, higher rates of economic growth;[3] by failing to engage more openly and courageously with the relatively moderate structuralist/ post-Keynesian/social democratic economic ideas and policy recommendations coming out of their own think tank, MERG; by giving political backing to those (white) academic economists mainly from the liberal universities who, eager to place themselves at the top of the list for future government positions, set about brutally rubbishing the ideas of comrades such as Vella Pillay, John Sender and Ben Fine, simply because they were 'foreigners' or 'British communists'; by failing to engage in structured debate on ideas and policies within the democratic movement at branch and regional levels, giving favour instead only to the views of the top leadership of the ANC, in this way losing touch with one of its greatest moral and political assets, the 'need(s) of the people on the ground' (Hani in Saul and Bond 2014: 135).

It is not our role or place to criticise the decision made in terms of the 'sunset clauses' proposed by Joe Slovo in the 'Record of Understanding' of September 1992, among which was a guarantee that white civil servants would retain their pensions and their jobs for five years of the incoming administration. We were not there directly, and we would not presume to know of the pressures, tensions and risks that drove the decision.[4]

Yet, just this single decision for the economics of the transition was damaging to the policy formulation of the kind of socio-economic restructuring that was so essential to the goal of making 'freedom and democracy worthwhile to ordinary South Africans' (Hani in Saul and Bond 2014: 135). In those crucial few years on both sides of 1994, the die was cast on many policy issues, including abandoning MERG and the RDP and embracing GEAR, the ghost of which lives with us even today.

No less an authority than Wolpe (1995: 88) drew attention in a prescient paper on the 'uneven transition from apartheid' as to whether a 'fundamental transformation' of South African society was posed by the implementation of post-apartheid government policy through the mechanism of the RDP in its drastically revised post-election White Paper form. In his paper, Wolpe (1995) agreed with the argument presented by Asghar Adelzadeh and Vishnu Padayachee in their own paper (1994) that the RDP in the revised form of the White Paper represented a fundamental retreat from the redistributive impetus of the original RDP Base Document, evidenced in the dropping of consideration of mechanisms of redistribution, such as nationalisation, for example, and the introduction of privatisation into the policy lexicon of the new state (referred to euphemistically as the 'sale of state assets'). Wolpe argued that the RDP, while operating on a deeply contested terrain, eradicated sources of contradiction and conflict by either presuming or asserting harmony, and, on the basis of this premise, conceptualised the state as the unproblematic instrument of the RDP. He further argued that the impressive empirical accounts of welfare, housing and educational delivery of the first year of the first democratic government could not be assessed in relation to the claimed goal of the RDP White Paper of a 'fundamental transformation', as, taken on their own, they represented an important but largely disparate set of sectoral objectives, which were not clearly indicated as part of an overall agenda of social change. The achievement of these important empirical objectives of delivery was nonetheless '*perfectly consistent with something far less than systematic "fundamental transformation"*', putting at issue, for Wolpe, the use of the term in the RDP White Paper (Wolpe 1995: 91, emphasis added). Of course, it is pertinent to pause and draw attention here that it is precisely the failure of these sectoral objectives in education and welfare to be sustained in the current era, most tellingly represented in service delivery failures, that points to the absence of a coherent strategy of systematic 'fundamental transformation', which Wolpe drew attention to 24 years ago. What then is the overarching political strategy for achieving fundamental transformation? This critical question Wolpe posed then has perhaps an even more profound relevance today and in a sense is one of the primary questions our book attempts to offer a response to.

THE ROLE OF THE INTERNATIONAL MONETARY FUND AND THE WORLD BANK

Many commentators have attributed the shift in ANC economic policy to the influence of the IMF and the World Bank. In particular, they cite the impact of the 1993 IMF loan to South Africa on the eve of the democratic elections as a central factor.[5] In a report based on his latest book, Allan Boesak, an anti-apartheid activist, clergyman and United Democratic Front (UDF) leader, makes the following claim: 'This negotiated settlement was sold to the ANC by Western economists and institutions such as the International Monetary Fund and the World Bank, which argued for the adoption of a neo-liberal capitalist system and property ownership model, warning that the alternative was an outdated communist model which would damage the economy' (2017: n.p.).

This line echoes that of Terreblanche (2012). There can be little doubt that the IMF and the World Bank would have used moral suasion to argue against any sort of socialist or communist model for a post-apartheid economy; that is after all to be expected. However, we argue that neither institution had a suitable vehicle to force a neo-liberal policy platform down the throats of the ANC unless the latter had itself come to that view through other means. As we claim here, a combination of internal forces – including local business, the late apartheid state's residual power and the views of *some* top ANC economic leaders – was more influential in the ANC's rightward drift to neo-liberalism.

The IMF and the World Bank were established at the Bretton Woods conference in New York State in 1944. Typically, since at least the early 1980s, they played two key roles in influencing economic policy in developing countries. Firstly, they both acted to some extent as idea banks, based on their ideology, their research and comparative experiences. Secondly, they influenced borrowing countries through what is referred to as 'conditionality' – the policy measures such nations had to comply with as a pre-condition for an IMF loan. The ideological underpinnings of the IMF and the World Bank have been described as neo-liberal by many on the left, and even by the IMF itself (Ostry, Loungani and Furceri 2016). It consisted of a package of market-driven policies favouring liberalisation of trade and financial flows, fiscal conservatism, flexible labour markets and the like. In their article 'Neoliberalism', Jonathan Ostry, Prakash Loungani and Davide Furceri argue convincingly that despite many caveats, the IMF finally admitted, on the basis of the evidence, that it was wrong in some policy areas, such as its blanket endorsement of capital account liberalisation (2016).

The International Monetary Fund

South Africa under apartheid received its first loan from the IMF in the financial year 1957/1958 and its last in 1981; the latter was repaid in full in 1987. The IMF returned to South Africa after 1990 as a relatively quiet and minor player, and now mainly plays its role as a knowledge and ideas bank. In 1992, it published its first major report on the country, which focused on the growth policies it believed were needed in the country (Lachman and Bercuson 1992). The report was both predictable and pessimistic. It recommended that external trade and financial relations should be liberalised – exchange controls to be abolished, albeit gradually, as its later pronouncements made clear – as a strategy to eliminate balance of payments deficits (Padayachee 1997: 30ff.). Later, once sufficient consensus had in its view been reached about a more inclusive and democratic government in the negotiations, the IMF received an application through the TEC for a Compensatory and Contingency Financing Facility (CCFF) of US$850 million.[6] Padayachee observed that 'the loan was designed (purportedly) to support South Africa's balance of payments following the decline in agricultural exports and the increase in agricultural imports caused by the prolonged drought' (1997: 32). However, as Bond (2001: 68) has pointed out, the drought ended 18 months before then, thus raising concerns about the logic of the application. The IMF approved the loan on condition that a 'legitimate body gave its undertaking that the economy was responsibly managed' – in our view, a low- or no-conditionality approval. The Letter of Intent, which accompanied the loan, warned in general terms against the dangers of increases in real wages in both the private and public sectors, stressed the importance of controlling inflation, supported trade and industrial liberalisation, and repeatedly espoused the virtues of market forces over regulatory interventions. In the Letter of Intent, ostensibly drawn up by the borrowing government (in this case the TEC) but normally drafted by the IMF, the TEC also promised *to consider* the introduction of 'inflation targeting' and a cut in the budget deficit to 6 per cent of GDP 'within a few years' (Padayachee 1997: 32). These were far from the usual stringent IMF conditionalities. Thus, in our view, the loan came with no typical conditionalities, though there are differing opinions on the subject. Terreblanche argues that a close reading of the Letter of Intent reveals that 'it was the GEAR policy of 1996 in embryo form. The document committed the TEC to the ideologies of neo-liberalism and market fundamentalism' (Terreblanche 2012: 64; see also Bond 2000: 178–179).

Why do we differ? It has to be noted that if a country borrows within its Special Drawing Rights (SDR) quota – that is, if the loan could be accessed from its own reserves at the IMF (a reserve tranche drawdown) – there is normally minimal or no conditionality. That was the case here. South Africa borrowed only 45 per cent of its quota, and, if no other obligations were due in 1993 (as seems the case), there would have been no or very minimal conditions in terms of IMF policy (Cyrus Rustomjee, former special adviser to the deputy minister of finance and former South African representative at the IMF, email exchange, 11 December 2017). Sharing our view, Fine points out that 'the loan came without conditions. People think, oh, they took the IMF loan and therefore they had to implement the programme; the IMF loan came without conditions' (Fine interview, 30 June 2015).

IMF historian James Boughton argues from a more political angle that 'entering into a stand-by arrangement with the IMF, with all of the attendant policy conditions, would have been unthinkable for the authorities as well as for the IMF' (2012: 692).

Our interpretation is also shared by the then DEP deputy head, Tito Mboweni, later governor of the SARB. He strongly refutes the view that the ANC sold out by accepting a loan with specific conditionalities:

> The end result was that we agreed to that request by the then government to approach the IMF for the required balance of payments support called the Compensatory and Contingency Financing Facility (CCFF). There were no conditionalities attached since this was a soft loan as it were. However, we had to provide the IMF with a 'Statement on Economic Policy'. The statement was fairly simple: assure the IMF that the future government will pursue prudent macroeconomic policies. This was something that the ANC in particular had adopted as an approach as early as 1992 in a document entitled – Ready to Govern. We did not sell out! … I emphasise that any careful reading of the statement will find no contradiction with Ready to Govern. But that is a matter for political economists to sort out in due course (Mboweni 2004: 1–2).

So, what was the logic for the application? The Letter of Intent was clearly in preparation as early as November 1993, well before the TEC began its work. This does lend credence to the view that it was the National Party government that pushed for the loan (Mutize 2017). It should be no surprise that Finance Minister Keys was again an important player here. Waldmeir's account is somewhat simplistic but she does make an important point: '[Derek] Keys' *all party economic team*, the Economic Technical Committee', played a central role in persuading the parties of the value of such an application to the IMF. The ANC, she argues, 'had finally bought into the world consensus on good economic government, and was applauded internationally for so doing' (Waldmeir 1997: 258). She claims that the De Klerk regime 'could not believe their luck at the economic transformation of their adversaries, though Keys ensured that they judiciously avoided crowing about it, which might have jeopardised the conversion' (Waldmeir 1997: 258).[7]

On 5 November 1993, the DEP head, Trevor Manuel, requested comment from the MERG office on the draft IMF Letter of Intent, and especially its quantitative dimensions. Manuel sent the draft letter to MERG via the National Economic Forum. John Sender's cover letter to Manuel, following discussion held with some MERG researchers, who were then based at the Wits Department of Economics, is worth quoting in full, as it has never been referred to by any source before. Sender replied as follows:

Dear Trevor,

I think the 'quantification' is less important than some of the ideological biases, or the theoretical straight jacket that Keys/IMF would like to lock the next government into. If you accept, or make explicit, the sort of theory they are pushing, then a wide range of *policy* options become closed.

I have tried to eliminate the phrases which suggest acceptance of inadequate and failed theory, as well as those phrases likely to cause trouble with Cosatu. I don't think it is worth fussing too much about the quantification on page 4, since it is qualified by words like 'aim', 'about', 'projected'. There are all sorts of legitimate reasons why government's aims might be frustrated and approximate, projected targets not actually realised.

Finally, the *best* method of negotiating on these letters is to call upon the services of powerful people in Washington, rather than negotiate with [Leslie] Lipschitz or delegations to S.A. Have you considered approaching the Clinton administration directly, or lobbying the IMF representatives of the Scandinavian, Dutch countries who could put pressure on the Fund at the Executive Board level …

p.p. Signed John Sender (Vishnu Padayachee private archive, original emphasis)

An attachment of one and half pages sets out the changes, deletions and additions that Sender proposed (in Vishnu Padayachee private archive).

We do not know if Manuel followed Sender's suggestion to lobby likely allies (though we doubt he did), nor if the letter was debated at the DEP. What we do know is that the Letter of Intent was kept a secret for months until it was leaked to *Business Day* in March 1994. It only then became clear that none of the even relatively modest and pragmatic changes proposed by Sender made it into that final approved Letter of Intent. So either the proposed changes were presented by the ANC/TEC to the IMF and simply ignored by the latter, or they were never presented to the IMF by the South African side.

The Letter of Intent was signed off on 3 December 1993 by the IMF and on the South African side by Keys on behalf of the TEC, Dawie de Villiers on behalf of the National Party and Pravin Gordhan on behalf of the ANC Alliance. It was ratified on 7 December 1993 when the TEC formally came into effect. Bond was working as the co-ordinator of the RDP at the time, and he remarks that the IMF's managing director, Michel Camdessus, put intense pressure on the TEC to ensure the reappointment of Finance Minister Keys and SARB Governor Chris Stals (Bond 2000: 155ff.).

If we are correct in our interpretation, it suggests that the loan was not really needed for balance of payments reasons, but rather that it was a signal of the IMF's 'stamp of approval' for South Africa's democratic transition and its economic policies – in effect encouraging private international lending, trade and investment to the country. At that critical stage in South Africa's transition, such approval must have been regarded as important to Keys and the late apartheid government, even perhaps to some of the incoming ANC leadership. Boughton makes the point clearly: 'Major creditor countries recognized the global political importance of aiding the transition to democracy, but they also knew they had to have some assurance that committing money to the country would help and would not be wasted. The IMF, with its technical expertise and its regular dialogue with the authorities, was the natural conduit for determining when and how the international community could safely resume lending to South Africa' (2012: 692).

The ANC concern about likely IMF and World Bank interference with its sovereignty, and the potential of a popular backlash based on historically grounded understandings of the role of the IMF in other parts of Africa since the 1980s, came to the fore again once this interim stage was over. Effectively in power after April 1994, the ANC leadership was able to push its own policy stance. It resisted all early attempts by Camdessus to persuade the new government to accept more of its facilities. Misheck Mutize has this view on the ANC's stance: 'When the African National Congress (ANC) came to power after the elections in April 1994 it walked away from the IMF offer. Its concern was mainly that the IMF would undermine the sovereignty of the newly established democracy by imposing inappropriate policy choices that would have further harmed poor people' (2017: n.p.).

Boughton makes the same point:

> When the new government showed no inclination to seek the Fund's help, [Camdessus] sent Alassane Ouattara [deputy managing director][8] to Cape Town in February 1995 to discuss the matter with Mandela and other officials, but Ouattara found that much of the leadership was still hostile to the IMF. A visit by First Deputy Managing Director Stanley Fischer in December was no more productive. Bitter memories persisted of the Fund's past support to the minority government, and many political leaders believed that IMF lending would come with unacceptable restraints on economic policies and would threaten the country's sovereignty (Boughton 2012: 695).

After GEAR was in place and following a visit by Camdessus to Mandela's home in October 1996, an IMF loan looked a better than even bet. Why would the managing director himself visit Mandela unless something big was in the offing? But while the world awaited the formal announcement of an IMF loan to South Africa, the ANC informed the world that it had vetoed any new borrowings from the Fund (Boughton 2012: 698).

From Table 5.1, it appears that democratic South Africa repaid the CCFF loan in full in 1997 and 1998, disaggregated into eight separate quarterly payments over these two years. This was clearly delayed payment, as repayment for CCFF loans at the time had to be made within 30 days. Delays are typically recorded as such, but no such 'default' record can be found in this situation – clearly a case of condonation in the context of a perceived need not to take a hard line against Mandela's ANC government.

It has been much more difficult to track down whether (and despite its concerns) the ANC-led government, in fact, drew down on the US$850 million CCFF facility in order to strengthen its balance of payments, and (if it did) in what ways did it utilise the loan to this end? When interviewed on this matter, key state officials of that time were initially stumped. Cyrus Rustomjee argues that it may have been drawn down, but he is not certain (Email exchange, 11 December 2017). Many officials then at either the National Treasury or the SARB, when asked 25 years later, initially claimed (embarrassingly) not to remember whether it was drawn down or not. After further investigation and many leads, we received an email on 10 December 2017 from Johan Krynauw, a long-standing official of the Treasury and programme manager at the National Treasury's Public Debt Management division, who confirmed our suspicion. Speaking of developments after 1994, he states that 'I can't remember a time where the National Treasury of South Africa ever drew down on an IMF facility'.

This official confirmation strengthens our argument that the IMF loan was no more than a stamp of approval, pushed by Keys and the National Party, that it came with no or very low conditionality, and that it had little or no effect on the economic policy positions of the ANC or the ANC-led Government of National Unity. This conclusion, if correct, punches a hole in the Faustian pact argument of those claiming that the ANC was pushed towards neo-liberalism by the stringent 'conditionalities' imposed by the IMF on the 1993 CCFF.

So here is our ironic conclusion:

- The ANC leadership did not make use of the IMF loan for fear of compromising its sovereignty and a potential popular backlash.
- Yet, the ANC leadership was persuaded or pressurised by other (mainly internal) forces of the need for a (self-imposed) austerity programme to defend a perceived threat to the fiscus.
- The end result was arguably the worst possible outcome – IMF policies without IMF support![9]

Table 6.1: South Africa: Transactions with the IMF from 1 May 1984 to 30 November 2017 (in SDRs)

Year	General Resources Account			Poverty Reduction and Growth Trust[1,2]			Total		
	Purchases		Charges Paid	Loans		Interest Paid	Purchases and Loans		Charges and Interest Paid
	Disbursements	Repurchases		Disbursements	Repayments		Disbursements	Repayments	
1999	0	0	462,100	0	0	0	0	0	462,100
1998	0	307,215,000	11,333,206	0	0	0	0	307,215,000	11,333,206
1997	0	307,215,000	24,476,971	0	0	0	0	307,215,000	24,476,971
1996	0	0	27,295,661	0	0	0	0	0	27,295,661
1995	0	0	33,020,481	0	0	0	0	0	33,020,481
1994	0	0	26,723,328	0	0	0	0	0	26,723,328
1993	614,430,000	0	0	0	0	0	614,430,000	0	0
1988	0	0	86,579	0	0	0	0	0	86,579
1987	0	397,500,000	16,520,044	0	0	0	0	397,500,000	16,520,044
1986	0	347,500,000	42,213,452	0	0	0	0	347,500,000	42,213,452
1985	0	0	52,126,186	0	0	0	0	0	52,126,186
1984	0	0	38,308,471	0	0	0	0	0	38,308,471

[1] Includes loans under the Structural Adjustment Facility and Trust Fund.
[2] Formerly Poverty Reduction and Growth Facility and Exogenous Shocks Facility Trust.

Source: Padayachee and Fine (2018), drawn from International Monetary Fund Confidential Staff Reports.

The World Bank

South Africa was a founder member of the World Bank. It received many large loans from the Bank for infrastructural development in the 1950s – for example, to establish Eskom. It received its last loan (to Eskom) in 1966, and had repaid this by 1976. After 1990, the World Bank sent many missions to South Africa to begin research and consultations with relevant parties, including the ANC. This was unusual, given that it did not typically engage in discussions with anyone other than elected governments and their agencies. That was why the TEC was key.

After discussions with the Bank president, Lewis Preston, and the Africa Region vice president, Edward Jaycox, between November 1991 and February 1992, Mandela gave the signal for the Bank to start preparing projects for an interim government, and the Bank's programme was accelerated (World Bank 1993b).

On 1 March, the Bank's Africa vice president wrote to Mandela, underlining 'the critical importance of an advance indication of the areas where the new South Africa would want World Bank investments to be directed and the institutional framework that it would want to support them' (Nelson Mandela Papers, Box 66, Folder 678). This letter was sent to the DEP. Yet, the DEP appears to have been reluctant to move forward with World Bank project financing. Manuel wrote a short note to the Office of the President under the subject reference 'World Bank': 'No, Don't want them to take policy matters out of our hands. We are involved in initiatives of Wiseman [Nkuhlu] and Eric [Molobi] and [at the] end of the day we would want to be calling the shots on issues.' Mandela replied to Manuel in what appears to be a rather terse handwritten note: 'Your brief response does not give me any indication whether "our calling the shots on the issues" means we have progressed to the degree of capability to get funds at the point of transitional government. Would you please favour us with a response that attempts to respond to the issues raised?' (Nelson Mandela Papers, Box 66, Folder 678).

This trail of correspondence from the archival papers then went cold on us.

Hirsch (2005) has traced the debates on and formulation of economic policy back to the numerous 'post-apartheid economy' international conferences involving various combinations of ANC Alliance constituencies and supporting intellectuals. He argues that the ANC was acutely aware of prevailing domestic and international conditions, and was preoccupied with 'not giving up sovereignty to international financial capital, private or multilateral' (Hirsch 2005: 5). Manuel makes a similar point: 'We were completely determined to retain our sovereign right to take decisions – this meant no borrowings from the Bretton Woods institutions – a record we retained until 2010 when we had to guarantee Eskom's borrowings' (Private email exchange between Manuel and Adam Habib, December 2010).[10]

What can one make of this argument about the 'need to maintain our sovereignty'? How real was this 'fear' of being forced to comply with the dictates of international organisations such as the IMF and the World Bank? Or, is this concern (with its echoes of anti-neo-colonial rhetoric) a proxy for some other factors at work at that time? It is true that since the mid-1980s some of us had warned about the dangers of becoming caught in the trap of IMF/World Bank conditionalities that would force us to give up progressive economic policy options in favour of the Washington Consensus line. Thus, in a paper given at the first conference to discuss the post-apartheid economy held at York in 1986, Padayachee argued: 'Revolutionary governments, especially in the developing world, have found that it has often been as hard to live with the IMF as it has been to live without its support … The IMF … can very well form an integral part of the formidable weaponry available to the West in shaping the emergence, nature and development of a post-apartheid South Africa (1988: 202).

But the concern expressed by Padayachee (1988) was clearly about the danger to a progressive economic stance from the side of the Bretton Woods institutions. Padayachee had no inkling at that time that he had to concern himself with an attack by the IMF on a government that would adopt a self-imposed form of Washington Consensus macroeconomic and development strategy.

So, when it became apparent that the ANC leadership had by sometime in 1992 already reconciled itself to an approach to the post-apartheid economic policy framework that was very close to the Washington Consensus line, what was there to fear from the IMF and the World Bank? It may be argued that it was the fear of being caught in a debt trap sometime in the future, based on fiscal ill-discipline in the early post-apartheid years. Hence the need to demonstrate fiscal discipline from the very beginning.

Presumably, given the latter consideration and within the context of a negotiated settlement, the ANC was left with little or no room to manoeuvre on economic policy options. There was simply no alternative! While fully aware of the alternative ideas proposed by, among others, the ANC's own policy think tank, the Macroeconomic Research Group, and recognising some useful research reports coming out of MERG, Hirsch (2005: 55–57) nonetheless argues that the MERG proposals were more 'muddled than revolutionary', in his view, but that is perhaps more a reflection of his own ideological disposition at the time. Furthermore, by placing such an onus on state-led development, MERG did not reckon with the realities of a likely incompetent, inexperienced and even treacherous bureaucracy and civil service (Hirsch 2005: 55–57). He points to MERG proposals, such as on the budget deficit (ironically, similar to that considered to be feasible by the World Bank at the time) and the independence of the SARB (Hirsch 2005: 57). As Freund observes: 'Yet the World Bank was well informed about South African conditions and was prepared to tolerate and even approve radical reform: it is from World Bank consultants that the ANC acquired the idea of the racial transfer of a substantial amount of land (30% of white owned land)' (2013: 526).

Of significance and worth pausing to mention in more detail here is the development of the ANC's policies on land reform in the transition era. The evidence suggests it mirrored the largely under-capacitated, poorly equipped policy-making processes in economic and social policy in both the transition era (1990–1993) and the democratic era (post-1994). In an illuminating account on this, Marinda Weideman (2004: 223–226) explains how the ANC before and by 1990 had no policy on land or agrarian reform and that it did not feature high on the ANC's policy-making agenda, citing influential ANC land policy researcher Helena Dolny's illustration that less than a handful of people attended a 1986 reading group she organised for the ANC to debate the relevance of land reform for a post-apartheid South Africa. In its engagement with land policy at a first conference in Lusaka in early 1990, nationalisation was still a dominant theme for the ANC, but this subsequently shifted at a second conference in Lusaka in May 1990 (after its unbanning) to more 'convoluted' discussions on, among other matters, regulated land markets and the reintroduction of share-cropping as a mechanism for addressing landlessness (Weideman 2004: 225). At the same time, the National Party and its well-resourced policy-making apparatus had produced its White Paper on Land Reform in 1991, which, while repealing racist legislation on land ownership, maintained the market-dominated status quo on land ownership (which remained privately owned) and the neo-liberal trend of liberalisation and deregulation established in agriculture in the 1980s (Weideman 2004: 220–221).

What is not disputable based on the available evidence is that the World Bank played a decisive role in influencing the ANC's land reform policy, as eventually set out in the ANC's 1993 document, 'Options for Land Reform and Rural Restructuring in South Africa' (World Bank 1993a). This document was preceded by a range of policy-oriented documents on land reform in 1991 and 1992, 'produced by prominent World Bank representatives, agricultural economists from the University of Pretoria, former staff of the Development Bank of Southern Africa (DBSA), and over a hundred (often "progressive") social scientists and lawyers, mostly contracted to the LAPC [Land and Agricultural Policy Centre, effectively the ANC's policy think tank on land in the transition and immediate democratic era]' (Weideman 2004: 223).

Prominent authors included Hans Binswanger, Masiphula Mbongwa, Klaus Deininger, Bill Kinsey, Heinz Klug, Robert Christiansen, Bongiwe Njobe, Nick Vink and David Cooper. According to Weideman: 'The World Bank managed to give legitimacy to its [land reform] research and proposals by hiring ANC-aligned and some "radical" South African researchers' (2004: 223). She quotes an interview with a senior researcher, then working for the progressive National Land Committee: 'Of course, the synthesis that the Bank [eventually] produced was distorted but, by then, the research was legitimated' (Weideman 2004: 223).

Prominent scholar of land Henry Bernstein tellingly recalls the subordinate position ANC-aligned land reform researchers found themselves in with regard to external experts such as those of the World Bank: 'A few individuals charged by the ANC with formulating (or conjuring) land and agricultural policies were overwhelmed by representations, models and prescriptions from a variety of quarters. South African and external ... ideological skill, policy analysis and advice were supplied by the World Bank and other agencies, the plane loads of consultants attached to them and the rest of the internationally mobile usual suspects' (Bernstein in Weideman 2004: 223). Or, according to a source who attended the first LAPC workshop in Swaziland, 'these guys were technically superior and excellent lobbyists, nobody from South Africa was at that level. We just sat there and were lectured to' (Weideman 2004: 223).

Returning again to the various twists and turns of the World Bank's role in South African economic policy-making processes in particular, Padayachee (1997: 33) points out that the Bank advanced a view that a judicious and targeted public sector investment related to infrastructural development to benefit the poor would be an important element of any growth strategy. How different was this from a principal MERG recommendation? Hein Marais quotes the Bank as saying that 'South Africa's unequal legacy cannot be reversed solely by market reforms' (Marais 2011: 102). In a World Bank Southern African Department working paper written by Pedro Belli, Michael Finger and Amparo Ballivian (1993), the Bank sets out its most progressive views on macroeconomic policy. The authors begin by reminding us that because of financial sanctions South Africa had an unusually low foreign debt to GDP ratio and that savings as a percentage of private disposable income were unusually high (Belli, Finger and Ballivian 1993: 7). Typically associated with prescriptions of reducing budget deficits and controlling inflation, the Bank (recognising some room to manoeuvre, as it were) proposed that as long as GDP growth of 5 per cent per annum could be attained, a fiscal deficit as high as 6 per cent of GDP might be sustainable (Belli, Finger and Ballivian 1993: 15). Furthermore, while too much should not be expected of monetary policy, it warned that South African monetary 'authorities need to consider the consequences for the real economy of quickly reducing inflation much below its present levels [about 8 per cent at the time of the 1994 elections]' (Belli, Finger and Ballivian 1993: 14). Of course, we need to be careful, even retrospectively, about being bowled over by all of this, because, as Marais also reminds us, the Bank's views on South Africa at the time 'were studded with contradictions' (Marais 2011: 101–102).

Our research, including the total picture that emerges from interviews with most of the key economic policymakers in the ANC, leads us to a somewhat controversial conclusion. That is that the ANC economic and political leadership appeared to have been convinced, rightly or wrongly, and perhaps somewhat naively, about the merits of economic liberalisation, the value of (orthodox) fiscal discipline, and the importance of an independent central bank. They viewed these policy stances as being 'progressive' moves to increase foreign capital inflows and trade, avoid borrowing from the IMF and, above all, to retain 'national sovereignty'. This view accords with those of London School of Economics anthropologist Jason Hickel based on his own independent interviews with early ANC appointees to the SARB and the National Treasury. Hickel maintains that these policymakers saw their stance as progressive, 'either by their own accord or by their interlocutors' (2016: 7).

It is for these reasons that we reject Boesak's contention with which we began this section.

A FAUSTIAN PACT? WHERE IS THE EVIDENCE?

Well-known and highly respected left-wing academic and solidarity activist John Saul leads a glittering cast of commentators (Bond, Terreblanche, Mbatha, among others) who have argued in essence that the ANC's elite bourgeois nationalist faction consciously betrayed and sold out the values of the movement's long 'noble struggle' by capitulating to powerful forces, such as local and international capital, to serve both their own class interests as well as the interests of local and international capital. While we accept that some element of this may have existed in the 1990s, the evidence leads us to draw different conclusions regarding the political process by which this was done. We found no hard evidence that suggests that the compromises that were made were the outcome of some kind of conspiracy – talks between the ANC and Western interests held at secret locations in the dead of the night – as claimed by Terreblanche (2012: chap. 4). What is his evidence?

Terreblanche refers to the regular meetings between Mandela and Oppenheimer at Anglo American's headquarters after Mandela's release. Here, it would seem, the limits of the ANC's policy of nationalisation and redistribution were laid out squarely before Mandela. These private meetings between two powerful South Africans were, according to Terreblanche, expanded to include other leadership figures from both business and the ANC where a deal was struck to downplay redistribution.

Kasrils (2013b) echoes Terreblanche and makes similar points in his piece in the *Guardian*. But he goes on to speak of the 'young ANC economists schooled in western economics [who] were reporting to Mandela, and were either *outwitted or frightened into submission* by hints of the dire consequences for South Africa should an ANC government prevail with what were considered ruinous economic policies' (Kasrils 2013b: n.p., emphasis added). This looks partly right to us, though there was surely no need for secret late-night meetings to get to that point, a point that Kasrils admits differentiates his view with that of Terreblanche's (Kasrils interview, 30 March 2017). We would extend this analysis to include the role of late apartheid leaders (including De Klerk and Keys) and economic institutions, such as the Department of Finance, the SARB and CEAS, in applying similar pressure on the 'young' ANC economists that Kasrils refers to.

ANC activist and one-time adviser to President Kgalema Motlanthe, Mbatha argues that MERG 'came to naught because in the secret negotiations that were running parallel to the political negotiations, the ANC leadership were being strongly influenced by white business to soften its stance on a number of positions, including nationalisation' (2017: 147). He, too, provides no evidence for this claim about secret negotiations.

Michael Spicer, at the time an executive director of Anglo American (South Africa), in turn refutes a claim first made in *Africa Confidential* (2000) that the ANC received a donation to the amount of R150 million for its election campaign from Anglo in return for policy favours by the ANC after the elections:

> I was in charge of all donations, including political. There was funding for all the major parties, but the DA remained by far and away the largest recipient – the leader of the DA in its then form was Zac de Beer, a former Anglo Exec and close protege of Harry Oppenheimer. The total political donations were a fraction of the sum mentioned … So suffice it to say there was no such contribution and no such 'deal' (Michael Spicer, email communication 14 April 2019).

We do not doubt that corporate South Africa used various channels to influence ANC economic policy but the quantum referred to here by *Africa Confidential* as going to the ANC only and the claim (lacking evidence) that it was extended in return for economic policy changes conducted during secret negotiations, appears far-fetched. Until evidence is presented, such policy influencing claims in return for electoral donations still remain 'unproven' in our view.

Even if the donation referred to was made, the conspiratorial direction of causation variously employed is tenuous to say the least. 'Secret' negotiations over the future of the economic policy of South Africa also allegedly involved American and British ambassadorial staff, the National Party, the IMF and the World Bank, and were then shifted to the DBSA where the 'meetings took place at night' (Terreblanche 2012: 63). These negotiations culminated in an agreement among the parties just before the formation of the TEC on 7 December 1993 that a future ANC government would not pursue its previously stated policy of 'growth through redistribution' and would toe the line of the Washington Consensus.

However, the problem for those who may be sympathetic to this argument, is that Terreblanche baulks at the very moment when we would expect him to provide the evidence for his bold claims about these late-night meetings. Though unnamed, Terreblanche clearly had close contacts at the DBSA at that time. There was a connection, he claims, between what was going on in formal negotiations at Codesa and these secret meetings over economic policy. Thus, he claims: 'In September 1992, the MEC[11] was satisfied that the ANC was boxed in sufficiently on economic issues in the secret negotiations, and so informed the NP [National Party] on 26 September 1992 that it could accept the "sunset" clauses" [the concessions made by the ANC to break the logjam at the formal negotiations]' (Terreblanche 2012: 69).

Apart from the fact that these dates do not make sense and that the sequence of events is implausible, what did happen on 26 September 1992?

We accept, of course, that South African capital did make concerted efforts to influence the ANC, much of this via Mandela. Thus, for example, 'new money', such as that represented by Douw Steyn, was also quick to seize opportunities to curry favour with Mandela. Steyn is reputed to have provided special accommodation for Mandela at his private estate on more than one occasion. Mandela's private secretary, Zelda la Grange, recalls:

> Douw invited Madiba [Mandela's clan name] and Mrs Machel [Mandela's third wife, Graça] to his farm Shambala in the Waterberg. It was a relaxed luncheon … When [they] returned they told me that Douw had offered to build a house on the farm for [their] use, where they could relax as no one would be able to disturb them there. [They] knew not to refuse the offer as Douw didn't take lightly to being refused. In no time he built [them]

the most beautiful house on the farm, before even completing his own (in Wrathall 2015).

What Steyn received for these favours is not known. Could he have influenced ANC thinking on issues such as nationalisation? We simply have no way of finding out, as Steyn chooses to remain reclusive and out of reach.

So, at this point, and until perhaps future researchers find the evidence, we are unable to corroborate Terreblanche's conspiracy theory. However, we did ask Erwin, then a leading Cosatu/ANC/SACP player in the negotiations, whether he was aware of such secret meetings. He responded as follows:

> Yes, there were lots of talks between us and the apartheid bureaucrats but no such thing as secret talks involving the IMF and Western governments. Then we started meeting, when Keys comes into power as finance minister, and we started meeting his top executives. So there were indeed meetings at the DBSA and elsewhere [involving Tito Mboweni, Jay Naidoo, Trevor Manuel, Derek Keys, Estian Calitz, Danie Smit, Japie Jacobs], but this thing that Sampie Terreblanche talks about, the secret meetings, no, he is talking crap … If it happened, then it is a secret to me also (Erwin interview, 23 October 2015).

Vella Pillay, the director of MERG, lends some support for the interpretation that some kind of collusion or conspiracy involving the ANC and National Party leadership and key foreign governments may have occurred, though he is short on specifics. In an interview with Padraig O'Malley, this is what Pillay contends:

> VP: You know that multi-party thing and CODESA was, in my judgement, maybe not Mac's [Mac Maharaj] but my judgement, a piece of theatre because below that other negotiations, more deeper, were taking place.
> POM: These were?
> VP: Some of the top leaders of the ANC and top leaders of the existing government, probably the British Ambassador and the American Ambassador, some of these guys, were sitting in a cabal and really thrashing these things out. At that CODESA there was the PAC [Pan Africanist Congress] and a whole series of other organisations and it was a huge jam. It's one of these big exhibition halls, all of these guys were there, all of these people were there. It was going on and on and speeches and speeches and speeches and so on, that somehow or the other the deal was being made somewhere else. I don't

know whether Mac will be prepared to reveal that. Maybe he wasn't part of it or if he was I didn't know.

POM: Did he talk about it to you? How did you know that other talks were taking place?

VP: Because I went down there once or twice.

POM: To Kempton Park?

VP: Yes, and I saw what was going on there. I once went to the ANC offices here at Shell House and I went to see Walter Sisulu, the old man, a very, very fine man, I have a great regard for him, and I had ready some of the questions about my doubts and so on, like what I was trying to do in MERG, the Macro Economic Research Group, and so on, and he said, and he held my hand, he said, 'Vella, hamba kahle. Go slowly, please, I beg of you'. I said, 'Why?' He said, 'I don't want to tell you. Please go slowly. You're a good friend of mine and I don't want you to be hurt'. Just like that (O'Malley interview archive, Vella Pillay, 30 December 2002).

Yet, Mac Maharaj, who had been Pillay's comrade since 1957, is sceptical of his interpretation:

> So Vella's picture is pure conspiracy, and again it suggests one possible major lacuna in the way he was thinking. He was assuming that what goes into the packages at MERG would feed back into the ANC and would lead to negotiations with the regime on economic issues, in which he would be playing some part, and because he does not see himself playing a part in it he feels it was happening behind the scenes, right, and therefore it's a cabal thing, right, and it can't be that the comrades have excluded him. It must be the bloody Brits and the Americans that did that (Maharaj interview, 16 August 2016).

Maharaj may be correct to argue that Pillay underestimated the degree to which the comrades, rather than the colonial or imperial powers, 'excluded' him.[12] But some MERG staff experienced at first-hand interventions (and bullying) by senior diplomats working at the British and other embassies who wanted to reduce the influence of Marxist economists on the research output. Besides, British diplomats have now gone on record to boast about their success in influencing ANC economic policy debates – and about the role of their 'spooks' (FCO 2013: 34; see also Padayachee and Sender 2018).

Those who were directly involved at the highest level in the MERG project would argue, admittedly with the benefit of hindsight, that while the kind of

'Western-inspired' conspiracy spelled out above may not have existed as such, there was a kind of, shall we say, 'internal conspiracy', in part against the economic stance being taken by MERG but also for what could only have been personal advancement with a view to positions in the democratic government. That grouping of some politicians and some academics, while initially supportive of MERG, came to use their power and behind-the-scenes lobbying in an attempt to advance their own standing in the movement, to undermine MERG and to viciously attack Pillay. How else does one explain why many of the ANC economic leadership and 'progressive' academics who were so much part of the MERG project suddenly became its greatest adversaries? This is evident by their words and actions on the day of the MERG launch on 3 December 1993 – almost as if someone had instructed them to do this. That is why we use the term 'internal conspiracy'. Here is Fine's take on this point:

> My view tends to be, with the benefit of hindsight, that whatever external conspiracy or pressures and inducements, there was at most some mild and manageable rumbling of discontent against MERG among some South African academic quarters before the publication of the MERG report – especially from researchers in the Industrial Strategy Project and some other conservative white academics. MERG otherwise was a stunning success in preparing policy proposals in a short time and in difficult circumstances (and the analysis and proposals might be considered to have passed the test of time). But, just prior to the publication of MERG, an internal 'conspiracy' of what was to become a long-standing side-lining of those involved was orchestrated, ultimately leading to the stigmatising of both Vella in particular and MERG in general as a condition of advancement within the ANC, from leadership down, and not least in forms and words that reflected total ignorance and lack of respect. Not only MERG as a document but also as a policy project was effectively killed off as if it had never existed, as most dramatically and symbolically revealed by the results of transitional negotiations and both the fate of the RDP and the emergence of the non-negotiable GEAR. At best, MERG and Vella were shamefacedly shunned out of political loyalty to the ANC by those who would otherwise have enthusiastically supported both. At worst, and fuelling his personal bitterness and frustration, Vella found himself and MERG treated with dismissive and arrogant contempt (Fine, email correspondence, 10 February 2017).

What we argue here is that the factors we believe influenced the final decision to dump MERG were mutually reinforcing, that there was some degree of both explicit and implicit political co-ordination about the line to take on the post-apartheid economy, and that these factors all interacted with the bigger picture of achieving a negotiated settlement.

That is the explanation we believe best fits the evidence for the dumping of MERG as seen by some of the direct participants in the MERG project. But that still does not fully explain the overall shift towards neo-liberalism within the ANC and its Alliance partners over the first half of the 1990s, of which the dumping of MERG was but one part. Other forces were at play.

ANC ECONOMICS TEAM OUTMANOEUVRED

There is another interpretation for the shift in ANC economic policy that is worth considering. This interpretation, while not being dismissive of a range of possible global and national forces, emphasises the residual policy role of the National Party and its access to and leverage over the key economic institutions at the time, including the Treasury, the SARB, the DBSA and CEAS. We also stress the role played by South African capital, old and new, through its well-funded and much-publicised scenario-planning exercises, as well as other informal contacts. In our view, the primary forces driving the economic policy debate were national and internal rather than external. This interpretation rejects as baseless (for now) the argument that the shift can be attributed to some kind of conspiracy (Terreblanche and others); it rejects, too, the notions that there was, in fact, no shift from the ANC's positions in the 1950s or that there was no alternative (Hirsch). Neither do we view the shift as representative of some kind of betrayal or sell-out or ideological conversion on the part of the ANC leadership (Bond and others). We point to the many failures and weaknesses on the side of the ANC, but we are not convinced that this represented an ideological capitulation to neo-liberalism in the ANC Alliance. However, it may indeed be the case that a few top leaders in the ANC economics team may have been converted to neo-liberalism in the transition.

The apartheid regime and local capital skilfully used their access to not inconsiderable political, economic and intellectual resources within South Africa to outfox and outmanoeuvre the then young, largely unevenly trained and inexperienced ANC economics team, and to convince them that a 'redistribution through growth model' was not an answer to the challenges of the post-apartheid economy. That these policy ideas more or less coincided with those of the Washington Consensus institutions was of course a major bonus: without any history or tradition of economic theorising, and with an inexperienced DEP in place, the ANC was easy prey to these combined forces. On some key issues, such as SARB independence, DEP economists had come, through their own routes, to the same position as the apartheid leadership and the SARB.

Barry van Wyk observes:

> Because the ANC had placed so little emphasis on economic policy formulation before 1990 the movement was positively on the defensive in terms of the South African economic debate ... the ANC were gradually tied as the policies and reforms initiated by the NP had created an irreversible momentum that could not be inverted for fear of alienating the now all-important market. Crucially ... in this way the antecedents of the preeminence of the economic balance of power was established in South Africa (2005: 150–151).

Though theirs is a somewhat different take on the macroeconomics of the transition because of their emphasis on technocratic capture, Aurelia Segatti and Nicolas Pons-Vignon come close to our interpretation of developments since the late 1980s in the first part of the quote below:

> This article has shown that the resilience of orthodox macro-policies in South Africa has hinged on the continuation of reform processes initiated during the late apartheid period. The expertise for economic thinking in the transition has largely drawn on 'indigenous' conservative forces, while the politically calculated ideological conversion to neoliberalism among the top leadership of the ANC was accompanied by a strategy of technocratic capture through the rise of the NT [National Treasury] and its role across government. It should therefore not be a surprise that macro-economic policy has been dominant, and the interests of finance and mining capital have continued to be well served in the post-1994 era (Segatti and Pons-Vignon 2013: 551).

Though differently expressed, both of these quotations accord in many ways with the findings of our own research. The ANC, playing catch-up after years of neglecting economic policy, struggling to establish its own capability and skills, and failing to draw on the rich democratic culture that the unions and the UDF had established in the 1980s, was indeed outmanoeuvred by the well-resourced late apartheid regime and an equally well-resourced local big business sector (including old money, such as Anglo, Old Mutual/Nedbank (Nedcor) and Sanlam). The ANC, while holding strong moral and political cards, was outmanoeuvred on the technical and economic details of the transition. This cannot be a surprising outcome if one considers the balance of forces across a range of arenas of the struggle; there was simply no need for secret conspiratorial talks to bring about the shift in economic policy thinking.

The argument we make here is not unique to South Africa's transition. Rommy Morales Olivares (2015), in a paper comparing economic policy choices in the transition to democracy in Chile and South Africa, arrives at very similar conclusions. She stresses continuation in policy inherited from previous regimes as key to the nature of the economic policy outcomes.

> What were the conditions or likelihood for alternatives in the years immediately after 1994 in South Africa and 1990 in Chile? The options of the governing elites of the time in both countries are rather clear. While the option of a radical economic agenda was not possible, with the pursuit of a logic of responsibility seen as essential, a weak version of a social-democratic agenda would nevertheless have been possible: in fact, it was even expected by the business community and other interest groups, as it had been around in electoral discourse. Historically different situations, as in the case of Chile and South Africa, are influenced by mechanisms of continuity and [these] mechanisms have managed to generate specific trajectories, where the institutions have changed semantically but only in order to keep the general socio-economic regimes of the [previously] authoritarian period in place (Morales Olivares 2015: 144–145).

The next two chapters present two case studies that provide further evidence in support of our general contentions. In chapter 7 we take a careful look at the debate over central bank independence as it evolved in the 1990s, and in chapter 8 we identify similar trends in one arena of the struggle over social policy – that is, the debate over a National Health Service.

7

South African Reserve Bank Independence

Since its establishment in 1921, the South African Reserve Bank (SARB) was both legally and practically subordinate to the Ministry of Finance and to the government of the day, despite the fact that it was wholly owned by private shareholders. It had neither the mandate to set independent goals to achieve nor full operational independence to realise them. Its mandate was eclectic and at various times included price stability, exchange rate stability and economic growth.

It is important at the outset to gain some understanding of government–SARB interactions in the late apartheid era to better understand the significance of what followed in the 'negotiations' over central bank independence in the 1990s. We learn from former President FW de Klerk that Gerhard de Kock regularly appeared at Cabinet meetings during his tenure as governor to make presentations on the economy, a practice that De Klerk apparently stopped soon after he became president in 1989. Yet, we also know that Governor de Kock met De Klerk in Hermanus (where both had holiday homes) from time to time to discuss economic issues in general terms. De Klerk's views on central bank independence may have arisen out of these meetings, but also from his general belief that the state should not interfere in economic matters, including the work of the Reserve Bank. De Kock was clearly an important influence on De Klerk on such matters (De Klerk interview, 28 January 2019).

De Klerk's decision to end the practice of the governor attending some Cabinet meetings appears to be in stark contrast to developments in the 1980s. There is a view that during PW Botha's term as prime minister, then president, he intervened directly in monetary policy matters (see Rossouw and Padayachee 2011: S60–61; Rossouw and Padayachee 2019). This is illustrated by the 'infamous' Primrose by-election on 29 November 1984, when President Botha allegedly instructed

Governor de Kock to reduce the interest rate in order to win the support of heavily indebted farmers in that constituency, in what appeared to be a close contest between the governing National Party and the opposition Conservative Party. Despite official denials, the governor complied with this directive from the president and dropped rates. A few months after the elections, in January 1984, interest rates were raised back to the pre-election level (Rossouw and Padayachee 2011: S60–61), suggesting a clear political motive.

In this chapter, we deal with arguably the most significant decision on economic policy taken at the constitutional negotiations in the early 1990s. This was the decision to grant the SARB independence from the state, to enshrine this in the Constitution (sections 222–224) and to give it a narrow price stability mandate in a context and moment where a broader growth, employment or developmental mandate would have been more appropriate to tackle the legacy of apartheid. How and why did this come about?

THE SIGNIFICANCE OF CENTRAL BANK INDEPENDENCE[1]

A noticeable trend in both developed and emerging market economies since the early 1990s was the increase in the number of central banks granted statutory independence. As Sylvia Maxfield points out: 'Between 1990 and 1995 at least thirty countries, spanning five continents, legislated increases in the statutory independence of their central banks. This represents a rate of increase in central bank independence many times greater than in any other decade since World War II' (1997: 3).

The question that arises is this: why would a democratic government voluntarily relinquish its power and authority over monetary policy to an independent central bank? A variety of factors, Maxfield argues, may account for this. The argument of her book rests on an explanation located in the changing global context within which economic policy has to be conducted. She argues that 'politicians use central bank independence to try to signal their nation's creditworthiness to potential investors' (Maxfield 1997: 4). Historically, but especially in the contemporary era of hugely globalised financial markets, developing countries have tended to grant increased authority, in one way or another, to central banks in order to attract scarce foreign capital.[2]

This raises questions about the democratic accountability and the representivity of central banks in contexts and conditions where the goals of growth, employment and distribution ought to feature more prominently on political and economic agendas than price stability. Policy decisions made by central banks, it can be argued, are not just technical decisions to be left up to a group of experts who will pursue what is optimal for society. They involve judgements about trade-offs – most fundamentally about whether inflation or unemployment is more of an economic priority in any particular society at any particular time. Ideally, the way decisions are made about such trade-offs should be representative of the values of those who comprise society.

Central bankers generally are not representative of society as a whole. They tend to be drawn from the ranks of the financial community and their policy prescriptions are likely to coincide narrowly with those of that community. Former World Bank chief economist Joseph Stiglitz is particularly severe on this point about representativeness. Central bankers, he argues, 'typically have little knowledge of these broader macroeconomic policy issues which should be their concern'; and they 'typically do not even have the training that makes them suited for judging the macroeconomic consequences of their policy decisions – arguably their central concern' (Stiglitz 1998: 19). It is, therefore, no real surprise, in his view, that central bankers tend to be more worried about inflation and less about unemployment (Stiglitz 1997: 14).

These issues are not without significance in the South African case. There, a central bank, which for most of its long history (from 1921 until arguably 1989) was subservient to political agendas, was granted full *constitutional* independence as part of the political negotiations process that brought the apartheid system to an end in 1994. Both the 1994 Interim Constitution and the final 1996 Constitution granted the SARB full independence, understood by most at that time to mean both goal and operational autonomy. Its primary goal and mission, as set out in the 1996 Constitution, is 'to protect the value of the currency', that is, to ensure price stability.

These developments occurred at a time when the need for close macroeconomic policy co-ordination, aimed at addressing and reversing the apartheid legacy of poverty, inequality and underdevelopment, was at its greatest. The ANC's own macroeconomic policy think tank, the Macroeconomic Research Group (MERG), argued that 'the independence of the Reserve Bank ... which divests the elected government of significant economic powers, is not a sound way to build international confidence in South Africa' and it called for the subordination of the Reserve Bank to the Ministry of Finance but with more operational independence than that which prevailed under apartheid (MERG 1993: 262, 264).

So, why did the ANC, the dominant anti-apartheid movement involved in the negotiations, choose to grant full constitutional independence to the SARB? Was it ignorance about the real significance of losing control over monetary policy, given the movement's historical neglect of economic policy matters? Was it traded

away, despite its significance, in return for other more important, though not publicly disclosed, concessions from the National Party government, for example on
national security or labour rights? Was the ANC outmanoeuvred into accepting
this position (against its will) by the outgoing National Party government, which
appeared determined to ensure that the SARB did not fall into the hands of a potentially populist ANC government? Or did the ANC consciously promote and cham-
pion SARB independence in order to assure international capital markets of its
credibility and willingness to play by the rules of the international game, and so
secure the foreign capital needed to bolster its low domestic savings ratio?

Given its economic isolation since the early 1960s, the importance of South
Africa's reintegration into the global economy would have struck negotiators on
all sides, and especially the outgoing National Party government and the ANC, the
likely incoming government. Both main parties may well have recognised (perhaps
at different stages in the negotiations and for different reasons) that an independent
SARB would be important to their cause: the ANC for reasons of displaying its credibility on economic management; the National Party to keep what they perceived to
be a populist and 'socialist-inclined' ANC away from the levers of monetary policy-
making. Jason Hickel makes the case for the National Party's position clear:

> Knowing that the ANC were going to assume political power, the National
> Party wished to insulate economic policy as much as possible from their con-
> trol ... An independent Reserve Bank with a low inflation mandate was cen-
> tral to this strategy. The National Party had presided over a state-controlled
> central bank for decades and knew how powerful it could be: they did not
> trust the ANC to wield this power, probably fearing that the latter would
> engage in 'loose' monetary policy for populist ends which would undermine
> creditors, people with accumulated wealth and businesses seeking foreign
> finance – all of which were disproportionately represented in the white com-
> munity whose interests the National Party sought to secure. This move to
> tie the hands of its successor government is recognised in the literature as a
> classic motive for enshrining central bank independence (2016: 4–5).

Yet, as we shall see, few of the key players on any side really appear to have a clear
picture today of how the movement to secure constitutional independence for the
SARB actually unfolded during negotiations, especially from July 1993 when this
issue was under consideration. Many of those directly involved in the negotiations
(Mac Maharaj, Pravin Gordhan) were not able to shed much light on how this
important matter was debated and decided at the negotiations. This is surprising,

given the significance of the issue. Others (Tito Mboweni) failed to respond to repeated formal attempts to interview them. As a result, there remain some gaps of our understanding of these processes. So much so that a relatively minor participant, Mario Oriani-Ambrosini, an Italian-born adviser to the president of the Inkatha Freedom Party (IFP), Mangosuthu Buthelezi, could claim credit for the relevant clauses of the constitution (RSA 1996a: 222–225) in his posthumous memoir.

We now trace the origins and evolution of this complex and sometimes confusing policy debate over the period of South African negotiations for a new constitution (referred to as Codesa), in which we try to make as clear as possible what the positions of the different parties were and how they evolved to a point where consensus was reached.

THE CONVOLUTED POLITICS OF THE DEBATE OVER CENTRAL BANK INDEPENDENCE

The position of the apartheid regime and the National Party

If anyone among the parties to the final negotiations always knew exactly what it wanted for a post-democracy SARB, both in terms of independence and mandate, it was the apartheid regime – the government and the ruling National Party. The apartheid government had been considering these matters very seriously for about a decade. As early as 1986, the De Kock Commission into monetary policy recommended that while the Treasury and the SARB should share broad responsibility for monetary policy, the SARB 'should primarily be charged with the responsibility for maintaining monetary stability and protecting the internal and external value of the currency' (Rossouw and Padayachee 2011: S62). The SARB's 1990 Mission Statement, the first one to be published since 1921,[3] stated that the Bank's 'primary aim was the protection of the internal and external value of the rand'; these words signalling a price stability mandate are virtually the same as those that entered the final Constitution in 1996 (Rossouw and Padayachee 2011: S62). This interpretation, confirming the direct link between the 1990 (late apartheid) Mission Statement of the SARB and the democratic Constitution, is confirmed by the following statement in the 2011 SARB publication commemorating the 90th anniversary of the SARB: 'In 1990 the SARB accepted a formal mission statement for the first time, which stated that its aim was to protect the internal and external value of the rand. This objective, albeit in a revised format (i.e., to protect the value of the currency), is also contained as the primary goal of the SARB in the Constitution of the Republic of South Africa,

1996' (SARB 2011: 17–18). Even more significantly, the direct link is confirmed by Chris Stals, the governor of the SARB at the time the Mission Statement was approved. In an email to Wits Professor Jannie Rossouw (copied to Vishnu Padayachee), Stals explicitly notes that it is important to acknowledge 'where the wording' of the relevant clauses of the Constitution comes from, and then mentions the origin as the 1990 SARB Mission Statement (email to Jannie Rossouw, 11 April 2019; see also Rossouw and Padayachee 2019). No more authoritative source establishing the role of the (old) SARB in the formulation of these critical economic policy clauses in the democratic Constitution can possibly be established.

In a paper he gave at the Bank of England's tercentenary symposium in June 1994, Governor Stals admitted that the SARB had used the early 1990s quietly to consolidate its stance over monetary policy. As reported by the Centre for Research into Economics and Finance in Southern Africa (CREFSA), Stals argued that the political transition in South Africa had meant that politicians had had 'little time for the central bank and for monetary policy' (CREFSA 1995: 3). He noted that the Reserve Bank used the opportunities presented during this time to transform the Bank in an attempt to make monetary policy more effective.

Stals informed us that sometime in 1992, in the context of the Convention for a Democratic South Africa (Codesa) negotiations, he was asked by the then minister of finance Barend du Plessis to draft a memo on the central bank's role and mandate going forward into the new dispensation (Telephone exchange with Padayachee, 23 November 2017; email exchanges with Padayachee, 17 February 2016 and 15 July 2016). According to Stals, the Governors' Committee and some senior staff drafted the memo, which he then sent to the minister. The content of that memo is not in the public domain, yet it is hard to imagine that it did not include a recommendation for SARB independence and a price stability mandate of some kind, as the argument had been consistently made since the mid-1980s (see Rossouw 2007). It does appear that some kind of line can be traced from the recommendations of the De Kock Commission, to the Mission Statement, to the memo to the finance minister, and to the interim and final constitutions over the role, mandate and status of the SARB, including the nature of its relationship to the government. All argued for more SARB independence and a price stability mandate.

The position of the ANC's Department of Economic Planning

The ANC's Department of Economic Planning (DEP) had begun the process to address the issue of central bank independence well before 1993:

You know, one of the things that happened was, in the DEP there was a little group of people who worked on the Reserve Bank … and it is a very important point to say that it included Tito Mboweni. Neil Morrison was part of that, Maria [Ramos] was part of it, and they took that discussion as far as, you know, crafting a model piece of legislation for the Reserve Bank. I'm sure that we could find it later because, you know, technology also changed from the WordPerfect 3.1 that we were using then (Manuel interview, 4 July 2016).

Our efforts to locate such a document proved fruitless.[4] We know a little about these internal DEP debates from some unscripted[5] remarks made by the current governor of the SARB, Lesetja Kganyago, at a ceremony at the official residence of the German ambassador to South Africa.[6] That event, which took place on 29 August 2016, was to welcome the first Bundesbank representative to South Africa. The governor reportedly remarked that it was then almost two weeks to the exact date 25 years ago – that would make it mid-1991 – that he was one of a group of ANC economists, along with Maria Ramos, who, following an invitation extended by the Bundesbank governor Karl Otto Pohl, had visited Germany. This followed an earlier meeting at Diepsloot between Nelson Mandela and Pohl. The South African economists visited the German Bundesbank and spent some time at a university in Germany. That visit, Kganyago observed (as reported to us privately by Jannie Rossouw), changed his views on central banking: he reached the conclusion that South Africa needed a politically independent central bank as was the case in Germany. On his return to South Africa, he said that it was necessary to convince his comrades at the DEP of this viewpoint to make sure it was reflected in the Constitution. This does suggest that the DEP economists initially held a different view on central bank independence.

In August 1992, Tito Mboweni, then deputy head of the DEP, set out his (and the DEP's) view about SARB independence in an interview with Padraig O'Malley. Mboweni was responding to a line of questioning by O'Malley about the ANC's response to the National Party government's line that there should be a clause in the Constitution guaranteeing SARB independence:

Among ANC economists the general mood is to have an independent central bank if you want your monetary policy to be of substance … but if it's independent [the government] can still determine who can be governor and who cannot be governor so their independence is really relative. But the critical thing for us is that whatever the outcome it has to be a Cabinet decision eventually, or it can be decided by the constitution-making body. But even if the constitution-making body agrees on an independent central bank it's meaningless. At the end of the day it will depend on the actual operations and the relationship of that to the Cabinet. If the future Cabinet decides to maintain a more interventionist financial policy from the Cabinet side they will do it. The critical thing is that there should be co-ordination between fiscal and monetary policy. There has to be co-ordination. You can't have a situation where fiscal policy is going in one direction and monetary policy in the other like in the current situation in South Africa (O'Malley interview archive, Mboweni, 18 August 1992).

We cannot fault Mboweni's logic and reasoning here.

Trevor Manuel maintains that the DEP at the time was working within the 'framework of the New Zealand model' (Manuel interview, 4 July 2016). We know that the Reserve Bank of New Zealand Act of 1989 was designed 'to give the New Zealand Reserve Bank greater independence from political influence, establish a single objective for monetary policy (price stability) and ensure accountability on the part of the Reserve Bank for the achievement of its policy objective' (Walsh 1995: 1179). It is significant, however, that all this was enshrined in an Act of the New Zealand parliament, and not in its Constitution, as it eventually turned out in South Africa.

This debate over central bank independence was taken up at the National Executive Committee (NEC) of the ANC around November 1993, where supporters of the competing DEP and MERG positions (see more below) battled it out. After some debate, it was apparently agreed to make the Bank's independence 'subject to the powers of parliament' (Bond 2000: 76; Steyn 1993), allowing both sides to claim victory.

Financial journalist Greta Steyn argued that 'A Battle Royal for the Economic Soul of the ANC' took place at the NEC a few days before the issue of SARB independence was to be debated at the technical committee of Codesa:

> The left-leaning Macroeconomic Research Group (MERG) ambushed the ANC's economic planning department [DEP] just days before negotiations at the World Trade Centre were due to debate central bank independence. MERG coordinator Vella Pillay argued for the Bank to be an arm of government. He was swiftly and publicly rapped over the knuckles. But Pillay found support in high places in the ANC. Pressure within the NEC led to the ANC negotiators suggesting an amendment to the final wording on the

central bank. After extensive debate, negotiators agreed to a clause which would make the Bank's independence 'subject to the powers of parliament' (Steyn 1993: n.p.).

While Vella Pillay claimed a small but important victory, the DEP insisted that the amendment did not change the basic principle of central bank independence (Steyn 1993). So both sides within the ANC claimed a victory.

We were informed by a senior SARB official (who wished to remain anonymous) that the ANC successfully argued at the technical committee for an insertion into the final wording to the effect that the Bank's monetary policy imperative to protect the currency had to be conducted 'in the interests of "balanced growth"'. This was a potentially important intervention by the ANC but it was poorly handled and, in the end, turns out to be rather meaningless. The insertion of the term cannot be viewed as indicative of a 'growth mandate' by any stretch of the imagination as it does not make economic growth a target but simply a vague contextual consideration. In any event, what could 'balanced growth' possibly mean in this context? The term 'balanced growth' has not been in contemporary use (being last employed in development debates in the early 1950s) and how it should be considered by the SARB decision-making is unspecified.[7]

The Rustomjee/Padayachee memo and the position of MERG

So, while a position around some kind of independence had emerged within National Party ranks and may have been emerging at the DEP, the ANC's macroeconomic policy think tank, the Macroeconomic Research Group, was moving in a different direction. Vella Pillay, director of MERG, requested Cyrus Rustomjee and Vishnu Padayachee, both researchers in the MERG project at the time, to draw up a memorandum on central bank independence to be presented to the ANC negotiations team for debate at the World Trade Centre negotiations in July 1993. The two researchers had one weekend to research and write up this paper. Here, in summary, is Rustomjee and Padayachee's argument:

> The CB's [central bank's] ultimate subordination to the Treasury is a norm in industrialised democracies as well as in democracies in developing countries. Within this normal framework, very substantial scope exists for operational independence of the CB. Constitutional independence of the CB is, by contrast, an extreme position and ought to be characterised as such. The

more substantial issue is the nature of the relationship between the CB and the Treasury: the extent of CB independence *within* government, not *from* government. The economic crisis facing SA requires far-reaching, innovative and new economic strategies, such as those proposed by the ANC.

Resolution of the crisis will require a high degree of coordination between the major components of economic decision-making. Hence the proposal for a degree of cooperation between the Treasury and the SARB, which accepts the integrity of their respective views; which is founded on the need for exceptionally close coordination of policy; which involves procedures for the resolution of conflicts as they arise; but which is ultimately underpinned by subordination of the CB to the authority of the democratic state, represents the only consistent institutional arrangement if the economic reconstruction programme is to be successfully concluded (Padayachee 2015: 25).

This line of reasoning informed the MERG recommendations. The MERG report, published on 3 December 1993, argued for the SARB's subordination to the Treasury, for an end of private shareholding (effectively for nationalisation of the SARB in line with most of the world's central banks) and for a broad development mandate. On 5 November 1993, Pillay delivered an opening address at the Oliver Tambo Memorial Lecture (given by Bishop Trevor Huddlestone) in which he pre-empted the MERG findings, after he was tipped off that the ANC was likely to reject the MERG recommendations. Mandela and senior officials of the DEP were present, as were members of the public and the media. Pillay presented some of the main findings of the MERG draft report, stating, among other recommendations, that MERG would present a case *against* SARB independence.

Pillay spelled out the MERG stance – that is, that 'the independence of the Reserve Bank … which divests the elected government of significant economic powers, is not a sound way to build international confidence in South Africa'; MERG, he stated, called for the subordination of the Reserve Bank to the Ministry of Finance (MERG 1993: 262, 264).

Not surprisingly, the response of the mainstream media, which in the main supported big business, was 'vitriolic'. Describing Pillay as 'an economic populist', an editorial in *Business Day* observed that Pillay's suggestion presented a 'clumsily interventionist economic role for government rather than a purely facilitative one … South Africa cannot afford experiments in socialist economics', it thundered. 'South Africa's present economic difficulties have their roots in the cavalier actions on interest rates and other mechanisms by earlier National Party governments' (*Business Day* 1993: 6).

Yet, there was much popular support for the MERG position. Referring to the MERG recommendation that the SARB be nationalised, the president of the South African National Civic Organisation, Moses Mayekiso, observed:

> Indeed MERG director Vella Pillay has earned the gratitude of many future generations by putting the issue of [the] Reserve Bank onto the public agenda. The MERG recommendation for a nationalised Reserve Bank is by no means out of step with international thinking. From my own dealings with the banking industry I certainly believe that the most powerful bank in our country, with responsibility for monetary policy and exchange controls [sic] must be controlled by the government of the people, not by an anonymous crowd of money mandarins (Moses Mayekiso, SANCO Press Release, 3 December 1993 in Vishnu Padayachee private archive).

The MERG position was immediately rejected by DEP deputy head Tito Mboweni (Bond 2000: 75). Mboweni emphasised that the MERG position was not ANC policy (*Business Day* 1993). He said that the ANC was developing its own approach to monetary policy, which would not require the Bank's nationalisation. It would be further recommended that an independent SARB would be constitutionally bound to consult the finance minister in conducting monetary policy, and that the Bank would act in support of the general economic policy of government. Here is precisely how Mboweni is quoted in *SouthScan*: 'However, we have to break with the past, and as such, the Bank should be constitutionally bound to consult the Finance Minister in conducting monetary policy' (*SouthScan* 1993: 325). Again, in the circumstances, we cannot fault Mboweni here. Sadly, this precise and important wording did not make it into the Constitution[8] and Mboweni's own stance on such obligatory consultation when he was governor was at odds with his view as expressed here – a point we shall return to at the end of this chapter.

Developments during the multi-party negotiations, 1993

So how did discussions on this policy issue unfold at the negotiations? Some clues have since emerged that help us understand at least the broad context of these debates during the negotiations in 1993, though much still remains unknown. In their book *The Politics of Transition: A Hidden History of South Africa's Negotiated Settlement*, Richard Spitz and Matthew Chaskalson (2000) point out that in the debates dealing with Constitutional Principles, the National Party and the apartheid government (which each had separate delegations) argued strongly for the independence of a number of 'state' institutions, including the SARB, the Public Service Commission, the Auditor General and the Public Protector, while the ANC prioritised its arguments around guarantees of trade union rights. In the end, after some 'tit for tat debate' (Spitz and Chaskalson 2000: 84), it would appear as if some kind of trade-off occurred, with each side getting its way on the matters closest to them.

Spitz and Chaskalson argue that the ANC had the power to stand its ground on the SARB independence debate *but chose not to do so*:

> As the likely majority party in the Constitutional Assembly [*sic*],[9] the ANC did not need a Constitutional Principle guaranteeing trade union rights and collective bargaining. It would have been able to ensure the enactment of the necessary provisions in the final constitution merely by using its strength in the Constitutional Assembly [*sic*]. It could, therefore, have stood its ground against the inclusion in the principles of a constitutional guarantee of the independence of the Reserve Bank and the Public Service Commission. Given the dynamics of the negotiating forum, however, it seemed easier to give the NP [National Party]/government its principle on [SARB] autonomy in return for getting the ANC principle on labour rights (Spitz and Chaskalson 2000: 84).

What is of interest is that Spitz and Chaskalson acknowledge assistance they received from the IFP's Mario Oriani-Ambrosini in their analysis and in coming to their conclusions on this and other constitutional matters (Spitz and Chaskalson 2000: vii). This begs the question: what role did Oriani-Ambrosini play, if any, in the drafting of the clauses about the SARB? In his book, former SARB non-executive director Stephen Goodson (2014: 124) acknowledges the role of Oriani-Ambrosini in the drafting of the constitutional clauses relating to SARB independence.

Oriani-Ambrosini has since died, but in June 2015 we were granted access[10] to the following extract from his book manuscript, which was later published posthumously:

> Another one of my regrets are the constitutional provisions relating to the South African Reserve Bank. It is unusual for a constitution to entrench the position and functions of the central bank. I admit that *when I drafted those provisions* I did not have a clear understanding of what a central bank does and I ascribed to them entirely benign functions that had to be protected from

a potential evil ANC government [*sic*]. I drafted the provisions regarding the central bank first in the constitution of KwaZulu-Natal of 1992 and then in the constitutional proposals that the IFP submitted at the World Trade Centre. Comparing the language of what I drafted with what can be found first in the Interim Constitution and then in the final Constitution shows how it was indeed the case that the entrenchment of the central bank of South Africa *came from my pen*, so much so that it is a set of unusual provisions in most modern institutions and neither the ANC or the NP or DP [Democratic Party] had any proposal with respect of the central bank. The greatest regret is that *I drafted language* entrenching what I referred to as the ordinary functions of a central bank, which is still the language of section 225 of the Constitution which states that the South African Reserve Bank must perform those powers which are 'customarily exercised and performed by central banks'. The fact is that at the time I did not have a clear idea of what those powers and functions were and neither did most of those at the World Trade Centre. As a result, *those provisions were included with little awareness of their enormous implications* (Oriani-Ambrosini 2017: 356, emphasis added).

We respect Oriani-Ambrosini's version but there is little corroboration of his version from anyone else directly involved in the debate. Who was Oriani-Ambrosini, most asked? Mboweni refuted any claim that Oriani-Ambrosini was involved in any way in the writing of these sections of the Constitution. He argues instead that the position adopted on the SARB was in fact the common position of the ANC's DEP and the National Party government of the day (Personal communication with Padayachee, 29 July 2015). Perhaps Oriani-Ambrosini was part of the technical, legal drafting team. If so, this would have been purely a functional role and not a substantive 'policy-making' role.

Pravin Gordhan, one of the ANC's chief negotiators at both Codesa and the World Trade Centre multi-party negotiations, also refutes Oriani-Ambrosini's claim, arguing that the decision was *in all likelihood* made through an agreement between the two major parties (the ANC and the National Party), as policies were sometimes traded off between these two parties (Telephonic interview, 16 July 2015). But Gordhan did indicate that he had not been directly involved in this particular matter and his recollections were somewhat vague.

Mac Maharaj, who was the principal ANC negotiator at the talks (alongside the National Party's Fanie van der Merwe), claims that the matter of SARB independence was not debated at the formal final stages of the negotiations and appears to have simply gone through to the legal drafters 'unflagged':

> Now you've raised the question of the independence of the Reserve Bank. There were these sub-committees, constitutional committees, etcetera, meeting, and all of them had different versions of what happened. So [on] Reserve Bank independence, I remember the issue coming up at the Negotiating Committee. I don't remember anybody saying, 'flag this critical problem, there is a debate behind this problem'. I remember it coming through as a non-issue. Yes, *they* want independence … That is how it appeared (Maharaj interview, 16 August 2016, emphasis added).

By 'they' he is likely to have meant all, or at least both, the main parties.

The SARB governor at the time, Chris Stals, is particularly insistent that the version of Oriani-Ambrosini's involvement is totally incorrect (Telephone conversation with Padayachee, 23 November 2017) and, given his position and knowledge of such matters, we have no reason to doubt his view on this point. So we must conclude that the Oriani-Ambrosini claims are for unknown reasons either incorrect or exaggerated.

The archival research carried out by London School of Economics graduate student Jasmine Bide (2016) suggests strongly that some agreement or understanding about SARB independence had been reached by the two main parties as early as mid-1993. Drawing on the negotiations archives, Bide points out that the principle of a constitutionally independent central bank was agreed as binding in the Multi-Party Negotiations Forum on *2 July 1993*. Our own archival research suggests that the principle of central bank independence was agreed to by the parties on *13 July 1993*. The proposal read: 'The independence and impartiality of a Commission of Administration, a Reserve Bank, an Auditor General and an ombudsman shall be provided for and safeguarded by the Constitution in the interests of the maintenance of effective public finance and administration and a high standard of professional ethics in the civil service' (Leon Wessels Papers, PV 883, 1/02/2/4/1/6).

So the dates are slightly different but not significant. According to Hickel (2016: 6), an associate professor at the London School of Economics, Manuel and Mboweni had by this stage been persuaded of the importance of central bank independence either by their own logic or by that of 'their interlocuters' (presumably meaning the apartheid government) in the negotiations process. However, as we shall see, the matter comes up for debate again in November 1993, by which time the horse had certainly bolted.

We know that the debate was then taken up at a technical committee of all parties at the World Trade Centre sometime in mid-November 1993. The South African Communist Party's (SACP's) Joe Slovo was clearly unhappy with the eventual outcome. Slovo informed academic and activist Patrick Bond 'that he was most upset about losing the November 1993 battle over whether [the SARB] would become "independent". This conversation happened, according to Bond, outside Slovo's house in late 1993 (Email correspondence with Bond, 22 June 2017).

The SACP's Jeremy Cronin had a more positive take on the outcome of that technical committee meeting. On 11 November 1993, in a fax to Vella Pillay, Cronin writes, 'It seems as though (after a tough fight *late last night*) a much-improved section on the Reserve Bank got through out at [the] World Trade Centre' (Vella Pillay private archives, emphasis added). Although Cronin's one-liner does not make it clear what was 'much improved', given Slovo's view that the battle was lost, it does appear that a 'tough' debate about the future of the SARB took place in November 1993.[11]

Whatever the case, we know from Derek Keys that the battle was truly over by around 20 November 1993. We know that in the end the Interim Constitution did not include the words 'subject to the powers of parliament' but only that 'there must be regular consultation between the Bank and the Cabinet member responsible for national financial matters'. Here is what Keys said in the exchange with O'Malley:

> DK: The ANC has been very careful to distance itself from MERG in exactly the same way as I kept saying, and I still keep saying, that the Normative Economic Model (NEM) is not government policy, it's the advice that I get from my economists. The ANC, I'm pretty happy to note, are saying that the MERG report doesn't represent their policy, it represents the advice that they are getting from MERG which is an accurate statement. And in one case where the ANC has had to act so far is on the MERG recommendation, the one about the Reserve Bank, the ANC has firmly slapped it down and has agreed to the fact that the new constitution enshrines the independence of a Reserve Bank.
>
> POM: Is that right? This has been done then in the last —?
>
> DK: Last two weeks.
>
> POM: Two weeks. I would have thought that control of the central bank would be a big issue for them, that one man should not have control over the state of the economy with respect to interest rates and inflation.
>
> DK: There it is in the constitution (O'Malley interview archive, Keys, 5 December 1993).

Developments at the Constituent Assembly, 1994–1996

Following the approval of the Interim Constitution, one of the first tasks after the 1994 democratic elections was that of forming a Constituent Assembly, in which the elected parliament would debate and finalise the Constitution. According to Manuel, the ANC deputed Alec Erwin and Rob Davies to represent it at the post-1994 negotiations – the Constituent Assembly – to finalise the mandate, functions and powers of the SARB (Manuel interview, 4 July 2016). The Constituent Assembly was the body charged with debating and approving the Interim Constitution. Cronin, then a member of the Central Committee of the SACP and a member of the ANC's NEC, informs us that Davies, also a senior SACP member, still argued at the Constituent Assembly that the SARB should only be granted *operational independence and not full independence* (Cronin interview, 25 July 2017, emphasis added). Clearly, that position did not win out at the Constituent Assembly. The final approved Constitution of the Republic of South Africa, which was adopted in 1996, reads: 'The South African Reserve Bank, in pursuit of its primary object, must perform its functions independently and without fear, favour or prejudice, but there must be regular consultation between the Bank and the Cabinet member responsible for national financial matters' (RSA 1996a: s.224(2)).

Manuel, who became minister of finance in April 1996, has argued that the requirement for regular consultation was met in the first few years. Stals also observed that the governor, the minister of finance and senior Department of Finance officials met at least once a month (CREFSA 1995: 10). Manuel confirms that these regular meetings did not continue after 8 August 1999, when Mboweni became governor. The new governor, Manuel maintains, appeared to have been 'heavily invested in formal and ceremonial occasions and was high on strict adherence to protocols'. As a result, according to Manuel, Mboweni was not as keen as former Governor Stals on meeting regularly with the Ministry of Finance (Manuel interview, 9 September 2016).[12]

The SARB's main mandate, as defined in terms of the South African Reserve Bank Act No. 90 of 1989 (as amended in March 1996 and in section 224(1) of the 1996 Constitution) is 'to protect the value of the currency in the interest of balanced and sustainable economic growth in the Republic' (RSA 1996a).

Other post-1994 developments

The independence of the SARB was enshrined in the Interim Constitution in 1994 and ratified in the final Constitution in 1996. But between these two dates, an important seminar on central bank independence and accountability took place at the Reserve Bank on 9 and 10 January 1995. The seminar was jointly organised by the Bank and the London-based Centre for Research into Economics and Finance in Southern

Africa, whose director was Jonathan Leape. According to Leape, Maria Ramos, who was a research officer at CREFSA at the time, was a leading member of the organising committee (Email exchange with Padayachee, 8 September 2016). Twenty-one people representing a variety of local constituencies, including the Treasury, labour and the Bank as well as some high-powered experts in central banking, participated and gave papers. The international participants included Andrés Bianchi, the first governor of an independent Chilean Central Bank, and Charles Goodhart, once chief adviser and later Monetary Policy Committee member at the Bank of England. Other participants included deputy finance minister Erwin, Ebrahim Patel representing the Southern African Clothing and Textile Workers' Union, as well as Brian Kahn and Gill Marcus, then chair of the Joint Standing Committee on Finance in parliament.

Some highlights of the seminar in relation to our mandate in this book are:

- Stals's observation, as noted earlier, of the need for regular monthly meetings with the minister of finance.
- The suggestion that the SARB did not have *goal* independence but only operational independence, a matter that remained unsettled until the adoption of inflation targeting in 2000.
- Stals quoting Stan Fischer (an ex-chief economist at the World Bank and ex-first deputy managing director of the International Monetary Fund) to the effect that, because of the undemocratic nature of central bank independence, there must be a process by which the government could override the decisions made by the central bank, citing examples of New Zealand and Canada, where this was possible under certain limited conditions. No one appears to have followed up on this useful proposal.
- Erwin's comment that the Reserve Bank had a special position within the National Economic Development and Labour Council as part of the government's consensus-seeking approach on economic policy. (We have not been able to verify if the SARB took its place at Nedlac after the latter was set up.)
- Goodhart's observation that while the theory suggested that independence would allow the authorities to reduce inflation with minimal loss in employment, there was no evidence of this. He also raised the issue of the SARB considering the adoption of an inflation-targeting regime (CREFSA 1995).

Some interesting issues emerged in this seminar, but it had little or no status beyond an academic exercise.

Over the past two decades, the appropriateness of the SARB mandate, its somewhat unique private shareholding structure and the appropriateness of its inflation-targeting policy have been raised in academic, union, political and civil society debates and circles. This chapter assesses developments in the early to mid-1990s, so we do not cover these post-1996 developments in any detail.

In a recent commentary, Luke Jordan (2017) questions why the mandate of the SARB had to be enshrined in the Constitution in the first place, when in nearly all comparable countries such matters are incorporated in ordinary legislation, that is, in statute law. He continues:

> But the fundamental issue is what the [SARB] mandate is doing in the Constitution in the first place. We are the only country, to my knowledge, that has the mandate in the Constitution. In the 1990s it was understandable why reasonable and well-intentioned negotiators and officials would have accepted the argument for a strict mandate. But that could have been accepted, as in all other countries, in legislation. Instead, it was inserted in the Constitution, where it would be almost impossible to change. *It was inserted through closed-door negotiations, at the back of the document. It has embedded, deep in the heart of our economic governance, a bias towards the status quo, as it existed in 1994* (Jordan 2017: n.p., emphasis added).

When Jordan queries how this mandate ended up in the Constitution, he implicitly raises the questions: by which parties and through what process? Importantly for our purposes here, he makes the point that the result was the entrenchment of the status quo.

Alan Hirsch, University of Cape Town professor, a senior policy civil servant in the Mbeki administration and a vocal supporter of the ANC's approach to post-apartheid economic policy-making, admits that had it not been 'constrained by concerns for economic stability' the ANC could have been more insistent on granting the SARB a full employment mandate like the United States central bank (2015: n.p.).[13]

In April 1996, when Manuel joined the Treasury as minister, he came to discover the extent and severity of the country's net open forward position (NOFP) – or dollar debt in layman's terms – and appeared to lament his powerlessness as minister to interfere in the independent SARB to address this matter. Here is Manuel's view:

> Now at the point of democracy the reserves that we had were minus $24 billion; that was the size of the net open forward position … so we have to work that 24 billion down to zero and start building up a positive position.

... one day Chris Stals calls me and he says, minister, I have to see you. And again, I can play the movie. I didn't know what this was about. We were having one of our early *bosberaads* out in the North West and I flew in from Cape Town, stopped at the Reserve Bank ... we had just been together; we were actually travelling together; we were at a conference of the Institute for International Finance – first the conference in Rome, then we went to Perugia – all this was just the previous week and now we are back. He says, something happened while we were travelling. He says, I'm afraid what I have for you is not very good news. He says, the net open forward position has risen to $27 billion. I said, what? He said, the NOFP is now $27 billion. I said, how did that happen? He says, well, you know, when there was a little attack [on the rand] and *the chaps here* ... they threw money at trying to protect the exchange rate of the rand and then blew reserves and put us into that negative territory ...

In fact, we had a visit here from [Robert] Rubin when he was the US Treasury secretary. He came to South Africa and then we went off to Swakopmund [in Namibia] where he met all the SADC [Southern African Development Community] finance ministers. *We were talking about this and he said, when I hear the story about this gambling on the exchange rate, I must say I haven't actually ever heard a stronger case for a dependent central bank that would be directly accountable to the Finance Ministry for their actions.* Later Chris Stals makes way for Tito [Mboweni], and in the budget speech of 2000 we announced formally the introduction of inflation targeting (Manuel interview, 4 July 2016, emphasis added).

It is not clear who Stals meant by 'the chaps here', though it must refer to other senior Reserve Bank executives, so exonerating him from the decision to defend the rand. In his interview with us, Manuel expressed some exasperation at the Treasury's lack of power on this matter. Though not directly related to the growing dollar debt, the move to inflation targeting in April 2000 (where the democratic government set the monetary policy target for the Bank to give effect to) may have been a direct response to the general lack of Treasury power over the SARB.

CONCLUSION

The ANC economics leadership may well have genuinely believed that central bank independence was important for the future of the economy under a democratic government. They may have reckoned that a financialised capitalist economy like South Africa, always connected to the global economy even during the darkest days of apartheid and isolation but on the verge of reintegrating under different political conditions, would need foreign capital and credit and the stamp of approval from the global financial community. Credibility in global markets would be critical. For that reason, they pushed for independence for its flagship monetary policy-making institution, the SARB, despite differences within the ANC and the Alliance. They ensured that such matters were kept out of broader debates within the democratic movement, which included the radical trade unions and civil society organisations, not all of whom could be relied upon to be as disciplined as their own inner circle. That this goal was so easily achieved can be put down to the fact that their principal opponents in the negotiations, the National Party and the apartheid regime, also wanted the same thing, albeit for different and narrower ends, and had started planning for this eventuality as early as the mid-1980s, well before anyone had even thought about negotiations for a democratic South Africa.

8

The Politics of Health Policy-Making in the Transition Era, 1990–1996

After its unbanning, the ANC faced the dilemma of how to move from opposing apartheid to presenting social policy alternatives that would change a radically unequal, racialised system of health and welfare. The legacy of pre-democratic South Africa established structures of class and race inequality that aimed to uphold the 'good society' for a white minority at the consequent expense of the black majority, creating for the latter what could, drawing on Richard Titmuss (1974: 75), be aptly described as a racialised 'diswelfare' state. In health care, the key mechanisms through which this racialised 'diswelfare' state was achieved in the apartheid era were: (i) differential allocation of funding to public health on the basis of race; (ii) a racialised labour market and the consequent unequal access to private and public health on the basis of race and class (income, employment status); (iii) the fragmentation of service delivery among 14 administrations, all of which were constituted on a racial basis; (iv) an inappropriate balance between the primary preventive and tertiary curative level components of health care, tipped in favour of the latter, in the context of the impoverished social conditions of the majority of South Africa's black inhabitants.

The structuring of health policy to provide for the health needs of the inhabitants in South Africa was fundamentally conditioned by the relationship between the public and private sector. The racial and income dualism of the labour market and the manner in which it influences access to social provision in South Africa is most tellingly revealed in the case of private health care. Historically, the private health care sector in South Africa has been a more significant sector in human resource and budget terms than the public sector. It was estimated that private finance accounted for 61 per cent of all health care expenditure by 1992/1993 – a year before the democratic transition (FFC 1998: 35). Private health care in South Africa (referred to as medical aid schemes) are a form of private occupational health care. These private medical schemes offer variable 'packages' of health care services, provided by private general practitioners and hospitals contracted into the medical aid schemes, and provide health care services on a strict fee-for-service basis. Excluded are only the most sophisticated and expensive specialist care, such as heart transplants, which are provided by the public health sector (Söderlund, Schierhout and Van den Heever 1998). Most of these medical schemes are employment-based. However, only a privileged 18 per cent of the population are covered by such medical aid schemes, with the remaining 82 per cent mainly black section of the population reliant on the public health care system.

The schemes are also indicative of the funding differentials between private and public health care in general. It is estimated that by 1995, medical aid schemes spent more than four times as much as the public sector per head of covered population (Söderlund, Schierhout and Van den Heever 1998: 3). Access to the private medical schemes is dependent, furthermore, on adequate levels of income to pay contributions and reflects the racialised duality of the labour market whereby those in employment and with the economic means have benefited disproportionately from such private health schemes. They have predominantly been whites and, to a lesser degree, coloureds and Indians, particularly public sector workers. By 1960, 80 per cent of whites had medical scheme cover and thus had significantly less need to utilise the public health sector (Söderlund, Schierhout and Van den Heever 1998: 3). A striking feature in the transition era, however, was the rapidly increasing coverage of blacks by medical schemes, accounting for 23–24 per cent of those insured in 1990 and increasing to 36 per cent by 1995 (Söderlund, Schierhout and Van den Heever 1998: 4). This was the historical context in the health care sector that confronted the ANC after its unbanning and which required a policy response.

As discussed in chapter 2, the historical demand at the core of ANC health policy since the 1940s was the establishment of a state-run national health service (NHS). The question was how this agenda was to be established in the new context of negotiations. A noted health policy analyst and activist, Cedric de Beer (1992: 272), comments that the prospect of nationalising the health services raised three daunting concerns for the ANC and its allies. Firstly, the separation of funding between the public and private sectors raised questions about whether the ANC in government would be able to double the tax rate to replace the revenue lost by nationalisation of the private sector health care industry. Secondly, half of the doctors worked in the private sector, and at issue was whether they could be attracted or compelled into the public sector at levels of remuneration equivalent to that of the private sector without many emigrating or creating a 'black market' in private health care. Finally, what political costs would need to be borne by nationalisation and could the ANC sustain such costs (De Beer 1992)?

These issues of feasibility and sustainability of social policy were not unique to the health sector, but occurred in all areas in which policy was contested, ranging from land reform to the restructuring of education.[1] The larger concern, which loomed over these debates, was what economic strategy could simultaneously meet the demand for economic growth and respond to demands for equity in the social sectors? This is discussed in greater detail below.

As discussed in chapters 4 and 5, a dominant current in the ANC on the debate on economic and social restructuring in the immediate post-1990 period was defined by thinking emerging from the Macroeconomic Research Group (MERG 1993). MERG favoured a redistributive growth strategy whereby the state would perform a prominent, interventionist role in economic restructuring, with substantially increased expenditure in the social sectors to meet equity imperatives. As demonstrated in chapter 5, the influence of those supporting this current was summarily displaced by an increasingly market-friendly group centred around Thabo Mbeki as the debate on social and economic restructuring leading up to the first democratic elections in 1994 gained momentum.

Other moderating interests, influenced but not necessarily dictated to by the World Bank, reinforced the politics of pragmatic social change in a policy elite within the ANC as it considered its tasks as a future government.

The counter-positioning of the initial radical and then cautious positions of the largely exiled ANC leadership with that of a radical, redistributive impetus in health policy reform of many leading health activists aligned to the mass democratic movement (MDM) is revealing of the tensions. Progressive health campaigners tended to cohere around a 'pro-NHS' position as a way to address the stark inequalities of apartheid-era health care.

Leslie London, a public health medical doctor, MDM activist and member of the progressive National Medical and Dental Association (NAMDA) recollects:

> There was a lot of resistance to private-sector gain at the expense of the public good, and there was a lot of support for a national health service … for socialised medicine, at least equal medicine … The people involved in the private sector in NAMDA were basically GPs [general practitioners]; they were not making mega-bucks … But definitely my recall was that the dominant position in NAMDA was very much pro-public sector, pro-NHS … a little bit suspicious of this [health] insurance stuff … The one

NAMDA conference [in 1987][2] was a conference on the national health service drawing on international experience ... There was never discussion about the national insurance system; it was a national health service ... All the things I was connected with were talking about a national health service ... (London interview, 21 August 2018).

Although organised around a broad NHS position, there were no detailed, clearly articulated and specific policy alternatives in the MDM for the transformation of health care. This was explained by Irwin Friedman, director of the National Progressive Primary Health Care Network, as follows:

Our position pre-1990 was oppositional; we engaged in struggle ... we saw everything [the government was doing] in terms of strengthening apartheid. As a progressive health sector, our approach was to, wherever we could, oppose whatever the government of the day was doing, and our contribution there was to put together a theoretical rationale from a health point of view as to why health policies of the time were wrong.

...

With the unbanning of the ANC and the liberation movement in general, it was realised there that in fact very little policy had been formulated – apart from policy that had been formulated in relation to the liberation struggle; it did not relate to how to govern. And in the health sector, for example, there was a need to put in place all the kinds of policies that the new department [of health] would need to implement when they came to power (Friedman interview, 11 November 1998).

Ralph Mgijima, who performed a leading role in the exiled ANC's health service in various African states as well as in the development of its post-apartheid health policy, described the health focus of the exiled ANC as inescapably a mainly applied one. This involved direct health service provision for MK and ANC activists in the context of building an armed struggle to defeat the apartheid regime and activities directly aimed at exposing the health care system under apartheid as part of a wider international mobilisation against apartheid:

We ran a health service of some sort in exile for the ANC and there were a few doctors. I was in the fortunate position of having to coordinate most of those from time to time ... so that's how I got into health policy ... policy for me at that time meant how do you ensure that there is efficiency in the delivery of health services for basically ANC [aligned] South Africans ... under difficult and trying conditions ... [And] ... we would use the platform of the World Health Organization to expose the atrocities of apartheid in South Africa and also to tabulate the state of health services in South Africa ... in the United Nations Assembly (Mgijima interview, 13 November 2018).

By 1991, however, the language of opposition and resistance changed to that of reconstruction, mediated through negotiations with the National Party government. There was an increasing reliance on internal and international researchers, experts and consultants to assist in shaping social policy in health. Strategies of political mobilisation, with their emphasis on mass-oriented participation in the oppositional period, were increasingly displaced in favour of research by policy elites. Although consultative conferences and forums still provided the mechanisms through which policy was debated, these elites became the primary influence of policy proposals. This change was exemplified in an early landmark conference on health and welfare held in Maputo, Mozambique, in April 1990, which brought together for the first time the recently unbanned ANC and a range of activists and academics from internal opposition movements organised around health and welfare issues.

London, a delegate to the Maputo conference, recalls the mood of that conference as follows:

My impressions of it was that it wasn't so much what was discussed but that [the conference] actually happened – that was what was important. The actual discussions were not particularly new or novel in terms of the content of what was said and what was going on in NAMDA and other organisations inside South Africa ... The fact that the ANC in exile was there was the big thing.

...

But I also got the impression that there were other things being organised ... I remember stumbling on a meeting that I was not supposed to be in, and an ANC representative was deep in conversation with four or five people, and there was clearly a kind of, not a hidden agenda, but another agenda going on, which was clearly related to the ANC's political objectives related to a national health system.

...

There was a not a heavy-handed fist being exercised over what you could or could not say, though ... The discussions were quite open and I don't remember any kind of power dynamics clamping down discussion. I think the actual discussions were quite vibrant and positive and 'here's our chance' but I remember being totally aware that there was another agenda at the same time and they co-existed and it was just accepted … We did not worry about it as it seemed the other agenda was very socialist, very socialised and the ANC was intent on driving an NHS kind of health system (London interview, 21 August 2018).

The organising committee of the Maputo conference included representatives of the ANC, the National Education, Health and Allied Workers' Union, NAMDA, the Organisation for Appropriate Social Services in South Africa, the South African Health Workers' Congress, the Welfare Co-ordinating Committee, the United Democratic Front and select affiliates, the Congress of South African Trade Unions (Cosatu) and public health organisations such as the Progressive Primary Health Care Network, South African Black Social Workers' Forum, the Health Workers' Society and the Islamic Medical Association. Also represented were the Ministry of Health of Mozambique and public health solidarity activists from international solidarity movements in the UK and the US, as well as the World Health Organization. A wide representative cross-section of the progressive public health movement in South Africa and senior members of the ANC in exile deliberated on future strategies for health and welfare transformation in a post-apartheid South Africa. More than 60 papers were presented, spanning themes and topics from community health personnel education, HIV, health services, a health charter and health personnel, to special issues such as women, occupational health, family and children, and returnees. Attention was also paid to the crucial issue of financing and restructuring the future health system. The key presenters included: public health doctor and policy specialist HM (Jerry) Coovadia on a new health policy; activist academics Leila Patel and Cedric de Beer on the status of health and welfare services under apartheid; academic Rachel Jewkes on the experiences and lessons of the British National Health Service; trade unionist Sisa Njikelana on the challenges of industrial relations in the health sector in South Africa; academic Laetitia Rispel on the future providers of primary health care; academic and social welfare activist Francie Lund on the financing of welfare in a post-apartheid South Africa; ANC senior policy analyst and academic Rob Davies on the economic framework underpinning future health care services; academic and public health activist Kamy Chetty on the provision of hospitals and clinics in South Africa; academic and health policy analyst Max Price on a framework for conceptualising the financing of health care; health policy analysts Jonathan Broomberg and Cedric de

Beer on whether national health insurance was the first step in achieving equity in health care financing; and Merrick Zwarenstein on the role of the private sector in a future national health service. A provocatively entitled paper on the practical steps to building a welfare state was also presented by ANC member Nombulelo Hlatshwayo.

Setting the scene in the keynote address to the conference was the ANC chief representative in Maputo, Walter Seathe. He unequivocally presented the position of the ANC as supportive of a national health service: 'As an integral part of the struggle of our people against the inequities of the apartheid system, health workers have become involved in the struggle to establish a *national health service* in South Africa, based on the principle of primary health care and geared towards a programme of health for all by the year 2000. The ANC endorses this goal as the basis of the health policy of a future democratic, non-racial, unitary South Africa' (Seathe 1990: 7, emphasis added).

In the same presentation, Seathe also said the ANC unequivocally condemned the regime's programme of privatising health services, arguing further that 'by starving the state sector of resources, privatisation policies seek to guarantee that a substantial part of the existing health infrastructure will remain available to provide privileged access to services for a minority with the means to pay. Health ... must become a right and not a privilege' (Seathe 1990: 7).

This position was reinforced at the conference by the ANC Health Department in response to a question about how the ANC envisaged a future system of health care in South Africa: 'The ANC is strongly in favour of a *national health service and of a service with a strong bias towards the primary health care approach.* The democratic state will have a duty to ensure that health services provision will reach out to those most in need. Resources will have to be put into this' (ANC Health Department 1990: 56, emphasis added).

These positions of the ANC in support of a national health service are perhaps unsurprising. They reflect a direct continuity with the social imagination or the 'big idea' for fundamental health care transformation that informed ANC health policy in the 1940s (African Claims) and the 1950s (Freedom Charter). Indeed, this position of continuity with the earlier policy thinking of Albert Luthuli, in particular, was strikingly reinforced by Hlatshwayo, who argued: 'The Freedom Charter and the ANC's Constitutional Guidelines *set the basis for a welfare state in a post-apartheid South Africa.* The people's government will intervene in the economy and in the provision of social security for the people. It will institute a national health service and introduce free and compulsory education for all' (Hlatshwayo 1990: 15, emphasis added).

At the same conference, health policy analysts De Beer and Broomberg argued that the route to an equitable health care system should be through a national health insurance system, which, in their view, was the obvious mechanism as the post-apartheid state would not be able to afford the additional expenditure required to equalise health care provision against other competing social priorities. In this scenario, legislation would be enacted that would compel employers and employees to contribute to a single national health insurance scheme, the membership of which would be compulsory and the payments of which would be to the state (through the Department of Health). They further argued that the 'basic aim of centralised state funding is the eradication of the two-tier health system' as such a system excluded those who did not have the ability to pay and differentially favoured a privileged stratum of society that had the means to afford private health care. Their conclusion was that implementing such an equity-driven system of centralised state funding in health care would result in the 'end of the [private] medical aid system as we know it' but with the caveat that the route to achieving this would need to be negotiated (De Beer and Broomberg 1990: 29). Furthermore, they concluded that it was important to accept that the private health care sector would be around for the 'foreseeable future' but that the private sector would need to be carefully regulated and that the 'centralisation of funds in the hands of the Department of Health could provide this major mechanism for the effective regulation of the private providers of health care' (De Beer and Broomberg 1990: 29).

London observed the irony that Broomberg went on to become the CEO of Discovery Health in 2012, the most significant provider of private health insurance schemes in the health care system:

> Looking at the [1990 Maputo conference] report I am kind of gob-smacked at what people were saying then … Like there's Jonny Broomberg writing with Cedric [de Beer] saying things that he would never dream of putting in his mouth today … He talks about doing away with the medical aid and subsidy for private insurance … He talks about the eradication of the two-tier health system … by definition an end to the medical aid system as we know it … He's talking about preventing the private sector from expanding in already well-served areas … that's exactly what Discovery Health does … (London interview, 21 August 2018).

In the light of the powerful commitments to an equity-driven agenda based on the concept of a redistributive national health service to underpin the transformation of the health care system, the actual formal declaration that finally emerged from the Maputo conference seemed timid and studiously cautious by contrast.

The 'Declaration on Health and Welfare in Southern Africa' expressed a commitment to:

> (i) transforming the existing health and social services in South Africa into a non-racial, accessible, equitable, *cost-effective* and democratic national health and welfare system.
>
> …
>
> (v) emphasising the importance of *making realistic assessments* of the resources required to meet national health and welfare needs equitably, and of researching means for mobilising such resources. In line with the above commitments *high priority must be placed on applied health and welfare research and training.* The conference devoted particular attention to the problems of financing future national health and welfare … and *recognised the need for further research.*
>
> …
>
> (T)hese debates need to be placed in the context of the specific characteristics of a *mixed economy* (*Critical Health* 1990: 4, emphasis added).

Despite the pragmatic caution that started to seep into the policy discourse, the ANC was under pressure from its working-class constituency and trade union federation ally Cosatu to provide a decisive rupture with the policies of the apartheid-era state. The National Party state was attempting to reform the health sector following the appointment of Rina Venter as the new (and last) National Party health minister in 1989.

By May 1992, following its annual policy conference, the ANC still expressed an unequivocal commitment to establishing a national health service as expressed in its policy document 'Ready to Govern: ANC Policy Guidelines for a Democratic South Africa' (ANC 1992).

The document's sub-section on 'Principles of ANC Health Policy' is prefaced by the statement that the 'provision of equitable health care should be guided by the aspirations of our people as enshrined in the Freedom Charter and by principles which reflect the Primary Health Care Approach …' (ANC 1992: n.p.).

The policy guidelines then propose 'the creation of a comprehensive, equitable and integrated *National Health Service (NHS)*' with a 'single governmental structure dealing with health for the whole country', which would 'coordinate all aspects of both public and private health care delivery'. It would 'be accountable to the people of South Africa through democratic structures'. It further advocates that 'in line with the ANC commitment to a mixed economy, the provision of health care by the private sector will continue to be acknowledged and regulated' (ANC 1992: n.p., emphasis added).

Gonda Perez, an activist in the health policy debate who had been in exile with the ANC, commented:

> The underlying principle was that people wanted equity and everything else came from that broad principle ... trying to ensure that everyone in the country had access to similar kinds of services. I think we had no choice but to put in place these policies ... We had documents like the Freedom Charter that set out policy long before we had an inkling of what these policies would cost, but we had to implement it and try and redress some of the inequities (Perez interview, 11 November 1998).

The commitment to democratisation and the attempt to involve, or at least to be seen to be involving, a broader constituency was a distinguishing feature of the policy-making process in the social sectors of the ANC and its allies compared to that of the apartheid state and what may have been occurring in other sectors of the ANC policy-making apparatus. This could also be viewed as an attempt to present a unified approach and to recognise legitimate attempts by the apartheid government to restructure the health and welfare system along more egalitarian lines.

The attempts at unilateral restructuring were evidenced in 1990 when Venter, the minister of health, declared that all formerly white hospitals were to be opened to black patients. Ironically, this decisive break with apartheid health care was not quite as revolutionary a step for the government as it seems at first glance. This was because no legislation had to be repealed, as none existed that barred access to hospitals – it had merely been a norm applied by health professionals and administrators, a fact that Venter discovered to her surprise (Venter interview, 10 November 1998).

De Beer suggests that the administrative framework, within which the decision was made to deracialise hospital services, provided insight into Venter's resolve to reform health care. For example, the whites-only hospitals in the then Transvaal Province had been transferred to the white 'own affairs' department in 1989, suggesting that 95 per cent of the patients in these hospitals were white patients; 'the minister apparently felt no discomfort at overriding this constitutional imperative' of white departments only providing services to whites 'with immediate effect' (De Beer 1992: 275).

The ANC and its allies had to respond to a government that was not only developing alternative health policies but implementing them. These policies were attempting to respond to the criticisms of being financially and racially inequitable. The government was also trying to effect structural changes in the management, human resourcing and balance of private and public health care provision, which would have serious long-term implications for a new government.

In response, the ANC and its allies attempted to meet these demands through the Patriotic Health Front. This was a loose coalition that unified a range of oppositional political parties, non-governmental organisations (NGOs) and social movements in opposition to what was described as the 'unilateral restructuring' of health and welfare services being undertaken by the state (Perez and Friedman interviews, 11 November 1998). The duality of roles related to a situation in which '… the ANC and its allies were putting in place policies for the long-term future but did not want these policies to be stopped in their tracks by structural changes prior to the elections. So one was engaging the state … and stopping these structural changes. [However] there was another process in place to ensure that policies were being developed and put in place. It was the time when the ANC Health Plan was being developed' (Perez interview, 11 November 1998).

The Patriotic Health Front sought to develop a national health plan through a wide-ranging consultation process. The idea was for ANC branches to establish health committees that were tasked to reflect the health needs of their communities through a range of workshops. This was then supposed to be reported to a regional health conference, and then finally compiled at national level by a team of ANC-aligned health experts in defined areas, such as nutrition, health promotion, and maternal and child health, with assistance from the World Health Organization. While the process far exceeded the capacities of the average ANC branch, there was a concerted attempt to be accountable and inclusive.

While the primary impetus was towards establishing a community-oriented health care system based on the primary health care approach, a working group was also established to examine tertiary medicine. This group revolved around Jerry Coovadia at the University of Natal. According to globally recognised public health specialist and socialist scholar David Sanders, 'this group had formed itself, because I think it was quite worried that somehow academic medicine, specialist medicine, was going to be marginalised' (Sanders interview, 19 August 2017).

The imperative around defending tertiary medicine, which consumed nearly 65 per cent of the provincial health budgets, was to take on increasing significance as the health policy debate unfolded in the period leading to and after the democratic elections in 1994.

Meanwhile, the first draft of a national health plan was produced and circulated to ANC branches and progressive NGOs, and regional conferences were held on the draft proposals. These were finally produced after refinement by ANC health experts working with the World Health Organization and UNICEF, as a 100-page document entitled 'A National Health Plan for South Africa' (ANC 1994a). This document was an unequivocal restatement of the ANC's transformative health policy trajectory since the 1940s as reflected in the African Claims policy document of the 1940s, confirmed in the Freedom Charter of the mid-1950s and reflected in the 1992 Ready to Govern policy guidelines.

The primary objective, as reflected in this document, in fact largely restated the Ready to Govern policy guidelines: 'A single, comprehensive, equitable and integrated *National Health System (NHS)* must be created. There will be a single governmental structure dealing with health, based on national guidelines, priorities and standards. It will co-ordinate all aspects of both public and private health care delivery, and will be accountable to the people of South Africa through democratic structures … All racial, ethnic, tribal and gender discrimination will be eradicated' (ANC 1994a: 2, emphasis added).

In order to reflect continuity with the positions emerging from the mandate of the 1992 ANC National Policy Conference, the national health system that was being advocated had to be 'in line with the ANC's commitment to a mixed economy', while 'the provision of health care by the private sector will continue to be *acknowledged* and *regulated*' (ANC 1994a: 2, emphasis added).

The proposals under the rubric of a national health system can be summarised as follows. Firstly, the document proposed the transformation in the perceived curative, bio-medical ethos of the health service through application of the community-oriented primary health care approach, adopted at Alma-Ata in the then USSR.[3] It was envisaged that this would 'inevitably bring about some radical transformations, not only of the health infrastructures … but also of the mentality of both health providers and those demanding health care services' (ANC 1994a: 5).

Secondly, the delivery and management of health services at local level would take place in conjunction with communities organised into a district health system.[4] The bodies envisaged to administer the programme were community health committees, which would co-manage community health centres with health care providers to the extent of examining budgets and determining local policies. The community health centres were proposed to be the backbone of the national health services. They would provide comprehensive promotional, preventive, curative and rehabilitative care. Crucially, community health workers – who were not formally regulated, trained or accredited by the state but who worked in conjunction with health care NGOs – were to act as catalysts for effecting community development from a health perspective. It was proposed that they should be integrated into the national health system and remunerated according to their skills either by the community or by government. The community-level services, both public and private, would fall under the auspices of a district health authority, which would be allocated a budget for the provision of public health care services.

In the nine new provinces, it was proposed that a provincial health authority be established to support and supervise the district health authorities by controlling specialist hospitals and services and co-ordinating health personnel training. Alongside these would be a provincial health advisory body composed of members of the private sector and civil society. Finally, at central or national level, a national health authority would have overall responsibility for the development and provision of all health care, with specific responsibility for allocation of budgets to provincial health authorities as well as policy and planning and the development of norms, standards and guidelines.

Thirdly, funding of the national health system was to derive from general tax revenue; the charging of user fees, other than for insured patients, would be abolished. It was also posited that 'the reduction in fragmentation and duplication of service provision and administration among different health authorities could release certain resources' (ANC 1994a: 5).

The private sector was acknowledged as important to the national health system. However, it was believed that the 'current structure of the private sector has created incentives which detract from the ultimate objective of health for all, and instead has created incentives which allow financial interests to take precedence over the patients' interests' (ANC 1994a: 5). Thus, it was proposed that 'the state will no longer subsidise the private sector. A better regulatory framework will be applied to the licensing of private sector facilities. Other systems of remuneration will be investigated to replace fee-for-service payments in private health facilities to reduce the incentive to over-service' (ANC 1994a: 5).

There is a striking similarity between these objectives of the ANC's National Health Plan and the far-reaching health transformation proposals of the 1944 Gluckman Commission on a National Health Service of the segregation era (Union of South Africa 1944), which preceded it by 50 years and was supported by the ANC of the time under AB Xuma. The similarity with the Gluckman Commission proposals is particularly evidenced in the attempt at a community-oriented democratisation of health care delivery, with an emphasis on preventive care and community health centres, as well as the diminished role envisaged for the private sector. The one significant exception was that under the Gluckman proposals of 1944, hospitals would be controlled at national level by government. The intention was to enforce a rationalised system of health care organisation throughout the three different levels of service delivery (national, provincial and local), and to ensure the ending of provincial control over government health budgets, which provinces were empowered to use for purposes other than health. This proposal contributed to the defeat of the Gluckman proposals (Van Niekerk 2012).

These proposals in the 1994 ANC National Health Plan were also fully consistent with the policy proposals advocated by MERG (1993) the year before. The health section of the MERG document was finalised by the noted Marxist economist and international solidarity activist Ben Fine.

The MERG proposals were unequivocal in locating the inequities in health care provision in the distribution of resources between the private and public sectors and the drive towards privatisation of health care services by the last apartheid-era government.

MERG identified the central problem as being the private sector's domination of the health human resource structure, which only benefited a small minority of the population:

> Currently [1993] the private sector employs half the doctors, 80 to 90 per cent of dentists, nearly 20 per cent of nurses and absorbs half the money spent on health. Most of this expenditure arises out of private insurance, yet only 16 per cent of the population are covered – 70 per cent of whites and under 4 per cent of blacks. The rapid growth for the latter, from a negligible base, indicates the inadequacies of resources devoted to public provision, rather than the superiority of a private health care system (MERG 1993: 110).

Furthermore, MERG drew attention to the correlation between income inequality and the poor socio-economic well-being (particularly of the black population) under the apartheid regime. It concluded that the 'the extreme incidence of ill-health will be further compounded by differentiation in access to treatment, the more so to the extent this depends upon the ability to pay' (MERG 1993: 110). It drew out the consequences of privatisation as compounding these identified inequities:

> In the light of the extreme inequalities in the distribution of income, privatisation inevitably tends to the over-treatment of the wealthy and, by the criteria of social efficiency and equity, the inefficient crowding-out of the

treatment of the impoverished. Moreover, privatisation is often linked to occupational insurance schemes, which widen existing inequalities between the employed and unemployed. Similarly, health provision amongst the employed will be unequal, as health care as a form of fringe benefit will reflect and magnify occupational stratification (MERG 1993: 107).

The MERG proposals also drew attention to the negligible provision of comprehensive public health care for the majority of (black) inhabitants with a minority (white) enjoying such care, with health care provision based on market principles inevitably privileging those who already had access to health services (MERG 1993: 107). It further drew attention to the curative bias of health care at the expense of preventative health care and the failure to adequately account for industrial health and safety – a neglect that would be compounded through privatisation, it argued (MERG 1993: 109).

In response to the problems and inequities identified, MERG unequivocally proposed – and was fully consistent with ANC policy on health up to that point – a national health service as the mechanism to transform the apartheid-era health care system: 'South Africa requires a *unitary national health service* available to all citizens without user charges, and based on a rolling programme of basic health services, which will be extended over time to include more services, as well as specialist treatment at higher levels on a selective basis' (MERG 1993: 112, emphasis added).

The institutional vehicle for the achievement of this objective was to propose that a 'single department of health be implemented, responsible for planning health services and providing basic health care' with 'government expenditure and health policy directed towards preventive measures and primary health care' (MERG 1993: 112).

The report further recommended that the role of the private sector be 'regularly reviewed' and that the privatisation of services be 'discouraged and where appropriate, reversed'. Reflecting its primary orientation to a national health service, MERG also proposed that the health service be funded through 'general government revenue' and that the union-based private health care schemes being negotiated by Cosatu be 'integrated into the developing national health service' (MERG 1993: 112).

However, and as a precursor to the policy displacement that occurred following the 1994 elections, the MERG policy proposal on a national health service was summarily dismissed by influential figures within or aligned to the dominant ANC policy-making apparatus.

Fine relates this as follows:

> As far as I was concerned, the idea of a national health service was going to be uncontroversial. That doesn't mean there was not going to be a big battle over a very powerful insurance industry. There were issues like that, but not whether there was going to be a national health service … I mean, the arguments about what happens if you allow a parallel system, everyone knows this, particularly in the context of South Africa where the command of resources in the private sector would have been extraordinary (Fine interview, 30 June 2015).

The health proposals were to be introduced to the ANC policy-making elite at the MERG launch conference on 3 December 1993. Instead, they were summarily dismissed (see chapters 4 and 5 for details). No alternatives were presented or debated at the launch conference in response to the MERG health proposals (Fine interview, 30 June 2015). What was telling was the realignment of key progressive health policy activists around a cautiously pragmatic position on health care reform that ultimately acquiesced to the private sector-dominated status quo. It is worth repeating a point made earlier by Fine:

> On health, to my astonishment, Max Price [a leading public health policy researcher aligned to the progressive movement at the time] gave the response on behalf of the Department and it was very much one of, 'we are short of resources, therefore it is better to keep the private health system going for those who can afford it and then that would mean that we'll have lesser charges on what we can provide', and so on. So these positions came as a great surprise to me, in part because in doing the research for those sections of the MERG report, I travelled around the country, talking to policymakers and activists to see what they saw as the ways forward, in part on the basis of their experiences and struggles. But in many ways, I don't think the issue was one of what was the substance of the reply or the response. It's not clear they had alternative policies that they had to put forward. It's that they disagreed, I mean that was it (Fine interview, 30 June 2015).

It is also instructive to compare the synergies of the ANC's 'A National Health Plan for South Africa' policy document with the proposals developed and contained in MERG and the Reconstruction and Development Programme (RDP) (ANC 1994a, 1994b).

With regard to health care policy, the RDP Base Document released before the 1994 elections advocated: 'One of the first priorities is to draw all the different role players and services into the NHS [national health system] … Reconstruction in the health sector will involve the complete transformation of the entire delivery system … The whole NHS must be driven by the Primary Health Care (PHC) approach. This emphasises community participation and empowerment, intersectoral collaboration and cost-effective care …' (ANC 1994b: 51).

The mechanism for achieving the transformation in health care is described in the following fiscally redistributive terms: 'The RDP must significantly shift the budget allocation from curative hospital services towards Primary Health Care to address the needs of the majority of the people. This must be done mainly by reallocating staff and budgets to district health services … within a period of five years a whole range of services must be available free to the aged, the disabled, the unemployed …' (ANC 1994b: 51).

However, a policy schism emerged between the frameworks developed for the health sectors – such as those contained in the MERG document, the National Health Plan and the RDP Base Document – and their subsequent iteration, when the ANC became the government in 1994.

Ralph Mgijima, influential head of the exiled ANC Health Department, was actively involved and influential in both the development of the ANC National Health Plan and the health section of the RDP Base Document. Already in the early years after the unbanning of the ANC in 1990, he detected disquiet with the redistributive impetus in health policy in the RDP Base Document compared to the direction of economic policy in the same document. For Mgijima this was at variance with the historical 'social' underpinning of ANC policy-making:

> You know when we were debating the Reconstruction and Development Programme in 1992, '93 … when they come to the health section it would be quiet … it would be like you have dropped something, you know … it would be quiet … because the other aspects of the RDP were talking basically [about] modified capitalism … they were not looking at a comprehensive social solution which is what the basis of ANC policy is all about. The soul of ANC policy is social. To ensure the well-being of all citizens and people is protected (Mgijima interview, 13 November 2018).

The early disquiet in the 1990s of sections of the ANC policy-making elite on redistributive social policy was to be more fully reflected in the receptivity to neo-liberal tenets in post-election policy documents, which emphasised 'fiscal discipline'. This was a new, overarching discourse in Nelson Mandela's speeches and in government policy documents, such as the White Paper for Reconstruction and Development in 1994 and the Government of National Unity programme in 1994 to restructure the social and economic system after coming to power.

FISCAL DISCIPLINE AND THE DISPLACEMENT OF THE ANC'S 'BIG IDEA' OF ESTABLISHING A NATIONAL HEALTH SERVICE

The dominant activity of the ANC-led Government of National Unity (GNU) in the three years following the first democratic election centred on policy-making in all spheres of government. Its aims could be seen as threefold. Firstly, the ANC under Mandela attempted to legitimate itself as the new government rather than as an oppositional liberation movement. Secondly, it was unsure of the exact strategy that it would need to achieve the objectives that were presented in broad form in its pre-election policy frameworks and declarations. Thirdly, it lacked a detailed awareness and understanding of the depth and extent of the fragmented, unequal apartheid state it had inherited and was aiming to transform.

The time-consuming process of extensive policy consultation and development, combined with public expectations of urgent delivery in the 'honeymoon' period immediately following the 1994 elections, provided a space in which the new government could not only consolidate, but also revise its position and the expectations placed on it. The process of policy displacement and distancing from substantive accountability to mass-based formations, which occurred in the pre-1994 period, gradually gained added momentum when the ANC came to power and could draw on its legitimacy as the ruling party in a democratic government.

The process of policy development between 1994 and 1996 was characterised by an avalanche of Green Papers, White Papers, Bills and Acts. In this period, pre-election policy papers came under intense scrutiny by a new policy order consolidated under Thabo Mbeki. Many of the redistributive proposals for social policy previously developed by the ANC, Cosatu, the SACP and the MDM were displaced or diminished by the ANC after it became the ruling party.

A fuller assessment is emerging of this period of policy-making (Lund 2008; Plagerson et al. 2018). Plausible reasons for the policy displacement in health include that new civil servants and political appointees in provincial and national government, the majority aligned to the ANC but many from other parties in the GNU, were not necessarily part of the prior processes of policy-making. Neither could the new civil servants be considered supportive of the detail of the pre-election policy frameworks, as exemplified, for example, by the new minister of health, Nkosazana Dlamini-Zuma.

While a staunch and unequivocal advocate and supporter of the broad primary health care and redistributive thrust of ANC health policy, she had not been prominent in the pre-election policy-making process. She thus did not feel compelled to implement the pre-election health proposals, with some of which, such as the strong role envisaged for community health workers, she did not agree (Friedman interview, 11 November 1998).

Many members of the new GNU who were given crucial portfolios – such as welfare (Abe Williams, replaced by Patrick McKenzie after financial irregularities were uncovered) and finance (Derek Keys) – were members of parties traditionally opposed to the ANC, including the National Party, which had ruled in the apartheid era. These critical portfolios were returned to the ANC in 1996 when the National Party left the government.

A second and perhaps more significant reason for the displacement was that much of the pre-election redistributive health policy had given little thought to fiscal considerations, and this was to have serious implications for implementation. As discussed in chapters 4 and 5, the government's new approach was oriented to fiscal restraint and the reduction of the budget deficit through cuts in government expenditure and improved tax collection. These emerging economic objectives were consolidated in the Growth, Employment and Redistribution (GEAR) policy released in 1996 (see chapter 5).

In the social policy sector, the most dramatic impact of the displacement of prior ANC and MDM policy positions was felt in the health sector. Health had a coherent non-governmental sector and active social movements that had participated extensively in the pre-election policy development process, as discussed earlier. However, when the new government took power, there was a discernible shift in the positions of many activists, especially when they joined the government.

David Sanders, active in the pre-election ANC health policy-making process, described it as follows: 'There was this kind of schizophrenia, almost. That all these people who had been involved in these [prior] policy debates then arrive in government. Government essentially adopts neo-liberal policies in the health sector, and all these people implement them, almost unquestioningly, not seeing them as part of neo-liberal reforms – i.e. [structural adjustment] in the health sector' (Sanders interview, 19 August 2017).

Sanders illustrates this paradox with reference to a public policy discussion at the University of Cape Town (UCT) in response to a major policy report on health released by the World Bank in 1993. The report, 'Investing in Health', argued inter alia for the pursuit of economic growth policies that would 'benefit the poor', including 'where necessary, adjustment policies that preserve cost-effective health expenditure' and promoting 'diversity and competition in provision of health services' through encouraging 'social or private insurance (with regular incentives for equitable access and cost containment) for clinical services outside the essential package' (World Bank 1993b: 6). This market-oriented framework for health reforms is accompanied with the continued, albeit not uncritical, advocacy of user fees, a direct contradiction with the policy impetus in ANC-aligned policy-making in the pre-1994 era (World Bank 1993b: 172).

However, despite the contradictory position of the World Bank report in relation to the redistributive policy impetus of ANC health policies, the report received significant support among key ANC-aligned policymakers and activists.

Sanders provided a critique of the World Bank policy report at the discussion at UCT, detailing why he considered it the 'bible of neo-liberal health reforms'. He reported that he was somewhat stunned at the lack of response from the progressive policymakers: 'I did raise some serious concerns about [the 1993 World Bank report] and I can remember that all in the room, they just didn't get what I was on about. There was almost like a Jekyll and Hyde thing. Here were people who had been involved in elaborating the ANC health policy document, which is a very good document, and then when it came to actually going into government, they actually implemented a kind of selective primary health care and structural adjustment' (Sanders interview, 19 August 2017).

He commented on this policy 'schizophrenia' as follows:

> I think it was more that people that were now policymakers within the health sector were actually quite naive, had not fully apprehended what comprehensive primary health care and a national health system à la the ANC health plan really meant. And were easily swayed by the [UK King's Fund] and people coming from outside the country, you know, mostly from the US and the UK, with all sorts of new ideas, which fitted in well with the thrust of the World Bank's World Development Report. And there were only a few of us who had any kind of critical approach to that. And that created great surprise among comrades at UCT. They couldn't understand why I was in any way unhappy with the World Bank World Development Report (Sanders interview, 19 August 2017).

Following the appointment of Dlamini-Zuma as minister of health in 1994 and provincial health ministers (referred to as provincial Members of the Executive

Council, MECs), a series of Strategic Management Teams were established at provincial level. They were composed of academic experts and consultants, members
of NGOs and government functionaries, including those of the previous government. These were tasked with advising the provincial governments on the restructuring and integration of the provincial health system in accordance with the move
to create a single national public health system.

At the national level, the minister of health appointed two special advisers and
established a number of ministerial technical committees composed of academics,
government personnel, including those from the previous government, and the
NGO community. Foreign experts, funded by major donor agencies and international institutions, became prominent in government policy-making circles.

The ministerial committees were charged with developing policy and plans in
areas such as human resources, financing and management (Tollman and Rispel
1995: 78). These technical committees, however, conducted their deliberations in
private with little public participation. Draft technical documents were released in
1995 as discussion documents, partly in response to this criticism. The Ministry
of Health responded to the wide-scale public criticism led by health professionals
by including public consultation in the deliberations of the Committee of Inquiry
into a National Health Insurance System (Tollman and Rispel 1995: 80). It was
becoming clear that post-election policy-making would be consultative, but select-
ively so. More fundamentally, there would not be continuity with the redistributive ANC National Health Plan, in which the ANC-aligned NGO sector and health
social movements had invested their energies.

When this became apparent, it caused consternation and a great deal of
uncertainty:

> We were all stunned [in the NGOs]. We had expected that there would be
> the rapid adoption of the of the ANC Health Plan and all the various sub-
> committees that had done all that work – or at least that the work would
> have been acknowledged – and that anything that was set up would have
> used that as sources, but all that work disappeared ... There was a continual
> jettisoning and reinvention of the wheel ... and a complete unwillingness to
> recognise policies that had been developed not only by the NGOs but even
> within the ANC itself (Friedman interview, 11 November 1998).

Some spectacular advances were made in elements of the health reform agenda
under the new health minister, such as a presidential project advocating the implementation of free health care for pregnant mothers and children. At the same

time, however, a gradual conservative recalibration of policy was occurring, which circumscribed the health policy agenda. This was informed by the increasingly dominant, new market-friendly, neo-liberal imperative of fiscal discipline, the cumulative effect of which was to subordinate and ultimately displace the larger vision of a broadly social democratic 'good society'. The latter had been reflected in ANC social policy since the 1940s under AB Xuma, the 1950s under Albert Luthuli, the MERG policy framework in the early 1990s and the RDP Base Document before the 1994 election. It is this recalibration under a policy elite in the ANC, supported by Mandela, which eschewed a neo-Keynesian (and ultimately democratic socialist) redistributive possibility for South Africa. For us, this explains the abandonment of the social democratic imperatives that historically underpinned ANC social policy.

The evidence for this shift to fiscal conservatism is found in a range of post-election policy documents and official government statements, in particular by President Mandela, which reflected the gradual distancing of the GNU from the pre-election social democratic and redistributive policies advocated by Cosatu, the SACP and civil society groups. It is worth reflecting on the scale, intensity and depth of this overriding policy commitment to fiscal discipline within which health policy was to be circumscribed in the post-apartheid era.

In his State of the Nation address to the Houses of Parliament in 1994, Mandela says the following:

> Precisely because we are committed to ensuring sustainable growth and development leading to a better life for all, *we will continue existing programmes of fiscal rehabilitation*. We are therefore determined to make every effort to contain real general government consumption at present levels and to manage the budget deficit with a view to its continuous reduction. Similarly, we are agreed that a permanently higher general level of taxation is to be avoided. To achieve these important objectives *will require consistent discipline* on the part of both the central and the provincial governments (Mandela 1994a: n.p., emphasis added).

The creeping fiscal conservatism gradually hardened in the government's 'RDP White Paper: Discussion Document' (RSA 1994) released in September 1994, and the finalised and gazetted White Paper for Reconstruction and Development released in November of that year. Proposals for nationalisation and state interventionism in the economy found in the original RDP Base Document were either dropped or moderated. While retaining the broad principles of the Base

Document, the 'White Paper: Discussion Document' introduced a new language of fiscal austerity, reflecting the influence of discourses consistent with those found in the World Bank, such as 'affordability' and 'cost containment', and mechanisms such as privatisation (euphemistically referred to as 'sale of state assets') and 'user charges' as key objectives of government economic policy:

> All levels of government *must pay attention to affordability given our commitment to fiscal discipline* and to achievable goals (RSA 1994: para. 1.3.2, emphasis added).
>
> ...
>
> The GNU draws on the following basic strategy to achieve its objectives: *financial and monetary discipline* in order to finance the RDP, reprioritise public sector activity, and facilitate industrial restructuring and the establishment of *fair and equitable user charges* (RSA 1994: para. 3.3.1, emphasis added).
>
> ...
>
> ... not only has the RDP Fund financed with these [fiscal] constraints in mind, in the overall process for taking forward the RDP, *it is geared to cutting government expenditure* wherever possible (RSA 1994: para. 3.3.4, emphasis added).

Mandela's role in facilitating the shift in policy discourse has been discussed in chapter 5 above and cannot be underestimated. In the preface written by Mandela to both the RDP 'White Paper: Discussion Document' and the subsequent finalised RDP White Paper, he states that '*the Government is firmly committed to the gradual reduction in the fiscal deficit, thereby avoiding the debt trap*' (RSA 1994: 4). As discussed, a fear existed that further borrowing would lead to a dependency cycle of debt repayment to the World Bank and International Monetary Fund (Padayachee 1997). This is stated explicitly in the White Paper: 'The deficit has reached disturbingly high levels in recent years and any future borrowing strategy will be based on caution, particularly with respect to foreign loans. The Government is committed to the progressive reduction of the overall deficit. The Government's commitment to maintaining *fiscal discipline* is a tool to ensure sustainability of the RDP in the medium to long term' (1994: para 4.1.2, emphasis added).

This message of fiscal discipline is also well represented in Mandela's speeches to parliament, labour and business in the 1994/1995 period. In the opening address to the President's Budget Debate after his first 100 days in office, for example, Mandela stated: 'The Cabinet started last week to discuss guidelines for the 1995/96 budget.

We are confident that more fundamental restructuring will be introduced, *without undermining the requirement for fiscal discipline*' (Mandela 1994b: n.p., emphasis added). The following month, at an address to the Fifth National Congress of Cosatu on 7 September 1994, he stated: '… our basic standard to gauge progress [of the RDP] is the rate at which various departments are changing their priorities in line with the programme as a whole. Along with this, *is the challenge of ensuring fiscal discipline* and efficiency, so that the RDP can be implemented in a sustainable manner. The RDP White Paper, to which the trade union and other formations have made an important contribution, seeks to address these issues' (Mandela 1994c: n.p., emphasis added).

In a speech to the Business Initiative against Corruption and Crime in August 1995, he presents the matter in the following terms: 'We have laid particular stress on steps by the private sector towards increased and *more effective self-regulation* because this would bring double benefits. It would help to cut crime; but it would also reduce the scale of public resources required to combat tax evasion and fraud. *That would strengthen our national drive for fiscal discipline*' (Mandela 1995a: n.p., emphasis added). This was yet again repeated in a speech by Mandela at the inauguration of Gencor's new head office and celebration of Gencore's Centenary in Johannesburg on the 29 September 1995: 'The consensus we enjoy has also allowed us to establish an economic policy framework that is conducive to sustained growth and development. *Fiscal and financial discipline*; the rational use of public resources; the opening of our economy; and reduction of foreign exchange controls are key elements in that framework' (Mandela 1995b: n.p., emphasis added).

This veritable onslaught of fiscal conservatism informing policy came accompanied with a diminution of fiscal resourcing of the RDP programme, which was arguably the last hope for implementing the broadly social democratic agenda in the post-election era of democracy, relegating it to a relatively minor programme of government. The chiselling away at the redistributive imperatives and principles, which informed pre-election policy-making, was evident in the budgeting arrangements for the RDP in post-election government policy.

The RDP White Paper limited expenditure on the Reconstruction and Development Programme to 'savings' from government departments that would be placed in an RDP Fund: 'The RDP Fund consists of funds which have been removed from departmental allocations and can be reassigned to them subject to compliance with the new priorities' (RSA 1994: para. 2.3.2). The actual RDP funds assigned from such 'savings' were a minuscule 2 per cent of the total government budget in 1994/1995 (Blumenfeld 1997: 73).

Even with the doubling in expenditure seen in subsequent years, the RDP budget formed a small part of total government expenditure in the White Paper: 'In the 1994/95 Budget R2.5 billion was allocated to the RDP Fund. This amount will increase to R5 billion in 1995/96 and will progressively increase to R10 billion in 1997/98 and R12.5 billion thereafter' (1994: para. 2.3.2).

Institutionally, the RDP was run by Jay Naidoo as an anonymously titled 'minister without portfolio'. His ministry was established in the Presidency with the task of implementing the RDP provisions through influencing the budgets of government departments and funding special Presidential Lead Projects in health, school feeding, rural water provision and infrastructure development. Paradoxically, Naidoo, as a minister with significant challenges of delivery in the immediate post-apartheid era, seemed to encourage a more limited role for the RDP Ministry as well as imbibing the language of fiscal conservatism. He believed that his ministry's role was to realign government expenditure to the point that the entire budget would be informed by the RDP within a five-year period: 'We don't want to up the Budget. We don't want to increase state expenditure in such a way that it leads to inflation and undermines fiscal discipline. Fiscal discipline is not an Internal [sic] Monetary Fund or World Bank term. It is fundamental to achieving the RDP on a sustainable basis' (in Harber 1994: n.p.).

The RDP Ministry experienced a number of management failures and, after slow delivery, it was incorporated into the Office of the Deputy President under Thabo Mbeki in 1996.

The scale and depth of the post-apartheid government's near obsessional policy commitment to fiscal discipline had real consequences for achieving equity. This was clearly illustrated in the new budgeting arrangements introduced for health care in the immediate post-election era.

EQUITY, BUDGETARY ARRANGEMENTS, GOVERNANCE AND HEALTH POLICY IMPLEMENTATION IN THE POST-ELECTION ERA

The most serious potential problems standing in the way of achieving equity in provision of health and welfare services relate to the constitutional arrangements for budgeting between the three levels of government. The estimate of government expenditure on health care in 1992/1993 was R30 billion, equivalent to 8.5 per cent of gross domestic product. The division between public and private *sources* of expenditure was 38 per cent from general tax revenue and 40 per cent from private medical schemes. The remaining sources were from 'out-of pocket' payments (14 per cent) and other forms of expenditure (8 per cent) (McIntyre 1995: n.p.).

Within the public sector, non-hospital primary-level services comprised only 11 per cent of total health expenditure (Makan, McIntyre and Gwala 1996: 73–74).

The achievement of an integrated NHS oriented to primary health care services depended to a substantial degree, however, on the restructuring of funding from tertiary to lower secondary and primary levels of care. This expenditure pattern in health care was also contrary to the professed policy aims and objectives of the new health system as contained in the government's White Paper for the Transformation of the Health System in South Africa, which was 'to unify the fragmented health services at all levels into a comprehensive and integrated NHS' and to 'to reduce disparities and inequities in service delivery and increase access to improved and integrated services, based on primary health care principles' (DoH 1997: 6).

The restructuring of financing arrangements for health care, informed by the post-apartheid policy obsession with fiscal discipline, shifted the policy momentum further from the equity imperative underpinning a national health service – a redistributive model of health financing based on general taxation as the primary source of health care funding, in which private funding would play an insignificant role.

The change to equity in health financing at provincial level first occurred in 1994, and in relation to the 1995/1996 budget. It was undertaken at national government level through a Health Functions Committee, which included representatives of the national and provincial departments of health, finance and state expenditure (McIntyre et al. 1999: 33).

The joint determination by the health and finance departments of the provincial health allocations for the 1995/1996 budget was based on a weighted capitation formula that took account of the need for public health services in the different provinces (DoH 1997). This formula for achievement of equity used variations in per capita provincial spending on health as a proxy for socio-economic status, and determined allocations on the basis of equalising these variations. Differences in health status as indicated in morbidity and mortality figures and differential access to health care services between the private and public sectors were also factored in as arguably more equitable indicators of health needs in the South African context. This was because per capita spending provided no indication of use of services, as citizens with access to medical aid schemes would very rarely use the public sector, other than for infrequent emergency care or specialist care. Secondly, some provinces had larger health needs than their total population suggested due to specific health conditions, such as KwaZulu-Natal, which had the highest prevalence of HIV and the greatest number of Aids-related patients in the post-apartheid era (McIntyre et al. 1995: 164–165).

With the promulgation of the 1997 Intergovernmental Fiscal Relations Act No. 97, however, a new 'fiscal disciplining' budgetary system came into effect. It aimed to determine the appropriate share of revenue between the national, provincial and local levels of government as well as to achieve inter-provincial equity. The intention was to establish mechanisms for making provinces more accountable for their expenditure by providing them with greater autonomy over their prioritisation and allocation of functions (such as education, health and welfare) at provincial level. The Act also intended to overcome problems of 'unfunded mandates' – the process whereby national government set policy and norms for provincial-level service delivery but did not provide sufficient funds for its implementation, resulting in either the decline of service delivery or unchecked provincial expenditure to meet commitments, which the national government was then required to sustain (FFC 2011).

The Financial and Fiscal Commission (FFC) replaced the Health Functions Committee. Established in terms of Section 198 of the Constitution of the Republic of South Africa, Act No. 200 of 1993 and confirmed in Section 220 of the Constitution of the Republic of South Africa Act No. 108 of 1996 as amended, its tasks included: 'Render advice and make recommendations to the relevant legislative authorities … regarding the financial and fiscal requirements of the national, provincial and local governments, including – (a) financial and fiscal policies; (b) equitable financial and fiscal allocations to the national provincial and local governments from revenue collected at the national level …' (RSA 1993).

The FFC recommended that allocations to national governments should grow more slowly as the constitutional allocation of functions for delivery of health, welfare and education services occurred mainly at provincial level, comprising up to 85 per cent of provincial budgets. The FFC further recommended that total provincial allocations be based on a provincial grants formula with a minimum national standards grant for provinces to specifically provide primary and secondary education, and district health care to their residents (FFC 1995).

The health component of this provincial grant was determined by a combination of demographics, policy and cost. Unlike the previous formula of the Health Functions Committee, it separated provincial public users of health services from users covered by medical aid schemes. It did this by apportioning an equity-targeted weighting of 3.5 visits to primary-level health clinics of public users as opposed to 0.5 visits for private users.[5] The advantage of the formula with regard to equity of access is that it separated citizens covered by medical schemes in the private sector from those who were reliant solely on public care. It did not, however, address the concern of differential morbidity and mortality ratios between provinces.

KwaZulu-Natal, for example, had a potentially much greater need and thus a higher 'qualifying population', with potentially high HIV and Aids-related care and contact with health facilities required (McIntyre 1995: n.p.). Provincial-level determination of per capita weightings also obscured the large intra-provincial differentiation in access to and need for health care; a solution to that requires determination of the formula to be decentralised to local government level.

The major threat for health funding represented in this restructuring and the introduction of the new budgeting arrangements informed by the policy discourse of fiscal discipline is that they did not entrench health funds at provincial level. The nine provinces were, in effect, allocated a cumulative block grant, including for health services, which was determined using a formula aimed at achieving inter-provincial equity. Once they 'received' this grant from the national government, provinces were entitled to allocate the funds according to their own provincially determined priorities, alongside the nationally agreed upon norms and standards. These arrangements established a 'path dependency' in health policy-making in the post-apartheid era that the sector has yet to recover from, as evidenced in poor delivery of health care services in under-served provinces such as the Eastern Cape.

A previous provincial MEC for health in the Eastern Cape and community-health-oriented public doctor and activist, Trudy Thomas, revealed the depth of health care delivery failure as a consequence of the federalist fiscal budgeting arrangements (an underpinning feature of the market-oriented GEAR), which did not ring-fence health expenditure in the province: 'It seemed that in its services GEAR was in reverse and, as usual, its teeth were biting deepest into the poorest. Instead of growth, employment and redistribution, the new financial policies were associated with increasing unemployment, poverty and deteriorating services [in the Eastern Cape]' (Thomas 2001: n.p.).

The evolution of the 'big idea' of establishing a national health service, first identified as a necessary institutional objective to overcome health care inequality in South Africa in the detailed research and proposals of the segregation-era Gluckman Commission of 1944 and finding full consensus in the proposals of African Claims, the Freedom Charter, the RDP Base Document, MERG and all key ANC health policy statements until the introduction of GEAR, was then displaced by the overarching narrative of 'fiscal discipline' in the post-1994 era. As discussed in detail in chapters 4 and 5, this narrative cumulatively formed part of an ideological shift in the ANC to a market-friendly agenda, which undermined the coming to fruition of the social democratic possibility that lay at the core of the ANC's emancipatory agenda, including for health policy.

9

Interpretation and Conclusion

Ruling national liberation movements, not least in southern Africa, were stagnating partly as a result of internal weaknesses and largely as a result of horrific apartheid destabilisation. The social democratic tradition was a pale and rather cynical shadow of its former self. Neo-liberalism appeared to be the only show in town. Thabo Mbeki bought into it, and it bought into him. There was an affinity in temperament. Shock therapy was the recipe. Out of the blue, zap the economy with undebated, written in stone, macro policy. What's the point of policy debate when all the answers are pre-given and managerial in character? All the old isms (as someone put it) had now become wasms. Ideology was dead, history had ended (Cronin 2016: n.p.).

OUR INTERPRETATION

Evidence from three years of research on this project leads us to argue that the narrative and the subsequent explanations for the compromises of the 1990s are far more complex than most monocausal explanations suggest. Some nascent ideas about economic and social policy can be traced back to African Claims (1943) and the Freedom Charter (1955), and to the Morogoro Conference (1969). But the intensity and contestation over such policy escalated considerably as democracy neared. As we have shown, economic and social policy debates in the transition era occurred at formal constitutional negotiations as well as through a variety of research think tanks, such as the Macroeconomic Research Group (MERG), within institutions of the state, in and through the progressive union movement and in business through various scenario-planning exercises.

So as to avoid any misunderstandings, we stress that our conclusions are based only on the areas of the research we have chosen to investigate – that is, on aspects of economic and social policy debates from 1943 to 1996. As far as formal constitutional negotiations are concerned, from Mac Maharaj, Ronnie Kasrils, Pallo Jordan and Jeremy Cronin, among others, we came to hear that other policy debates, especially over constitutional principles, security and defence, were very different and we have no reason to doubt their versions. In these (mainly political) areas, the ANC negotiating teams were better prepared and clearly emerged as 'winners'.

In the end, the ANC rightly prevailed in most areas and it delivered to us our celebrated democracy, partly because it was the bearer of the democratic dream, and through the 'Madiba factor'. Nïel Barnard (2017) points out that in fact neither side was very well prepared in all negotiating areas. And he is far from complementary of FW de Klerk's negotiating strategy. Chris Stals, in turn, makes the very valid observation that far more direct attention should have been placed on the economics of the transition by both major parties (Stals, telephone conversation with Padayachee, 23 November 2017).

Yet, in economic and social policy, both inside and outside formal negotiating forums, our evidence shows that the National Party was able to turn to some well-resourced economic institutions and individuals with decades of experience in economics, and which had been at the forefront of the development of market-friendly economic policy reforms since PW Botha's days. For some time in the 1980s and before his death in 1989, Gerhard de Kock appears to have had an important influence on the government's economic thinking. So, too, did Simon Brand, who headed the Development Bank of Southern Africa (DBSA) at a crucial time around the negotiations. The powerful, affable and seductive figure of Derek Keys, appointed as minister of trade and industry and of finance by De Klerk, was one such individual who emerges in the early 1990s as central to the nature and character of the economic policy debates. Keys used his deep knowledge of finance and budgeting gleaned in both the private and public sector as well as his access to state resources, his charm and his diplomatic skills to win over the younger and inexperienced ANC economic cadres. Against all this, the ANC economics team, while streetwise and sharp, was small and understandably unevenly trained and inexperienced. Less understandably, they appear to have turned their backs with undue haste on alternative progressive policy ideas and advice from their own research think tanks. They failed to engage with the power of the democratic movement in formulating economic policy, choosing instead to form themselves into a tightly knit and self-referential circle who trusted only themselves.

In summary, our findings reveal that the ANC economics team too eagerly imbibed a few weeks of crash-course training in economics provided to them by the World Bank, JP Morgan and other corporate ideologues. We set these events in the context of the hurly-burly of the transition, which saw these individuals over-stretched in trying to satisfy multiple and often seemingly trivial calls on their services. We show that the ANC economics team failed to engage sufficiently with its own historically informed traditions and with its rich mass democratic base to develop and defend its historical line from African Claims and the Freedom Charter. We argue that in terms of economic policy debates, the ANC was eventually outmanoeuvred by the outgoing government and state institutions, which had been shifting steadily towards a market-friendly approach to economic policy since the early 1980s. South Africa's powerful conglomerates also played a supporting role in this exercise in persuasion. In the end and given all this, the ANC bought into an essentially neo-liberal economic approach, with economic outcomes that have mostly had damaging consequences for the constituency of poor, marginalised and mainly black people, on whose behalf it had with nobility and distinction waged the struggle for democracy over many decades. By the 1990s, a dogmatic and arrogant (yet shallow) adherence to neo-liberal orthodoxy had already firmly embedded itself into ANC economic policy thinking.

In government after 1994, Ben Turok has observed with great insight in our view:

> Although the ANC had done some work on a future programme for government in the Reconstruction and Development Programme and Ready to Govern, these were only broad policy documents. There was no plan of how an ANC government would actually take over the administration of the country, nor did it have trained personnel to run the country. Consequently it took over most of the personnel from the apartheid regime and only replaced them incrementally in the following years. *Hence the actual arrangements of transition were carried out by apartheid officials, especially in the Treasury* (Turok 2017: n.p., emphasis added).

The influential ANC educationist and civil servant John Samuel, who worked in Nelson Mandela's Presidency, writing in July 2017 and speaking about the early years of the democratic government, makes a broadly similar point: 'Despite much preparation, we were not at all prepared for the subterranean text on the walls of the old government offices we moved into. The absence of guidelines shaped by the ideals of the struggle, coupled with pervading old apartheid culture, was a toxic mix' (Samuel 2017: n.p.).

Our research project is based on more than 35 in-depth interviews with key informants directly involved in the transition and negotiations of the late 1980s and early to mid-1990s, on shorter and more directed interviews with key activists, on archival research mainly at the University of Fort Hare Heritage Archives and on some private archival collections, on documentary analysis, and a review of the key economic and business journals and newspapers of the period. Based on all that, we have come up with the conclusions laid out in the next section.

GENERAL FINDINGS

(I)   Throughout its long history, the ANC failed (arguably with reason) to give any detailed attention to economic policy, so it entered negotiations in the late 1980s without any history of economic theorising behind it. It did so facing a well-resourced set of opponents, while it was itself unarmed and vulnerable to countervailing forces from all sides. It was unprepared for the implications of an evolutionary process of change, which it had never anticipated or planned for.

(II)   If one attempts (in the absence of specifics) to impute some very broad theoretical stance on the ANC's economic and social policy thinking, then neither a label of 'black nationalist bourgeois' nor 'communist/socialist' would appear to be appropriate. Rather one discerns ideas – especially in African Claims, the Freedom Charter and the Reconstruction and Development Programme (RDP) Base Document – which could better be described as social democratic (even if the ANC eschewed the use of this European-derived concept), whatever the South African Communist Party (SACP) then or now may argue. It is this social democratic and redistributive tradition, and not some imagined socialist vision, that the ANC leadership conceded by rejecting MERG in December 1993 and the RDP in April 1996.

(III)   There is evidence that the way in which the ANC worked on policy in general was highly fragmented, compartmentalised and, to some extent, personalised. Each National Executive Committee meeting of the ANC, including the Department of Economic Planning (DEP), worked in its own silo, hugely influenced by who was at the top of these committees. There was little or no reference to what other complementary policy committees were doing, with little or no co-ordination from the centre driving towards a common goal. There were only very tenuous links to the formal negotiations in the Convention for a Democratic South Africa and the multi-party talks, where crucial economic policy issues, such as central bank independence, were being led and finalised by apartheid regime bureaucrats and politicians.

(IV) Significantly (and ultimately disastrously), no evidence exists that the DEP group made itself accountable for its economic and social policy positions negotiated with the National Party government and the corporations. It did not engage with ANC branches and the core democratic structures of the movement through open, substantive and sustained engagements. For whatever reason (including arguably a fear of creating disunity), the ANC turned its back on its greatest asset and resource – the people of South Africa. A culture lacking in democracy and accountability but high on ego and arrogance were key features of the DEP's approach in the transition years. The unit was, in our assessment, a self-referential group, accountable only to themselves and working under the protection of both Mandela and Thabo Mbeki. This culture clearly carried into the new government, where the Growth, Employment and Redistribution (GEAR) programme was produced largely in secret by a small group of 'establishment' economists, led first by Alec Erwin and later by Trevor Manuel. As we all know, that document was made public in mid-1996 with the stunning announcement that it was 'non-negotiable'. The impact of the absence of both the Congress of South African Trade Unions (Cosatu) (with its mass base) and of the SACP (with its historical revolutionary mission) as forces in many of these economic policy processes in the 1990s is noticeable. In the end, it was just a handful of (arguably well-meaning) individuals who drove all these critical policy debates across the years of the democratic transition.

(V) Despite the fact that MERG was set up as a Tripartite Alliance initiative, the DEP failed seriously to engage with any of the policy positions and ideas produced by this most coherent economic policy alternative over the two to three years of its existence. For the ANC to argue that there was no alternative on the table is disingenuous. Note this comment by Turok: 'There were indeed critical voices which sought to introduce more radical economic and social policies which were rejected by the top leadership. The RDP was one such voice which was soon closed down on spurious grounds such as budget allocation difficulties. And there were others such as MERG (Macro Economic Research Group). *The main problem seemed to be that the leadership did not have a sense of what economic development meant and how it could be promoted*' (Turok 2017: n.p., emphasis added).

(VI)   ANC participation in MERG workshops and steering committee structures
         was formalistic and not substantive, reflecting both the organisation's unwill-
         ingness to engage with the MERG academic leadership and research teams
         and a certain growing disdain for any ideas that did not fit in with the sim-
         plistic pro-market positions of various institutions and organisations (both
         internal and external), which they appeared to have swallowed hook, line
         and sinker. The SACP and the South African National Civic Organisation
         had little or nothing to say about economics within MERG, and Cosatu
         had effectively nailed its mast to the RDP process and not to MERG, thus
         rendering the Alliance approach to economic policy highly fragmentary. In
         the context of the 1990s, if you did not recognise that 'we had no alternative',
         you had to be an 'economic dinosaur'.

(VII)   There is to date no credible evidence of any conspiracy theory involving the
         ANC, Western governments, the apartheid state and the international finan-
         cial institutions to repudiate the ANC's perceived programme of radical
         economic transformation. On the other hand, there is clear evidence that
         the market-friendly GEAR programme was initiated well before the cur-
         rency crash of February 1996 and driven in secret by a small hand-picked
         group of centre-right South African and international economists. Their
         meetings appear to have been held at the DBSA headquarters in Midrand,
         near Johannesburg. There is a strong possibility that some commentators,
         such as Sampie Terreblanche, may have mixed up these post-1994 meetings
         with those that ostensibly occurred secretly at the DBSA sometime in mid-
         1992 or mid-1993. Jay Naidoo's book *Fighting for Justice* (2010) also brings
         out aspects of Mandela's role in providing very open support and political
         cover for these secret GEAR talks. The key players, such as Manuel and
         Erwin, clearly and genuinely believed that GEAR was the only approach
         that could have been taken in that context and, as is evident from our
         interviews with them, they stand by this even today.

(VIII)   Overall, we find no credible evidence that the International Monetary Fund
         and the World Bank had any suitable vehicle through which they exerted any
         direct influence on ANC economic thinking. In some ways, the World Bank
         adopted a fairly sympathetic and accommodative stance towards the ANC.
         Ironically, the ANC on some policy issues opted for Washington Consensus
         ideas, on which the Bank was slowly turning its back. The World Bank's efforts
         to influence Mandela and the DEP to accept a package of loans in support of its
         public investment in physical and social infrastructure were, in effect, rejected
         by the ANC, which feared losing policy control and sovereignty to the Bank.

(IX)   The late-apartheid government, though weakened in some significant ways, nevertheless retained control of the not inconsiderable capacity and resources of key economic institutions, including the Treasury, the South African Reserve Bank (SARB), the Central Economic Advisory Services, Central Statistical Services, and agencies such as the DBSA and the Land Bank. All of them had bought into market-friendly economics since the days of the National Party's economic reforms, beginning in the late 1970s. The positions tabled by the National Party – including on SARB independence, the national debt and fiscal policy, as well as on the number and composition of provinces – carried the day almost by default as the ANC/DEP were underprepared to engage on such issues from their own platforms. These key economic institutions remained untouched across the pivotal years of the transition to democracy and were allowed the freedom to continue to retain a disproportional influence in shaping economic policy thinking immediately after 1994. These forces argued that an interventionist Keynesian, left social democratic or 'redistribution through growth' model was not an answer to the challenges of the post-apartheid economy. That these policy ideas more or less coincided with those of the Washington Consensus institutions was of course a major bonus.

Without any history or tradition of economic theorising, without the backing of its former Soviet supporters (Burawoy 1997), with an inexperienced DEP at the helm, having rejected any *substantive* engagement with the alternative progressive ideas coming out of the MERG and the RDP processes, and having rejected an inclusive democratic engagement on economic policy with its own internal constituency, the ANC was easy prey to a variety of influences. In this view, the ANC, through its DEP, was outmanoeuvred by the apartheid regime and local, big (white) capital: there was simply no need for secret talks in the dead of night to bring this about.

CONCLUSION: A SHADOW OF LIBERATION

The late-apartheid regime that the ANC negotiated with in the early 1990s may have been weakened by international sanctions and internal resistance, not to mention the psychological impact of the armed struggle, but it remained a formidable opposition. Its modern industrialised capitalism, its powerful financial, banking and physical infrastructure, its major conglomerates, its strong and well-educated white minority, and its powerful and well-resourced economic institutions were not a pushover, however weakened politically and internationally. To recognise that the ANC had to concede more than it might have wanted in this context is hardly surprising. Nevertheless, those compromises and that unnecessary lurch to economic conservatism have undoubtedly had serious negative consequences for the South African economy and for the poor and the working class. In this broad condemnation of the ANC's essentially neo-liberal policy choices in the lead-up to democracy and in power, we are at one with John Saul, Patrick Bond, Sampie Terreblanche, Ronnie Kasrils and other fierce critics of the ANC's policy choices. We simply but respectfully disagree with these scholars and activists in explaining how and why the ANC came to embrace neo-liberalism.

Finally, we hope that this book offers a significant and distinctive set of more complex – and yes, messier – arguments about why the transition in respect of economic and social policy unfolded in the way that it did. We believe that it demonstrates the weakness of arguments based on conspiracy theory, and that it debunks the myth of a coherent 'goose-stepping' neo-liberal project under the DEP group of the ANC. We further believe that the consequences of the catastrophic missteps on economic and social policy during the transition era cast a pall on the emancipatory social-democratic policy project (which historically lies at the heart of the ANC) developing further and eventually coming to fruition.

NOTES

PREFACE

1   This is the description of Minsky by a respected former chairman of the UK Financial Services Authority (see Rapley 2017: 378).

CHAPTER 1

1   Yet Harris (1990: 26) maintains that the ANC was still better placed than most other liberation movements in developing its overall economic programme.

2   The term 'warts and all' was used by Alec Erwin in encouraging us to undertake this research project. Erwin, like others, will not agree with all of our arguments – it is hard to think of a single person from any side who will agree with them all – but we hope he and others accept that we applied our minds to a complex set of concerns and interpreted these based on the best available evidence we could uncover.

CHAPTER 2

1   The CPSA was formed in 1921, but was banned by the apartheid National Party government in 1950. It reconstituted itself in 1953 as the South African Communist Party. The SACP functioned underground until FW de Klerk lifted the ban in February 1990.

2   The 'minimum programme' originally emerged out of a CPSA conference against fascism in 1936, which urged the formation of a 'people's front' against fascism, and which included communists forming an alliance and working with non-communist 'national movements' around the common minimal goals of fighting for and establishing democracy as part of an anti-fascist programme (Raman 2005: 232–233).

3   The Fort Hare protests refer to the boycott by students at the University of Fort Hare of the Student Representative Council elections in 1940 over poor-quality food in the boarding hostels, which led Mandela to resign from the SRC elections in protest that year and which he further recalls was a turning point in his political awakening (Mandela 1994d: 48–50).

CHAPTER 3

1   On Robben Island itself reading anything at all was no easy matter, especially in the 1960s, and reading was a 'right' that had to be struggled for. But read they did.
2   Of course, the Marxist Workers' Tendency, 'a far-left faction' (later expelled from the ANC), was committed to a (one-stage) worker-led revolution that would 'dismantle capitalism in South Africa as part of an inevitable world transition to communism' (Gerhart and Glaser 2010: 126). But its position was a marginal one in the debate over nationalism and socialism, where both Congress-aligned Robben Island groups more or less accepted a two-stage revolution.
3   We borrowed this phrase for the title of our book.
4   The Five Freedoms Forum was an extra-parliamentary organisation formed in the wake of the state of emergency in 1987. It consisted of progressive business leaders, lawyers, students, church people and other organisations, which were in the broadest sense opposed to the apartheid regime.
5   For more on this environment of revolutionary black and Asian life in London in the twentieth century, see Marc Matera (2015).
6   Segal, who escaped from South Africa in 1960, set up, funded and edited *Africa South* magazine (later *Africa South in Exile*). He was also the editor of the iconic Penguin African Library.
7   The National Economic Forum was a stakeholder body between big business, labour and the state, established during the negotiations era (1990–1993) to address issues of labour and business in the context of the political transition from apartheid.
8   Most of this section is drawn from and pieced together from a number of papers, notes, letters and documents in the Nelson Mandela Papers, Box 237, Folders 12–17.

CHAPTER 4

1   See further details by Michael Savage at http://www.sahistory.org.za/article/chronology-meetings-between-south-africans-and-anc-exile-1983-2000-michael-savage#sthash.vfHwReHX.dpuf (accessed 19.04.19).
2   Ngoasheng, formerly a sociology lecturer at the University of Natal, and not himself an economist, went on to to develop a deep loyalty to Thabo Mbeki and served in the Mbeki administration in the early 2000s as an economic policy adviser. He is now a business person.
3   The speech was reputedly drafted by Marxist ANC economist Jaya Josie (Interview, 30 January 2015).
4   Mandela's opening address on the occasion of the signing of a statement of intent to set up a national capacity for economic research and policy formulation, November 1991, in the Vishnu Padayachee private archives.
5   The book *Making Democracy Work* was also published in paperback by Oxford University Press (New York, 1994). As part of the preparations for democratic elections, the book was translated into isiZulu and published by the Community Law Centre under the title *Ukwenza Intando Yeningi Isebenze* (Wilson 1993).

CHAPTER 5

1   As an interesting aside, it is worth noting that Thuli Madonsela was present at the RTG conference where the office of an independent Public Protector was approved (*Business Day*, 15 October 2015).

2   The National Institute for Economic Policy was set up by the ANC and Cosatu after the end of the MERG process to provide economic advice and policy research. NIEP's first director was Renfrew Christie and its first research director was Asghar Adelzadeh. The description of NIEP as *die vader* (the father) of MERG is therefore incorrect.

3   HOP = RDP.

4   The Select Committee of parliament oversaw the drafting of the White Paper.

5   The passage was translated by Vishnu Padayachee and checked and corrected by Professor Jannie Rossouw, School of Economic and Business Sciences at the University of the Witwatersrand.

6   See https://www.datapacrat.com/True/INTEL/CSIS/COM44E.HTM (accessed 19.04.19).

7   Despite these weaknesses, and arguably to cover up their obvious shortcomings, there was on display in the 1990s no small amount of ego and arrogance and a singular lack of humility among some of the ANC's economic leadership team. That has not changed much today.

8   Cronin must have been referring to the Economic Trends Research Group, discussed in chapter 4.

9   Kasrils is referring to political developments, corruption and what has come to be termed 'state capture' under the Zuma administration post-2009. These issues are outside the scope of this book. See Pauw (2017) and Kasrils (2017) for more on these contemporary matters.

CHAPTER 6

1   Both authors were once active members of the ANC and/or the Alliance, especially during the period covered in chapters 4, 5 and 6. We still regard ourselves a part of the Congress tradition of Albert Luthuli, Oliver Tambo and Nelson Mandela in our commitment to non-racialism, non-sexism, democracy and the struggle for a socially just and economically prosperous South Africa.

2   Hirsch (2005: 66–67) contends that Keys was offered a top post at the UK office of Gencor, the Afrikaans mining conglomerate he had once headed. He may have felt that this represented a conflict of interest.

3   Padayachee expressed scepticism that the end of apartheid and the embrace of neo-liberalism would see foreign capital pouring into the country after apartheid. International experience, he indicated, suggests that 'clarity over development strategy and a sound macroeconomic framework (whatever the mix of market and state inter-vention) are the most important factors determining successful development, which, in turn, encourages inflows of some forms of foreign capital' (Padayachee 1995a: 174).

4   Interestingly, Pallo Jordan made the point to us that a group of top ANC leaders, including (he claims) Thabo Mbeki, Jacob Zuma and Aziz Pahad, had proposed a similar deadlock-breaking measure earlier in the negotiations. That proposal was

rejected by the ANC's National Working Committee, where Jordan and Kasrils, among others, expressed their strong opposition. But when it came back again later, presented this time by Slovo (undoubtedly with the support of Mandela), it was accepted (Jordan interview, 4 August 2017).

5   For a full account of the IMF's 1993 loan to South Africa, see Padayachee and Fine (2018).

6   The IMF uses its own non-traded currency called Special Drawing Rights (SDRs). The loan amounted to SDR614 million.

7   But this was surely not something that De Klerk had left to 'luck'. He and his team had worked hard and shrewdly since the early 1990s to secure such an outcome on economic policy options, as we have shown throughout our narrative.

8   And later prime minister and president of Côte d'Ivoire.

9   We thank Ben Fine for drawing out these conclusions so clearly.

10 This email correspondence between Habib and Manuel was shared with us by Adam Habib.

11 The minerals-energy complex (MEC) is a proxy term Terreblanche used for South African capital, but lacking the logic or precision of Fine and Rustomjee's (1996) usage of the term.

12 Sylvia Neame insists that the ANC and the Congress movement as a whole should be regarded as 'complex historical phenomena' and their approach to negotiation did not 'come out of the blue', but was consistent with Mandela's long-standing recognition of the importance of the 'centre', together with his appreciation of the need to retain the typically Congress core of the ANC (Lissoni and Neame 2015: 142).

CHAPTER 7

1   This section draws on a review article in the *International Review of Applied Economics* (see Padayachee 2000).

2   When he became British prime minister in 1997, one of Tony Blair's first decisions (following Margaret Thatcher's long tenure) was to increase the independence of the Bank of England, again in order to demonstrate the Labour Party's credentials to wary global markets.

3   According to Chris Stals, the need to have a Mission Statement for the SARB was inspired by the local and global debates over Codes of Corporate Governance, which had proposed that companies should have a Mission Statement and a Board Charter (Telephone conversation, 23 November 2017). Note, however, that the King Code on Corporate Governance in South Africa was only formally published in 1992.

4   Trevor Manuel did not get back to us on his promise to find it. Maria Ramos and Tito Mboweni failed to respond to our numerous requests for an interview despite emails to their PAs.

5   An official in the office of the governor confirmed that these remarks were not in the official text of the speech.

6   Reported to us by Professor Jannie Rossouw, head of Economic and Business Sciences at Wits University and a former company secretary and former deputy general manager at the SARB, who attended the function.

7   'Balanced growth' had some currency in the development literature of the 1950s associated with Rosenstein Rodan, but it is a nebulous term in the modern development economics and macroeconomics literature. (See Fleming 1955.)

8   The Constitution says that 'there must be regular consultation between the Bank and the Cabinet member responsible for national financial matters' but does not specify that such consultation must take place over monetary policy operations.

9   Should read Constituent Assembly.

10   By the IFP's archivist Anthony Mitchell, through the kind intervention of IFP chief whip Narend Singh.

11   Cronin was not able to recollect these events when we interviewed him.

12   Despite many written email requests via his PA at Goldman Sachs for an interview, we were not able to secure an interview with Mboweni to hear his take on this and other matters.

13   This response was made in the wake of a critique of Nelson Mandela's policy choices by the president of the Economic Freedom Fighters, Julius Malema, in his Oxford Union address on 25 November 2015. Malema argued that some mistakes were indeed made by the ANC and Mandela on matters of economic policy during the negotiations in the early 1990s.

CHAPTER 8

1   See Moss and Obery (1992) for a detailed background and discussion of these policy debates.

2   See Owen (1987).

3   The Alma-Ata Declaration emerged from the International Conference on Primary Health Care held at Alma-Ata, USSR, 6–12 September 1978. The conference attempted to redefine the objectives of health within an explicit socio-economic context of rights, and saw the vehicle to its achievement as the primary health care approach. This involved devolving control of health care to the lowest level and delivering services through district health services, involving communities in assessing the quality and quantity of health services, and emphasising preventive rather than curative solutions to health problems.

4   The district health system referred to the devolution of health care provision to the lowest administrative level of government – which in South Africa were the local authorities. It was specifically proposed that three local authorities would form a district, each comprising 200 000 to 750 000 people, with a total of 100 health districts envisaged for the country.

5   Medical aid scheme users are calculated as using public facilities once in two years on average as opposed to twice a year for non-medical scheme users. The provincial target over 10 years is 3.5 visits per year.

PRIMARY SOURCES

Interviews

Almost all of the interviews were one-on-one and lasted for between two to three hours. They were conducted by Vishnu Padayachee, Robert van Niekerk or both. A few interviews extended over two or more sessions. One or two were telephonic and sometimes emails were used to clarify information or raise specific new points after formal interviews.

Calitz, Estian, former director general of the National Treasury and professor of economics, University of Stellenbosch. Stellenbosch, 1 March 2015 and Pretoria, 12 January 2017.

Cronin, Jeremy, former first deputy secretary general, South African Communist Party, and deputy minister of public works. Cape Town, 14 March 2016 and Johannesburg, 25 July 2017.

De Klerk, FW, former president of South Africa and deputy president in the first democratic government. Interviewed by Jannie Rossouw and Vishnu Padayachee, Cape Town, 28 January 2019.

Dommisse, Ebbe, former editor of *Die Burger* and a participant in the Mells Park talks. Stellenbosch, 10 March 2015.

Erwin, Alec, former Cosatu official and former deputy minister of finance, former minister of trade and industry, and former minister of public enterprises. Johannesburg, 23 October 2015.

Esterhuyse, Willie, professor of political philosophy and convenor and interlocuter of the pre-1990 'talks about talks' between the South African government (National Intelligence Agency) and the ANC in exile. Stellenbosch, 10 March 2015.

Fine, Ben, professor of economics and MERG researcher, London, 30 June 2015, and numerous email exchanges in and around April–September 2016 and February 2017.

Friedman, Irwin, director of the National Progressive Primary Health Care Network, Johannesburg, 11 November 1998. Originally interviewed by Robert van Niekerk for his MPhil research project completed through the University of Oxford, 1997/1998.

Godsell, Bobby, former CEO of Anglo-Gold Ashanti and former executive director of Anglo American Corporation. Johannesburg, 5 April 2017.

Jordan, Z Pallo, ANC revolutionary, intellectual and Cabinet minister in both the Mandela and Mbeki administrations. Cape Town, 4 August 2017.

Josie, Jaya, ANC activist, MK soldier, former and first co-ordinating secretary of MERG. Cape Town, 30 January 2015.

Kasrils, Ronnie, ANC activist, MK soldier and former Cabinet minister in the Mbeki administration. Johannesburg, 30 March and 17 May 2017.

Kathrada, Ahmed, (late) ANC stalwart, Robben Island prisoner and member of the ANC's National Executive Committee. Johannesburg, 9 October 2015.

Keeton, Gavin, former chief economist of Anglo American Corporation and professor of economics, Rhodes University. Grahamstown, 12 June 2015.

Le Roux, Pieter, member of the 'Mount Fleur' scenario planning team and former professor of development economics, University of the Western Cape. Cape Town, 29 January 2015.

London, Leslie, public health scholar, activist, professor and head of the Division of Public Health, University of Cape Town, and member of the National Medical and Dental Association. Cape Town, 21 August 2018.

Maharaj, Sathyandranath (Mac), senior ANC negotiator during 1990s negotiations, ANC activist, revolutionary, soldier, exiled member of the ANC (London, Lusaka), leading member of Operation Vula, member of parliament, Cabinet minister in the Mandela administration, and author. Durban, 16 August 2016.

Manuel, Trevor, UDF activist, former head of the ANCs Department of Economic Policy, later minister of trade and industy, and minister of finance in the first Mandela government and under Mbeki until 2009, later minister in the Presidency under Zuma. Johannesburg, 4 July and 9 September 2016.

Mgijima, Ralph, head of the exiled ANC's health service in various African states, ANC health policy adviser in the transition era, ex-head of the Department of Health, Gauteng Province. Johannesburg, 13 November 2018.

Mlangeni, Andrew, ANC stalwart, revolutionary and Robben Island prisoner. Makhanda, 6 October 2015.

Mouton, Jannie, CEO of PSG Group. Stellenbosch, 11 March 2015.

Perez, Gonda, ANC health activist and head of the office of the minister of welfare in the first democratic government. Pretoria, 11 November 1998. Originally interviewed by Robert van Niekerk for his MPhil research project completed through the University of Oxford, 1997/1998.

Renwick, Lord Robin, former UK high commissioner to South Africa, telephone and email exchanges facilitated by the British high commissioner in South Africa, from 18 February 2015.

Sanders, David, global public health specialist, scholar, activist and emeritus professor of public health, University of the Western Cape, and member of the ANC National Health Plan drafting group. Cape Town, 19 August 2017.

Sender, John, former research director of MERG, emeritus professor of economics at the School of Oriental and African Studies (SOAS) and former professor of economics, Wits University. Sandton, 10 September 2015, and numerous email exchanges on and around 15 July 2016.

Sisulu, Max, one time head of the Department of Economic Planning in Lusaka, revolutionary, former member of parliament, former speaker of the South African parliament. Johannesburg, 25 August 2016.

Terreblanche, Mof, business person, non-executive director of Sanlam, participant in the pre-1990 'talks about talks' between the South African government (National Intelligence Agency) and the ANC in exile. Stellenbosch, 9 March 2015.

Terreblanche, Sampie, emeritus professor of economics, University of Stellenbosch, and participant in the pre-1990 'talks about talks' between the South African government (National Intelligence Agency) and the ANC in exile. Stellenbosch, 9 March 2015.

Turok, Ben, stalwart, activist, author, exiled ANC member (London and Lusaka) and former member of parliament. Cape Town, 31 May 2014 and 29 January 2015, and an email exchange on 20 May 2015.

Venter, Rina, last minister of health under the apartheid government. Pretoria, 10 November 1998. Originally interviewed by Robert van Niekerk for his MPhil research project completed through the University of Oxford, 1997/1998.

Zita, Langa, activist, past SACP member and director general of agriculture. Makhanda, 10 August 2017.

Notes

1. We exchanged emails (often more than one) with, made direct phone calls to, or held short discussions with some key informants on specific issues. Our project was always explained and we kept recordal notes. Emails were saved. Vishnu Padayachee held a telephonic interview specifically about developments in the South African Reserve Bank (SARB) with Chris Stals, former governor of the SARB, on 30 July 2015, and exchanged emails with him on 17 February 2016, 15 July 2016 and 23 November 2017. Padayachee further had a discussion with him and former SARB company secretary Jannie Rossouw over lunch in Pretoria in July 2016. Padayachee also held a telephone conversation with Pravin Gordhan about how the SARB issue was dealt with in the negotiations. Gordhan was head of the ANC's management committee at the Codesa and multi-party negotiations in the early 1990s. Padayachee had a discussion over dinner with Tito Mboweni about the alleged role of the late Mario Oriani-Ambrosini in the drafting of the constitutional clauses related to the SARB's independence and associated matters. In addition to our formal interviews with Alec Erwin and Trevor Manuel, we also sought clarity from them by email over specific issues. John Sender held a conversation with

Patsy Pillay (widow of Vella Pillay) in London on 28 June 2017 to discuss Vella's expulsion from the SACP in the early 1960s Personal and email communications were held with Patrick Bond in July 1997 and on 22 June 2017, Jonathan Leape on 8 September 2016, Johan Krynauw on 10 December 2017, Cyrus Rustomjee on 11 December 2017, and Michael Spicer on 14 April 2019.

2. We had conversations (not full interviews) on the record and on specific issues with a number of comrades active in ANC branches, mainly in Cape Town and Durban in the early 1990s, including Leslie Watson and David Abrahams in Athlone, Western Cape, Shepi Mati (now in Makhanda) and Enver Motala, Durban (now in Port Elizabeth).

Archives

> [Our archives] should be packed with young researchers – it would
> be a tragedy if these are the preserve of only aged … historians. We
> have to continue to tell our own story as a young nation, and that
> requires us to dig deep into our past, beyond the point of discomfort
> — Hennie van Vuuren, *Apartheid, Guns and Money*

AB Xuma Papers, Historical Papers Research Archives, William Cullen Library, University of the Witwatersrand, Johannesburg.

ANC Lusaka Mission, including Boxes 24, 37, 57, 58, 84, 126 and 157 on the ANC's Department of Economic Planning, University of Fort Hare Heritage Archives, Alice.

FW de Klerk Papers, PV 734, Archives of Contemporary Affairs (ARCA), University of the Free State.

Hansard, Republic of South Africa, Parliament Debates, 1996. Vol. 10, 1996, 3092, National Library, Pretoria.

Hansard, Union of South Africa, Parliament Debates, 1942, Vol. 43, National Library, Pretoria.

Leon Wessels Papers, PV 883, Archives of Contemporary Affairs (ARCA), University of the Free State.

Nelson Mandela Papers, including Boxes 11, 31, 66, 84, 126, 130, 135, 172, 203 and 237 on all matters related to the economy, Department of Economic Planning, as well as correspondence to and from the office of the ANC president, University of Fort Hare Heritage Archives, Alice.

O'Malley 'The Heart of Hope' interview archive, hosted by the Nelson Mandela Centre of Memory, https://omalley.nelsonmandela.org/omalley/index.php/site/q/03lv01508.htm (accessed April 2019):

- Keys, Derek, 5 December 1993. https://omalley.nelsonmandela.org/index.php/site/q/03lv00017/04lv00344/05lv00730/06lv00825.htm (accessed April 2019).
- Maharaj, Mac, 12 December 2002. https://omalley.nelsonmandela.org/omalley/index.php/site/q/03lv03445/04lv03689/05lv03714/06lv03747.htm (accessed April 2019).
- Mboweni, Tito, 18 August 1992. https://omalley.nelsonmandela.org/omalley/index.php/site/q/03lv00017/04lv00344/05lv00607/06lv00695.htm (accessed April 2019).
- Pillay, Vella and Patsy, 30 December 2002. https://omalley.nelsonmandela.org/omalley/index.php/site/q/03lv03445/04lv03833/05lv03858/06lv03890.htm (accessed April 2019).

Oliver Tambo Papers, Boxes 039, 040, Folder 357, Department of Economic Planning, University of Fort Hare Heritage Archives, Alice.

Roelf Meyer Papers, PV 912, Archives of Contemporary Affairs (ARCA), University of the Free State.

Ronnie Kasrils Papers, Historical Papers Research Archives, William Cullen Library, University of the Witwatersrand, Johannesburg.

Vella Pillay private archives, covering his life and work in London since c.1950 and his engagement as director of the MERG project (1991–1993), Muswell Hill, North London.*

Vishnu Padayachee private archives, covering his engagement with the Economic Trends Research Group and the Macroeconomic Research Project (1987–1993), Westville North, Durban.*

Note

* These private archives are available on request from Vishnu Padayachee at Vishnu.padayachee@wits.ac.za. On completion of the project, both sets of archives will be deposited with the Historical Papers Research Archives in the William Cullen Library at the University of the Witwatersrand, Johannesburg.

SECONDARY SOURCES

Adelzadeh, A. 1996. 'From the RDP to GEAR: The Gradual Embracing of Neo-Liberalism in Economic Policy'. *Transformation* 31: 66–95.

Adelzadeh, A. and V. Padayachee. 1994. 'The RDP White Paper: Reconstruction of a Development Vision'. *Transformation* 25: 1–18.

Africa Confidential. 2000. 'South Africa: Heading North'. *Africa Confidential* 41 (2). https://www.africa-confidential.com/article-preview/id/787/Heading_north (accessed 19.04.19).

Alexander, N. 1979. *One Azania, One Nation*. London: Zed Books.

Alexander, N. 1994. *Robben Island Dossier*. Cape Town: UCT Press.

Alexander, N. 2002. *An Ordinary Country: Issues in the Transition from Apartheid to Democracy in South Africa*. Pietermaritzburg: University of Natal Press.

ANC (African National Congress). 1943. 'African Claims in South Africa', including 'Atlantic Charter from the Standpoint of Africans within the Union of South Africa' and 'Bill of Rights'. In *From Protest to Challenge: A Documentary History of African Politics in South Africa, 1882–1964: Volume 2: Hope and Challenge, 1935–1952*, edited by T. Karis and G.M. Carter, 1987, 209–223. Stanford: Hoover Institution Press.

ANC. 1992. Ready to Govern: ANC Policy Guidelines for a Democratic South Africa: Adopted at the National Conference 28–31 May. Johannesburg: African National Congress.

ANC. 1994a. 'A National Health Plan for South Africa'. Unpublished report prepared by the ANC Department of Health with the support and technical assistance of WHO and UNICEF.

ANC. 1994b. *The Reconstruction and Development Programme*. Johannesburg: Umanyano Publications.

ANC. 1997. 'Strategy and Tactics'. Statement adopted by the ANC at the Morogoro Conference, Tanzania, 25 April – 1 May 1969. In *From Protest to Challenge: A Documentary History of African Politics in South Africa, 1882–1990: Volume 5: Nadir and Resurgence, 1964–1979*, edited by T. Karis and G.M. Gerhart, 387–393. Bloomington, IN: Indiana University Press.

ANC. 2001. 'Document 21. Memorandum on ANC "Discord" Smuggled out of Robben Island, 1975'. https://omalley.nelsonmandela.org/omalley/index.php/site/q/03lv01538/04lv01600/05lv01634/06lv01635.htm (accessed 20.04.19).

ANC Health Department. 1990. 'Interview: ANC Health Department'. *Critical Health* 31/32: 55.

Anon. (Cosatu member). *c.*1992. 'Lunch at the Charlton with Bobby and the Boys'. Photostat copy in Vishnu Padayachee private archive.

Barber, S. 2004. *Mandela's World*. Oxford: James Currey.

Barnard, N. and T. Wiese. 2017. *Peaceful Revolution: Inside the War Room at the Negotiations*. Cape Town: Tafelberg.

Barron, C. 2015. 'Bethual Setai: Underground ANC operative and academic'. *Sunday Times*, 31 May. https://www.pressreader.com/south-africa/sunday-times-1107/20150531/282106340243532 (accessed 18.04.19).

Bell, R.T. 1997. 'Trade Policy'. In *The Political Economy of South Africa's Transition: Policy Perspectives in the Late 1990s*, edited by J. Michie and V. Padayachee, 71–90. London: Dryden Press.

Bell, T. 2007. 'Fighting Spirit of Vella Pillay Moves in Alliance Battles'. *Business Report*, 31 May. https://www.iol.co.za/business-report/opinion/fighting-spirit-of-vella-pillay-moves-in-alliance-battles-715730 (accessed 18.04.19).

Bell, T. 2016. 'ANC Legacy of Corruption Is SA's True Danger'. *Network 24*, 26 April. https://www.fin24.com/Opinion/anc-legacy-of-corruption-is-sas-true-danger-20160426 (accessed 18.04.19).

Belli, P., M. Finger and A. Ballivian. 1993. 'South Africa: A Review of Trade Policies'. Informal discussion paper on aspects of the economy of South Africa; No. 4. Washington, DC: World Bank.

Benneyworth, G. 2011. 'Armed and Trained: Nelson Mandela's 1962 Military Mission as Commander in Chief of Umkhonto we Sizwe and Provenance for his Buried Makarov Pistol'. *South African History Journal* 63 (1): 78–101.

Bernstein, R. 1999. *Memory Against Forgetting: Memoir of a Time in South African Politics 1938–1964*. London: Viking.

Bide, J. 2016. 'Why Was the South African Reserve Bank Granted Constitutionally Enshrined Independence in the 1993 Interim Constitution?' Honours thesis, London School of Economics.

Blumenfeld, J. 1997. 'From Icon to Scapegoat: The Experience of South Africa's Reconstruction and Development Programme'. *Development Policy Review* 15: 65–91.

Boesak, A. 2017. 'The ANC Sold Out'. *City Press*, 20 August. https://www.news24.com/SouthAfrica/News/boesak-the-anc-sold-out-20170820-2 (accessed 19.04.19).

Bond, P. 1991. 'The ANC's Economic Manifesto: Can It Satisfy the Majority's Needs?' *Work in Progress* 75 (June): 17–22.

Bond, P. 1996. 'The Making of South Africa's Macroeconomic Compromise'. In *Transformation in South Africa?* edited by E. Maganya and R. Houghton, 15–34. Johannesburg: Institute for African Alternatives.

Bond, P. 2000. *Elite Transition: From Apartheid to Neo-Liberalism in South Africa*. Pietermaritzburg: University of Natal Press.

Bond, P. 2001. *Against Global Apartheid*. Cape Town: UCT Press.

Bond, P. 2004. 'From Racial to Class Apartheid: A Critical Appraisal of South Africa's Transition'. Paper presented to AIDC's 10 Years of Democracy Conference, Cape Town, 27 November.

Borgwardt, E. 2002. *An Intellectual History of the Atlantic Charter: Ideas, Institutions, and Human Rights in American Diplomacy, 1941–1946*. Cambridge, MA: Belknap Press of Harvard University Press.

Botha, J. 2002. 'Down Memory Lane: The Economic Society of South Africa – Past Presidents, 1925–1963'. *South African Journal of Economics*, special issue, September. https://www.essa.org.za/memory_lane.pdf (accessed 18.04.19).

Boughton, J.M. 2012. *Tearing Down Walls: The International Monetary Fund, 1990–1999*. Washington, DC: IMF.

Bruce, P. 2016. *Sunday Times*, 17 January.

Bundy, C. 2012. *Govan Mbeki*. Johannesburg: Jacana.

Burawoy, M. 1997. 'Neo-Liberal Pitfalls: South Africa through a Russian Lens'. Paper presented at the Harold Wolpe Memorial Trust Inaugural Conference, University of the Western Cape, 1–2 April.

Business Day. 1993. 'Comment: Left Bank'. 8 November.

Butler, A. 2007. *Cyril Ramaphosa*. Johannesburg: Jacana and Oxford: James Currey.

Coutts, K. and L. Laskaridis. 2019. 'Financial Balances and the Development of the Ethiopian Economy'. In *The Oxford Handbook of the Ethiopian Economy*, edited by F. Cheru, C. Cramer and A. Oqubay, 213–229. London: Oxford University Press.

CREFSA (Centre for Research into Economics and Finance in Southern Africa). 1995. *Independence and Accountability: The Role and Structure of the South African Reserve Bank*. London: London School of Economics.

Critical Health. 1990. 'Declaration on Health and Welfare in Southern Africa'. *Critical Health* 31/32: 4–5.

Cronin, J. 1997. *Weekly Mail*, 20–26 June.

Cronin, J. 2016. 'Jeremy Cronin: My Response to Thabo Mbeki'. *eNCA*, 21 January. https://www.enca.com/opinion/jeremy-cronin-my-response-thabo-mbeki (accessed 19.04.19).

De Beer, C. 1992. 'Health Policy in Transition? The Limits to Reform'. In *South African Review 6: From 'Red Friday' to Codesa*, edited by G. Moss and I. Obery, 267–278. Johannesburg: Ravan Press.

De Beer, C. and J. Broomberg. 1990. 'Financing Health Care for All: Is National Health Insurance the First Step?' *Critical Health* 31/32: 26–29.

De Klerk, F.W. 1998. *The Last Trek: A New Beginning*. London: Macmillan.

Desai, A. and H. Bohmke. 1997. 'The Death of the Intellectual, the Birth of the Salesman'. *Debate* 3: 10–34.

DoH (Department of Health). 1997. 'White Paper for the Transformation of the Health System in South Africa'. https://www.gov.za/sites/default/files/gcis_document/201409/17910gen6670.pdf (accessed 18.04.19).

Edwards, C. 1995. 'Restructuring the New South Africa'. *International Review of Applied Economics* 9 (1): 101–108.

Ellis, S. 2015. *External Mission: The ANC in Exile, 1960–1990*. London: Hurst.

Ellis, S. and T. Sechaba. 1992. *Comrades against Apartheid*. London: James Currey.

Erwin, A. 1990. 'South Africa's Post-Apartheid Economy: Planning for Prosperity'. *South Africa International* 20 (4) (April): 205–210.

Erwin, A. 2016. 'Interview'. In *The Thabo Mbeki I Know*, edited by S. Ndlovu and M. Strydom, 138–155. Johannesburg: Picador Africa.

Esterhuyse, W. 2012. *Endgame, Secret Talks and the End of Apartheid*. Cape Town: Tafelberg.

FCO (Foreign and Commonwealth Office). 2013. 'South Africa Witness Seminars: The Role and Functions of the British Embassy/High Commission in Pretoria: 1987–2013'. Institute of Contemporary British History, the Foreign and Commonwealth Office and the Arts and Humanities Research Council. gov.uk/fco.

FFC (Financial and Fiscal Commission). 1995. *Framework Document for Intergovernmental Fiscal Relations in South Africa*. Pretoria: Government Printer.

FFC. 1996. The Allocation of Financial Resources between the National and Provincial Governments: Recommendations for the Fiscal Year 1997/8. Pretoria: Government Printer.

FFC. 1998. Public Expenditure on Basic Social Services in South Africa: An FCC Report for UNICEF and UNDP. Pretoria: Government Printer.

FFC. 2011. 'The Impact of Unfunded Mandates in South African Intergovernmental Relations'. In *Submission for the Division of Revenue 2011/12*. https://ffc.co.za/docs/submissions/dor/2012/FFC%20SDOR%20-%20Approval.pdf (accessed 18.04.19).

Filatova, I. 2012. 'The Lasting Legacy: The Soviet Theory of the National Democratic Revolution and South Africa'. *South African Historical Journal* 63 (3): 507–537.

Filatova, I. and A. Davidson. 2013. *The Hidden Thread: Russia and South Africa in the Soviet Era*. Cape Town: Jonathan Ball.

Fine, B. 2010. 'Engaging the MEC: Or a Few of My Views on a Few Things'. *Transformation: Critical Perspectives on Southern Africa* 71: 26–49.

Fine, B. 2019. 'Post-Truth: An Alumni Economist's Perspective'. Department of Economics Working Paper No. 219, SOAS, University of London.

Fine, B. and V. Padayachee. 2000. 'A Sustainable Growth Path?' In *South African Review 8*, edited by S. Friedman, 269–281. Pretoria: HSRC Press.

Fine, B. and Z. Rustomjee. 1996. *The Political Economy of South Africa: From Minerals Energy Complex to Industrialisation*. Johannesburg: Wits University Press and London: Hurst.

Fleming, M. 1955. 'External Economies and the Doctrine of Balanced Growth'. *The Economic Journal* 65 (258): 241–256.

Frankel, G. 2016. *Rivonia's Children*. 2nd ed. Pretoria: Jacana.

Freund, W. 2013. 'Swimming against the Tide: The Macroeconomic Research Group in the South African Transition 1991–94'. *Review of African Political Economy* 40 (138): 519–536.

Freund, W. 2015. 'Debate: Post-Apartheid South Africa under ANC Rule: A Response to John S. Saul on South Africa'. *Transformation: Critical Perspectives on Southern Africa* 89: 50–75.

Freund, W. 2019. *The Development State*. Cambridge: Cambridge University Press.

Fukuyama, F. 1992. *The End of History and the Last Man*. New York: The Free Press/ Macmillan.

Garcia, F. 2016. 'My Tip-off Led to Mandela's Arrest'. *Mercury*, 16 May. https://www.iol.co.za/news/south-africa/my-tip-off-led-to-mandelas-arrest-cia-spy-2021941 (accessed 18.04.19).

Gelb, S., ed. 1991. *South Africa's Economic Crisis*. Cape Town: David Philip and London and New Jersey: Zed Books.

Gerhart, G.M. 1978. *Black Power in South Africa: The Evolution of an Ideology*. Berkeley, CA: University of California Press.

Gerhart, G.M. and C.L. Glaser, eds. 2010. *From Protest to Challenge: A Documentary History of African Politics in South Africa, 1980–1990: Volume 6: Challenge and Victory, 1980–1990*. Bloomington, IN: Indiana University Press.

Gevisser, M. 2007. *Thabo Mbeki: The Dream Deferred*. Johannesburg and Cape Town: Jonathan Ball.

Gevisser, M. 2016. *Thabo Mbeki: The Dream Deferred*. International ed. Johannesburg and Cape Town: Jonathan Ball.

Giliomee, H. 2003. *The Afrikaners: Biography of a People*. London: Hurst.

Giliomee, H. 2009. 'True Confessions, End Papers and the Dakar Conference: A Review of the Political Arguments'. http://www.scielo.org.za/scielo.php?script=sci_arttext&pid=S0041-476X2009000200003 (accessed 19.04.19).

Giliomee, H. 2012. *The Last Afrikaner Leaders: A Supreme Test of Power*. Cape Town: Tafelberg.

Gish, S. 2000. *Alfred B. Xuma: African, American, South African*. New York: New York University Press.

Good, K. 2011. 'The Capacities of the People versus a Predominant, Militarist, Ethno-Nationalist Elite: Democratisation in South Africa, c.1973–1997'. *Interface* 3 (2): 311–358.

Goodson, S.M. 2014. *Inside the South African Reserve Bank: Its Origins and Secrets Exposed*. Cape Town: Privately published.

Green, P. 2008. *Choice, Not Fate: The Life and Times of Trevor Manuel.* Johannesburg: Penguin.

Gumede, W. 2007. *Thabo Mbeki and the Battle for the Soul of the ANC.* 2nd ed. London: Zed Books.

Gurney, C. 2000. '"A Great Cause": The Origins of the Anti-Apartheid Movement, June 1959 – March 1960'. *Journal of Southern African Studies* 26 (1): 123–144.

Habib, A. 2004. 'The Politics of Economic Policy-Making: Substantive Uncertainty, Political Leverage, and Human Development'. *Transformation: Critical Perspectives on Southern Africa* 56: 90–103.

Habib, A. 2013. *South Africa's Suspended Revolution: Hopes and Prospects.* Johannesburg: Wits University Press.

Habib, A. and V. Padayachee. 2000. 'Economic Policy and Power Relations in South Africa's Transition to Democracy'. *World Development* 28 (2): 245–263.

Hamilton, L. 2014. *Are South Africans Free?* London: Bloomsbury.

Harber, A. 1994. 'The RDP Minister Who Would Like to be Redundant'. *Mail & Guardian,* 19 August. https://mg.co.za/article/1994-08-19-the-rdp-minister-who-would-like-to-be-redundant (accessed 18.04.19).

Harris, L. 1989. 'The Mixed Economy of a Democratic South Africa'. First In-House Seminar of ANC Economists, Lusaka, August 14–17 1989. Unpublished. Vishnu Padayachee private archive.

Harris, L. 1990. 'The Economic Strategy and Policies of the African National Congress: An Interpretation'. In *McGregor's Economic Alternatives,* edited by B. Godsell, L. Harris, A. Jammine, L. Louw and R. McGregor, 25–73. Cape Town: Juta.

Harris, L. 1993. 'South Africa's Economic and Social Transformation: From "No Middle Road" to "No Alternative"'. *Review of African Political Economy* 20 (57): 91–103.

Hart, K. and V. Padayachee. 2013a. 'A History of South African Capitalism in National and Global Perspective'. *Transformation: Critical Perspectives on Southern Africa* 81/82: 55–85.

Hart, K. and V. Padayachee. 2013b. 'Introducing Varieties of Capitalism into the South African Debate: Uses and Limits'. *Transformation: Critical Perspectives on Southern Africa* 81/82: 5–32.

Harvey, R. 2001. *The Fall of Apartheid: The Inside Story from Smuts to Mbeki.* Basingstoke: Palgrave Macmillan.

Hayo, B. and C. Hefeker. 2002. 'Reconsidering Central Bank Independence'. *European Journal of Political Economy* 18 (4): 653–674.

Hickel, J. 2016. 'The (Anti) Politics of Central Banking: Monetary Policy and Class Conflict in South Africa'. Unpublished paper presented at the workshop on Capitalism in the Global South, LSE-Wits-Michigan Research Group, London School of Economics, 26–28 April, pp. 1–17.

Hirsch, A. 2005. *Season of Hope: Economic Reform under Mbeki and Mandela.* Pietermaritzburg: University of Natal Press.

Hirsch, A. 2015. 'How Compromises and Mistakes Made in the Mandela Era Hobbled South Africa's Economy'. *The Conversation,* 23 December. http://theconversation.com/how-compromises-and-mistakes-made-in-the-mandela-era-hobbled-south-africas-economy-52156 (accessed 18.04.19).

Hlatshwayo, N. 1990. 'Building a Welfare State: Conceptual Framework and Practical Steps'. *Critical Health* 31/32: 15–16.

IDRC (International Development Research Centre). 1991. *Economic Analysis and Policy Formulation for Post-Apartheid South Africa*. Ottawa: IDRC.

Johnson, R.W. 2016. *Brave New World: The Beloved Country since the End of Apartheid*. London: Allen Lane.

Jordan, L. 2017. 'It's Time to Debate the Central Bank's Mandate'. *Daily Maverick*, 23 June. https://www.dailymaverick.co.za/opinionista/2017-06-23-its-time-to-debate-the-central-banks-mandate (accessed 18.04.19).

Jordan, Z.P. 1984. 'The African Petty Bourgeoisie: A Case Study of NAFCOC, 1964–84'. ANC Occasional Research Papers, ANC Research Unit, Department of Information and Publicity, Lusaka.

Jordan, Z.P. 1986. 'Socialist Transformation and the Freedom Charter'. *African Journal of Political Economy / Revue Africaine d'Economie Politique* 1 (1): 142–161.

Jordan, Z.P. n.d., *c.*1988. 'The African Bourgeoisie: A New Look'. Unpublished memo.

Jordan, Z.P. 1988. 'Socialist Transformation and the Freedom Charter'. In *Whither South Africa?* edited by B. Magubane and I. Mandaza, 89–110. Trenton, NJ: Africa World Press.

Kaplinsky, R. 1994. 'Economic Restructuring in South Africa: The Debate Continues: A Response'. *Journal of Southern African Studies* 20 (4): 533–537.

Karis, T. and G.M. Carter, eds. 1977. *From Protest to Challenge: A Documentary History of African Politics in South Africa, 1882–1964: Volume 3: Challenge and Violence, 1953–1964*. Stanford: Hoover Institution Press.

Karis, T. and G.M. Carter, eds. 1987 [1973]. *From Protest to Challenge: A Documentary History of African Politics in South Africa, 1882–1964: Volume 2: Hope and Challenge 1935–1952*. Stanford: Hoover Institution Press.

Karis, T. and G.M. Gerhart, eds. 1997. *From Protest to Challenge A Documentary History of African Politics in South Africa, 1882–1990: Volume 5: Nadir and Resurgence, 1964–1979*. Bloomington, IN: Indiana University Press.

Kasrils, R. 2013a. *Armed and Dangerous: From Undercover Struggle to Freedom*. Johannesburg: Jacana.

Kasrils, R. 2013b. 'How the ANC's Faustian Pact Sold out South Africa's Poorest'. *Guardian*, 24 June. https://www.theguardian.com/commentisfree/2013/jun/24/anc-faustian-pact-mandela-fatal-error (accessed 19.04.19).

Kasrils, R. 2017. *A Simple Man: Kasrils and the Zuma Enigma*. Johannesburg: Jacana.

Keable, K. 2012. *London Recruits: The Secret War against Apartheid*. London: Merlin Press.

Kentridge, M. 1993. 'Turning the Tanker: The Economic Debate in South Africa'. Centre for Policy Studies Research Report, 72.

Klein, N. 2007. *The Shock Doctrine: The Rise of Disaster Capitalism*. New York: Metropolitan Books.

Lachmann, D. and K. Bercuson, eds. 1992. *Economic Policies for a New South Africa*. Washington, DC: International Monetary Fund.

Leach, G. 1989. *The Afrikaners: Their Last Great Trek*. Johannesburg: Macmillan and Southern Book Publishers.

Lehohla, P. 2017. 'Statistician-General Tells of Flight from Lesotho and Work in South Africa'. *Cape Times*, 15 August. https://www.pressreader.com/south-africa/cape-times/20170815/282007557498392 (accessed 18.04.19).

Levy, N. 2011. *The Final Prize: My Life in the Anti-Apartheid Struggle*. Cape Town: South African History Online.

Lissoni, A. and S. Neame. 2015. 'The Following Piece is Based on an Interview, Conducted by Arianna Lissoni, with Author Sylvia Neame on the Occasion of the Launch of her

Book, *The Congress Movement: The Unfolding of the Congress Alliance, 1912–1961*, vols 1–3 (Cape Town, HSRC Press, 2015)'. *African Historical Review* 47 (2): 132–152. DOI: 10.1080/17532523.2015.1130248 (accessed 19.04.19).

Lombard, J. n.d. *A Strange Intermezzo: Memoirs of a Political Economist.* Privately published (highly restricted circulation).

Lombard, J. 1978. *Freedom, Welfare and Order: Thoughts on the Principles of Political Co-Operation in the Economy of Southern Africa.* Pretoria: Benbo Publishers.

Lonsdale, J., ed. 1988. *South Africa in Question.* Cambridge: Cambridge University Press.

Louw, R. 1989. *Four Days in Lusaka: Whites in a Changing Society.* Proceedings of a Five Freedoms Forum–ANC Conference in Lusaka. Johannesburg: Five Freedoms Publication.

Lund, F. 2008. *Changing Social Policy: The Child Support Grant in South Africa.* Cape Town: HSRC Press.

Luthuli, A. 1952. 'The Road to Freedom is Via the Cross'. Statement issued by Chief A. Luthuli. In *Voices of Liberation: Volume One: Albert Luthuli*, edited by G. Pillay, 2012. Pretoria: HSRC Press.

Luthuli, A. 1953. 'Interview with Luthuli'. *Drum*, May (n.p.). https://www.sahistory.org.za/archive/interview-drum-may-1953 (accessed 16.06.19)

Luthuli, A. 1955. 'The Implications of the Freedom Charter'. In *Voices of Liberation: Volume One: Albert Luthuli*, edited by G.L. Pillay, 2012. Pretoria: HSRC Press.

Luthuli, A. 1956. 'A Reply by Albert Luthuli to Mr Jordan K. Ngubane's Attacks on the African National Congress, 5 June 1956'. https://www.sahistory.org.za/archive/reply-albert-luthuli-mr-jordan-k-ngubanes-attacks-african-national-congress-5-june-1956 (accessed 18.04.19).

Luthuli, A. 1962. 'What I Would Do if I Were Prime Minister'. *Ebony*, 5 February.

Macmillan, H. 2013. *The Lusaka Years: The ANC in Exile in Zambia.* Johannesburg: Jacana.

Makan, B., D. McIntyre and P. Gwala. 1996. 'Financing and Expenditure'. In *South African Health Review 1996*, 73–84. Durban: Health Systems Trust.

Malinga, P. 1990. 'Nationalisation or Free Enterprise? The Economic Policy of the National Democratic Revolution'. *African Communist* 123: 20–33.

Maloka, E. 2002. 'The South African Communist Party in Exile: 1963–1990'. Africa Institute of South Africa Research Paper No. 65, Pretoria.

Mandela, N. 1956. 'In Our Lifetime'. *Liberation: A Journal of Democratic Discussion* 19 (June): 4–8.

Mandela, N. 1990. Address by Nelson Mandela at Options for Building an Economic Future Conference convened by the Consultative Business Movement attended by South African business executives (23 May). http://www.mandela.gov.za/mandela_speeches/1990/900523_econ.htm (accessed 29.07.19)

Mandela, N. 1991. 'Opening Address on the Occasion of the Signing of a Statement of Intent to Set up a National Capacity for Economic Research and Policy Formulation', Johannesburg, 13 November. https://www.sahistory.org.za/topic/opening-address-cde-nelson-mandela-occassion-signing-statement-intent-set-national-capacity-ec (accessed 20.04.19).

Mandela, N. 1994a. '1994 – President Mandela, State of the Nation Address, 24 May 1994 (After National Elections)'. https://www.sahistory.org.za/archive/1994-president-mandela-state-nation-address-24-may-1994-after-national-elections (accessed 18.04.19).

Mandela, N. 1994b. 'Opening Address by President Nelson Mandela in the President's Budget Debate after 100 Days in Office', 18 August. http://www.mandela.gov.za/mandela_speeches/1994/940818_budgetopen.htm (accessed 18.04.19).

Mandela, N. 1994c. 'Address by President Nelson Mandela at the 5th National Congress of COSATU, 7 September 1994'. http://www.sahistory.org.za/archive/address-president-nelson-mandela-5th-national-congress-cosatu-7-september-1994 (accessed 18.04.19).

Mandela, N. 1994d. *Long Walk to Freedom*. Johannesburg: Macdonald Purnell.

Mandela, N. 1995a. 'Opening Speech by President Nelson Mandela at the Business Initiative against Corruption and Crime, Kempton Park, 15 August 1995'. https://www.sahistory.org.za/archive/opening-speech-president-nelson-mandela-business-initiative-against-corruption-and-crime-kem (accessed 18.04.19).

Mandela, N. 1995b. 'Speech by President Nelson Mandela at the Inauguration of Gencor's New Head Office and the Celebration of Gencore's Centenary Johannesburg, 29 September 1995'. https://www.sahistory.org.za/archive/speech-president-nelson-mandela-inauguration-gencors-new-head-office-and-celebration-gencore (accessed 18.04.19).

Mandela, N. 1997. 'Speech by President Nelson Mandela at 6th National Congress of Cosatu, 16 November 1997, Johannesburg'. https://www.sahistory.org.za/archive/speech-president-nelson-mandela-sixth-national-congress-cosatu-johannesburg-16-september-199 (accessed 20.04.19).

Mandela, N. and M. Langa. 2017. *Dare Not Linger: The Presidential Years*. New York: Fararr, Straus and Giroux.

Manuel, T. 2006. Newsmaker of the Year acceptance speech, Sandton, 6 September.

Marais, H. 2011. *South Africa: Pushed to the Limit: The Political Economy of Change*. Cape Town: UCT Press.

Marshall, T.H. 1950. *Citizenship and Social Class and Other Essays*. Cambridge: Cambridge University Press.

Mashele, P. and M. Qobo. 2014. *The Fall of the ANC: What Next?* Johannesburg: Picador Africa.

Masilela, E. 2007. *Number 43 Trelawney Place*. Cape Town: David Philip.

Masinga, P. 1990. 'Nationalisation or Free Enterprise?' *African Communist* 123 (Fourth Quarter).

Matera, M. 2015. *Black London: The Imperial Metropolis and Decolonisation in the Twentieth Century*. Oakland, CA: University of California Press.

Mathebula, M. 2017. *The Backroom Boy*. Johannesburg: Wits University Press.

Matisonn, J. 1998. 'South Africa: How the ANC Battled to Balance the Ideological Books'. *Mail & Guardian*, 6 November. https://allafrica.com/stories/199811060119.html (accessed 18.04.19).

Maxfield, S. 1997. *The International Political Economy of Central Banking in Developing Countries*. Princeton, NJ: Princeton University Press.

Mbatha, K. 2017. *Unmasked: Why the ANC Failed to Govern*. Johannesburg: KMM Publishers.

Mbeki, G. 2015. *Learning from Robben Island: The Prison Writings of Govan Mbeki*, compiled by C. Bundy. Cape Town: Kwela Books.

Mbeki, T. 1984. 'The Fatton Thesis: A Rejoinder'. *Canadian Journal of African Studies* 18 (3): 609–612.

Mboweni, T. 1994. 'Formulating Policy for a Democratic South Africa: Some Observations'. *IDS Bulletin* 25 (1): 69–73.

Mboweni, T. 2004. 'The Foundation Has Been Laid'. Speech at the Black Management Forum Corporate Update Gala Dinner, Gallagher Estate, 18 June.

McIntyre, D. 1995. 'Financing and Expenditure'. In *South African Health Review 1995*. Durban: Health Systems Trust. http://www.hst.org.za/publications/South%20 African%20Health%20Reviews/sahr95.pdf (accessed 20.04.19).

McIntyre, D., G. Bloom, J. Doherty and P. Brijlal. 1995. *Health Expenditure and Finance in South Africa*. Durban: Health Systems Trust and World Bank.

McIntyre, D., S. Thomas, S. Mbatsha and L. Baba. 1999. 'Equity in Public Sector Health Care Financing and Expenditure'. In *South African Health Review 1999*, 27–52. Durban: Health Systems Trust.

McKinley, D.T. 2017. *South Africa's Corporatised Liberation: A Critical Analysis of the ANC in Power*. Johannesburg: Jacana.

Meredith, M. 1997. *Nelson Mandela: A Biography*. London: Hamish Hamilton.

MERG (Macroeconomic Research Group). 1993. *Making Democracy Work: A Framework for Macroeconomic Policy in South Africa*. Bellville: Centre for Development Studies, University of the Western Cape.

Michie, J. and V. Padayachee, eds. 1997. *The Political Economy of South Africa's Transition: Policy Perspectives in the Late 1990s*. London: Dryden Press.

Michie, J. and V. Padayachee. 1998. 'Three Years after Apartheid: Growth, Employment and Redistribution'. *Cambridge Journal of Economics* 22 (5): 623–635.

Mkandawire, T. 2005. *African Intellectuals: Rethinking Politics, Language, Gender and Development*. Dakar: Codesria and London: Zed Books.

Mkandawire, T. 2014. 'The Spread of Economic Doctrines and Policy Making in Post-Colonial Africa'. *African Studies Review* 57 (1): 171–198.

Morales Olivares, R. 2015. 'Inconsistencies between Social-Democratic Discourses and Neo-Liberal Institutional Development in Chile and South Africa: A Comparative Analysis of the Post-Authoritarian Periods'. In *African, American and European Trajectories of Modernity: Past Oppression, Future Justice*, edited by P. Wagner, 125–148. Edinburgh: Edinburgh University Press.

Morris, M. 1996. 'Methodological Problems in Tackling Socio-Economic Policy Issues in the Transition to Democracy in South Africa'. In *Methodological Challenges of Inter-Disciplinary Research in the Social Sciences*, edited by J. Gaspankova, V. Bakos, N. Pillay and C. Prinsloo, 251–272. Pretoria: HSRC Press.

Morris, M. and V. Padayachee. 1988. 'State Reform Policy in South Africa'. *Transformation: Critical Perspectives on Southern Africa* 7: 1–26.

Morris, M. and V. Padayachee. 1989. 'Hegemonic Projects, Accumulation Strategies and State Reform Policy in South Africa'. *Labour, Capital and Society* 22 (1): 65–109.

Moss, G. and I. Obery, eds. 1992. *South African Review 6: From 'Red Friday' to Codesa*. Johannesburg: Ravan Press.

Mutize, M. 2017. 'Why South Africa Shouldn't Turn to the IMF for Help'. *The Conversation*, 8 August. https://theconversation.com/why-south-africa-shouldnt-turn-to-the-imf-for-help-82027 (accessed 18.04.19).

Mzala/Nxumalo, J. (also pseudonyms 'B.L.' and 'Comrade Mzala'). 1982. 'Discussion Article: The National Democratic Revolution', *Sechaba*, Official Organ of the African National Congress, October: 11–16.

Mzala/Nxumalo, J. 1988. *Gatsha Buthelezi: Chief with a Double Agenda*. London: Zed Press.

Naidoo, J. 2010. Fighting for Justice: A Lifetime of Political and Social Activisim. Johannesburg: Picador Africa.

Naidoo, J. 2017. *Change: Organising Tomorrow Today*. Cape Town: Penguin.

Nattrass N. 1994. 'Politics and Economics in ANC Economic Policy'. *African Affairs* 93 (372): 343–359.

Ndebele, N. and N. Nieftagodien. 2004. 'The Morogoro Conference: A Moment of Self-Reflection. In *Road to Democracy in South Africa, Volume 1 (1960–1970)*, edited by SADET, 573–599. Cape Town: Zebra Press.

Neocosmos, M. 1997. 'Intellectual Debates and Popular Struggles in Transitional South Africa: Political Discourse and the Origins of Statism'. Paper presented at the African Association of Political Science Eleventh Biennial Congress, University of Durban-Westville.

Ngoasheng, M. 1992. 'Policy Research inside the African National Congress'. *Transformation: Critical Perspectives on Southern Africa* 18/19: 115–124.

O'Malley, P. 2007. *Shades of Difference: Mac Maharaj and the Struggle for South Africa*. New York: Viking.

O'Meara, D. 1983. *Volkskapitalisme: Class, Capital and Ideology in the Development of Afrikaner Nationalism, 1934–1948*. Johannesburg: Ravan Press.

Oriani-Ambrosini, M. 2017. *The Prince and I: A South African Institutional Odyssey*. Cape Town: Privately published.

Ostry, J., P. Loungani and D. Furceri. 2016. 'Neoliberalism: Oversold?' *Finance and Development* 53 (2): 38–41.

Owen, C.P., ed. 1987. *Towards a National Health Service: Proceedings of the 1987 NAMDA Annual Conference*. Cape Town: NAMDA.

Padayachee, V. 1988. 'The Politics of International Economic Relations: South Africa and the IMF, 1975 and Beyond'. In *After Apartheid: The Renewal of the South African Economy*, edited by J. Suckling and L. White, 191–204. London: James Currey and Trenton, NJ: Africa World Press.

Padayachee, V. 1995a. 'Foreign Capital and Economic Development in South Africa: Recent Trends and Post-Apartheid Prospects'. *World Development* 23 (178): 163–177.

Padayachee, V. 1995b. 'Afterword'. In *Building a New South Africa, Volume 2: Urban Policy*, edited by M. van Ameringen, 51–78. Ottawa: IDRC.

Padayachee, V. 1997. 'The Evolution of South Africa's International Financial Relations and Policy, 1985–95'. In *The Political Economy of South Africa's Transition: Policy Perspectives in the Late 1990s*, edited by J. Michie and V. Padayachee, 27–54. London: Dryden Press.

Padayachee, V. 1998. 'Progressive Academic Economists and the Challenge of Development in South Africa's Decade of Liberation'. *Review of African Political Economy* 25 (77): 431–450.

Padayachee, V. 2000. 'Independence in an Era of Globalisation: Central Banking in Developing Countries'. *International Review of Applied Economics* 14 (4): 495–500.

Padayachee, V. 2013a. 'Corporate Governance in South Africa: From "Old Boys Club" to Ubuntu?' *Transformation: Critical Perspectives on Southern Africa* 81 (1): 260–290.

Padayachee, V. 2013b. 'Lost and Found: The South African Transition through a Stellenbosch Lens'. *International Review of Applied Economics* 27 (6): 834–841.

Padayachee, V. 2015. 'South African Reserve Bank Independence: The Debate Revisited'. *Tranformation: Critical Perspectives on Southern Africa* 89: 1–25.

Padayachee, V. and B. Fine. 2018. 'The Role and Influence of the IMF on Economic Policy in South Africa's Transition to Democracy: The 1993 Compensatory and Contingency Financing Facility Revisited'. *Review of African Political Economy*. DOI: 10.1080/03056244.2018.1484352.

Padayachee, V. and J. Sender. 2018. 'Vela Pillay: Revolutionary Activism and Economic Policy Analysis'. *Journal of Southern African Studies* 44 (1): 149–167.

Padmore, G. 1963. *History of the Pan-African Congress: Colonial and Coloured Unity, A Programme of Action*. London: Hammersmith Bookshop. https://www.prisoncensorship.info/archive/etext/countries/panafrican/pac1963.pdf (accessed 18.04.19).

Padmore, G. and N. Cunard. 1942. *The White Man's Duty: An Analysis of the Colonial Question in the Light of the Atlantic Charter*. London: W.H. Allen.

Papenfus, T. 2010. *Pik Botha and His Times*. Pretoria: Litera Publications.

Parsons, R. 2007. 'The Emergence of Institutionalised Social Dialogue in South Africa'. *South African Journal of Economics* 75 (1): 1–21.

Parsons, R. and A. Parry. 2018. *Good Capitalism, Bad Capitalism: The Role of Business in South Africa*. Johannesburg: Jacana.

Pauw, J. 2017. *The President's Keepers: Those Keeping Zuma in Power and out of Prison*. Cape Town: Tafelberg.

Pillay, G., ed. 1993. *Voices of Liberation: Volume One: Albert Luthuli*. Pretoria: HSRC Press.

Pillay, V., writing as P. Tlale. 1964. 'The Apartheid Economy Today'. *African Communist* 18 (July–September): 48–59.

Pillay, V. 1989. 'Some Problems of a Mixed Economy in South Africa: A Response to the Paper Presented by Laurence Harris to the In-House Seminar of ANC Economists, Lusaka, 14–17 August 1989'. Unpublished, London, 9 October. Wits Historical Papers Research Archive, University of the Witwatersrand. http://www.historicalpapers.wits.ac.za/inventories/inv_pdfo/A3299/A3299-G1-3-2-001-jpeg.pdf (accessed 18.04.19).

Plagerson, S., L. Patel, T. Hochfeld and M. Ulriksen. 2018. 'Social Policy in South Africa: Navigating the Route to Social Development'. *World Development* 113: 1–9.

Plaut, M. 2012. 'The Uneasy Alliance'. In *Who Rules South Africa? Pulling the Strings in the Battle for Power*, edited by M. Plaut and P. Holden, 3–29. Johannesburg: Jonathan Ball.

Pogrund, B. 1990. *How Can Man Die Better: The Life of Robert Sobukwe*. Johannesburg: Jonathan Ball.

Rajab, K. 2017. *A Man of Africa: The Political Thought of Harry Oppenheimer*. Cape Town: Zebra Press and Random House.

Raman, P. 2005. 'Yusuf Dadoo: A Son of South Africa'. In *South Africa's 1940s: Worlds of Possibilities*, edited by S. Dubow and A. Jeeves, 227–245. Cape Town: Double Storey Books.

Rapley, J. 2017. *Twilight of the Money Gods: Economics as a Religion and How It All Went Wrong*. London and New York: Simon and Schuster.

Renwick, Lord Robin. 2015. *Mission to South Africa*. London: Jonathan Cape.

Rossouw, J. 2007. 'Inflation in South Africa: 1921–2006: History, Measurement and Credibility'. PhD thesis, University of KwaZulu-Natal, Durban.

Rossouw, J. 2009. *South African Reserve Bank: History, Functions and Institutional Structure*. Pretoria: SARB.

Rossouw, J. 2011. 'A Selective Reflection on the Institutional Development of the South African Reserve Bank since 1921'. *Economic History of Developing Regions*, special issue on the occasion of the 90th anniversary of the South African Reserve Bank, July.

Rossouw, J. and V. Padayachee. 2011. 'Reflecting on Ninety Years of Intermittent Success: The Experience of the South African Reserve Bank with Inflation since 1921'. *Economic History of Developing Regions*, special issue on the occasion of the 90th anniversary of the South African Reserve Bank, July.

Rossouw, J. and V. Padayachee. 2019. 'The Independence of the South African Reserve Bank: Coming Full Circle in 25 Years?' Paper presented to the biennial conference of the Economic Society of South Africa, September.

RSA (Republic of South Africa). 1993. *Constitution of the Republic of South Africa Act No. 200 of 1993*. https://www.gov.za/documents/constitution/constitution-republic-south-africa-act-200-1993 (accessed 18.04.19).

RSA. 1994. 'RDP White Paper: Discussion Document'. September. Pretoria: Government Printer. http://www.anc.org.za/content/rdp-white-paper-discussion-document (accessed 18.04.19).

RSA. 1996a. *Constitution of the Republic of South Africa Act No. 108 of 1996*, http://www.justice.gov.za/legislation/constitution/SAConstitution-web-eng.pdf (accessed 24.06.19).

RSA. 1996b. *The Growth, Employment and Redistribution Strategy*. Pretoria: Government Printer.

Russell, A. 2009. *Bring Me My Machine Gun: The Battle for the Soul of South Africa from Mandela to Zuma*. New York: Public Affairs.

SACP (South African Communist Party). 1962. *The Road to South African Freedom: Programme of the South African Communist Party*. London: Inkululeko Publications.

SACP. 1981. *South African Communists Speak: Documents from the History of the South African Communist Party 1915–1980*. London: Inkululeko Publications.

SACP. 1989. 'The Path to Power: Programme of the South African Communist Party as Adopted at the Seventh Congress, 1989'. http://www.sacp.org.za/docs/history/1989/power1989.html (accessed 18.04.19).

SAIRR (South African Institute of Race Relations). 1978. *Laws Affecting Race Relations in South Africa (to the end of 1976)*. Johannesburg: SAIRR.

Samuel, J. 2017. 'We Kept Quiet out of Loyalty – And Bred a Culture of Fear that Eroded Public Morality'. *Times Live*, 30 July. https://www.timeslive.co.za/sunday-times/opinion-and-analysis/2017-07-29-we-kept-quiet-out-of-loyalty--and-bred-a-culture-of-fear-that-eroded-public-morality/ (accessed 19.04.19).

SARB (South African Reserve Bank). 2011. Commemorative Publication to Mark the 90th Anniversary of the SARB. Pretoria: SARB.

Saul, J. 2005. *The Next Liberation Struggle: Capitalism, Socialism and Democracy in Southern Africa*. Pietermaritzburg: University of KwaZulu-Natal Press.

Saul, J. and P. Bond. 2014. *South Africa: The Present as History, from Mrs Ples to Mandela and Marikana*. Oxford: James Currey.

Schumpeter, J. 1942. *Capitalism, Socialism and Democracy*. London and New York: Routledge.

Seathe, W. 1990. 'Keynote Address'. Health and Welfare in Transition. Critical Health, Johannesburg.

Segal, N. 2007. *Breaking the Mould: The Role of Scenarios in Shaping South Africa's Future*. Stellenbosch: Sun Press.

Segatti, A. and N. Pons Vignon. 2013. 'Stuck in Stabilisation? South Africa's Post-Apartheid Macro-Economic Policy between Ideological Conversion and Technocratic Capture'. *Review of African Political Economy* 40 (138): 537–555.

Sender, J. 1994. 'Economic Restructuring in South Africa: Reactionary Rhetoric Prevails'. *Journal of Southern African Studies* 20 (4): 539–543.

Setai, B. 1977. *The Political Economy of South Africa: The Making of Poverty*. Lanham, MD: University Press of America.

Slovo, J. 1994. 'Development and Reconstruction'. Presentation to a Davis Borkum Hare seminar, Johannesburg, 26 January.

Smith, J. and B. Tromp. 2009. *Hani: A Life too Short*. Johannesburg: Jonathan Ball.

Söderlund, N., G. Schierhout and A. van den Heever. 1998. 'Technical Report to Chapter 13 of the South African Health Review 1998: A Report to Health Systems Trust by the Centre for Health Policy'. In *South African Health Review 1998*, edited by A. Ntuli. Durban: Health Systems Trust. http://docplayer.net/7793719-Private-health-care-in-south-africa.html (accessed 20.04.19).

South African Foundation. 2002. 'Business and Economic Policy: South Africa and Three Other African Cases'. Occasional Paper No. 2, February, Johannesburg.

South African History Online. 2011. *John James Issel*. 3 May. https://www.sahistory.org.za/people/john-james-issel (accessed 03.05.19)

South African History Online. 2012. ' Delegations and Dialogue between ANC and Internal Non Government Groups'. https://www.sahistory.org.za/topic/delegations-and-dialogue-between-anc-and-internal-non-government-groups (accessed 18.04.19).

SouthScan. 1993. 'Economic Dispute inside ANC Breaks into the Open on Reserve Bank Issue'. *SouthScan: A Bulletin of Southern African Affairs* 8 (42), 12 November: 325.

Spicer, M. 2016. 'Government and Business: Where Did It All Go Wrong?' *Business Day*, 15 November. https://www.businesslive.co.za/rdm/politics/2016-11-15-government-and-business---where-did-it-all-go-wrong/ (accessed 19.04.19).

Spitz, R. and M. Chaskalson. 2000. *The Politics of Transition: A Hidden History of South Africa's Negotiated Settlement*. Johannesburg: Wits University Press.

Star (article). 1986, 22 January.

Steyn, G. 1993. 'A Battle Royal for the Economic Soul of the ANC'. *Business Day*, 17 November.

Steyn, G. 1993. ' MERG Poses Serious Challenge to Government's Economic Model', *Business Day* 1 December.

Stiglitz, J. 1997. 'Central Banking in a Democratic Society', Tinbergen Lecture, Amsterdam, 10 October.

Stiglitz, J. 1998. 'Redefining the Role of the State: What Should it Do? How Should it Do it? And How Should these Decisions be Made?' Paper presented at Tenth Anniversary of the MITI Research Institute, Tokyo.

Suckling, J. and L. White, eds. 1988. *After Apartheid: Renewal of the South African Economy*. London: James Currey and Trenton, NJ: Africa World Press.

Sunter, C. 1987. *The World and South Africa in the 1990s*. Cape Town: Human and Rosseau.

Tambo, O. 1987. 'South Africa: Strategic Options for International Companies'. Statement by Oliver Tambo to Business International Conference, London, 27 May. https://www.sahistory.org.za/archive/south-africa-strategic-options-international-companies-statement-oliver-tambo-business-inter (accessed 18.04.19).

Terreblanche, S.J. 2012. *Lost in Transformation*. Johannesburg: KMM Review Publishing.

Thomas, T. 2001. 'And So the Babies Die'. *Mail & Guardian*, 21 September.

Titmuss, R.M. 1974. *Social Policy: An Introduction*. London: George Allen and Unwin.

Tollman, S. and L. Rispel. 1995. 'Organisation, Planning and Management'. In *South African Health Review 1995*, 75–88. Durban: Health Systems Trust.

Trotsky, L. 1931. 'For a Workers' United Front Against Fascism'. https://www.marxists.org/archive/trotsky/germany/1931/311208.htm (accessed 18.04.19).

Turok, B. 2003. *Nothing but the Truth*. Johannesburg and Cape Town: Jonathan Ball.

Turok, B. 2014. *With My Head over the Parapet*. Cape Town: Jacana.

Turok, B. 2015. 'Reflecting on the Struggle for Democracy: A Reply to John Saul'. *Transformation: Critical Perspectives on Southern Africa* 89: 45–49.

Turok, B. 2017. 'Explaining Mandela's Strategy in 1994'. *Daily Maverick*, 19 February. https://www.dailymaverick.co.za/opinionista/2017-02-19-explaining-mandelas-strategy-in-1994/ (accessed 19.04.19).

Union of South Africa, National Health Services Commission. 1944. Report on the Provision of an Organised National Health Service for All Sections of the Union of South Africa (U.G.30). Pretoria: Government Printer.

University of the Witwatersrand Seminar. 2016. `Were Business Schools to Blame for the 2008 Financial Crisis?' by J. Michie. Parktown Management Campus, Wits Business School, 23 November. (Notes of seminar, Vishnu Padayachee).

United Nations. 2018. '1941: The Atlantic Charter'. http://www.un.org/en/sections/history-united-nations-charter/1941-atlantic-charter/index.html (accessed 18.04.19).

Van Ameringen, M., ed. 1995. *Building a New South Africa: Volume 1: Economic Policy*. Ottawa: IDRC.

Van Kessel, I. 2009. 'The United Democratic Front's Legacy in South Africa: Mission Accomplished or Vision Betrayed?' In S. Ellis and I. van Kessel (eds). *Movers and Shakers: Social Movements in Africa,* (Vol. 8 of *African Dynamics*), 197–220. Leiden and Boston: Brill.

Van Niekerk, R. 2012. 'The Historical Roots of a National Health System in South Africa'. In G. Ruiters and R. van Niekerk (eds). *Universal Health Care in Southern Africa: Policy Contestation in Health System Reform in South Africa and Zimbabwe*. University of KwaZulu-Natal Press: Durban.

Van Niekerk, R. 2013. 'Social Policy, Social Citizenship and the Historical Idea of a Social Democratic Welfare State in South Africa'. *Transformation: Critical Perspectives on Southern Africa* 81/82: 115–143.

Van Niekerk, R. 2017. 'The African National Congress: Social Democratic Thinking and the Good Society, 1940–1962'. In E. Webster and K. Pampallis (eds). *The Unresolved National Question in South Africa: Left Thought Under Apartheid*. Johannesburg: Wits University Press.

Van Niekerk, R. and B. Fine. 2019. 'Conclusion: Harold Wolpe: Towards a Politics of Liberation in a Democratic South Africa'. In *Race, Class and the Post-Apartheid Democratic State*, edited by J. Reynolds, B. Fine and R. van Niekerk. Pietermaritzburg: University of KwaZulu-Natal Press.

Van Vuuren, H. 2017. *Apartheid Guns and Money: A Tale of Profits*. Johannesburg: Jacana.

Van Wyk, B. 2005. 'The Balance of Power and the Transition to Democracy in South Africa'. MA thesis, Department of History, University of Pretoria.

Visser, W. 2004. 'Shifting RDP into GEAR: The ANC Government's Dilemma in Providing an Equitable System of Social Security for the "New" South Africa'. Paper presented at the 40th ITH Linzer Konferenz, Linz, Austria, 16–19 September.

Vuk'unzenzele. 2018. 'A new dawn for South Africa'. *Vuk'unzenzele* 1 (March). Government Communications (GSIS). https://www.vukuzenzele.gov.za/new-dawn-south-africa (accessed 03.05.19)

Waldmeir, P. 1997. *Anatomy of a Miracle: The End of Apartheid and the Birth of the New South Africa*. London: Penguin and Viking.

Walsh, C.E. 1995. 'Is New Zealand's Reserve Bank Act of 1989 an Optimal Central Bank Contract?' *Journal of Money, Credit and Banking* 27 (4): 1179–1191.

Walshe, A.P. 1970. 'Black American Thought and African Political Attitudes in South Africa'. *The Review of Politics* 32 (1): 51–77.

Webster, E. 1997. 'Research, Policy-Making and the Advent of Democracy: A Reply to Max Price'. *Transformation: Critical Perspectives on Southern Africa* 33: 70–79.

Weideman, M. 2004. 'Who Shaped South Africa's Land Reform Policy?' *Politikon* 31 (2): 219–238.

Williams, G. 1988. 'Celebrating the Freedom Charter'. *Transformation: Critical Perspectives on Southern Africa* 6: 73–86.

Wilson, J. 1993. *Ukwenza Intando Yeningi Isebenze: Making Democracy Work*. Zulu translation by T. Cele. Durban: Community Law Centre.

Wolpe, H. 1990. *Race, Class & the Apartheid State*. Trenton, NJ: Africa World Press.

Wolpe, H. 1995. 'The Uneven Transition from Apartheid in South Africa'. *Transformation: Critical Perspectives on Southern Africa* 27: 88–101.

World Bank. 1993a. 'Options for Land Reform and Rural Restructuring in South Africa'. Washington, DC: World Bank. http://documents.worldbank.org/curated/en/707271468302672976/Options-for-land-reform-and-rural-restructuring-in-South-Africa (accessed 18.04.19).

World Bank. 1993b. *World Development Report 1993: Investing in Health*. New York: Oxford University Press.

World Bank. 1993c. *The East Asian Miracle: Economic Growth and Public Policy*. Oxford: Oxford University Press.

Wrathall, C. 2015. 'Mandela's South Africa Safari Hideaway'. *Financial Times*, 29 May. https://www.ft.com/content/cd92f194-009b-11e5-a908-00144feabdc0 (accessed 18.04.19).

YouTube. 2011. *Johnny Issel: the Final Address 14 January 2011*. https://www.youtube.com/watch?v=45T3-GO8cc8 (accessed 03.05.19)

A

Adelzadeh, Asghar 102, 117, 158, 237n2

African Bill of Rights 5, 12

African Claims in South Africa document
    4–6, 9, 11, 18, 25, 69, 73, 140, 205, 210,
    227, 229–230
    Bill of Rights 12–13, 19
    support for health care transformation
        205, 226
    trade union influence on 11–13

African National Congress (ANC) 2–3
    Constitutional Guidelines 44–45,
        62, 205
    Kabwe conference 41–42
    liberal reformist politics 5–6, 10, 147
    moral standing of 2, 7, 157, 178
    National Working Committee (NWC)
        67–68, 89, 138, 237n4
    radicalism/radicalisation of 5, 13, 22, 24,
        26, 46
    unbanning of 1, 58, 66, 68, 102, 143, 168,
        199–200, 202–203, 215
    views on economic emancipation 3–4,
        6–7, 16, 37–38, 42, 59, 234
    Youth League 18, 21
    see also armed struggle; Congress
        alliance; Morogoro 'Strategy and
        Tactics' statement

African nationalism 13, 16, 38,
    44–45, 147

agrarian question 51, 54, 168
    redistribution of land 60, 16

Amsterdam 38, 43, 78

ANC Alliance 2, 4, 62, 70, 74, 93, 108, 116,
    130–132, 162, 166, 231

ANC Alliance leadership 10–12, 18, 32,
    96, 127
    intellectual seduction/retreat of 135, 139,
        144, 155, 171
    interaction with MERG 92–97 *see also*
        Macroeconomic Policy Framework
        report: ANC's rejection/dumping of
    National Executive Committee (NEC)
        38, 41, 44, 56, 59, 65, 67, 145, 194

ANC economic policy 14, 17, 44
    1991 Economic Manifesto 86–87, 112
    influences on 8, 13–15, 44, 47, 55, 91,
        146, 149, 151–152, 154–159, 171,
        233 *see also* IMF; SACP: influence on
        ANC economic policy; Washington
        Consensus
    institutional developments 72
    weaknesses/failures of 3, 8, 53, 64–68,
        82, 85, 93, 103, 116, 133, 136, 176,
        229–231, 237n7
    see also Department of Economic
        Planning; Economics Unit, Lusaka;
        MERG; mixed economy model;
        nationalisation; neo-liberalism, ANC
        shift to; redistributive ANC economic
        policies

ANC/SACP exile years 5, 26, 31, 35–36, 65,
    80, 146
    health service 202–203
    1987 Moscow conference 55
    see also London/UK exile community;
        Lusaka, ANC in

Anglo American Corporation 1, 65, 75, 116,
    144, 150–154, 170–171

Angola 33–34

Anti-Apartheid Movement 7, 50, 52, 54
  Boycott South African Goods campaign
    50–51
apartheid regime 1, 5, 15, 51
  economists/economic institutions 1, 73,
    76, 90, 154–155
  economic legacy of 3, 25, 53, 146, 181
  sanctions against 1, 50–51, 75–76, 81,
    169, 233
  racialised economy of 52–53, 55, 80
  racialised health and welfare systems 199,
    202–203, 208
  role in shaping ANC economic policy
    154–157, 229
  see also inequality: apartheid legacy of;
    National Party
apartheid repression 16, 18–19, 32
  bannings 5, 23, 26–27, 29, 51, 78, 82
  censorship/restrictions 28–30
  states of emergency 23, 76
armed struggle 6, 24, 56, 202, 233
  MK 39, 41, 52, 58, 63, 202
  Operation Mayibuye 30
  Wankie campaign 36–37
Asmal, Kader 50–51, 69, 115
Atlantic Charter 10–13
Attlee, Clement 21, 25
Australia 70, 136

B
Ballivian, A 169–170
Barnard, Niël 15, 84, 115, 228
Bell, Terry 36, 108
Belli, P 169–170
Bernstein, Lionel 'Rusty' 14–15, 53, 136
black economic empowerment (BEE)
  144, 148
Boesak, Allan 158, 170
Bohmke, Heinrich 83–84
Bond, Patrick 87, 112–115, 143–144,
  157, 160, 162, 170, 176, 186, 189,
  192–193, 234
Botha, PW 74, 123–124, 156, 179, 228
Botha, Roelof (Pik) 119, 122
Botswana 42, 52
Brand, Simon 75, 78–80, 228
Brenthurst meetings 151–152, 154
Britain see United Kingdom

British colonialism 2, 5
Broomberg, Jonathan 204, 206
Bundy, Colin 29–30

C
Calitz, Estian 80, 124–125, 127–128,
  155–156, 173
Cambridge University
  Department of Applied Economics 61, 78
Camdessus, Michel 162–163
Canada 70, 88, 90–91, 195
capitalism, South African 1–2, 9, 37, 51–52,
  62, 144, 176, 233
  African-style capitalism of 15, 147
  integration into global/international
    circuits 59, 107, 132, 144–145, 150,
    159, 180, 182, 198
  neo-feudal 2
  racialised/racist 10, 29, 55, 80–81, 200
  see also minerals-energy complex;
    neo-liberalism: ANC shift to
Carolus, Cheryl 70, 100, 114
Carter, Gwendolen 15, 19, 23
Cassim, Fuad 79–80
central bank independence 75, 170, 178,
  238n2
  New Zealand model 186, 195
  significance of 180–181
  see also South African Reserve Bank,
    independence of
Central Economic Advisory Services
  (CEAS) 1, 76, 124, 155, 171, 176, 233
Central Statistical Services (CSS) 1, 76,
  117–118, 233
Centre for Research into Economics and
  Finance in Southern Africa (CREFSA)
  184, 194–195
Chaskalson, Matthew 189–190
China 29, 70, 123
  State Bank, London 48–50, 54, 77
Chinese Communist Party 47–49
Christie, Renfrew 102, 237n2
citizenship, universal rights of 4–5, 10,
  11–13, 18
  ANC's campaigning around 17–18,
    22–23
  see also African Claims in South Africa
    document; Atlantic Charter

civil society organisations 83, 103, 110, 196, 198, 211, 220
class
and citizenship 13
black bourgeoisie/middle class 15–16, 117, 147–148
capitalist 60, 68, 170
interrelationship with race 51, 199
middle 108
power 59, 95–96
see also working class
class conflict/struggle 33–34, 62
Coleman, Colin 68, 139
colonialism of a special type 38, 52
communism/communist ideology 5, 31, 41
Soviet-style 21–22
Suppression of Communism Act 18
Communist Party of Great Britain (CPGB) 40, 51, 57
Communist Party of the Soviet Union (CPSU) 48–49, 57
Communist Party of South Africa (CPSA) 4, 11, 17, 26, 47, 147, 235n1&2
Compensatory and Contingency Financing Facility (CCFF) 160–161, 164
Congress alliance 4, 8, 14–16, 45, 47–48, 51, 237n1 *see also* ANC Alliance
Congress of South African Trade Unions (Cosatu) 2, 7, 78, 99, 116, 162, 216, 220
on economic policy 53, 60, 86, 103, 110, 231
Economic Trends Research Group (ET) 74, 77, 80–82, 84, 129, 146
emergence/formation of 63, 72, 76
health care initiatives 204, 207, 213
RDP initiative 114, 116–117, 232
socialist ideology of 62–63, 84
see also ANC Alliance leadership; NUMSA
Consolidated Goldfields 78, 85
Constituent Assembly 117, 190, 193–194
Constitution of Republic of South Africa 54, 180–181, 183–184, 191, 194, 196, 225, 239n8
constitutional negotiations 2, 23, 63, 65, 69, 117–118, 123, 180, 182, 185, 189–190, 192, 227–228
Interim 115, 181, 184, 191, 193–194

proposed bill of rights 85
Convention for a Democratic South Africa (Codesa) 63, 71, 172–173, 183–184, 186, 191, 230 *see also* negotiations towards transition to democracy; World Trade Centre negotiations
Coovadia, Jerry 204, 209
corruption/personal wealth accumulation 2–3, 36, 237n9
Business Initiative against Corruption and Crime 222
Council for the Development of Social Science Research in Africa (Codesria) 39, 43
Cronin, Jeremy 57, 60, 63–64, 113, 131, 136, 140, 148, 193–194, 227–228
deputy general secretary, SACP 7
formulation of RDP 113, 140
on MERG report 102, 106
UDF underground 36
cronyism *see* corruption/personal accumulation
Cuba 29, 39, 60, 62, 138

D

Dadoo, Yusuf 14, 47–49
Dakar conference 85–86
Davies, Rob 44, 61, 77, 194, 204
Davos 138, 151, 156
de Beer, Cedric 200–201, 204–206, 208
de Klerk, FW 1, 40, 74, 119–125, 127, 153–155, 161, 171, 179, 228, 235n1, 238n7
de Kock, Gerhard 227 *see also under* South African Reserve Bank
De Kock Commission 75, 183–184
de Villiers, Dawie 119, 162
Democratic Party (DP) 118, 191
democratisation 5, 7, 208
of economy 86, 110, 116
global 10–11
Department of Economic Planning (DEP) 35, 39, 42–45, 52, 65–66, 77, 110, 166, 230
Economic Transformation Committee 126, 129, 132
lack of accountability in 137–140, 180, 231
land commission 69

Department of Economic Planning (*continued*)
  lack of capacity/training of 67–70, 86–88,
    145–146, 233
  policy formulation and coordination
    70–72, 91, 138, 140, 157
  relationship with MERG 69–70, 72, 89,
    92–94, 96–102, 140
Desai, Ashwin 83–84
Development Bank of South Africa (DBSA)
    55, 76, 79, 168, 172–173, 176, 228,
    232–233
  New Development Bank 92
  see also under GEAR
Dlamini-Zuma, Nkosazana 217–218
Dolny, Helena 44, 61, 168
Dreyer, Jan 124, 155
du Plessis, Barend 120, 123, 184
du Toit, Treurnicht 117–118

E
Economic Commission for Africa
    (ECA) 38, 42
economic liberalism 75–76
  critique of statism 83
  see also neo-liberalism, ANC shift to
Economic Research on South Africa
    (EROSA) 39, 43, 52, 77
Economic Trends Research Group *see under*
    Cosatu
Economics Technical Committee 155, 161,
    192 *see also* Transitional Executive
    Council
Economics Unit, Lusaka 35, 38–40, 42, 45
  Research Unit 38, 40, 42–43, 52, 54
education 4–5, 9, 12, 19, 24–25, 60, 105
  adult basic 104
  free and compulsory 205
  teacher training 104
elections 1994 112–115, 118–119, 123,
    128, 151, 158, 163, 170–171, 193, 201,
    209, 215
  policy displacement following 213,
    216–217, 219–220
Ellis, Stephen 38, 47, 56
Erwin, Alec 109, 231–232
  cabinet minister 62, 108
  deputy finance minister 125, 127–129,
    132, 135, 194–195

MERG Steering Committee member 95,
    98–99, 102–103
  role in NEF 62, 125–127
  trade unionist 62, 81–82, 113–114, 148,
    154–155, 173
Eskom 70, 80, 166–167
Esterhuyse, Willie 61, 84–85

F
facism 4–5
  struggle against 9–10
Fine, Ben 40, 43, 52, 57, 77, 80, 82, 89,
    94–96, 100–101, 157, 175, 212, 214
Finger, M 169–170
First, Ruth 14, 50, 146
fiscal discipline, policy discourse of 114,
    122, 167, 170
  impact on health funding 215–216,
    220–224, 226
  see also neo-liberalism, ANC shift to
Fischer, Stanley 163, 195
Five Freedoms Forum 45, 236n4
foreign investment 116, 156–157
Free Market Foundation 75, 86
Freedom Charter 18, 62, 69, 86, 148,
    227, 229
  inauguration/adoption of 17, 19,
    103, 110
  SACP influence on/support for 14–15,
    56–57, 147–149
  social democratic impetus of 5–6, 9,
    14–16, 20–21, 23, 25, 30–31, 42, 44,
    102, 230
  support for health care transformation
    205, 207, 226
  vision for 'good society' 12, 22, 24–26,
    199, 220
  see also under nationalisation;
    redistributive ANC economic policies
Friedman, Irwin 202, 209, 217, 219
Freund, Bill 62, 68, 95–96, 107–108, 132,
    149, 168

G
Gelb, Stephen 78, 84, 129
  concept of racist Fordism 81–82
Gencor 122–123, 126, 222, 237n2
Gerhart, Gail 33–34, 38, 41, 44, 62, 147

Germany 90
    Bundesbank 70, 185
Gerwel, Jakes 78–80
Gevisser, Mark 65, 72, 132, 136, 138,
    147, 157
Giliomee, Hermann 62, 74, 86, 123,
    153–154
Glaser, Clive 33–34, 41, 44
Gluckman Commission 211–212, 226
Godsell, Bobby 152
Goldman Sachs 70, 79, 150
Gorbachev, Mikhail 55, 64
Gordhan, Ketso 68, 71, 111
Gordhan, Pravin 162, 182, 191
Gouws, Rudolph 78, 153
Government of National Unity (GNU) 75,
    119, 120–122, 127, 135, 140, 155, 164,
    216, 220–221
    NP departure from 217
Green, Pippa 68, 106, 123, 134–135,
    154, 157
Growth, Employment and Redistribution
    (GEAR) programme 4, 30, 74, 96, 103,
    109, 140, 151, 154, 160, 163, 217, 226,
    231–232
    and closure of RDP office 122–123, 128,
        130, 144, 151, 157, 175, 230
    DBSA involvement in 124–125, 128–129,
        133, 135
    non-negotiability of/lack of consultation
        over 129–137, 175, 231–232
    NP support for 127, 135
Gurney, C 50–51

H
Habib, Adam 95, 102, 167
Hamilton, Laurence 5–6, 102
Hanekom, Derek 69, 71
Hani, Chris 36–37, 40–41, 58, 63, 138,
    150, 157
    assassination of 96
Harmel, Michael 14, 49
Harris, Laurence 6, 39–44. 52, 54, 57,
    59–61, 66, 77–78, 95–96, 103
health care policy, post-1994 218–220,
    223–224
    delivery failure 224, 226
    expenditure/budget 223–225

Financial and Fiscal Commission
    (FFC) 225
health care system, pre-1994 4–5, 9–10, 12,
    19, 25, 60, 102, 104–105, 110
    private 199–200, 206, 212
    public 199–200
    see also National Health Service
Health Functions Committee 224–225
Helleiner, Gerry 88, 91, 96
Hickel, Jason 170, 182, 192
Hirsch, Alan 15–16, 45, 143, 146–147,
    149, 166–168, 176, 196, 237n2
housing, delivery of 100–102, 104–105,
    110, 112
Huddlestone, Trevor 50, 99, 188

I
industrialisation 43, 105, 187, 233
inequality, apartheid legacy of 3, 16, 24, 41,
    85, 107–108
    in health care 199–201, 209–210,
        212–213, 226
infrastructure development 104, 108, 110,
    112, 205, 210, 223, 232–233
    transport 134
Inkatha Freedom Party (IFP) 122, 183,
    190–191
Institute for Democratic Alternatives in
    South Africa 62
International Development Research
    Centre (IDRC) 53, 77, 82, 88
International Monetary Fund (IMF)
    69–70, 114, 120, 145, 170, 172–173,
    195, 221, 223
    influence on Normative Economic
        Model 127
International Monetary Fund loans 118, 156,
    158–159, 163–165tab, 167, 232, 238n5
    Letter of Intent 160–162

J
Jacobs, AS (Japie) 120–121, 124–125, 173
Japan 9, 64
Jaycox, Edward 70, 166
Jordan, Pallo 5, 28, 45, 52–55, 77, 89–90,
    138, 148–159, 228, 237n4
    head of Economics Unit 38–40, 54
Josie, Jaya 39–41, 66, 155

K

Kaplan, David 78–79

Karis, Thomas 15, 19, 23, 38, 62

Kasrils, Ronnie 7, 35, 63, 94, 101, 125,
135–136, 138–139, 141, 228, 234, 237n4
criticism of ANC's economic policy shift
144–146, 171, 234

Kathrada, Ahmed 26, 28, 32–33, 50

Keeton, Gavin 150–151, 154

Keys, Derek 116, 120, 123–126, 128, 193,
217, 237n2
role in democratic transition 153–157,
161–164, 171, 173, 228

Kganyago, Lesetja 70 see also under SARB

Kotane, Moses 11, 56

L

Labour and Economic Research Centre
77, 81

labour movement see trade union
movement

labour rights 25, 182, 190

Land and Agricultural Policy Centre 69,
168–169

Land Bank 76, 233

land, redistribution of see under agrarian
question

land reform policy 112, 168, 201
NP White Paper on 168
World Bank influence on 168–169

Langa, Bheki 39, 42, 79, 122

Lausanne conference 78–79

le Roux, Pieter 78–80, 153

Lehohla, Pali 117–118

Levy, Norman 38, 54–56, 60–61

liberalisation 13, 157, 159–160, 168, 170
see also neo-liberalism, ANC shift to

Liebenberg, Chris 120, 128

Lombard, Jan 74–76, 78, 80, 124–125, 155

London, Leslie 201–202

London/UK exile community 27, 43, 39–41,
43, 46, 66
Africa Committee 51
economic research capacity 52
education policy research 54
policy debates/research 46–48, 77–78
see also MERG; York University
conferences

London School of Economics (LSE) 48, 66,
111, 170, 192

Louw, Leon 75, 86

Loxley, John 88, 91, 96

Lund, Francie 204, 216

Lusaka, ANC in 27, 30, 41, 46, 58–59,
65–67, 80, 89–90
divisions within ANC in 36
see also Department of Economic
Planning; Economics Unit, Lusaka

Luthuli, Albert 17, 22, 37, 45, 56, 147,
205, 220
views on social democratic welfare state
20–21, 24–26, 32

M

Maasdorp, Leslie 67–68, 91

Macmillan, Hugh 27, 35

Macozoma, Saki 138–139

Macroeconomic Policy Framework report
53–54, 91–92, 124, 188, 227
ANC Alliance's rejection/dumping of
97–103, 106–108, 119–121, 140, 171,
175–176, 188, 230–232
recommendations of 99, 101–105, 169,
193, 212
significance/value of 102–103, 106–108

Macroeconomic Research Group (MERG)
67, 112, 151, 167–168, 201
DEP's relationship with 69–70, 72, 89,
138, 161
Donors Steering Committee Forum 90–91
Economics Research Committee 90
health policy proposals 212–213, 215,
220, 226
neo-Keynsianism of 144, 157
Pillay's directorship of 47, 53–54, 66,
89–90, 92, 98–103, 106–109, 134, 157,
173–175, 186–189
role of international economists in
88–93, 95, 102, 105–106
Steering Committee 89–90, 92–93, 98,
102–103
training and capacity building
programme 91–92, 104
see also ANC Alliance leadership:
interaction with MERG; DEP:
relationship with MERG

Maharaj, Mac 36, 46, 115–116, 150, 182,
    191–192, 228
    on exile in London 46
    friendship with Vella Pillay 48–51, 54, 89,
        173–174
    on Robben Island 31–34
    Transport Minister 129, 132–134
Malaysia 46, 70
Mandela, Nelson (Madiba) 48, 53–54, 56,
    93, 109, 111
    arrest and imprisonment 27–28, 150
    on Freedom Charter 15–16, 20, 22,
        32–33, 146
    international support for 7
    involvement with MERG 88–90, 96–98
    membership of ANC youth league 18
    release of 1, 86, 151, 156, 170
    support for RDP 114, 116, 119, 122, 129
    views on socialism/Marxism 30–31,
        138, 149
Mandela presidency 4, 9, 55, 62, 119, 122,
    125, 220, 229
    shift in economic policy under 128–129,
        131–132, 135, 138–139, 145, 152,
        154–156, 163–164, 166, 185, 221–222
Manuel, Trevor 106, 149, 152, 166–167, 173,
    194, 231–232
    and formulation of RDP 112–116, 123
    as head of DEP 62, 66–70, 72, 80, 87–90,
        93–95, 97–102, 111, 126, 138, 151, 153,
        161–162, 185–186, 192
    support for GEAR 127–128, 130–135,
        141, 154, 231
    Treasury Minister 196–197
Marais, Hein 169–170
Marcus, Gill 128, 130, 195
Marxism 5, 33, 28, 34, 51–52, 62, 77, 91,
    149, 174, 212
    African Communist 63
    Inqindi and 33–35, 59
mass-based mobilisation 16, 23, 203
    civil disobedience campaigning 13, 19, 23
    Defiance Campaign 17–19
mass democratic movement (MDM) 58–59,
    103, 137, 140, 201–202, 216–217
    ANC failure to engage with 228–229
Matisonn, John 93
Matthews, Joe 49, 147

Matthews, ZK 11, 14
Mayekiso, Moses 106, 189
Mbatha, Khulu 147, 170–171
Mbeki administration 50, 62, 146, 196,
    201, 216
    support for GEAR 134–135
Mbeki, Govan 11, 29–30
Mbeki, Moeletsi 94, 96
Mbeki, Thabo 30, 51, 60–61, 65, 67, 70,
    72, 93, 150
    and ANC Economics Unit 39–40, 66
    economic vision 148
Mboweni, Tito 55, 61, 79–80, 102–109, 118,
    152, 173, 183
    Labour Minister 79, 103, 129, 154,
        194, 197
    MERG Steering Committee member
        93–95, 97–99, 108
    role in DEP 66, 68, 70–71, 79, 111, 139,
        161, 185–186, 189, 191–192
    reconstruction levy 112
    views on GEAR 132–133, 135
    see also under SARB
McMenamin, Vivian 68, 111
Mgijima, Ralph 202–203, 215
Michie, J 54, 132
minerals-energy complex 53, 69, 77, 238n11
    mining 2
Ministry of Finance 1, 135, 155, 179, 181,
    188, 194, 197
mixed economy model 39–40, 59–60, 62,
    64, 110, 150, 207–208, 210
    role for private sector in 44–45, 59
Mlangeni, Andrew 17, 26, 28, 31–32
monopoly capitalism 15, 22, 24, 29, 39, 44,
    60, 86, 147
Mont Fleur scenario-planning exercises
    149, 153–154, 176, 227
Morogoro 'Strategy and Tactics' statement
    3, 37–38, 57, 59, 62, 147, 227
Morris, Mike 74, 82–83
Morrison, Neil 67–68, 70, 118, 185
Mozambique 33–34, 45
    1990 Maputo health and welfare
        conference 203–207
Mutize, Misheck 161, 163
Mzala, Comrade (Nxumalo, Jabulani)
    58–59

N

Naidoo, Jay 70, 82, 102–103, 114, 123, 125, 127–130, 173, 223
  as Cosatu leader 53, 155
  as driver of RDP 114, 223
  Fighting for Justice 232
  as MERG Steering Committee member 99, 102–103, 126
  involvement in NEF 126–127
National African Federated Chamber of Commerce and Industry (Nafcoc) 39, 41
national democratic revolution 6, 38, 59
  see also national liberation struggle
National Economic Development and Labour Council (Nedlac) 120, 129, 134, 195
National Economic Forum (NEF) 62, 125–127, 161, 236n7
National Health Service 178, 200–205, 207–208, 226
  community health centres as backbone of 210–211, 217
  funding of 211, 213
  health insurance mechanism for 201, 205–206, 211–212
  National Health Plan 209–213, 215, 217–219
  policy dismissal/displacement 213–214, 216–217
  Primary Health Care (PHC) approach 215
  role of private sector in 206, 209, 211, 213
National Institute for Economic Policy (NIEP) 102, 121–122, 133, 237n2
national liberation struggle 30, 33–34, 148
  multi-class alliance 15, 26, 32
  see also Congress Alliance
National Medical and Dental Association (NAMDA) 201–204
National Party (NP) 15, 17–18, 22–23, 48, 84, 101, 116, 162, 153, 172
  market-oriented economic reform 74–76, 123, 135, 155, 228–229, 233
  Ministry of Health 207–209
  relationship with IMF 127, 155–156, 161–162, 164
  response to MERG and RDP 118–122

  see also Normative Economic Policy
National Progressive Primary Health Care Network 202, 204
National Union of Metalworkers of South Africa (Numsa) 82, 84
nationalisation 14–15, 37, 44, 59–62, 64, 85, 151–152, 161, 191
  ANC shift on 109, 117, 139–140, 155–156, 158, 168, 170–171, 173, 220
  Freedom Charter on 19–22, 24–26, 32–34, 41, 45, 55, 86, 139, 147
  see also health care system: National Health Service debate
nationalism/socialism debate 44–45, 56, 230, 236n2
nazism 10–11
Ndulu, Benno 88, 91
negotiations towards transition to democracy 1–4, 7–8, 40, 58, 60, 71–72, 86, 93, 115, 118, 157, 228
  key economic debates/conferences 61, 73, 76–80, 84–86, 103, 105, 116, 124, 153, 166, 227–228, 231
  outmanoeuvred ANC economics team 73, 135, 176–178, 182, 229, 233
  role of (white) business in 1, 73, 78, 84–86, 102, 126, 129, 132, 136, 139, 149–155, 171–172, 229
  sell-out/conspiracy argument 8, 73, 141, 144, 157, 161, 170–176, 178, 232
  see also central bank independence; Codesa; MERG; TEC
Neocosmos, Michael 83
neo-liberalism, ANC shift to 46, 67, 84, 94, 127, 159–160, 164, 176–177, 215, 217, 227, 229, 234, 237n3
  capitulation to market-friendly approach 95, 103, 140, 144, 149, 231–233
  in GEAR 122, 140–141
  in RDP 115, 117
  see also fiscal discipline, policy discourse of
Ngoasheng, Moss 52, 67–68, 77, 79, 87, 111, 236n2
Ngubane, Jordan K 21–22
Nkuhlu, Wiseman 125, 166
non-racialism 2, 5–7, 13, 16, 23, 31, 205, 207, 237n1 *see also under* trade unionism

Normative Economic Model (NEM)
106–107, 121, 123–124, 127, 155, 193

O

O'Malley, Padraig 46, 48, 51, 116, 132–133,
173–174, 185–186, 193
Oppenheimer, Harry 132, 144, 149–150,
152, 170–171
Oriani-Ambrosini, Mario 183, 190–192

P

Padmore, George 10, 31
Pahad, Aziz 51, 148, 237n4
Pahad, Essop 51, 61–62, 77, 108
Pan-Africanism 10
Pan Africanist Congress (PAC) 21, 23, 28, 173
Papenfus, Theresa 119, 122
Perez, Gonda 208–209
Pillay, G 18, 21
Pillay, Patsy 47–48, 50
Pillay, Vella 44, 51, 54, 79, 92, 95, 115, 136
    role in Anti-Apartheid Movement
        50, 52
    role in economy policy analysis
        46–47, 52–53
    role in EROSA 77
    as SACP representative in Europe 47–50
    see also under MERG
Planact 77, 113
Plaut, Martin 1–2
Pogrund, B 28–29
populism 110
    macroeconomic 105, 119, 154, 182, 188
    versus workerism 63, 83
poverty 3, 9, 41
Price, Max 100–101, 204, 214
private ownership 14, 45, 147, 168
privatisation 86, 109, 111, 117, 124, 131,
158, 205, 212–213, 221

R

racial discrimination/oppression 2, 12, 20,
25, 51, 168, 210
racial segregation 10, 48, 211, 226
racial supremacy see white supremacy
Ramaphosa, Cyril 68, 93, 152
Ramos, Maria 67–68, 70, 79–80, 92–93, 96,
111, 118, 135, 185, 195

Ready to Govern (RTG) document 69,
109–112, 161, 207, 210, 229, 237n1
Reconstruction and Development
    Programme (RDP) 6, 74, 105, 107,
        111–112, 114–116, 118, 162, 229–230
    Base Document 117, 119, 121, 140, 158,
        215, 220–221
    budget allocations/expenditure for 215,
        221–223, 231
    support for national health system
        214–215, 220, 226
    White Paper 117, 120–121, 158, 216,
        220–222, 237n4
    see also NP: response to MERG and RDP
redistributive ANC economic policies 4,
    26, 37, 41, 43, 45, 85, 110, 130, 140,
    144, 147
    ANC shift regarding 60, 151, 154, 158,
        171–172, 201
    Freedom Charter emphasis of 6, 20, 22,
        25, 86, 230
    national health service 206–207, 218–219
    see also RDP; GEAR
Relly, Gavin 150–151
Rivonia Treason Trial 17, 22, 28, 147
Robben Island 17, 26, 28–34, 59, 236n1&2
    education/discussion/debates on 28–29,
        31–33, 59
Rossouw, Jannie 122, 179–180, 183–185
Roux, André 79, 135
Russia 21, 29, 49 see also Soviet Union
Rustomjee, Cyrus 137, 160, 164, 187

S

Sanders, David 209, 217–218
Sanlam 1, 149, 177
Saul, John 144, 157, 170, 234
Second World War 1, 9, 11
Seme, Pixley ka Isaka 5, 12
Sender, John 46, 50–51, 61, 78, 157, 174,
    244n1
    MERG research director 91–96, 98,
        103, 114, 161–162
Serote, Mongane Wally 61, 77
service delivery 110
    failure 3, 158
    see also under health care policy,
        post-1994

Setai, Bethuel 55–56
Sexwale, Tokyo 139, 152
Sharpeville 23, 50, 75
Simons, Jack 36, 62
Sisulu, Max 39–40, 53, 56–58, 66–69,
  77, 80, 98
  role in DEP 42, 46, 55, 66, 68, 71,
    89–90, 97
  views on economic transformation 67
Sisulu, Walter 111, 174
Slovo, Joe 14, 30, 41, 50, 53, 157, 192–193
  general secretary of SACP 63–65, 93, 101,
    111–113, 136, 138, 145
  'No Middle Road' 57, 60, 147
Smuts, Jan 9–10, 13
Sobukwe, Robert Smangiliso 28–29
social democracy 5, 9, 178
  as basis of ANC 4–7, 10–11, 13, 15–16,
    20–21, 32, 41, 44–45, 148, 82, 220
  central role of labour in 32, 136
  Keynesian approach 22, 61, 78, 140
  see also under Freedom Charter; Luthuli,
    Albert
socialism 4–5, 14–15, 20, 22, 26, 29–34, 37,
  40–41, 51, 81, 83–84, 86, 96, 204
  Fabian 21
  two-stage theory 33, 60–61, 149,
    236n2
  see also nationalism/socialism debate
socialist economy 59, 64, 68, 95, 127, 138,
  146, 148, 151, 159, 188
South African Communist Party (SACP)
  2–5, 78, 216, 220
  Central Committee 7, 48, 50–51, 94, 194
  influence on ANC economic policy 38,
    56, 62, 110, 146–148
  Marxist-Leninist tradition 58
  Minimum Programme 14, 149, 235n2
  1962 programme 37–38, 56
  Soviet-style socialism of 44–45, 48–49,
    56–58, 62–63
  support for RDP 113, 115
  tensions over economic policy 58–61,
    63–64, 135–136, 230
  unbanning of 64, 235n1
  views on negotiated settlement 60–61
  see also mixed economy model
South African Foundation 41, 153

South African National Civic Organisation
  (Sanco) 7, 90, 99, 106, 110, 189, 232
South African Reserve Bank (SARB) 53,
  110, 120–121, 124, 135, 233, 238n3
  apartheid era 1, 76, 155
  calls for nationalisation of 106
  Chris Stals as governor of 126, 157, 162,
    184, 192, 194–195, 197
  Gerhard de Kock as governor of 74–75,
    179–180, 183–185
  Lesetja Kganyago as governor of 68,
    91, 185
  Tito Mboweni as governor of 55 79,
    96, 161
South African Reserve Bank, independence
  of 2, 71, 95, 98–101, 115, 168, 170, 177,
    196–198
  DEP/MERG argument over 181,
    184–189, 191–193
  negotiations over 179–184, 186–187, 189,
    191–193, 231, 233, 239n8
  NP position on 182–183, 189–191,
    198, 231
  1995 seminar on 194–195
Soviet Union 39, 42, 51, 66–67, 70
  collapse of 7, 63–64, 79–80, 146
  Moscow 22, 39, 47, 49, 55, 62, 78,
    90, 146
  see also Communist Party of the
    Soviet Union
Soweto 17, 33–34, 58, 96
Spicer, Michael 116, 151–153, 171
Spitz, Richard 189–190
Stalinism 4, 47–49, 57–58, 130
Stals, Chris 118, 228, 238n3
  see also under SARB
Steyn, Douw 152, 172–173
Steyn, G 107, 186–187
Stellenbosch University 80, 84–85, 106,
  135, 144
Strauss, Conrad 79, 152
Suckling, John 61, 78
Sweden 24, 90, 136

T
Tambo, Oliver 6, 16, 18, 27, 36–37, 44, 47,
  50, 55–56, 58, 69, 80, 99, 150
Tanganyika 46, 50

Tanzania 39, 46, 54, 58, 91
  see also Morogoro 'Strategy and Tactics' statement
Taylor, Lance 91, 93
Terreblanche, Sampie 61, 84–85, 144–146, 157, 159–160, 170–173, 176, 232, 234, 238n11
Thatcher, Margaret 122, 141
trade union movement 4, 53, 63, 81, 92, 110, 198, 227
  non-racial 76, 83
  see also Cosatu
trade union rights 25, 105, 190
Transitional Executive Council (TEC) 55, 102, 155, 160–162, 166, 172
  Sub-Council on Finance 118
Tripartite Alliance *see* ANC Alliance
Turok, Ben 14–16, 18, 26, 56–57, 85, 109–110, 114, 147, 229, 231

U

unemployment 3, 53, 181
  insurance/benefits 10, 12, 19, 44
  mass 105, 108
Unisa 28–29
United Democratic Front (UDF) 7, 36, 58, 76, 137, 158, 177, 204
United Kingdom (UK) 7, 11, 24, 48, 50, 58, 61, 66, 68, 70, 77, 85, 90, 204, 218
  Labour Party 10, 14, 21, 25, 96, 238n2
  see also Anti-Apartheid Movement; London/UK exile community
United Party government 9, 12–13, 17
  social democratic impetus of 10
United States (US) 11, 21, 24, 90, 196
  CIA 27
  Clinton administration 7, 162
  Declaration of Independence 12
universal franchise 5, 13, 19, 23
University of Cape Town (UCT) 43, 79, 196, 217
University of Fort Hare 18, 45, 69, 235n3
University of London 28, 51, 66, 69, 91, 96–97, 230, 235n3
  SOAS 42, 54, 61, 101
University of Sussex 39, 65, 77
University of the Western Cape (UWC) 36, 78–79, 91, 104

University of the Witwatersrand (Wits) 47, 91, 108, 114, 152, 161, 184

V

van der Berg, Servaas 79, 106, 135
Venter, Rina 207–208
Verwoerd, Hendrik 22–23, 52, 124

W

Waldmeir, Patti 152, 154–155, 161
Washington Consensus 115, 146, 149, 157, 167, 172, 176, 232–233
Weideman, Marinda 168–169
welfare 5, 9–10, 24–25, 100, 217
  industrial 12
Western Cape 71, 120
White, Landeg 61, 78
white supremacy 3, 15–17, 37
Williams, Gavin 19–20
Wolpe, Harold 51–52, 54, 61, 77–79, 148, 157–158
working class 4, 20, 57, 94, 96, 117
  role in liberation struggle 33–34
  constituency, ANC 5, 207
World Bank 93, 100, 114, 118, 124, 156, 158–159, 163, 172, 181, 201, 221, 223, 232
  economic courses/training 67, 69–70, 229
  loans/project financing 166–167, 169
  policy report on health 217–218
World Health Organization 203–204, 209–210
World Trade Centre negotiations 186–187, 191–193

X

Xuma, AB 4–5, 10–13, 18, 26, 45, 211, 220

Y

York University conferences 61, 77–78, 167

Z

Zuma, Jacob 3, 141. 337n9